D0712284

Heidegger
and
Asian Thought

Heidegger
and
Asian Thought

edited by
Graham Parkes

UNIVERSITY OF HAWAII PRESS
HONOLULU

Library of Congress Cataloging-in-Publication Data

Heidegger and Asian thought.

  Bibliography: p.
  Includes index.
  1. Heidegger, Martin, 1889–1876—Views on Asian
thought.   2.   Philosophy, Oriental.   I.   Parkes, Graham,
1949–   .
B3279.H49H34   1987   193   87–19073
ISBN 0–8248–1064–3

To the memory of my parents

Contents

Acknowledgments

Thanks are due to the editors of the following journals for their permission to reprint:

The Eastern Buddhist, for Keiji Nishitani's "Reflections on Two Addresses by Martin Heidegger," which originally appeared in vol. 1, no. 2, 1966.

International Philosophical Quarterly, for J. L. Mehta's "Heidegger and Vedānta: Reflections on a Questionable Theme," which appeared in vol. 18, 1978.

The Journal of Chinese Philosophy, for Joan Stambaugh's "Heidegger, Taoism, and the Question of Metaphysics," which appeared in vol. 11, no. 4, 1984.

I am also grateful to my colleague Eliot Deutsch, who first suggested the idea of an anthology on this topic, and provided encouragement along the way when it all seemed like too much work.

Finally I should like to thank the University of Hawaii Foundation for financial support for the translators' fees, and also the National Resource Center for East Asian Studies at the University of Hawaii for a travel grant which enabled me to go to Japan for consultations with the Japanese authors.

Introduction

The prospects for a thinking that strives to correspond
to the essential being of language remain veiled in their
vastness. And so I do not yet see whether what I am trying to think as the being of language is *also* adequate to
the nature of East Asian language—whether ultimately
. . . the thinking experience can be reached by a being
of language that would ensure that Western European
and East Asian saying can enter into dialogue in such a
way that there sings something that wells up from a single source.

> "A Dialogue on Language between
> a Japanese and an Inquirer"
> *On the Way to Language*

I

Some speculate that Plato or his predecessors had contact with India. It is
in any case instructive to compare Plato's understanding of things with
ideas in early Hindu and Buddhist thought, comparative philosophy
being generally more enlightening between unconnected philosophies.
Leibniz's encounter with the philosophy of Neo-Confucianism and also
the *I Ching* is the first case of a major Western thinker's seriously engaging Asian philosophy.[1] Interest in Oriental thought developed gradually,
until Hegel, commanding a more expansive view of history than any
before him, declared his philosophy (not without justification) to be the
culmination of Western metaphysics. Eastern thought he considered to
have remained in a state of relative immaturity—even though some of its
products were worthy of being incorporated into his own system. Schopenhauer, as more Asian texts began to be available in better translations, saw greater depth in those philosophies, and maintained that Western thought had much to learn from the wisdom of the East. Nietzsche
considered his "revaluation of all previous values" finally to have overcome the Western metaphysical tradition. His understanding of Indian
philosophy appears to have gone deeper than Schopenhauer's, and while
his attitude toward Buddhism is ambivalent, he acknowledges parallels
between aspects of Buddhist philosophy and his own subversive lines of
thought.[2]

Much of Heidegger's lengthy engagement with Nietzsche is concerned
with depicting him as still trapped in the Western metaphysical tradition,
and with presenting himself as the first to re-open the question of Being

and thus as the ultimate overcomer of metaphysics in the West. Recently, however, Jacques Derrida has criticized Heidegger's thinking, from a perspective that takes full account of the difference between languages with phonetic and nonphonetic scripts, for being too "logocentric" and thereby still enmeshed in the Western metaphysical tradition. We may therefore have to wait even longer for the last overcoming.

Rather than pursue this issue further, I should like simply to suggest that Heidegger's claim to be the West's first thinker to have overcome the tradition should be taken more seriously if his thought can be brought to resonate deeply with ideas that arose in totally foreign cultural milieus, couched in more or less alien languages, over two millennia ago. (The same applies, naturally, to the radicality of Nietzsche's subversion of the Western tradition.) The question of influence—of Eastern thought on Heidegger's work—while interesting, is of secondary significance in comparison with the independent congruence of ideas. This last contention, and my initial claim that comparative philosophy is most fruitful between unconnected philosophies, perhaps call for some expansion.

"East-West" comparative philosophy is in principle no different from "comparative" philosophizing within a single tradition—and most philosophy practiced with an appropriately historical sensibility involves comparisons. In order to understand, say, Kant's theory of causality, it is clearly helpful, if not indispensable, to know Hume's ideas on the relations between cause and effect. In order fully to appreciate Schopenhauer's views on almost anything, we have to understand Kantian philosophy. But these are perhaps simply examples of doing philosophy in a historically responsible way—in which we try to understand the nature of the problems a thinker takes over from the tradition, what he retains from the answers of his predecessors, and in what ways his responses differ from theirs. The philosophy of Plato in particular can serve as a kind of pattern, or map, to give the student a basic orientation in the cosmos of Western philosophy. It often helps in acquainting oneself with the ideas of subsequent thinkers if one pictures the later philosophy in relation to the structure of Plato's thought.

Perhaps the image of a network of interconnections inscribed on some transparent sheet can be helpful. In drawing a picture of the thought of Plotinus, for example, one can begin by placing the blank transparency on top of the Plato diagram in order to guide the initial sketching in of the broad outlines. The Plato map can then be put aside in order to allow one's readings of Plotinus' texts to fill in the details of the new pattern more freely. When the drawing gets difficult, it can help to pick up the Plato picture again and slip it underneath. And as in the course of time one's understanding of Plato becomes more sophisticated, one can go back and redraw some of the lines on the original transparency.

The comparative approach is equally helpful, though in a somewhat different way, in cases where there is relatively little influence, or where the thinkers are in different but overlapping disciplines. It is illuminating, for example, to compare the ideas of libido and *erōs* in Freud with the notion of *erōs* in Plato. Freud read and revered the latter enough to refer to him as "the divine Plato," but the context and goals of his inquiry were obviously different. Nevertheless, a thorough comparison of the similarities and divergences between the two conceptions can serve to hone our understanding of both philosophical psychologies.

Then one can compare two ideas across philosophies in the same tradition (which are thereby subject to similar influences), but between which there is no influence either way. Kierkegaard's and Nietzsche's understandings of time and eternity are two complex theories of temporality which diverge from traditional treatments in some fascinatingly similar ways. To compare the roles played by the "moment" (Kierkegaard's *Øjeblikket* and Nietzsche's *Augenblick*) in their respective theories provides bilateral insights, in spite—or even because—of the fact that neither influenced the other. This is not to deny that the tracing of the influence of one thinker upon another can be an interesting exercise in the history of ideas. The major concern of comparative philosophy, however, is an understanding of the philosophies themselves—and thereby, to a greater or lesser extent, of the world. And the deepening of such understanding can take place independently of a study of influence.

Finally there is the case of two philosophies from different cultural contexts in which the possibility of influence can be ruled out completely. In lifting the philosophies out of their historical context we do, of course, lose something. But as long as our interpretations of the texts keep the appropriate linguistic and historical contexts in view, and refrain from projecting anachronistic or culturally incongruous meanings on to them, the losses can be outweighed by the gains. More important than the contexts themselves are the situations of the thinkers in relation to their backgrounds. It would be perverse, for example, to compare Nietzsche's philosophy with the thought of the Legalists in Chou dynasty China. However, though the contexts of Nietzsche and Chuang-tzu are totally disparate, and Nietzsche seems to have known little or nothing about Taoism, their relationships to their respective traditions have enough in common to make a comparison of their philosophies worthwhile.

What are the gains from such comparisons? Let us suppose that we can sketch out some fairly broad morphological congruences between the two philosophies. The lines we draw on the transparencies do not represent anything absolute but rather denote connections among the major ideas of the discourses. We might, for example, find that the representation of the notion of *te* (power, *virtus*) in Chuang-tzu in its relationships to other major elements of his thought constitutes a pattern that is remarkably similar to that generated by sketching out the notion of *Wille zur Macht* ("will to power") on the Nietzsche slide. These are both difficult and generally poorly understood ideas, and so a careful mapping of each on to the other can first of all serve to dispel major misconceptions about them. Then comes the more interesting part. Looking through both transparencies, given that we see considerable areas of overlap, the places in which one pattern does not have a counterpart in the other will be conspicuous (especially if we imagine them drawn in different colors). Or, put another way: we follow out a particular parallel for some distance until we find that in one pattern the line of thought stops sooner than in the other. This can send us back to the texts and set us thinking: does this idea really have no counterpart in the other pattern? Sometimes the answer will be "no"; but often we may find that there *is* a corresponding feature in the second philosophy which commentators have persistently overlooked. And where there are differences, we can take it upon ourselves to articulate them as clearly as possible. The fruits of these labors consist in a better understanding of both philosophies and of the topic in question.

However, given a comparison which demonstrates congruity between totally unrelated philosophies or systems of thought, there may be a temptation to say something more—perhaps that both thinkers are "saying the same thing about the same thing." Suppose we discern substantial similarities between, say, the Presocratic notion of *logos* and the Taoist understanding of *tao*, would some (part) of us not want to say that these terms refer to the same non-Thing—*das Selbe*, or Being? But Heidegger, though he sometimes speaks of Being as *das Selbe*, would be reluctant to speak of "the same" between languages as different as ancient Greek and classical Chinese. Or one could go further and side with Nietzsche and the Derrideans, who would deny the existence of any "transcendental signified" outside the various realms of discourse.

What prompts us to want to say that in such cases thinkers from disparate traditions are saying the same thing is the desire, when faced with congruent patterns in different discourses, to posit some *ground* for the congruences, to say that the discourses are being patterned by the same thing, or event, or process. But if one is uncomfortable with anything approaching a *Weltgeist*, one could hypostasize less by saying that the patterns reflect underlying similarities in "forms of life," or deeper truths about what it is to be a human being.

There can be a genuine problem concerning the significance of the "and" in titles of books or papers which engage in comparisons, and the question "So what?" can often be posed legitimately as the final page is turned. But ultimately the criteria for the success of a comparative study of two thinkers from different traditions are no different from those pertaining to a discussion of a single philosopher. The question in both cases is, simply: does the study enhance our understanding of the philosopher's thought, of the problems engaged by it—and of ourselves and the world?

II

Hans-Georg Gadamer, the foremost living thinker among Heidegger's many eminent students, has said that Heidegger studies would do well to pursue seriously comparisons of his work with Asian philosophies.[3] This kind of research has, however, been slow to be undertaken—especially in view of Heidegger's considerable interest in Asian thought. The grounds for this relative lack of enthusiasm deserve some consideration.

The major reason is that both Heidegger's thinking and Asian philosophy have been regarded—at least until fairly recently—as quite marginal enterprises by the mainstream of the Anglo-American philosophical tradition. For decades Heidegger was dismissed by many eminent analytical philosophers as a hopelessly pompous and muddle-headed obscurantist. It seems now, however, thanks in part to the work of such broaderminded thinkers in the analytic tradition as Richard Rorty, that Heidegger's place in the annals of twentieth-century philosophy as a whole is finally secured. The increasing number of competent translations and greater sophistication in the secondary literature published in the past several years provide further confirmation.

The same kinds of analytical philosophers who dismissed Heidegger have generally been even more dismissive of Asian philosophy, often questioning with blatant chauvinism whether such a thing is not clearly a contradiction in terms. However, as the number of scholars with sufficient training in the appropriate languages and in Western philosophy increases, the field of Asian and comparative philosophy is becoming more firmly established, though full acceptance by the philosophical community at large will presumably take some time.

A major source of resistance to both Heidegger's and Asian thought stems from a complex of prejudices to the effect that: the proper medium for philosophical writing is the treatise rather than any more literary form; philosophy must work with intellectual concepts rather than play with poetic images; in such work reason is primary and imagination secondary, if not downright counter-productive; and rational and logical argumentation is the only appropriate method. If these are taken as criteria for philosophy, then most of Heidegger's writings and the majority of the major texts of Asian thought fail to qualify. Heidegger's claims that his thinking is more rigorous (*strenger*) than the exactness of logical ratiocination fall on deaf ears, as do the warnings of Asian specialists that standards of exactness set up by Western philosophy are simply inapplicable to most kinds of thinking conducted in languages unrelated to the Indo-European family. However, as the approaching bankruptcy and increasing irrelevance of the narrowest forms of analytical philosophy become apparent, there are signs that the Western conception of what counts as philosophy is gradually broadening once again.

Another factor that has hindered the acceptance of Asian thought on a larger scale is the difficulty of finding an appropriate terminology into which to translate Asian philosophical materials. The understanding of such texts in the West was initially vitiated by the tendency on the part of the early translators to translate them into the language of traditional (Platonic/Christian) metaphysics. While this language was appropriate for some works, it subjected the majority to gross distortion. The employment of the vocabulary of contemporary analytic philosophy does not generally fare much better. The realization has dawned recently, however, that the European Continental tradition—and existentialism and phenomenology in particular—has developed philosophical terminologies that are far more in harmony with many strains of Asian thought than are those of Anglo-American philosophy.

Much of Heidegger's language, because it reflects and embodies a way of thinking that is quite different from traditional Western metaphysics, appears to offer a wealth of resources for comparative endeavors. There is good reason to suppose that the development of comparative researches on Heidegger will be bilaterally illuminating: if done well, they should induce people interested in Heidegger to be more open to Asian thought, and on the other hand can provide Asian specialists (and especially translators of philosophical texts) with an appropriate vocabulary and numerous points of reference in a contemporary thinker whose understanding of the history of Western philosophy is rivaled by few others. Western comparativists can look to the East for encouragement in these endeavors, since Heidegger's interest in Asian thought has generated considerable reciprocal interest in his work on the part of the Oriental philosophical world.

A further reason for the relative lack of enthusiasm for comparative work on Heidegger (relative to the general resurgence of interest in his thinking over the past several years) is probably that the extent of his knowledge of Asian philosophy is not yet widely appreciated. The few, relatively cursory references to Asian thought in Heidegger's published writings do not suggest that he was any better acquainted with it than the average German scholar of his day. The story related by William Barrett in his introduction to *Zen Buddhism: Selected Writings of D. T. Suzuki* about Heidegger's laudatory remarks about Zen is, if not apocryphal, at least worn thin through constant citation (usually without further reflection). It will come as a surprise to many Heidegger scholars to learn from Professor Pöggeler's contribution to the present volume the extent of Heidegger's interest in and acquaintance with Asian culture in general—and particularly that he was familiar with the work of at least one Taoist thinker as early as 1930.

Given this information, the question arises: if Heidegger was so impressed by and enthusiastic about Taoist thought over a period of half a century, why then did he mention it only twice during those fifty years of publishing works of philosophy? I put this question to Professor Gadamer not long ago, and his response is well worth relating (though it is impossible to convey a sense of the subtle smile which accompanied his answer): "You have to understand that a scholar of the generation to which Heidegger belongs would be very reluctant to say anything in print about a philosophy if he were himself unable to read and understand the relevant texts in the original language."

While a number of articles have appeared comparing Heidegger with various Eastern thinkers and philosophies, no book-length study has appeared on the topic. A symposium on "Heidegger and Eastern Thought" was held at the University of Hawaii in 1969 in celebration of his eightieth birthday. In a letter sent to the organizers of the conference Heidegger wrote: "Again and again it has seemed urgent to me that a dialogue take place with the thinkers of what is to us the Eastern world." During the past fifteen years such a dialogue has been pursued in various forums, one of the major voices having been that of Chang Chung-yuan, Professor Emeritus at the University of Hawaii, who has published the only book devoted to a study of Heidegger and Taoism.[4] Hawaii therefore seems an appropriate location for gathering the fruits of some of these subsequent reflections—essays by authors of seven different nationalities relating Heidegger's thought to Indian, Chinese, Japanese and Tibetan philosophies. Most of the papers have been written especially for this volume or are appearing in English for the first time. Of particular interest are the contributions by the five Japanese philosophers, since so little modern Japanese thought has so far been available in translation.

III

Given the tradition of interest in Indian thought on the part of such philosophers as Hegel, Schelling, Schopenhauer and Nietzsche, combined with continued enthusiasm from his contemporaries (Rudolf Otto, Max Scheler and Karl Jaspers, for example), it is remarkable that Heidegger hardly ever mentions Indian philosophy. J. L. Mehta in his essay on Heidegger and Vedānta suggests that a partial explanation for this lack of interest was Heidegger's critical attitude towards the neo-Kantian presuppositions with which most of his older contemporaries approached Eastern thought. Also, Sanskrit, being an Indo-European language, is close to Greek (and far from East Asian languages) in having a subject-verb-object structure which tends to promote "metaphysical" thinking. Nevertheless, while Heidegger wants to "think what remains unthought" in the beginnings of philosophy with the ancient Greeks, he is still attempting this by way of an Indo-European language—and so in spite of his apparent lack of interest in "how Sanskrit speaks," the comparison with another of the world's great beginnings in philosophy is fruitful. Rather than undertaking morphological comparisons between Heidegger's sense of Being and Śaṃkara's understanding of Brahman, Professor Mehta's essay explores both paths of thinking *as questioning,* paying careful attention to the medium as an integral part of the message. By focusing on the non-dual aspect of Advaita Vedānta (which corresponds to the theme of "the between"—*das Zwischen*—in Heidegger, though Mehta does not mention the term in this context), the author uncovers some significant similarities among the differences between Vedānta thinking and Heidegger's, as in the dimension of the Holy they both attempt "the thinking of the unthought in what has been thought."

Otto Pöggeler is, next to Gadamer, the foremost Heidegger scholar in Germany, and has written his essay on Heidegger and Taoism especially for the present anthology. Given the paucity of references to Chinese philosophy in Heidegger's published works so far, it will be a revelation to most readers to learn of Heidegger's interest in Asian culture generally dating from quite early in his career. Professor Pöggeler provides a fascinating account of the extent of Heidegger's acquaintance with Chuang-tzu and Lao-tzu, of his contacts with scholars from Asia, and of his interest in Oriental art and culture. One of the author's major theses, which needs to be taken into account by subsequent studies of the development of Heidegger's later thinking, is that his engagement with Chinese philosophy, and with the *Tao Te Ching* of Lao-tzu in particular, exerted a decisive effect on the form and direction of his later thinking. The significant factor here is Heidegger's encounter with a philosophy couched in a language with a structure totally different from that of Indo-European languages.[5]

Paul Shih-yi Hsiao's contribution is a personal account of his collaboration with Heidegger on a partial translation of the *Tao Te Ching* during the summer of 1946. The essay presents a vivid picture of Heidegger as a painstaking questioner—such an industrious inquirer into the Chinese language that the translation proceeded at a rate of only a line or two per week—and above all a modest and attentive listener in his conversations with guests from the Orient. One hopes that the fruits of these collaborative labors, which are presumably buried amid piles of Heidegger's unpublished materials, will some day come to light.

Joan Stambaugh, herself an accomplished translator of Heidegger's work into English, offers some delightful meditations upon the related themes of *Weg* (way) and *Gelassenheit* (releasement), which point up their resonances with Taoist ideas. While the primary focus is upon later texts and on ideas such as *Ereignis* (appropriation) and *Inständigkeit* (indwelling), her discussion of the early appearances of the notion of *Weg* serves to point up the essential continuity of Heidegger's path of thinking.

My own contribution to the discussion is concerned to show the extent to which there appears to have been a "pre-established harmony" between Heidegger's thinking and Taoism, by uncovering a number of quasi-Taoist themes in Heidegger's early work—and in *Sein und Zeit* in particular—on the assumption that this work antedated his contact with Chinese philosophy. To see that the germs of the later poetic meditations on themes such as "releasement toward things" are already there in the early work again enhances our sense of the integrity of the development of his thought.

The reception of Heidegger in Japan has been the most enthusiastic of any country—perhaps even including Germany itself. A remarkable indication of the zeal with which Heidegger scholarship has been pursued there is the fact that a Japanese translation of *Sein und Zeit* was published only twelve years after the book's first appearance in 1927, and that during the following thirty years no fewer than *five* further translations were published. By contrast, the first translation into English did not appear until 1962, and though this valiant effort can now be perceived to be woefully inadequate, no further English translation has reached print.

Japan's foremost living philosopher is Keiji Nishitani, who for many years was the "Dean" of the Kyoto School of philosophy, and since his retirement from Kyoto University has been teaching at Otani Buddhist University in Kyoto. Heidegger's influence on Nishitani has been greater than on any other prominent Japanese philosopher, and the latter's understanding and assimilation of Heidegger's thought is deeper, in my opinion, than that of his predecessors or contemporaries. This is most evident from his major work, *Shūkyō to wa nani ka?*, which was recently translated into English as *Religion and Nothingness*.[6] I am reprinting here (with the author's kind permission, and with slight modification of the translation) his commentary on two addresses by Heidegger delivered in his home town of Messkirch, since it is the earliest example published in English of a view of Heidegger's thought from the perspective of Zen.

In this connection it is worth mentioning the source of Heidegger's acquaintance with Zen ideas, as related by Professor Nishitani in his foreword to one of the volumes of the Japanese edition of the *Collected Works* of D. T. Suzuki. In 1938 Nishitani was doing research in Freiburg, where Heidegger was teaching, and ordered from Blackwells in England the first volume of Suzuki's *Essays in Zen Buddhism,* which he presented to Heidegger for his birthday. Shortly thereafter, Heidegger sent a card inviting Nishitani to visit him at his home; it turned out that he had already read Suzuki's book and was eager to discuss it. He was particularly interested in the well-known story in the *Rinzai Roku* (the *Lin-chi Records*) about Rinzai and Ōbaku (Chinese: Huang-po) and Daigu. Rinzai, while a pupil of Ōbaku's, went to the monastery of Daigu, another Zen master, and on being asked what Ōbaku had to say, Rinzai replied: "I asked him three times what was the essence of Buddhism, and three times he beat me." When he went back to Ōbaku the latter asked him what Daigu had to say, and Rinzai told him what had happened. Ōbaku then said, "Just wait, I'll beat you up!"—to which Rinzai replied, "What do you mean about waiting? Get it right now!" and accordingly struck his master with considerable force. Nishitani explained to Heidegger the "living logic . . . of the oneness of Rinzai's affirmation and negation of Ōbaku" and the "complex transformation between self and other" evidenced by "Rinzai's identifying Ōbaku with Daigu . . . and himself with Ōbaku." Heidegger then said with a smile that he had got "a rough idea" (no pun in the Japanese) of what Zen was about.[7] Heidegger's interest in Zen was such that Suzuki's book prompted him to take out and read the only book on Zen he could find in the university library (*Zen: der lebendige Buddhismus in Japan,* by Ohazama and Faust), which he found "also very interesting."[8]

Yasuo Yuasa provides a comprehensive account of the salient details of the history of the reception of Heidegger's thought in Japan beginning from the early twenties. It is well known that the development of the Kyoto School of philosophy was considerably influenced by Heidegger's thinking, but the details are inaccessible to the Western scholar who does not read Japanese. Professor Yuasa's essay is thus of particular interest insofar as it discusses Heidegger's influence on three prominent philosophers of the Kyoto School whose work is almost unknown in the West: Hajime Tanabe, Shūzō Kuki, and Kiyoshi Miki. The essay concludes with an account of Heidegger's influence on the somewhat better known philosopher Tetsurō Watsuji, and an evaluation of the latter's understanding and criticisms of Heidegger's thought.

Akihiro Takeichi examines the problem of nihilism in Heidegger, orienting us to the issue by way of a preliminary discussion of its genesis in Nietzsche's thought. He discusses the way in which the oblivion of Being in Western metaphysics has led to a distorted and deficient view of beings that is manifest in the "enframing" *(Ge-Stell)* of modern technology. Through invoking the notion of *karma* and related ideas from Mahayana Buddhism, the author outlines a corresponding understanding of nihilism in the Eastern tradition and reflects on ways in which the Buddhist response to the issue of karma might illuminate Heidegger's discussion of the problems generated by the age of technology.

Kōhei Mizoguchi, in his essay on Heidegger's Bremen lectures of 1949, undertakes something that has not, as far as I know, been attempted in the secondary literature in English—namely, an examination of all four lectures together that focuses on their internal relations. While the author alludes to a comparison of Heidegger's thought with that of Kitarō Nishida, the founder of the Kyoto School, his essay consists mainly of a close and careful reading of Heidegger's four texts. These lectures are particularly important because they constitute a critical transition between Heidegger's "middle period" and his later thought, and Professor Mizoguchi's discussion circles around these four presentations in a pleasingly hermeneutical manner.

The hermeneutical approach informs the last of the Japanese contributions, an essay by Tetsuaki Kotoh on the roles of language and silence in the process of self-inquiry according to Heidegger on the one hand and Zen on the other. The author shows that while language, as "the house of Being," has always been of crucial importance in Heidegger, it has its ultimate source in a certain kind of silence—and that in this respect his position (which is more or less unique in the Western tradition) is remarkably close to that of Zen philosophy.

The topic of *the body* has not been a prominent one in Western philosophy. In general, it has been taken up only to be put down in unfavorable comparison with the soul or mind. Under the influence of the ascetic aspects of Plato and the Christian tradition the body has been largely dismissed as a proper object of philosophical reflection—except as it encroaches upon the sphere of the psychical and mental through the phenomena of sensation and perception, the emotions and instincts, and so on. Nietzsche was the first Western philosopher in a long time to rectify the impression that man is only contingently embodied by devoting a considerable amount of thought to the body and its mysteries. Merleau-Ponty has continued the trend by undertaking comprehensive phenomenological analyses of human embodiment. However, a number of contemporary phenomenologists—and not just devotees of Merleau-Ponty—reproach Heidegger for furthering the traditional philosophical neglect of the body. The analytic of *Dasein* in *Being and Time* is often accused of being overly mentalistic and of dismissing the somatic aspects of our being-here. Such criticisms stem from short-sighted literalism, based presumably on the fact that the words *Leib* and *Körper* appear only rarely in the text. But one of Heidegger's major motives in choosing to use the term *Dasein* was to undercut the Cartesian dualism of mind and body. The language of *Being and Time* has more body to it than that of most philosophical texts, being—especially in the original German—quite muscular, if not always supple, prose. If one insists on making the distinction between mind and body, then the existential structures elaborated by Heidegger refer just as much to our somatic presence as to our psychical or mental being.[9]

Attending as much to the somatic as to the psychical, Hwa Yol Jung opens the discussion out into a more cosmopolitan arena, beginning by situating Heidegger's encounter with Eastern philosophy in the context of the previous European engagement with Oriental thought from Hegel through Husserl to Merleau-Ponty. The *leitmotiv* of this essay is "the piety of thinking," where thinking is understood as a *Handwerk,* a work of the hand, the consummate product of which would be the Chinese ideogram as a manifestation of "the human body in graceful motion." Thinking and speaking and doing are inseparable in Heidegger—just as in Chinese philosophy, and especially for Confucius, the words of the thoughtful person have extraordinary ("performative") power. Professor Jung explicates the piety of thinking, with its emphasis on the closeness of the aural rather than the distance of the visual, as the appropriate mode or pathway for "gathering or orchestrating our thoughts—both Eastern and Western."

If the problematic of the body appears to be no more prominent in the Eastern tradition than in the West, this is not merely because the body has been similarly summarily dismissed by certain ascetic philosophies (as in some forms of Hinduism and Buddhism). The deeper reason is that in other philosophies, such as most Chinese and Tibetan thought, the human being is regarded *in toto* rather than as split into dichotomies. One of the concerns of David Levin's essay, "Mudra as Thinking," is "to interpret Heidegger in a way that brings out the embodiment implicit in his thinking," thereby rectifying a number of misconceptions of the nature of his enterprise. At the same time the author presents some corresponding ideas from Tibetan Buddhist philosophy—a field not yet well known or understood in the West—and shows through a carefully phenomenological discussion the importance of somatic awareness on the path of enlightenment in the Vajrayana Buddhist tradition.

IV

In his letter to the organizers of the East-West Philosophers' Conference in Hawaii, Heidegger wrote:

The greatest difficulty in the enterprise [of a dialogue between Eastern and Western thinking] always lies, as far as I can see, in the fact that with few exceptions there is no command of the Eastern languages either in Europe or the United States. . . . May your conference prove fruitful in spite of this circumstance.

The conference has borne fruit, and the exceptions have become more numerous. Still, the difficulty remains hard to overcome, since most of the scholars who are competent in Asian languages are in fields other than philosophy. To learn sufficient Sanskrit or Chinese or Japanese to be able to read what needs to be read is a long and arduous task—as is the acquisition of a good understanding of Heidegger's thought, together with the requisite grounding in ancient Greek and subsequent Western philosophy. Few mortals have time and energy to undertake both. Nevertheless, even a modest acquaintance with Asian languages can help; and the more one understands the language, the deeper one's understanding of the philosophy. Many philosophers in Asia have learned Western languages; if we are to respond to Heidegger's call for "planetary thinking" it is time to make a reciprocal effort. If we in the West can add our voices to the dialogue in other tongues and learn to read with wider opened eyes and ears, we may then be able to engage Asian thought in such a way that "there sings something that wells up from a single source."

It was in connection with the necessity of making our way back to the place from which nihilism and metaphysics can be overcome that Heidegger wrote of "planetary thinking."[10] It involves cultivating the polysemy of the saying of thinking (die Sage des Denkens)—though Heidegger expressed doubts, back then in the fifties, as to whether we were equal to the task. However, the words he used encourage the spirit in which the present anthology is presented:[11]

[These doubts hold] equally for both European and East Asian language, and above all for the realm of their possible dialogue. Neither side can of itself open up and establish this realm.

Notes

1. See Gottfried Wilhelm Leibniz, *Discourse on the Natural Theology of the Chinese,* trans. Henry Rosemont, Jr. and Daniel J. Cook (Honolulu: University Press of Hawaii, 1977); and David E. Mungello, *Leibniz and Confucianism: The Search for Accord* (Honolulu: University Press of Hawaii, 1977).

2. An excellent treatment of this topic is Freny Mistry, *Nietzsche and Buddhism* (Berlin and New York: de Gruyter, 1981), which will be of interest to readers concerned with comparative approaches to Heidegger also (though he is not explicitly discussed). Mistry deals exclusively with early Buddhism; for some points of comparison with contemporary Buddhist thought, see Graham Parkes, "Nietzsche and Nishitani on the Self through Time," *The Eastern Buddhist* 17, no. 2 (1984).

3. Personal communication, 1985.

4. Chang Chung-yuan, *Tao: A New Way of Thinking* (New York: Harper and Row, 1975).

For a bibliography of the secondary literature, see Hans-Martin Sass, *Martin Heidegger: Bibliography and Glossary* (Bowling Green, Ohio: Philosophy Documentation Center, 1982). This is a most comprehensive work containing several useful indexes, a glossary of Heideggerian terminology in numerous languages, and a broad selection from the voluminous secondary literature in Japanese.

5. In this connection see the latter half of Johannes Lohmann's insightful and thorough study, "Heidegger's Ontological Difference and Language," in J. J. Kockelmans (ed.), *On Heidegger and Language* (Evanston: Northwestern University Press, 1972), pp. 303–363.

6. Keiji Nishitani, *Religion and Nothingness,* trans. Jan Van Bragt (Berkeley, Los Angeles, London: University of California Press, 1982); *Was Ist Religion?,* trans. Dora Fischer-Barnicol (Frankfurt: Insel Verlag, 1982). The German translation is particularly recommended since it was completely proofed by the author and in the process considerably expanded. Part 2 of Hans Waldenfels, *Absolute Nothingness* (New York: Paulist Press, 1980) offers an exegesis of Nishitani's work with frequent reference to Heidegger, though more from a theological than a philosophical perspective. Also of interest in this context is Yoshinori Takeuchi, *The Heart of Buddhism* (New York: Crossroad, 1983), a profound and lucid exposition of the "existential" aspects of Shin Buddhism that makes frequent and illuminating reference to Heidegger.

7. Suzuki recounts only the first part of the story: see D. T. Suzuki, *Essays in Zen Buddhism, First Series* (New York: Grove Press, 1961), pp. 306–307. The fuller story can be found in *The Zen Teaching of Rinzai,* trans. Irmgard Schloegl (Berkeley: Shambhala Publications, 1976), pp. 78–79.

8. My thanks are due to Dr. Shigenori Nagatomo for translating these excerpts from Professor Nishitani's essay.

9. If we look at the basic elements of the words Heidegger uses to denote the structures of being-in-the-world we find: hand-ling *(das Zuhand*en*e/Vorhand*ene*),* grasping *(er*greifen*),* holding *(Ver*halten*),* standing *(Ver*stehen*; Selbst-*ständigkeit*; Ek*stasen*),* stretching *(sich er*strecken*),* throwing *(Ge*worfen*heit; Ent-*wurf*),* jumping *(voraus-*springend*),* running *(vor*laufen*),* falling *(das Ver*fallen*),* and so on.

The section entitled "Intoxication as an aesthetic condition" *(Der Rausch als ästhetischer Zustand)* in the first volume of Heidegger's *Nietzsche,* one of the few occasions on which he speaks explicitly of the body *(Leib),* shows the central importance Heidegger accords to the phenomenon of human embodiment. There he writes, for instance, "We do not 'have' a body but rather 'are' bodily [*wir 'sind' leiblich*]" and "we live in as far as we 'body' [*wir leben, indem wir leiben*]" *(Nietzsche* [Pfullingen: Neske, 1961], pp. 118–119; English translation by David F. Krell, *Nietzsche: The Will to Power as Art* [New York: Harper and Row, 1979], sec. 14).

10. In the letter to Ernst Jünger which constitutes the text of *Zur Seinsfrage* (1955), in *Holzwege* (Frankfurt: Klostermann, 1967); *The Question of Being,* trans. William Kluback and Jean T. Wilde (New York: Twayne, 1958).

11. *Holzwege,* p. 252.

J. L. Mehta

Heidegger and Vedānta:
Reflections on a Questionable Theme

What is questionable can sometimes be worthy of thought, and what is unthinkable can sometimes be glimpsed as that which thinking is about. Both Heidegger and Vedānta thought amply illustrate this. No other justification can be offered for the following very questionable enterprise of bringing together two disparate ways of thinking, so wide apart in time and in their entire context. The attempt can have unquestioned validity only for those who believe, like Nicolai Hartmann and many contemporary comparativists, that there are "eternal problems" in philosophy, everywhere and at all times the same, or, with Paul Deussen, that it is the same voice of the Eternal Truth that is heard by thinking spirits everywhere.[1]

Perhaps, however, the task of thinking, in the comparative sphere, is not limited to the search for what is common to the thought-content (the thoughts, the *Gedanke,* the answers given) of two different philosophical traditions, or the construction of new concepts overarching them, nor to the quest of motifs in another tradition that may supplement a deficiency in one's own and so "enrich" it. Perhaps there is, beyond this, the more exciting, in the end even more rewarding, task of trying to see and lay open the hidden truth of the paths taken by thinking (the *Denken,* the movement of thinking, the questions asked) in each, and letting questions arise in the process and stay with us, without seeking to come up with precipitate answers. This involves a movement of thought that is less like an arrow in flight toward its target than a roving and a rambling, a movement to and fro, between two different realms of discourse and vision, an exploration of two different topologies. There are no predetermined rules for a game of this kind, only the playing of the game can generate the rules, if at all. So much by way of apology for the following fragmentary, somewhat Heideggerian, remarks on this questionable theme.

I

Deussen quotes the following passage from Śaṃkara's *Commentary* on the *Brahmasūtra* (I, iii, 33) as "characteristic for Śaṃkara's period as well as for his theological conception":

> For also, what is for us imperceptible was for the ancients perceptible; thus it is recorded, that Vyāsa (the author of the Mahābhārata) and others used to meet the Gods and [Rishis] face to face. But if some would assert that, as for those now living so for the ancients also it was impossible to meet with gods and the like, they would deny the variety of the world; they might also maintain that, as at present, so also in other times, there was no world-swaying prince *(sārvabhaumaḥ kṣatriyaḥ)* and thus they would not acknowledge the injunctions referring to the consecration of kings; they might further assume that, as at present, so also in other times, the duties of castes and Āśramas had no stable rules, and thus treat as vain the canon of law which provides rules for them. We must therefore believe that the ancients, in consequence of pre-eminent merits, held visible converse with Gods and [Rishis]. The Smṛti also says (*Yogasūtra* 2, 44): "through study [is gained] union with the beloved godhead." And when it further teaches, that Yoga bestows as reward the mastery of nature, consisting [in the freedom from embodied being and its laws, and thereby] in the ability to become as small as an atom and the like, this is not to be rejected out of hand by a mere dictatorial sentence. [2]

Śaṃkara goes on to quote the *Śruti* (*Svetāśvatara Upaniṣad* II, 12) proclaiming the greatness of Yoga, and adds that we do not have "the right to measure by our capabilities the capability of the Rishis who see the mantras and Brāhmaṇa (i.e., the Veda)." Śaṃkara remarks in conclusion,

> From all this it appears that the itihāsas and purāṇas have an adequate basis. And the conceptions of ordinary life also must not be declared to be unfounded, if it is at all possible to accept them. The general result is that we have the right to conceive the gods as possessing personal existence, on the ground of mantras, arthavādas, itihāsas, purāṇas, and ordinary prevailing ideas. [3]

Here, the gods are absent but they are not denied; they have withdrawn from man's sight but still form a presence on the horizon. A world has passed, but its links with the present are not broken. The present, though impoverished, is still seen, understood and interpreted in the light of a nobler past and as continuous with it. Śaṃkara would not perhaps have said, with Heraclitus, that "Here too there are gods," but would have found little to quarrel with Catullus when he said of the golden age: then indeed did the gods come down and visit with men. Life, in this Upaniṣadic tradition, was still experienced as touched by the Divine, and the dimension of the holy provided the context for all inquiry into reality and into the nature and destiny of man, and for the pursuit of freedom and immortality. The quest for truth was still a quest for the truth of life, for the living truth, and its articulation into a coherent body of argued and examined statements; it was not just a matter of detached theoretical contemplation. It was a profoundly religious quest, and yet a passionately intellectual one.

The eighth century in India, when Śaṃkara probably lived and wrote, was the century that experienced the impact of the Buddhist thinker Dharmakīrti, of Kumārila and Prabhākara, thinkers of the Pūrva Mīmāṃsā school, of Maṇḍana Miśra, the lone-wolf in the history of Advaita Vedānta, as he has been aptly described, and a century which was heir to the imposing and strikingly original work of the Speculative Grammarians. But the India of this century, and of many more centuries to come, was not yet under the shadow of what Nietzsche called "the spirit of Socratism," and its thinking was not primarily an operation with concepts about a reality understood solely in terms of being, but had something of the quality of meditation, reflection, and remembrance, even in the midst of the lively give and take of argument and debate so characteristic of the Indian philosophical scene. What is to be heard, thought about, and meditated upon is not a bare ontological principle or a metaphysical ultimate, ground, or *archē,* but a reality experienceable and experienced as sacred. And the hearing, the reflecting and arguing, the meditating, the learning and teaching, the composition of commentaries and independent critical or creative works, all these activities are carried on within the dimension of the holy and the ambience of the Divine.[4]

The medium is not irrelevant to the message and is often part of it. But concern for the "philosophy" of the Upaniṣads and the Vedānta, for their content, has stood in the way of sufficient attention being paid to the medium: the literary structure and style; the poetry and not just the prose of these writings; the rhetoric and what appear to be minor embellishments; the magico-mythic elements still clinging to an endeavor where they do not seem rightfully to belong (for example, the role of the sacred syllable *Oṃ*); above all, the verses of obeisance and praise to be found at the beginning and conclusion of most Vedānta works.[5] It is not just a matter of convention and good form when Gauḍapāda concludes his *Kārikā* with a salutation to "the state of non-multiplicity" or when Śaṃkara begins and concludes his commentary on the same work with an obeisance to "that Brahman which destroys all fear in those who take shelter in It," and when, at the commencement of *Upadeśasāhasrī* XVIII, he bows down "to that Eternal Consciousness, the Self of the modifications of the intellect, in which they merge and from which they arise"; or when Sūreśvara, in the opening verse of the *Naiṣkarmyasiddhi,* offers obeisance to "that Hari, the witness of the intellect, dispeller of darkness." And when, towards the end of this work, he speaks of the Vedānta as a "science flowing out from the holy foot of Viṣṇu," this is no figure of speech only.

Nor is the idea, and historically the fact, of a world-renouncer *(saṃnyāsin)* and a wandering monk as the only one competent to pursue the inquiry—not just any "secular" scholar—into this sacred reality, a mere sociological curiosity. For Vedānta, thinking is not simply an expression of that universal urge so crisply stated by Aristotle: all men by nature desire to know *(eidenai)*; the urge which becomes, when joined with the *pathos* of wonderment *(thaumazein),* the *archē* of all philosophy, as Plato said. Nor is it identifiable with that *epistēmē theoretikē* which, in Aristotle's words, inquires after the first principles and causes of being or with that pursuit which he described as "that which is sought both of old and now and forever and forever missed is, what is being *(ti to on)?*"[6] In the Upaniṣadic tradition, too, there is a seeking, to which the intellectual quest is integral, but there is also a finding, which does not consist in merely putting at rest the *pathos* of *thaumazein* or in the discovery of its inexhaustible power to nourish unceasing inquiry, but concerns the whole man and the transformation and fulfillment of his human state. And both, the seeking and the finding, presuppose the experienced dimension of the holy and the darkly seen presence of truth as sacred and saving.

II

Turning now to Heidegger, we find ourselves in a completely different life-world; it is the world of our present-day experience, life as we all experience it, irrespective of how we individually choose to respond to it. The world in which and for which Heidegger writes is a world which Nietzsche meant when he spoke of "how the influence of Socrates, down to the present moment and even unto all future time, has spread over posterity like a shadow that keeps growing in the evening sun"; a world under the domination of that "profound illusion," again in Nietzsche's words, which lies in "the unshakable faith that thought, using the thread of logic, can penetrate the deepest abysses of being, and that thought is capable not only of knowing being but even of *correcting* it."[7] It is, further, a world which has been determined by the spread of Christianity and its subsequent secularization, so that, in the words of Arend Theodoor van Leeuwen, "in the spread of modern Western civilizations throughout the world something of the spirit of 'Christianity incognito' is at work."[8] It is a world shaped by the Enlightenment and by the spirit of technology, a world disenchanted and desacralized, as Max Weber saw. As Heidegger has also described it, a characteristic feature of the modern world is the flight of the gods *(Entgötterung):*

This expression does not mean the mere setting aside of the gods, a crude atheism. The disappearance of the gods is a two-sided process. First, the world image is Christianized, in so far as the ground of the world is set up as the infinite, the unconditioned, the absolute; on the other hand, Christendom gives a new interpretation to its Christian character by transforming it into a world-view, thus adapting itself to modernity. Desacralization *(Entgötterung)* is the state of indecision regarding God and the gods. Christendom has the largest share in the emergence of this state. But desacralization does not exclude religiosity; indeed, it is through it primarily that the relationship with the gods is transformed into religious experience *(Erlebnis)* as a subjective process. Once it comes to this, then the gods have indeed fled. The consequent emptiness is filled up by the historical and psychological investigation of myth, as a substitute.[9]

The question of Being, as Heidegger poses it, is marked by a radical putting into question of all that has led up to this present state, of the entire Greek-Christian tradition of thought which he sums up under the word "metaphysics." Equally radical is his attempt to so transform "the question of Being" itself, from its original formulation by the Greek thinkers, through the thinkers of medieval Europe, down to his own initial manner of posing it, that this questioning itself becomes a path of preparing for a possible future in which the dimension of the holy may once again give meaning to our world, no longer forsaken by the gods, and man heal himself through a thinking which has freed itself at last from its tutelage to the Greek paradigm.

The world-historical context in which Heidegger raises the question of Being is one which he has described as "the darkening of the world, the flight of the gods, the devastation of the earth, the transformation of men into a mass, the hatred and suspicion of everything creative."[10] The essence of this darkening of the world is the absence of God, as Hölderlin experienced it, in this destitute time, to which we ourselves still belong. Heidegger's explanation of the neediness of this time is worth quoting in full:

For Hölderlin's historical experience, the appearance and sacrificial death of Christ mark the beginning of the end of the day of the gods. Night is falling. Ever since the "united three"—Herakles, Dionysos, and Christ—have left the world, the evening of the world's age has been declining towards its night. The world's night is spreading its darkness. The era is defined by the god's failure to arrive, by the "default of God." But the default of God which Hölderlin experienced does not deny that the Christian relationship with God lives on in individuals and in the churches; still less does it assess this relationship negatively. The default of God means that no god any longer gathers men and things unto himself, visibly and unequivocally, and by such gathering disposes the world's history and man's sojourn in it. The default of God forebodes something even grimmer, however. Not only have the gods and the god fled, but the divine radiance has become extinguished in the world's history. The time of the world's night is the destitute time, because it becomes ever more destitute. It has already grown so destitute, it can no longer discern the default of God as a default.[11]

The question of Being, as it unfolds in Heidegger's thinking, is directly relevant to this destitution of the present age, "for which the ground fails to come, hangs in the abyss"; it is a reaching down into the abyss, experiencing and enduring it, so that a "turning of the age" and the return of the gods may be prepared for through a rethinking of Being.

With all his originality and brilliance, Śaṃkara writes as at one with his tradition, a tradition mediated, it is true, by the passing of the Vedic age and by a long period of Buddhist intellectual and religious dominance, but yet unbroken. Heidegger, on the contrary, starts off, with Nietzsche as precursor, as a radical thinker in whom the crises of thought and sensibility in the sciences and philosophy, in theology and in literature, are gathered to a focus. Śaṃkara too was not just a traditionalist intent on restoring the Vedic tradition but was a thinker moved by the experience of his age as destitute, pervaded by an absence and hanging in the abyss. The rise and development of the Buddhist schools (as of some others) in the preceding centuries was only a symptom of this, bringing to the surface a corrosion in the very substance of things, the abyss that was opening up in the very core of what is and summed up in the formula "Everything is without a self," and in the elevation of the subjective sphere as the ultimate frame of reference. It is from within this awareness that Śaṃkara understood his work and started on his way of thought, seeking to exhibit how it was still possible and supremely needful to think of life as grounded in Being (*ātman*), to show how experience is unmeaning and an unmitigated pain unless thought of as grounded in a "self," revelatory of it and therefore alive with "the radiance of the divine" (in Heidegger's sense). Śaṃkara said,

> This tree of *saṃsāra*, the round of worldly existence, which sprouts from action and constitutes the field of confusion and error, must be torn out from its very roots. Alone in pulling it out lies the fulfillment of life's purpose.[12]

A statement like this can easily be misunderstood as a classic example of a life-denying philosophy. In reality, what it denies is not life but the death-in-life that consists in taking things as empty of a self, without a ground in Being and yet holding us in their grip through the illusion of being all that there is, exercising this magic spell over us. The purpose of life is fulfilled in exorcising this spell and realizing that the spell arises from our disregard of the truth, the self, veiled under things, and is itself a reflection of our identity with this self or Being.

All great thinkers respond creatively to "the time of need," and so did Śaṃkara, massively, passionately and effectively, to the nihilism of his time, seeking to avoid the extremes of conceiving Being objectivistically, as an object of representation, and total subjectivism. But he did so in an age of divided history—of cultures, peoples, whole civilizations—and he thought from within the confines of a specific culture, and spoke to men sharing a common tradition, still felt as binding, with common ways of experiencing life and of speaking and inquiring about it. Heidegger's thinking, on the contrary, is a response, in full historical self-awareness, to the phenomenon of what he calls "world-civilization," to its correlate, the process of "the Europeanization of the Earth," and to its consequence, homelessness. As Heidegger puts it, "Homelessness has become a world destiny in the form of world-civilization."[13]

This homelessness has come about—has long been coming about, enveloping the future in this inexorable process, as Nietzsche perceived— as a consequence ultimately of the originally Greek comprehension of Being, of the way Being disclosed itself to the Greeks. More accurately perhaps, it is a consequence of the thinking generated by this disclosure (thinking as "philosophy," as metaphysics) and what remained unthought in this Greek understanding of Being. This comprehension, never made explicit, remained dominant in Western thought until Nietzsche's awareness of it as a prejudice, though he never succeeded in adequately formulating this awareness. It also determined the character and nature of this thinking itself, until Nietzsche subjected it to radical questioning, again without clearly seeing the way to a satisfactory formulation of his insight. It is precisely this that Heidegger seeks to accomplish, bringing Nietzsche's insight "to a full unfolding,"[14] inquiring about the predetermined perspective on which the Greek understanding of Being depended and trying to see how the dreary homelessness of our mode of being in the world today has come to pass. It is thus that Heidegger is able to bring Western thought, for the first time in its history, to an awareness of its specific limits, as something historically conditioned and "factitious," as based on specific presuppositions which have constituted its unthought, unverbalized, foundation. He has thus brought it to a realization of its own parochial character as Western thought, that is, as "philosophy," as distinct from other possibilities and modes of thinking, adumbrated or realized elsewhere, elsewhen.

III

But how has this homelessness, this transformation of home into wilderness, how has this harvest of what seems like death become a world destiny in the form of world-civilization? Why must the seeds sown once in Greece generate a desert bound to envelop the whole world of man? Much of Heidegger's thinking since the late thirties has been devoted to showing how Nihilism is not just an isolated phenomenon in the history of the West, nor even the central feature, but that it is the very law of this history, its "logic."[15] How this Western history has assumed in modern times more and more a world-historical character is a question that has been variously answered by Hegel, Marx, Nietzsche, and Christian theologians. Is it because of an inherent entelechy in the Greek idea of reason (the fountainhead of all philosophy and science) towards universal and glad appropriation, as Husserl thought, that a geographically localized history has become planetary? According to Heidegger, science and technology, themselves rooted in "philosophy" and in "metaphysics" as characteristically and uniquely Greek forms of thought, are universally triumphant because they are unrivalled instruments of power over that which is, over every being or entity *(to on, das Seiende),* as presented in the light of the conception of Being implicit in the Western metaphysical tradition. It is when beings are seen in this light that they acquire their character as sheer entities to be measured and manoeuvred. The "Europeanization of the Earth" is in reality the irresistible triumph of this light, through which things become entities and then (in the modern era of subjectivism) objects.

But a prerequisite for the irresistible power of this light is that it should itself remain invisible, that what has remained unthought in the Greek version of Being, its presupposition, should remain unthought. It is to the task of penetrating to this "unthought," of thinking it, that Heidegger addresses himself, and exhibits in his thinking how this power of "Being" can be broken and abated, how a turn in the world destiny of universal homelessness can be brought about. The world has become one only today, in the sense of being universally under the sway of the Greek mode of thinking as the thinking of Being, in terms of Being and as exhibiting everything under the aspect of Being. In seeking to think the unthought in all thinking of Being, Heidegger is the first world-historical, planetary thinker, a thinker who has attempted at the same time to rethink the nature of thinking itself as called for by his discovery of the truth, of that primordial dimension or region from which Being itself derives its nature, a region no longer Greek or parochial.[16]

Nietzsche saw the spectral presence of Nihilism, that uncanniest of guests, standing at mankind's door. Heidegger has succeeded in clearly seeing his visage, identifying and touching in thought this threatening shadow, tracking him down as to his provenance and pin-pointing the exact character of the threat he poses for the world. A danger hangs over the world and over man in it; its presence stalks the world. It is not the loss of religion in general or the brokenness of a particular faith which could be healed by taking the road East; it is not the Atom Bomb and the vividly present possibility of total annihilation for mankind; it is not even modern technology and its effects on human personality and culture. The danger comes from what Heidegger has called the "framework (Ge-stell)," the peculiar constellation of man and Being that lies hidden, unthought, in technology as its characteristic mode of concealment.

But, "where there is danger, there grows also what saves," Heidegger points out, quoting Hölderlin. Within that itself which has generated this danger, and is its unrecalled foundation, there lies the saving resource, forgotten, unthought, and therefore preserved and held in reserve. That same Western metaphysical tradition which has, inevitably, grown into a world-wide destiny contains, when we reach down into its ground, the remedy which alone can bring about a turn in this destiny. The cure must come from the source of the disease, if it is to be effective, because the disease itself is a destiny flowing from what has not been brought within the reach of thinking contained in this source itself, lying in it as a guarded treasure. It is this unthought of the Western tradition, lying beyond the Greek, out of which alone a planetary thinking adequate to the phenomenon of "world-civilization" can emerge. As Heidegger has said,

> The present day planetary-interstellar world situation is, in its essential ori-gin that can never be lost, through and through European-Western-Greek . . . What alters, is capable of doing so only out of that which still remains saved of its great origins. Accordingly, the present-day world situation can receive an essential alteration, or at least a preparation for it, only from that origin which has become fatefully determinative of our age.[17]

The thinking of the unthought of this imperishable Western beginning, however, is also the liberation of thought from its parochial mould and its meeting with the unthought of the other few, really great beginnings in human history. In no case can it be just a return to those beginnings, but only the gathering of resources for a novel beginning in the realm of thinking, for which perhaps, as Heidegger hopes, the initiative and the preparation can come from Europe, "this land of evening out of which the dawn of a new morning, of another world destiny can come."[18] Heidegger's thinking, as he himself conceives it, is a waiting and a prepa-ration for the arrival of what was glimpsed once as promise, but which came bearing a harsh visage, concealing itself behind it completely, and which can come again: the holy, the divine, God, without the "metaphys-ical" mask. Without living commerce with the Immortals, man has become incapable of truly experiencing himself as mortal, and the quest for immortality has become unmeaning. For "mortality," as conceived in terms of the metaphysical conceptions of Being and time, is only a sham and an evasion of the possibility of that awesome experience.

Heidegger's thinking has little to do with "cultural synthesis" or with the notion of a "planetary culture," or with the idea of a "universal philosophy" for the man of today, gathering together the complementary insights of the philosophies of the West and the East. His thinking is post-philosophical, in the sense of being no longer "metaphysical" and no longer operating on the presuppositions implicitly at work in all "philosophy." Yet it is finite, in the sense that it does not claim to make an absolute beginning but can emerge only as mediated by the course of the Western metaphysical tradition and its thinking of Being, as still linked to that which it seeks to overcome. It is, in a sense, the carrying forward through revolutionary transformation of the tradition of Western thought, beginning all over again, so to speak, an enterprise that remains imperishably, essentially Greek and Western; no longer "philosophy," yet, as thinking and asking, still concerned with questions that could be formulated only as mediated by the Greek-Christian course of Western philosophy, with unconcealment *(alētheia)*, opening *(Lichtung)* and presence *(Anwesenheit)*.

Heidegger mentions Indian philosophy (and Chinese) a couple of times in his writings, but only to point out that it is not "philosophy," a term which ought to be reserved for the uniquely Greek form, mode, and concern of thought. As compared with several pointed references to "East Asian thinking," he refers in a positive sense only once, and that, too, almost casually, to anything in Indian thought. This happens in the course of a discussion between him and Eugen Fink on Fragment 26 of Heraclitus, regarding the nature of sleep, where Heidegger remarks, "For Indians the state of sleep is the highest life," a remark dismissed by Fink with the words, "That may well have been the Indian experience."[19]

This unconcern is somewhat surprising in view of the attention given by Herder, the German Romantics, Schelling, Hegel, Schopenhauer, and Nietzsche to Indian philosophy, surprising in view of the fact that Deussen, who was a friend of Nietzsche, had brought, through his consummate scholarly work and enthusiastic appreciation, the philosophy of the Upaniṣads and the system of the Vedānta to the notice of the German academic world, assigning as he also did a position of importance to Indian philosophy in his *Allgemeine Geschichte der Philosophie*. It is not likely that Heidegger had no knowledge of these developments, or of the interest of his colleagues and contemporaries Rudolf Otto, Max Scheler, Georg Misch (Dilthey's pupil), and Karl Jaspers in Indian thought. It is clear that he deliberately steers clear of the tradition of Indian thought. His interest in "East Asiatic" ways of thinking (not so much in its content) is understandable, for here as in Meister Eckhart he finds the possibility of a non-conceptual, non-metaphysical way of thinking and speaking in some sense realized, and so of value to his own quest and to the matter *(Sache)* of his own thinking. But Heidegger is critical of the Neo-Kantian presuppositions with which his older contemporaries approached Indian thought; nor does he share Hegel's diametrically opposite concern for appropriating, subsuming, and cancelling all non-Western modes of thought, like all earlier stages of Western thought itself, into the total self-possession of the Spirit in the form of the Absolute Spirit. Therefore, in spite of being as mindful of the historicity of thinking as Hegel was, Heidegger is under no compulsion to incorporate non-Western achievements of thought in his thinking and exhibit them as consummated and superseded in it. Concerning himself with the opaque foundations of the Western thinking of Being in a ceaselessly backward movement of thought, rather than with the ever-progressive movement of the spirit toward complete self-transparency like Hegel, Heidegger leaves these traditions aside, lets them be, as repositories of a treasure which may be relevant, at some future time, to that planetary thinking for which he claims to do no more than prepare at this critical time of the in-break of world-civilization in our midst.

Deussen said in his *Allgemeine Geschichte der Philosophie,*

> One purpose will surely be served when the Indian world-view becomes known. It will make us aware that we, with our entire religious and philosophical thought, are caught in a colossal one-sidedness, and that there can be found yet a quite different way of grasping things than the one which Hegel has construed as the only possible and rational way.[20]

No less than Deussen and many others who have been saying this since, and far more acutely, Heidegger is aware of this "one-sidedness." But Heidegger is extremely suspicious of the concept of "world-view" and his way, therefore, has been that of becoming aware, through radical, persistent questioning and tracking down, of the origin and nature of this one-sidedness rather than of hastening to a premature answer like that of Deussen, an answer that is still rooted in his unexamined Schopenhauerian and Kantian presuppositions. Here, the Indian *Weltanschauung* remains an alternative image for mere aesthetic contemplation and it is an image which is in itself largely a projection of these presuppositions. As against Deussen's, the Heideggerian question is: Must not there be a different way of grasping things than the one which was launched by the Greeks, a way that needs to be fashioned yet by becoming aware of the implicit and unquestioned foundations on which they built? And must it not be, not an *alternate* way which can be substituted for the Greek, but rather a *foundational* way which can provide the Greek and the Western enterprise with the foundation of a more primordial awareness and thus break its appearance of absoluteness and independence? For there is no choice between two alternatives today. The Greek way *has* become world destiny. This is our world, and the only choice left is whether through another manner of thinking than the "metaphysical" we can enter into the region, yet to be recognized and articulated in language but not beyond reach, as the invisible basis of that world—the region of what Heidegger has called the event of appropriation *(Ereignis)*. The quest of thought here is not personal, the achievement by the single individual of his ultimate human purpose through insight into reality, but world-historical, as "philosophy" is world-historical—the quest of a common world of shared meaning and ways of speaking. It is thus not evident how the Indian tradition can help in this enterprise, as it is becoming evident, partly in consequence of Heidegger's thinking, that the Indian enterprise of self-understanding in respect of its tradition is by no means always helped by being translated in terms of Western conceptuality. This, too, may be a reason for Heidegger's lack of Schopenhauerian warmth for Indian philosophy.

And there is another, more crucial, point worth mentioning perhaps in this regard. Heidegger's quest for the "sense of Being" is at the same time a quest for the right or appropriate language in which to talk about it, in which the region from which Being itself gets its sense can find utterance. This region, as it finally comes into view in Heidegger's thinking is "that realm of the event of appropriation, vibrating within itself, through which man and Being reach each other in their nature, achieve their real nature by losing those qualities with which metaphysics has endowed them."[21] Thinking this "self-vibrating realm" is building with language "a self-suspended structure" expressive of this realm, inaccessible in the language of metaphysics. Here, "language is the most delicate and thus the most vulnerable vibration holding everything within the suspended structure of the appropriation."[22]

Heidegger's search for the appropriate language with which to build in this realm, that is to think it, leads him progressively away from metaphysical, conceptualizing ways of speaking and makes him even wonder whether Western languages, just because they are superbly suited for metaphysicial thinking, can ever lend themselves to non-representational utterance. For the thinking of Being the Greek language is paradigmatic, for it alone, Heidegger says, is *logos;* "what is said in it *is* at the same time in an excellent way what it is called. . . . What it presents (through its *legein*) is what lies immediately before us. Through the audible Greek word we are directly in the presence of the thing itself."[23] Because to the Greeks the nature of language is revealed as the *logos,* Greek is the language uniquely fitted for that "expressly adopted and unfolding correspondence which corresponds to the address of the Being of what is" which is philosophy, as Heidegger describes it, and for that very reason inadequate to the attempt at a thinking responsiveness to that other domain beyond the Being of what is, the domain of the truth of Being, from which Being itself derives. Since we can neither ever again return to this nature of language, nor simply take it over, Heidegger says, we must enter into a dialogue with the Greek experience of language as *logos*.

As Indo-European, Sanskrit also is in some measure "metaphysical," as distinct from the languages of the Far East, with the notions of Being embedded in it, grammatically and conceptually. It is metaphysical in being representational, concept-generating, and in being productive of ontological speculation about Being as the ground of all that is, and so giving the appearance of setting up a reality other and higher than this world, in the sense attacked by Nietzsche. Since *this* possibility of thinking has been fulfilled in its amplest and purest form in the Greek tradition, Heidegger is not interested in how Sanskrit speaks (in the sense in which, according to Heidegger, it is language that speaks, not man), nor in the tradition that has evolved out of it.[24] The extreme opposite of both Greek and Sanskrit, in their characteristic mode of disclosure, the Far Eastern languages hold greater promise for the thinking that reaches out to a non-representational mode of utterance. Thus, the very reasons for the delighted surprise and excitement with which the discovery of Sanskrit was hailed by European linguists, along with the thought forms in Indian philosophy by scholars such as Garbe and Deussen, are reasons for Heidegger's relative indifference to the Indian tradition.

IV

In this tradition, *Brahman* plays the same role as *Logos* in the Greek and *Tao* in the Chinese, corresponding to the notions of *verbum, oratio* and *ratio* respectively, as Johannes Lohmann has pointed out.[25] But whereas with the Greeks, by virtue of the very *logos* character of the language, attention was directed away from the light of the *logos* to what it illumined, that is, the world of entities, of what is, in the Indian case language itself entered, so to speak, into the reality it disclosed, shining forth itself also, while illumining and opening up the domain of meanings. The original Vedic sense of Brahman as poetic, creative and sacred utterance (as Paul Thieme has shown), sliding subsequently into the sense of the reality finding such utterance, the source of all utterance and itself beyond human speaking, manifested itself in the conception of *Vak* or speech as the primordial reality, in the extraordinary attention given to grammar (the invention of this discipline itself), finally in the emergence of the school of speculative grammar which culminated in the great *Vākyapadīya* of Bhartṛhari and the philosophy of Word-monism.

In the Upaniṣads themselves and in the schools of Advaita Vedānta which arose after Bhartṛhari this awareness of language, either as Word principle or as *Śruti,* is never absent. Śaṃkara's insistence on the inseparability of the liberating Brahman-knowledge and the Vedic word about this knowledge and on the immediacy of the relationship between the two is as good an example of this as any. That the word of the *Śruti* itself falls away and is left behind in the experience of what it has disclosed is no argument against the above, for all saying, as such, is a showing, a mode of disclosure, and the former is not just a tool for the latter but itself a reality inseparable from it, as Heidegger has insisted. The designation of the Veda, of even all primordial utterance sometimes, as the Śabda-Brahman—an aspect of Brahman or as the "lower" Brahman—and of the Word-principle as Brahman itself is not uncommon in Vedānta literature and expresses this whole way of thinking. When this is forgotten and language is understood as having a solely instrumental reality, Vedānta thought is easily treated as a kind of "theology."

It is not surprising that Professor Lohmann should take recourse to the concept of "magic" whenever he touches upon the beginnings of Indian thought. For "magic" is only the name of a category employed to indicate what a blind spot prevents one from seeing, what Lohmann's idealization of the Greek prevents him from thinking. Greek culture *is* paradigmatic, and perhaps we in India can do with even more emphatic reminders of this fact. But in the perspective of Heidegger's quest for what is "never Greek any more" and for "planetary thinking," in this age of world-civilization and man's homelessness, there is little meaning in such idealization. The presence of the Greek as world destiny is a hard reality to be faced and interrogated, now and for a long time to come, by thinking men everywhere. It requires a rethinking of the meaning, and the negative value, assigned by metaphysical thinking to the notions of the irrational, the magical, the mythic, the symbolic, the merely poetic and fanciful and so forth. It is a demand to rethink the relation between the contrasting spheres of "religion" and "philosophy," and the contrast itself, generated in Western thought by the coming together of the Greek and the Christian as major components in this metaphysical tradition, to rethink the concept of "mysticism" as a type of religious or philosophical view or position.

The value of a thinker such as Nietzsche, even more so Heidegger, lies in this, that they invite us to such "revaluation" and rethinking of concepts, categories and thought-forms, not in the solutions they supposedly offer to certain perennial philosophical "problems," nor in the philosophical doctrine or system they may be thought to teach or propound. Comparative philosophy so far has proceeded largely on the basis of an uncritical employment of these "metaphysical" concepts, assumed as obviously and eternally valid, in the understanding of "philosophies" such as those of India.[26] But something remarkable will be seen to happen when we take seriously Heidegger's talk of "the end of philosophy" and his "overcoming of metaphysics" (understanding these phrases in *his* sense, not just projecting an imaginary meaning into them, out of context): freedom from this metaphysical bias, the loosening of the hold of the "concept" on thinking, the liberation from prejudices functioning as norms and as standards of comparison, the openness to "the matter of thinking," wherever going on, East or West. For example, if "philosophy" is a synonym for the mode of thinking arising from the Greek venture and if there is no such thing as Indian or Chinese philosophy, as Heidegger insists, what happens to the concept of "comparative philosophy" itself? If the term philosophy is taken in this strict sense, as a proper noun, there is nothing to compare; if we still insist on comparing, it can only be for the sake of judging the non-Western, in the manner of Hegel, with the Greek-Western as the norm. But if we bring ourselves to share Heidegger's insight in this matter, we may also see the nullity of the contrast between "religion" and "philosophy" in the Western tradition (for, with the end of "philosophy," the opposite number of the pair also meets its "end"), and thus become open to the *Sache des Denkens* in those other ventures at thinking.

Comparative philosophy, if we still retain the name, would then be a name for the task, infinitely open, of setting free, bringing into view and articulating in contemporary ways of speaking, in new ways of speaking, the matter of thinking which, in what has actually been realized in thought, still remains unsaid and so unthought in the traditions of the East. Otherwise, comparative philosophy will amount to no more than an unthinking attempt at perpetuating Western "philosophy" by translating Eastern thinking into the language of Western metaphysics, taken as the universally valid paradigm. And this is bad, not because it is Western but because it hides an unthought opacity that stands in the way of adequately reaching out to the other, for it either prompts to an assimilation of the other or leads to a perpetuation of its otherness.

As Heidegger speaks of it, the end of philosophy as metaphysical thinking does not mean its termination but rather its consummation, the fact that it has reached "the place in which the whole of philosophy's history is gathered in its most extreme possibility."[27] It exhibits itself as "the triumph of the manipulable arrangement of a scientific-technological world and of the social order proper to this world. The end of philosophy means: the beginning of the world civilization based upon Western European thinking."[28] Are we to think of comparative philosophy as a continuation of this consummation or completion, a contribution to it required by the emergence of world-civilization and in its service? Or should we rather not think of it in terms of "the task of thinking" which, according to Heidegger, still remains reserved for thinking at the end of philosophy, a *first* possibility which was contained in its beginning but which it could not acknowledge or realize? Whether we choose the first or the second alternative depends upon whether or not we see this world-civilization as "the world destiny of homelessness," question it (not deny it, or want to substitute something else for it), and are willing to question the thought of Being as Ground which heralded its moment of birth.

For any one in search of "philosophemes" common to Heidegger and Vedānta, or of similar-looking ideas in them, there is a great deal to be found regarding man's nature, the world, and man's relationship to it, the unity of Being, the identity between man and Being. Each of these topics can provide the starting point of an examination in depth of the similarity and the differences between the two, and beyond these, to meditation on these central concerns of thought. There is, above all, the idea of Being (Brahman-Ātman) as the ground of all, that appears to offer an interesting point for comparison and contrast, for this is the basic concept of the metaphysical tradition and in Vedānta thought it is even more emphatically crucial. This is what made the arch-anti-Platonist Nietzsche describe the Vedānta as "the classical expression of the mode of thinking most alien to me," in his letter of 16. 3. 1883 to Deussen. Following Nietzsche, Heidegger also is engaged in the attempt to root out the very idea of a transcendent ground of things which seems most characteristic of Vedānta thought.

As one looks more closely, however, matters become more intriguing and complicated, calling for a fuller investigation than can be undertaken here. The second sūtra of Bādarāyaṇa's *Śārīraka-mīmāṁsā-sūtra* both sums up a long tradition and presents a task for centuries to follow when it declares: Brahman is that from which, by and into which, all this arises, is sustained and returns. Is this Anaximander all over again? Is it Aristotle? If Brahman is identified with the Greek notion of Being (not to speak of its scholastic variants), conceived as ground, then Heidegger's whole effort is to demolish this idea, for his entire thinking is a critique of just this single concept. Can Brahman be so identified? If not, then the "all this" of the Upaniṣads cannot just be identified with the "entity" of Heidegger or with the *to on* of the Greeks, for here the "this" is not thought of solely under the aspect of its being-ness. As for the notion of "ground," here again, despite the seeming similarity, different things were going on in the two traditions, with very different consequences. But into this fascinating problem, perhaps basic to the comparative enterprise, we cannot enter here.[29] Instead, let us discuss in what follows, though again only briefly, two questions of a more general character: Is Heidegger an ontologist, and is Vedānta an ontology? Is Heidegger a mystic and is Vedānta a mystical philosophy, is Śaṁkara a mystic? What makes these questions specially interesting is the fact that none of them can be answered with a simple "yes" or "no," that, *as* questions, they are themselves questionable.

V

Although taking the question of the "sense" of Being as his starting point, Heidegger is certainly not an ontologist, either in the traditional meaning of the term or in some new sense. The point hardly needs laboring, since he has expressed himself with all clarity on this matter in his later writings. He does not take ontology for granted as the first philosophy or as *metaphysica generalis* and then go on to make some original contribution to it, or provide a novel analysis of the "meaning" of Being but, on the contrary, subjects the very idea of ontology to the most radical questioning. For the first time in the history of Western thought, he exhibits the derivative, contingent, specifically Greek character of this whole notion, this whole manner of conceiving the matter of thought and of thought's response to the matter by which it is addressed. The Being of what-is emerged as the unique matter of thinking at the beginning of Western thought and this, Heidegger points out, is itself the beginning of the West, the hidden source of its destiny.[30] This great beginning of Western philosophy did not arise out of nothing but emerged in the process of overcoming "its extreme opposite, the mythical in general and the Asiatic in particular."[31] Heidegger's quest is for the source from which this thought of Being, indeed from which Being itself, emerged as the first and last for thinking, and a quest for that which remained unthought in this thinking, variously called by him Appropriation *(Ereignis),* Clearing *(Lichtung)* and Truth *(Alētheia),* or unhiddenness. And yet Heidegger is a thinker of Being from beginning to end, gnawing away at this marrow-bone (as Hamann said of his own concern with *Logos*) until he is able to dispel the darkness over this depth (luckier than Hamann, perhaps, to have found the key to this abyss).[32]

Throughout his work there is a strange, bewildering nebulousness or lack of precision in the use of the word "Being," apparent in the adoption of such expressions as "the truth of Being," "Being itself," and of variants such as *"Seyn"* and "Being" struck out with a cross mark, so that one can always pick out passages from different periods of his writing to prove that, after all, it is "Being" Heidegger is really talking about without being quite clear as to what he is trying to say. This would be a mistake, for this nebulousness is not confusion but part of the stringency or rigor (which is something quite different from "exactness," as Heidegger points out) necessitated by this path of thinking itself. It must be remembered, further, that for Heidegger thinking is a movement and a wayfaring, in which what is thought about itself undergoes continuous transformation, as thinking fashions its path and moves forward, that is, away from the matter as conceived at the starting point, and from the manner of thinking it, towards a destination of which it has no foreknowledge. Seeking for what can have no name until it is seen, Heidegger uses the word "Being" as a provisional first name for the greater part of his path of thinking, until the long drawn out act of renunciation is completed.

The starting point is the Greek thought of Being, but the path is one of continuous overcoming of this thought, until thinking is itself set free from its bondage to this thought and from the determination of its own nature by it. Heidegger is a thinker of Being, yet not an ontologist; he is a thinker of Being who has caught a glimpse of the truth covered over by the thought of Being. Heidegger said in 1935, "In the seemingly unimportant distinction between being and thinking we must discern the fundamental position of the Western spirit, against which our central attack is directed."[33] From the perspective of the successful carrying through of this attack in the following three decades, we can say that thinking is not, in its true nature, the sort of activity which can be *about* Being, with Being confronting it as its *Sache* or matter, but must be *of* Being; that Being is not the sort of thing which, eternally there, self-established and shining in its own light beckons thought to grasp it in its three-pronged onto-theo-logical movement; that both Being and thinking (man) belong together in a deeper unity (inaccessible to any form of dialectic), from which they both derive their nature and which exhibits itself, while yet concealing itself, as the proper matter of thinking that is no more a grasping, no longer a striving to form a system of concepts for what is beyond all conceptualizing.

VI

Neither the Upaniṣads nor Śaṃkara can be said to be concerned with a theoretical inquiry *(epistēmē theoretikē)* into being as being *(on hē on)* or into the *ontos on,* and their question is not identical with the Greek "What is Being *(ti to on)?"* or with Heidegger's questioning of the ambiguities and the unthought presuppositions of that question. Brahman, that one being *(sat)* which the wise speak of in many ways, is not identical with the *to on* of Aristotle, "spoken of in many ways"; and the Brahma-vidyā is not a *legein* of Brahman (so that it is as inappropriate to speak, with Paul Hacker, of Atomology as it would be to describe Vedānta as a Brahmology). It is not the conceptual knowledge of Being, though wisdom about Being *(sad-vidyā),* or about Brahman as Being, is part of it. Brahman is *sat* (Being), the ground of all that is, including my own being, which is of the nature of sheer, pure *cit* (awareness, of which "knowing" is itself a derivative mode) and potentially capable of rising above all otherness and, therefore, pure bliss. Thus Brahman is Being, but not in the sense in which it is other than what it is Being for or to, not in the sense of what knowing, thinking and speaking are about, other than them, as a reality confronting them, but inclusive of these as themselves modes of Being. It is *sat, cit* and *ānanda* in one and as one, and my being is one with it. We can, if we choose—and as metaphysics does—consider things (including my self) solely and exclusively under the aspect of their being (is-ness), only taking notice of the fact that they *are*. But this would be something like Blake's "Single vision and Newton's sleep," for no being, simple is-ness, is exclusive of the fact of being lit up, of lighting up, of being gathered into a unity with what it lights up and with where this lighting up occurs—in me, who am in essence (as *ātman*) just this lighting up itself and so identical with that is-ness. So regarded, however, is-ness (Being) becomes an aspect, though integral and essential, of something more "comprehensive" than it, thinkable separately and by itself, even as an aspect, only by an illegitimate abstraction. Brahman, therefore, is beyond Being and Non-being; "it cannot be spoken of either as being or as not being," as the *Bhagavadgītā* has it.

It has been rightly pointed out by Paul Hacker that Śaṃkara was wary and hesitant, for this reason, of dwelling too much on Brahman as Being, unlike his followers, but focused instead on Brahman as awareness *(cit)* and preferred hence an *ātman*-oriented approach to ultimate truth.[34] Being, taken by itself, carries a suggestion of objectivity, as being for another than it, for which reason K. C. Bhattacharyya also relegates metaphysics to the "philosophy of the Object." The self should first be realized as existing, but only as a stepping stone to the self-revelation of its essence, to which the ideas of being and not-being are not applicable, as Śaṃkara says.[35] In so far as Brahman, in itself devoid of all distinctions, is the basis (from our human perspective) of all diversification and the seed of all activity, it can be spoken of as existing; or, because only by thinking of it as being can we be prompted to realize it.[36] But, being beyond the reach of the senses, it cannot be an object of consciousness accompanied with the idea of either existence or non-existence, as we have it in ordinary experience. Further, Brahman does not belong to any class or genus, and therefore cannot be denoted by the word *sat*, for we cannot speak about anything that exists in the empirical mode without referring it to a class.[37] And if *sat* were itself regarded as only a class name, it would be no more than the "Being of or in beings" and cannot be the prior ground of all that is.[38] Brahman has a unitary nature and we cannot define it as merely "that which is *(sat)*," or as merely consciousness or thought *(bodha)* or as being made up of the two together; "for he who would maintain that Brahman is characterized by thought different from existence, and at the same time by existence different from thought, would virtually maintain that there is a plurality in Brahman."[39]

The *locus classicus* of the more ontologically oriented treatment of Brahman as Being *(Sad-Brahman)* is chapter VI of the *Chāndogya Upani-*

ṣad, and later Advaita thinkers have attached relatively greater importance to the notion of Brahman as *ens primum (Sattā)*, as Paul Hacker
points out. But it is in the *Brahmasiddhi* of Maṇḍana Miśra that we find
a view of Brahman as the universal Being that is presented in and animates all experience. Maṇḍana himself was probably influenced in his
ontological interpretation of Brahman by the speculative grammarian
Bhartṛhari, according to whom Brahman is the Highest Universal
(Mahāsāmānya), the Great Being *(Mahāsattā)* which expresses itself in
all words. For Śaṃkara, however, such a view would be intolerable
because it objectifies Brahman by making it an object of knowing. As he
says,

> The purport of this science is not to represent Brahman definitely as this or
> that object, its purpose is rather to show that Brahman as the eternal inward
> self is never an object, and thereby to remove the distinction of objects
> known, knowers, acts of knowledge, etc., which is fictitiously created by
> Nescience.[40]

We thus see that "ontology" hardly provides a basis for comparison
between Śaṃkara and Western thinkers like Parmenides, Eckhart, or
Aquinas. Deussen made use, though sporadically, of Greek ontological
concepts to illumine Śaṃkara's thought. More systematic attempts have
been made to compare Śaṃkara with Eckhart by Rudolf Otto and with
Thomas Aquinas by Richard De Smet and Paul Hacker. But in so far as
the final point of reference in these latter comparisons also perforce
remains the Greek notion of Being, they cannot be regarded as shedding
light on what *Brahma-vidyā* is about or what *Ātma-bodha* stands for. In
this respect, at least, a consideration of Advaita Vedānta in a Heideggerian perspective perhaps offers a better chance, for the thinking of Heidegger and Śaṃkara may be found to have a touching point somewhere in
that "region of all regions," beyond the thought of Being and Non-being,
in which it has its sojourn. About these two thinkers also it may with
some truth be said that they "dwell near to one another" though standing
"on mountains farthest apart."[41]

VII

Is Heidegger a mystic? It is true that he refers to Meister Eckhart and
Angelus Silesius, mentions Tao, speaks of Way and Topos and Leap, talks
of the identity of man and Being in a primordial belonging-togetherness,
of the abruptness of an unbridged entry into the region of the *Ereignis*.
There is enough evidence to show that Heidegger has been deeply
interested, from his early writings, in medieval mysticism in general and
Eckhart in particular, and in his later writings he borrows freely from the

vocabulary of Eckhart. As John D. Caputo has shown, Eckhartian concepts such as those of *Abgeschiedenheit* (detachment) and *Gelassenheit* (abandonment, releasement) have substantially contributed to his thinking.[42] Yet, it must be kept in mind that all this happens in the context of *thinking* and in its service. Heidegger appropriates what he finds to be genuine thinking contained in the works of the mystics, takes them as gestures of thought, as happenings on the path of thinking, never in the sense of finding access to a realm and an experience which lie beyond the reach of thinking, never as the necessary or even possible abrogation of thought. As he points out even in his early Duns Scotus book, the notion of mysticism in the sense of an irrationalistic *Erleben* (immediate inner experience) rests on an extreme rationalization of philosophy, on the conception of philosophy as a rationalistic structure divorced from life.[43] Almost a quarter of a century later, Heidegger makes the same point when he asserts that mysticism is the mere counterpart of metaphysics, into which people take flight when, still wholly caught in their slavery to metaphysical thinking, they are struck by the hiddenness in all revealment and lapse into unthinking helplessness.[44] When we abandon the presuppositions of such thinking and the traditional conception of *Lichtmetaphysik,* however, we can acknowledge this mystery of concealment as manifest, *as* concealment, in all disclosure, and can think it as such. "Mysticism" then loses all meaning and becomes both unneccessary and impossible. It should also not be forgotten that, according to Heidegger, pointing to and intimating something are gestures of thinking, not of the resignation of thought. As he says,

> What makes itself known only in such a way that it becomes apparent in its self-concealment, to that we can respond also only by alluding to it, indicating it. . . . This simple pointing is one of the distinctive marks of thinking.[45]

Such pointing in words is not a relegation of the *Sache* (the matter) to the realm of the ineffable and the unknown but a way of being related to it in thought, the seeing of what is pointed out. Thinking is a seeing of what comes into view and so a form of experiencing, the profoundest modality of experience in fact. The traditional, metaphysical contrast between entities known by reason (thought conceived as *ratio*) and what is experienceable breaks down.

Thus, Heidegger speaks of the *experience* of thinking, of thinking as itself an experience, appropriating within thinking the precious element of immediacy in all mysticism. Little attention has been paid to this extraordinary role of "experience" in Heidegger's writings. He speaks of the experiencing of Being, of the hiddenmost history of Being, of the basic experience of nothingness, of "undergoing an experience with language."[46] According to Heidegger, thinking is thus in a profound sense experiencing. "To experience," Heidegger says, "means *eundo assequi,* to obtain something along the way, to attain something by going on a way. . . . To experience is to go along a way."[47] And thinking is the pre-eminent mode of going along a way for man. Further, what one undergoes on the path of thinking is not just "intellectual insight" but experience in the most transforming sense. As Heidegger describes it,

> To undergo an experience with something—be it a thing, a person, or a god —means that this something befalls us, strikes us, comes over us, over-whelms and transforms us. When we talk of "undergoing" an experience, we mean specifically that the experience is not of our own making; to undergo here means that we endure it, suffer it, receive it as it strikes us and submit to it. It is this something itself that comes about, comes to pass, happens.[48]
>
> To experience something means to attain it along the way, by going on a way. To undergo an experience with something means that this something, which we reach along the way in order to attain it, itself pertains to us, meets and makes its appeal to us, in that it transforms us into itself.[49]

If we ponder these remarks and undergo, with Heidegger an experience with thinking, we may come to see that there is something wrong with the current and unquestioning characterization of Eastern thought as "mystical," especially by scholars of religion, and thus with the perpetuation of *Erleben* as the alternative to "mere" thought. Such an attempted perpetuation may be understandable in theologians like Rudolf Otto, with their quest for the "inner relationship of types of human experience and spiritual life,"[50] carried on in unexamined acceptance of "metaphysics" as the normative mode of thought. We can see what is wrong here if we understand why Heidegger, "having experienced theology in its own roots, both the theology of the Christian faith and that of philosophy, prefers to remain silent about God in the realm of thinking,"[51] and if we recall his remark in *Being and Time* about "those residues of Christian theology within the problematics of philosophy which have not as yet been radically extruded."[52] It is this extrusion which has enabled Heidegger to reclaim for thinking its proper plentitude, to set it free to reach out limitlessly to its *Sache,* and widen its sphere to an unbounded horizon. Such liberation of thinking can enable us to look out for the thinking going on in other religious and philosophical traditions. "Mysticism," too, is one such residue that has fused in recent religious thought with subjectivism, the form which metaphysics has assumed since Descartes, according to Heidegger, resulting in the present day pursuit of *Erlebnis* and the quest for types, patterns, and structures of inner experience or of its correlate, the world of objectivity as disclosed in such experience.[53]

VIII

From the perspective opened up by Heidegger's thinking we may seek in the Upaniṣads and in the tradition of Vedānta thought for "the thinking experience" of Uddālaka and Yājñavalkya, of Śaṃkara and his successors. For what is central, at least in the Advaita tradition of Vedānta philosophy, is the "way of knowledge," the way of insight through meditative thought, the way of "the experience of thought." Here, as in Heidegger, such realization of truth in and through thinking comprises a two-fold movement, the movement of "hearing" and the movement of questioning, with the former as basic and first, as in Heidegger. It culminates in a "seeing," which is not the act of a subject directed toward objective being, either in the Greek sense of *theōria* or in the modern subjectivistic sense, but as the shining forth of the *Sache* itself, in the sense of being appropriated by it and owned into an identity with it, prior and primordial, as in Heidegger. Finally, this whole process in which truth is realized in thinking experience occurs within the dimension of the holy, as Heidegger thinks it, as a sacred happening, within an experience of Being "which is still capable of a god," which is not yet "too late for the gods and too early for Being."

This comparison is not intended to establish any thesis about the similarity of two entities, the structure of Heidegger's thought (thus transforming it into a "philosophy") and Advaita Vedānta as a thought-form (thus devaluing its essentially religious character), but to imply that it is thinking that is happening in the latter, not just the rational justification of a set of assertions in the *Śruti,* in acknowledgment of it as an "authority," nor just the construction of an intellectually satisfying system of speculative philosophy, but a thinking which is experienced *as* thinking of ultimate concern. But this thinking is neither "no-more-metaphysical" nor "not-yet metaphysical" (in the sense Heidegger speaks of these in *Heraklit*); it has not been mediated by medieval Christianity, nor by the new awareness introduced into modern Western thought by the rise of historicism. It is not haunted by the reflective sense of the finitude of thinking as such, as Heidegger naturally is, in reaction against Plato and Hegel and the entire metaphysical tradition. As thinking, it moves straight ahead toward its *Sache,* not thematically mindful of its own character as a "thrown project," but seeking the impossible, fullness of light, all light, without shadows and dark corners, seeking the total elimination of pain and fear, of the ensnarement by things and all forms of objectivity and otherness in life, seeking the annulment of mortality.

But this naivety, if it must be called such, is minimal in the Vedānta tradition. For we have indeed here a vivid and energetic awareness of the possibility, ever present for thinking, of grasping, in Hegel's words, only "clouds of error instead of the Heaven of truth."[54] This is exhibited in the very extensive treatment of the problem of knowledge—its nature, sources and criteria of validity—and the nature of error in Vedānta, as in all schools of Indian thought. Guarded by the equally primal awareness of the voice of the Upaniṣadic word, undistracted from listening to it, Vedānta thinking could move on, however, without that fear of erring which, in Hegel's words again, is already the error itself. Is it not precisely in this straining towards the impossible, the Absolute, that the very passion, the ecstasy, and the moving power of all great thinking lie, in this incessant, relentless pushing beyond its ever incomplete accomplishment, in this unceasing self-transcendence, in this movement of unending self-overcoming which Nietzsche has so penetratingly seen and described, and which attains a straining and stretching to the utmost in the thinking of Heidegger, just because he is aware as no other thinker of the West of thought's finitude and in spite of his disclaimer that his thinking has no wisdom to deliver and is not put forward as a *Heilsweg,* a promise of salvation? What greater healing can there be than the thinking experience by man of being at one with that from which, in his all too human state, he experiences division, and of being freed from the tyranny of that thing out there, and this, here inside his mind, confronting him as an other to himself?

It is true that we find in the founders of systematic Advaita thought, Gauḍapāda and Śaṃkara, a great deal of insistence on setting aside, suspending and even nihilating the activity of the mind, so that we may have a vision of the true self and of what truly is, without being obstructed and tricked by this seed-bed of all seeming. A number of considerations, impossible to enter into here, account for this: the starting point with the self (rather than with the Being of beings, in the Greek sense), the prevailing conceptions about the mental faculty and the concern for distinguishing it from the self (which is the self or "being" of the mind itself), the discovery of the constructive, projective and representational functions of the mind as sources of error in our understanding of the world and ourselves by the Buddhist thinkers, and, above all the uncompromising resistance to the two "nihilistic" and "semi-nihilistic" ways of thinking dominant at the time (though as possibilities ever present threats to the Advaita mode of thinking), namely, the Mādhyamika and the Vaiśeṣika philosophies.

According to the first, thinking is the positing of an "it is" where there is in reality no entitative Being; according to the latter, thinking moves within and knows only the realm of entities and is intrinsically categorial in its procedure. In its concern to preserve the primal reality undiminished by the least vestige of opacity (somewhat in the Sartrean sense), the former replaces Being by Nothingness, giving to thinking the preliminary and solely negative role of a dialectical cancellation of its own thetic, positing activity. The latter takes cognizance only of beings, of Being only as a class concept and of Non-being as the absence of a being. Each denies Being as the ultimate "that from which"; each conceives thinking in accordance with its view of the *Sache* of thinking.

Advaita thinking lives in the tension between these two stances, refusing to go the way of systematic denial but acknowledging the illusions to which thought is ever exposed, and refusing also to accept the position that there is nothing for thinking to be addressed by except entities and that there is no other mode of thinking than the ontic-categorial. This is the Upaniṣadic way of "yea-saying," of saying yes to the realm of entities (for they are "beings in Being," upheld in and by Being, are grounded in a self; the "is" in any entity cannot be denied, for it is none other than the "is" that I myself am); of saying yes to the negativity infecting all mortal experience (for I, ever in the midst of entities, am "always already forfeited to them," am duped by them—*"genarrt durch das Seiende, dem Sein so entfremdet,"* as Heidegger puts it—am caught in the play of seeming, in this mirror-game of reflecting and being reflected in beings, confused between the realm of beings and the self of which and for which they are beings); of saying yes to that other dimension, beyond beings and yet in them, the dimension from which all is-ness derives, which is the primordial openness and truth and which is also the dimension of the holy, that *"Wesensraum"* of Divinity from which the real shines forth as the god, as God; of affirming that gesture of thinking which lies in saying, "It is." Does not the *Kaṭha Upaniṣad* (VI, 12 and 13) say, "Not by speech, not by mind, not by sight can he be apprehended. How can he be apprehended except by him who says, 'He is'?"? Intellection "dissolves" in such thinking of the self, Śaṃkara points out in his comment on this verse, but only as pregnant with a notion of existence *(satpratyayagarbhaiva vilīyate).*

The thinkers of the Upaniṣadic-Buddhist-Advaita tradition were acutely, intensely, and vividly alive to the havoc wrought by representational thinking because they lived in awareness of a dimension other than the workaday world in which such thinking is valid, perhaps inevitable as well as necessary. This sensitivity was all the more heightened by the fact that this "other" dimension was not thought of as wholly transcendent but as the truth of this workaday existence itself. However, the doctrine of two truths, or two levels of reality, as developed by Nāgārjuna and Śaṃkara in different ways and to different ends, is not quite the same as the distinction between the grasping, conceptual, and representational thinking generated in the metaphysical-philosophical tradition of the West and the notion of non-representational, meditative, reminiscent, topological, and preparatory thinking as we have it in Heidegger. Also,

Heidegger's distinction should not itself be understood in a "metaphysical" sense, or as a philosophical thesis about the nature of thinking, for it is itself part of a movement of thought that seeks to overcome and get behind, so to speak, the Greek metaphysical thought of Being, so that someday "the farewell from all 'It is' " may come to pass,[55] so that there may be a turn in the world destiny of homelessness.

The Brahman-Ātman of the Upaniṣads is not the same as the Being of Western thought; they are different starting points, each uniquely itself, for thinking in the two traditions, and they are untranslatable one by the other, for we do not yet have a name for what may be identical in them (though perhaps "Brahman" has the advantage of including in itself, but not being exhausted by, the notion of Being!). The history of Being, its mittence *(Geschick),* is the hidden history of the West, now overspreading the world and culminating in the all-consuming "Europeanization of the earth," in world-civilization and the loss of world as home for man. Brahman-Ātman, too, is *Geschick* and yet, not in the sense of historical destiny; perhaps a *Geschick* still, indeed in a more real sense so, when we have once achieved the "releasement toward things and openness to the mystery" of which Heidegger speaks in his address on *Gelassenheit.*[56]

Vedāntic thought or Vedāntism, in so far as it is a way of thinking and is not simply a name for what has at any time been actually thought in it (in respect of content, structure, and style), has been and will remain, like all genuine, original thinking, a thinking of the unthought in what has been thought, to speak in Heidegger's language, and a perpetually novel start. Historically, the challenge to this thinking has come from the existence of opposing systems and paths of thought and spirituality. It has therefore itself a history. The Upaniṣads do not say, could not have said, what Gauḍapāda found it possible and necessary in his time to say. Did he falsify the intent of the Vedic utterance, importing into its thought elements borrowed from alien sources, or was he able in some measure to set free the unsaid, implicit truth of those ancient thinkers, while appropriating a new language and speaking in a new age? Did Śaṃkara do this in respect of his predecessors, and in which regard and with what success? And so with his followers and with the other schools of Vedānta.

Much of Heidegger's work has been devoted to attempts at saying, by means of a series of "phenomenological interpretations" (as he described many of his early seminars on the great Western philosophers), what remains unsaid and unthought in their works. Should it not be possible to attempt the same with these Indian thinkers, "looking beyond the language which these philosophers employ to what they intended to say," in the words of Kant, or "wresting from the actual words that which these words 'intended to say,' " as Heidegger puts it?[57] To be able to do so, however, requires, as he goes on to point out, that

. . . the interpretation must be animated and guided by an illuminative idea. Only through the power of this idea can an interpretation risk that which is always audacious, namely, entrusting itself to the secret élan of a work, in order by this élan to get through to the unsaid and to attempt to find an expression for it.

With which "illuminative idea" have subsequent thinkers in the Vedānta tradition approached the earlier thinkers? Is there such a directive idea, capable of confirming itself by its own power of illumination, available to us today for the task of interpreting the thinkers of this tradition?

These thinkers themselves did not conceive their task in these terms but thought of themselves as continuators and defenders of a tradition— ahistorically, reaching the limits of impersonality and anonymity in their creative work. How could they ever come upon the idea that Śaṃkara's thinking, for example, drew its sustenance from its own unthought depths, that there was something he himself could not think, but which Sūreśvara or Padmapāda, his immediate disciples, could bring out into the open, but without their own thinking being totally transparent to themselves? Every great thinker has his own explicitly seen task, which he seeks to accomplish with the tools, the energy and the gifts at his command. But in the midst of what he actually manages to accomplish and sees himself as achieving, something else also goes on within his work, all unbeknownst to himself, to his contemporaries and immediate successors almost always, often to the entire tradition that springs out of his work. The continuity of the mostly hidden operation of this unknown and unsaid is the mittence *(Geschick)* which carries all history, giving it an inexhaustible potentiality of meaningfulness in the oncoming, endless future. Thus Vedāntic thinking has a history, that continuity of hidden unrest that pushes it forward. Can we say about it, as Heidegger does about the "end" of the Western tradition of metaphysical thinking with Hegel and Nietzsche, that it reached its completion with Madhusudan Saraswati, or even with K. C. Bhattacharyya? Perhaps not; perhaps the beginning (in the Upaniṣads) still hides a secret for future thinking and saying; perhaps Śaṃkara's thinking still contains a meaning, still awaiting the work of thought to be clearly seen, from which his school itself was sidetracked, even while bringing it to *one* consummation, carrying it to dizzying heights of intellectual effort in a white heat of luminous creativity rarely paralleled anywhere. If so, Vedānta thinking, far from being a closed and completed whole, remains a task for the open future.

Conclusion

In the world of today, in this one world of "world-civilization," our relationship to tradition is an irreparably broken one and our thinking is determined by an unheard-of simultaneity of times and places, all equally remote, all equally close. If the bringing together of "Heidegger" and "Vedānta" is to have any sense it can only lie in enabling us to see that there is more to Vedānta—something that is its very own and yet unfulfilled—than providing those who are in revolt against the establishment (the religious, the Western metaphysical), and in flight from thinking, with a "mystical" alternative; that as a way or path of thinking, not so much as a doctrine, Vedānta may also have some relevance to that other task to which Heidegger points, the task of planetary thinking, in an age of homelessness and of the coming together of East and West in the extremity of fate, in the task of overcoming this universal misery of lost home by "staying on the path, in genuine need, and learning, without straying from the path, even though faltering, the craft *(Handwerk)* of thinking."[58]

Notes

1. *Vedānta und Platonismus im Lichte der Kantischen Philosophie* (Berlin, 1922), pp. 40–41. The penultimate paragraph of this interesting study may be quoted here in full since it states most concisely and lucidly the approach to comparative philosophy most widely favored and which appears so questionable when we look at it from the perspective of Heidegger's thinking. Deussen says, "In allen Ländern und zu allen Zeiten, in allen Nähen und Fernen ist es eine und dieselbe Natur der Dinge, welcher einer und derselbe Geist betrachtend gegenübersteht. Wie sollte es da anders sein können, als dass der denkende Geist, sofern ihn nicht Traditionen und Vorurteile blenden, sofern er der Natur rein und unbefangen gegenübersteht, in seiner Erforschung derselben überall, in Indien wie in Griechenland, in alter wie in neuer Zeit zu den gleichen Ergebnissen gelangen musste! Wir haben die drei glänzendsten Erscheinungen der Philosophie, den Vedānta, Platon und Kant miteinander verglichen. Wir haben nicht an ihnen gedreht und gedeutet, gebogen und gerenkt, sondern wir haben jede Erscheinung in ihrer vollen individuellen Eigentümlichkeit bestehen lassen. Aber indem wir bei jeder von ihnen in die letzte Tiefe drängen, gelangten wir zu dem inneren Einheitspunkte, aus dem die Anschauungen der indischen, griechischen und deutschen Denker entsprungen sind, und diese ihre innere Übereinstimmung bei aller Verschiedenheit der Aussenseite ist eine nicht geringe Gewähr dafür, dass wir in allen dreien die Stimme der einen und mit sich einstimmigen Natur, dass in ihnen die Stimme der ewigen Wahrheit vernehmen."

2. Paul Deussen, *The System of the Vedānta* (Delhi: Motilal Banarsidass, 1972), pp. 38–39.

3. *The Vedānta Sūtras of Bādarāyaṇa with the Commentary by Śaṅkara*, translated by George Thibaut (New York: Dover, 1962), part 1, p. 223.

4. Keeping in mind Heidegger's conception of world as the "Fourfold *(Geviert)*" of earth and sky, divinities and mortals, a systematic examination of the meaning of *devatā* (divinity), of God and the gods, in the Upaniṣads (particularly in the *Bṛhadāraṇyaka*) and Śaṃkara's interpretation of it may prove rewarding. The comparative task here would be to differentiate this Vedic and post-Vedic conception from the Greek. In his early work, *Studies in Vedantism*, K. C.

Bhattacharyya gave an original interpretation of the notions of *devatā* and *loka* (region) as part of his treatment of "Vedantic metaphysics," but these suggestions have never since been examined or followed up. See Krishnachandra Bhattacharyya, *Studies in Philosophy* (Calcutta: Progressive Publishers, 1956), 1:31–68.

5. A major exception is Paul Hacker. See his remarks on Sūreśvara's style as compared with Śaṃkara's in *Untersuchungen über Texte des frühen Advaitavāda, I: Die Schüler Śaṅkaras* (Wiesbaden, 1951), pp. 16–21, and on verses of praise in Śaṃkara and the early Advaita writers in "Relations of Early Advaitins to Vaiṣṇavism," *Wiener Zeitschrift für die Kunde Süd- und Ostasiens* 9 (1965), and "Śaṅkara der Yogin und Śaṅkara der Advaitin," *ibid.* 12–13 (1968–1969) (Frauwallner *Festschrift*).

6. For references to these quotations from Plato and Aristotle, see Heidegger, *What Is Philosophy?* (New York: Twayne, 1958).

7. See *The Birth of Tragedy*, sec. 15 (*Basic Writings of Nietzsche*, ed. Walter Kaufmann [New York: Random House, 1968], pp. 93–95). These quotations by no means represent adequately Nietzsche's complex attitude to Socrates.

8. *Christianity in World History* (New York: Scribners, 1964), p. 18.

9. "Die Zeit des Weltbildes," in *Holzwege* (Frankfurt: Klostermann, 1950), p. 70.

10. *An Introduction to Metaphysics* (New York: Doubleday, 1961), p. 31.

11. *Poetry, Language, Thought* (New York: Harper and Row, 1971), pp. 91–92.

12. Śaṃkara's Commentary on the *Bṛhadāraṇyaka Upaniṣad* I.iv.7, beginning.

13. "Dankansprache von Professor Martin Heidegger" in *Ansprachen zum 80. Geburtstag* (Messkirch: Stadt Messkirch, 1969), p. 35. This is a recurrent motif in Heidegger's post-*Being and Time* writings, in which he keeps coming back to the ideas of "home," "world destiny," and "world-civilization" from the perspective of the question of Being.

14. *An Introduction to Metaphysics*, p. 30.

15. *Nietzsche II* (Pfullingen: Neske, 1961), p. 278.

16. On the notion of "planetary thinking, see *The Question of Being* (New York: Twayne, 1958), p. 107, and Kostas Axelos, *Einführung in ein künftiges Denken—über Marx und Heidegger* (Tübingen: Niemeyer, 1966), *passim*. See also this author's *The Philosophy of Martin Heidegger* (New York: Harper and Row, 1971), pp. 244–254, for this as well as the whole general topic of this paper.

17. "Hölderlins Erde und Himmel" in *Erläuterungen zu Hölderlins Dichtung* (Frankfurt: Klostermann, vierte, erweiterte Auflage, 1971), p. 177.

18. "Der Spruch des Anaximander" in *Holzwege* (Frankfurt: Klostermann, 1950), p. 300.

19. Martin Heidegger—Eugen Fink, *Heraklit* (Frankfurt: Klostermann, 1970), p. 212.

20. *Allgemeine Geschichte der Philosophie* (Leipzig, 1894–1917), 1:36.

21. *Identity and Difference* (New York: Harper and Row, 1969), p. 37.

22. *Ibid.*, p. 38.

23. *What Is Philosophy?*, p. 45.

24. Granting the metaphysical component in Sanskrit, however, it may be instructive to investigate the correctives it has developed against this representational or objectifying element, thus exhibiting its own unique genius: a mode of utterance in which representation and the cancellation of the representative force are held in tension and balance. Perhaps the uniqueness of Indian philosophy and

religion lies in this simultaneous de-objectification of the objectified, in the icono-clastic moment which is never for long absent from its iconism. If, as Heidegger admits (*Discourse on Thinking* [New York: Harper and Row, 1966], p. 46), thinking is of two kinds, calculative and meditative or representational and non-representational, it may yet be of significance to his concern to see how Indian thought took notice of the problem which it so explicitly recognized as crucial, the forms in which the problem presented itself as a haunting, ever-present task for thinking, and the solutions offered. Looked at from this point of view, the his-tory of Indian philosophy may prove to be not just an antiquarian, humanistic pursuit but a treasure house of direct promise to the Heideggerian quest.

25. See the preface in Latin to the first issue of *Lexis,* a periodical on compara-tive linguistics edited by Lohmann; also "Über den paradigmatischen Charakter der griechischen Kultur," in *Die Gegenwart der Griechen im neueren Denken* (Gadamer Festschrift. Tübingen: Mohr, 1960).

26. See this author's "Heidegger and the Comparison of Indian and Western Philosophy," *Philosophy East and West* 20 (1970), for a methodologically oriented consideration of the problem of comparative philosophy, as well as Eliot Deutsch's "Commentary" on the article in the same number. The entire issue is devoted to the subject of "Heidegger and Eastern Thought."

27. *On Time and Being* (New York: Harper and Row, 1972), p. 57.

28. *Ibid.,* p. 59.

29. Another, if possible even more basic and ultimate problem, concerns the meaning and nature of truth. The crucial, and culminating, point in Heidegger's thinking is how truth *(Wahrheit)* itself can be understood in terms of the pro-founder notion of *alētheia* or unhiddenness. In the Upaniṣadic tradition truth *(satya)* and Being *(sat)* are even more intimately connected than in the Greek. But, beyond this, we have also the conception of the truth of what is commonly called true. See *Bṛhadāraṇyaka Upaniṣad* II.i.20 for "the truth of truth *(satyasya satyam)*" as the secret name of the Self and Śaṃkara's commentary on this. How far the Advaita conception of *avidyā-māyā* (nescience-illusion) as the "seed" of all presentedness of entities is comparable to Heidegger's conception of *alētheia* as necessarily involving the element of hiddenness is also a question worth pursuing in this connection.

For a systematic and lucid exposition of Heidegger's life-long concern with truth as *alētheia,* see Walter Biemel, *Heidegger* (Hamburg: Rowohlt, 1973).

30. *Vorträge und Aufsätze* (Pfullingen: Neske, 1954), p. 227.

31. *Schellings Abhandlung über das Wesen der Menschlichen Freiheit (1809)* (Tübingen: Niemeyer, 1971), p. 175.

32. See the entire quotation from Hamann in Martin Heidegger, *Poetry, Lan-guage, Thought* (New York: Harper and Row, 1971), p. 191.

33. *An Introduction to Metaphysics,* p. 99.

34. Hacker has pointed this out repeatedly in a number of articles. See "Notes on the Māṇḍūkyopaniṣad and Śaṅkara's Āgamaśāstravivaraṇa," in *India Major,* ed. J. Ensink and P. Gaeffke (Leiden: Brill, 1972), pp. 125, 129–130, though he seems to be arguing from a position extraneous to the Vedānta (from the point of view of what we have called "the Greek thought of Being," as mediated in Hack-er's interpretation through the Christian Thomist tradition) when he finds that "the inadequacy of his argumentation landed Śaṅkara in that very nihilism which he made such valiant efforts to combat," and when he concludes that "Śaṅkara never succeeded in facing the overwhelming fact of existence." A statement like this, coming from the most competent scholar of Advaita Vedānta in the West since Deussen, brings to a focus the basic issues in the comparative enterprise,

whether in religion or in philosophy. See also Hacker's "Śaṅkara der Yogin und Śaṅkara der Advaitin" in *Beiträge zur Geistesgeschichte Indiens—Festschrift für Erich Frauwallner* (Wien: Gerold, 1968), p. 131 and "Essere e Spirito nel Vedanta," in *Filosofia e Vita*, 4 (1969), *passim*, where the problem of Being in Śaṃkara is dealt with extensively in the context of a comparison of Śaṃkara and Advaita generally with Thomas Aquinas.

35. Commentary on *Kaṭha Upaniṣad* II.iii.13.

36. Commentary on *Taittrīya Upaniṣad* II.vi.

37. Commentary on the *Bhagavadgītā* XIII.12.

38. Commentary on *Chandogya Upaniṣad* VI.ii.1.

39. Commentary on *Brahma Sūtra* III.ii.21.

40. Commentary on *Brahma Sūtra* I.i.4.

41. Heidegger says this about the hidden relationship between the thinker and the poet, quoting from Hölderlin's *Patmos*. See "What Is Metaphysics?" in Werner Brock, *Existence and Being* (London: Vision Press, 1949), p. 392.

42. See his articles "Phenomenology, Mysticism and the 'Grammatica Speculativa': A Study of Heidegger's 'Habilitationsschrift,' " *Journal of the British Society for Phenomenology* 5 (1974), and "Meister Eckhart and the Later Heidegger: The Mystical Element in Heidegger's Thought," *The Journal of the History of Philosophy* 12 and 13 (1974–1975), and also his book *The Mystical Element in Heidegger's Thought* (New York: Fordham University Press, 1986).

43. See *Frühe Schriften* (Frankfurt: Klostermann, 1972), p. 352.

44. *Nietzsche II,* p. 28.

45. *Vorträge und Aufsätze,* p. 134.

46. *On the Way to Language* (New York: Harper and Row, 1971), p. 57.

47. *Ibid.,* pp. 66–67.

48. *Ibid.,* p. 57.

49. *Ibid.,* pp. 73–74.

50. Rudolf Otto, *Mysticism East and West* (New York: Meridian, 1959), p. xvi.

51. *Identity and Difference,* pp. 54–55.

52. *Being and Time* (New York: Harper and Row, 1962), p. 272.

53. Recognizing "das Kreisen der Gedanken" in Sūreśvara and in Advaita thinkers generally and also the fact that they are all concerned with what is "ein einziger Gedanke" (both features so readily intelligible from a Heideggerian perspective), Paul Hacker does not find any special virtue here but, operating with the category of "mysticism," judges Sūreśvara's *Naiskarmyasiddhi* in the following words, "Die Naisk. ist für uns eine geistesgeschichtlich hochbedeutsame Mischung von Logik und Mystik, wobei die Mystik der Logik, auf die das Zeitalter doch nicht verzichten kann, immer wieder Gewalt antut" (*Untersuchungen über Texte des frühen Advaitavāda, I: Die Schule Śaṅkaras,* Wiesbaden, 1951). Would it not enable a reader of Sūreśvara's work to come closer to the thinking in it if he were to set aside, following Heidegger's critique, the concepts of "Logic" (which is not quite the same as the Indian *tarka*) and "Mysticism" as both suspect "in the realm of thinking"?

54. *Phänomenologie des Geistes* (Hamburg: Meiner, 1952), p. 65; 2nd paragraph of the "Introduction," *Phenomenology of Mind.*

55. *On the Way to Language,* p. 54.

56. *Discourse on Thinking* (New York: Harper and Row, 1966), p. 55.

57. *Kant and the Problem of Metaphysics* (Bloomington: Indiana University Press, 1968), p. 207.

58. *Vorträge und Aufsätze,* p. 185.

Otto Pöggeler
West-East Dialogue:
Heidegger and Lao-tzu

Bernhard Welte reports that on January 14, 1976, Martin Heidegger invited him to his house for the evening. Heidegger asked the theologian and fellow native of Messkirch if he would speak at his funeral in his hometown (which then took place shortly thereafter, on May 28). Because Welte was lecturing at that time on Meister Eckhart, this thinker became the topic of the conversation, and Heidegger's cautious questioning focused on the "detachment" *(Abgeschiedenheit)* of which the mystic had spoken.[1] In his youth Heidegger had not only dealt with the Scholastic doctrines of categories, logic and language, but had also promised a book on mysticism. As he became acquainted with Eckhart's "Opus tripartitum" during the twenties he was so enthusiastic that his students were constantly expecting a work on Eckhart from him.[2] However, in his lectures on Aristotle's *Metaphysics* from the summer of 1931, Heidegger said that Eckhart was in fact the only one in the Middle Ages to have had a solution to the questions that had found only an over-hasty answer in the doctrine of *analogia entis,* but that after a first approach he had given up his conception that "Being" was a finite predicate and could not be applied to God (who "is" precisely *intelligere,* the openness of knowledge).[3] The short essay "Der Feldweg" from 1947 connects a recollection of his youth and his Messkirch home with a word of "Eckehardt's, the old master of reading and living," to the effect that God was only God in the "unspoken" language of the "things" by the country path.

In 1979 Bernhard Welte published a book on Eckhart of which he was able to say that his last conversation with Heidegger, so close to the latter's death, had gone into it.[4] From Heidegger Welte rethinks the metaphysical tradition in such a way that *intelligere,* conceived "mystically," grants openness to Being, and thus metaphysics and mysticism, but also their traditions and Heidegger's new thinking, attain a seamless unity. This unity is also presupposed for both Western mysticism and East Asian contemplation and thereby for two quite different religious traditions. From the perspective of a philosophy influenced by Zen Buddhism, Keiji Nishitani has made clear to European and American readers, in his great book *Was Ist Religion? (Religion and Nothingness)*, how Heidegger made possible a new encounter between Eastern and Western thought.[5] Nishitani clears the way to the decisive questions with Heidegger starting from the experience of time: that which is in time not only hangs over the abyss of nothingness, but also has in the dimensions of past and future an infinite depth, out of which each one of them can interfuse itself with the whole of the other. It is true that the Mediterranean European tradition has in a twofold way understood this interfusion one-sidedly and falsely: from the Iranian and Judaic origins the uniqueness of history was discovered, and then again after Kierkegaard the personal and historical were set against the impersonality of a mythical eternal return and the mechanism of science. On the other hand one finds in Nietzsche and the willing of eternal return an attitude that gives itself no further illusions about that which is. Kierkegaard's theism, or his transformation of it into an existentialism, and Nietzsche's atheism remained final experiments on wrong paths; by contrast Meister Eckhart would lead by way of "releasement" *(Gelassenheit)* and detachment, and thereby through the death of the I, from God to the "absolute nothingness" of the Godhead. "In his preservation of the 'nothingness' of the Godhead in the ground of the personal 'God' he stands and develops his thinking 'on the other shore,' beyond theism and atheism, in the place where conversely the independence of the 'soul' is grounded in essential oneness with the being of God." And so it is Meister Eckhart in turn who supports Heidegger's attempt to lead us out of the Western metaphysical tradition and its aporias; and in as far as Eastern and Western thought engage in dialogue, the West as much as the East can find its way back to itself.

Heidegger himself in his lecture "What Calls for Thinking?" has discovered in the Western tradition the two culminations of wrong paths we have mentioned: on the one hand, the attempt to re-shelter the human will through repentance back into the will of God; on the other, the willing that in revenge against time and its "it was" paradoxically wills precisely the eternal return of the same.[6] In neither case would man find himself in time in the appropriate way—claimed by a call that calls for thinking to think. If Heidegger in his discussion of "releasement" in Eckhart finds much of value, he still sees in it a "throwing off of sinful self-centeredness and the letting go of the individual will in favor of the will of God." And so, would Eckhart not thereby also be the above-mentioned wrong path of the Western tradition? Such a criticism of Eckhart may well apply to the Eckhart of the "Pedagogical Discourses" *(Reden der Unterweisung)*, who provisionally, still attached to the traditional religious language, brings releasement and the "having of God" *(Gotthaben)* of detachment close to his listeners and readers; but it misses the Eckhart who lets God be for the sake of the Godhead, yet thereby experiences the spark of light in man as one with the life of the Godhead. Meister Eckhart quite "Neoplatonically" sets things aside for the sake of detachment; in this specific way he can then in harmony with the metaphysical tradition attain an onto-theology which wins back, from God as the highest being, that which is. However, what is decisive for Eckhart is that in his *last* "mystical" experiences he leaves the Neoplatonic and metaphysical path behind. And yet Heidegger seems to demand that the path of thinking be approached differently *from the very start:* in the renunciation of unconditionedness *(Unbedingtheit)* the Godhead should be found in the unspoken language of things and works (as Eckhart himself demands in the sermon "Misit dominus manum suam"). Can we presuppose that nothingness as mystical nothingness is pure light? Are not rather light and darkness given to us simultaneously from the beginning, but in such a way that in the language of each and every thing something unspoken, self-withholding, is the center, so that things themselves bring us into detachment, which releases us from control over things? It could have been Far Eastern meditation that encouraged Heidegger to take this different path to the determination of detachment starting from the "thing."

In the meantime there has been a great deal of evidence that Heidegger gladly acknowledged to visitors the closeness of his thinking to the Taoist tradition and to Zen Buddhism. When the University of Hawaii held a symposium entitled "Heidegger and Eastern Thought" on the occasion of his eightieth birthday, this closeness was particularly illuminated.[7] In fact since the fifties some people have sought to express this closeness by saying that Heidegger "identified aesthetic feeling with ontological experience" or with "pre-ontological experience." Heidegger is supposed to have attempted to free himself from representational thinking in order to engage in meditative thinking, to make the transition from "an analytical approach to a direct, intuitive one." But if one recalls the negative context in which the word "aesthetic" has always stood in Heidegger, one must treat these kinds of testimonies, which arise from conversations during brief visits, with some scepticism. In philosophical conversations Heidegger proceeded quite slowly, after adopting provisional orientations and conventions, toward the authentic questions, which then superseded the earlier formulations; and the English language still remained one which Heidegger scarcely understood, and for which he had little respect. In any case one hardly needs the testimony of hasty visitors, since a considerable number of Japanese philosophers have studied with Heidegger and with life-long effort have elaborated the intimations they gained.[8]

Nishida had built a bridge to German Idealism; while Schelling was in the foreground, there was also a novel accent through Hegel's insistence on mediation. This was attempted by Tanabe, who after studying in Freiburg was the first in Japan, in 1924, to have reported on "Heidegger's phenomenology of life" as "a new turn in phenomenology." Count Kuki explicated *Being and Time* to his Japanese colleagues, and later Nishitani attended Heidegger's lectures on Nietzsche. Nishitani, however, was to insist more than Tanabe on the ultimate immediacy of basic experience. And it was into Heideggerian language that the ancient Chinese Zen story of "The Ox and the Ox-herd," with interpretations by a contemporary Zen master, was translated in 1958 by Kōichi Tsujimura and Hartmut Buchner. On Heidegger's eightieth birthday Tsujimura spoke in Messkirch on "Martin Heidegger's Thinking and Japanese Philosophy." He sought to show that a Zen-influenced philosophizing could learn from Heidegger how better to reflect upon the contemporary situation—for us, the current advance of technology.

Already in the volume *On the Way to Language* Heidegger had included a conversation with a Japanese guest which had been written down between 1953 and 1954. In this kind of dialogue Heidegger by no means proceeded from a philosophy informed by Zen or meditation; rather he continually asked himself and others whether in the talk of nothingness in his lecture "What Is Metaphysics?" and in Japanese philosophers coming from different traditions something very different was not being thought. In the piece entitled "Conversation on Language" Heidegger tried in looking back on his own path, on which Being and language were ultimately connected, to retrieve his own concern in primal words of the Japanese language (the translation of which into German must of course be checked). Heidegger himself maintained, moreover, that from early on he had worked with Japanese scholars, "but had learned more from Chinese." In 1946 he collaborated with a Chinese scholar on a translation into German of the *Lao-tzu,* but they completed only eight of the eighty-one chapters.[9] In his "destruction" of the Western tradition, Heidegger did not stop with the almost already Hellenistic analyses and systemizations of Aristotle nor with late mysticism; he rather looked to the earliest thinkers for the beginnings that have constantly informed and also perhaps distorted the concern *(Sache)* of thinking. Did he not in his dialogue with the Far East have to go back similarly to the beginnings of those traditions, as we are able to construe them in Lao-tzu, for example, or in the work which was given that name?

In *Being and Time* Heidegger reclaimed for the *logos* of his phenomenological ontology, which was as universal as it was radical, the characterization "hermeneutics" and "hermeneutical." This philosophizing is to revert to *Dasein* as the openness of Being from which it arises; it is to be integrated into the current historical situation, and should reach through this situation to a concealed origin and thereby transform the situation in the direction of a new future. A philosophizing of this kind must be aware that the beginning of philosophy with the Greeks, viewed historically, is ultimately only one beginning of thinking among others and perhaps discloses the origin of thinking in a one-sided and distorted way. In this vein Georg Misch, for example—after having been able to reflect upon his philosophical ideas in the course of a journey around the world —in his philosophy textbook *The Way into Philosophy* (1926 and 1950) distinguished the *Logos* of Heraclitus from other primal terms such as the Indian *Brahman* and the Chinese *tao*. When Heidegger transposed his question of Being and time back into the *Ereignis* of truth as the place of the moment *(Augenblicks-Stätte)*, he conceived of time as "time-play-space" *(Zeitspielraum)* and thereby as a movement which as way and underway lets things rest in a stillness and stilledness, from which *logos* as language first arises. Thus in *On the Way to Language* he could invoke Lao-tzu: "Perhaps there lies concealed in the word 'Way,' *tao*, the mystery of all mysteries of thoughtful saying, as long as we let this name return to its unspokenness and are able to accomplish this letting. . . . All is Way."[10] The 1957 lecture "The Principle of Identity" adds to its own talk of *Ereignis* (event of appropriation) the Greek *logos* and Chinese *tao* as untranslatable guiding words of thinking.[11]

Lao-tzu did not become significant for Heidegger as a result of a universal and neutral historical contemplation, but rather in a quite definite context. When in 1945 National Socialism finally collapsed in its struggle for world domination, Heidegger was confronted with the fact that up to at least 1933 he had placed himself at the disposal of the new "breakthrough" in a delusion concerning the true goals of that movement. In December 1945, in the course of the de-Nazification proceedings—in the "Inquisition trial of the twenty-three questions," as he put it —Heidegger suffered a breakdown and had to be taken to a sanatorium for three weeks.[12] The small book written in his mountain cabin, *Aus der Erfahrung des Denkens* (From the Experience of Thinking), is not concerned with fir branches and the sound of cowbells; rather, in this piece thinking seeks in the manner of one severely ill and only now convalescing to right itself through the simple experiencing of seasons and times of day, and to reflect anew upon its task (as the interpretations of Japanese scholars have recognized).[13] Connected with this collection written *in extremis* is Heidegger's attempt at a translation of Lao-tzu. It is not surprising that his Chinese colleague sought to allay Heidegger's bitterness over the vagaries of politics with an adage from Mencius: "When heaven wishes to assign someone a great task, it first fills his heart and will with bitterness." Even though the Lao-tzu translation did not go very far, the attempt to confront the beginnings of Western thinking with the beginnings of one of the great East Asian traditions transformed Heidegger's language in a critical situation and gave his thinking a new orientation. If Heidegger loved Brecht's Lao-tzu poem, it was probably because he himself at that time wandered into the mountains like Lao-tzu and went against his epoch from an abiding distance, and yet nevertheless greatly affected it.

I

In the nineteenth and twentieth centuries people in Europe built various bridges to the traditions of the East; and Heidegger seems to have discovered Taoism quite early on. In his 1930 Bremen lecture on the essence of truth he struck out in a new direction, and the subsequent discussion became enmeshed in the question "whether a person could put himself in the place of another." This was the question of intersubjectivity, which dialogics thought it could direct critically against him. To the astonishment of the other participants Heidegger asked for the aphorisms of Chuang-tzu, and the host of the house was able to produce the Buber translation, whereupon Heidegger read aloud the story of the happiness of the fishes (chapter 17). In that episode Chuang-tzu remarks on the joy with which the fish in the stream leap out of the water. His companion asks him how he can know the joy of the fish since he himself isn't a fish. Chuang-tzu then remarks that he (his companion) isn't him (Chuang-tzu); so how could he know that he (Chuang-tzu) doesn't know the joy of the fishes? The conclusion says that we know the joy of the fishes by our joy at walking by the stream. This last proposition set to rest all inappropriate reflections upon the problem of putting oneself in the other's position. Heidegger could well have invoked an apposite understanding of *Being and Time,* where admittedly only some hints at the solution to this problem are given.[14]

The talk there is primarily about being-with *(Mitsein),* in which we are in agreement with others in "having an understanding about something" in such a way as not to distinguish between you and me. Heidegger speaks of *das Man,* and yet his analyses proceed primarily from examples of losing oneself in shared work, without considering, for example, the community brought about by the "nature" of races. This "inauthentic" mode of being-with is broken through in "anticipatory concern for others" *(vorausspringende Fürsorge),* in which *Dasein* helps fellow *Dasein* in need, in order to free it to find its way to itself. Here there arises an otherness that does not let itself be mediated into an encapsulated and disposable "we." Anxiety *(Angst)*, which is essentially anxiety in the face of death, individualizes *Dasein* into *solus ipse;* in the face of the "non-relatability" *(Unbezüglichkeit)* of death all being-with-others fails, and yet it is precisely the "unsurpassable possibility" of being-towards-death which allows *Dasein* to understand the possibilities-of-being of the other. And so, concerning the same "how-of-being" we have an understanding of the other that may not be adequate but cannot be denied. Chuang-tzu is able through his joy in wandering to share the joy of the fish in the stream. In "participation" and "struggle," that "destiny" can then be released from which the overarching community of a "people" can build itself over the generations. One might find lacking in this characterization of the relation to the other that "ethical" dimension in which the other takes responsibility for me, in which the "mythical" limiting oneself to one's own being and homeland is broken through by the messianic demand of peace for all.[15] It is precipitate to claim that in Heidegger the relation to the other is missing. It is simply viewed differently from the way it is in certain traditions—namely, as *friendship* in which the friends ultimately let each other be in their ownness and otherness, so that in each "the world stands there ready," not as *love of the neighbor (Nächstenliebe)* in which the one is dependent *(angewiesen)* on the other (as Nietzsche put it, rather abruptly and polemically, in the chapter of *Zarathustra* entitled "On Love of the Neighbor").

Heidegger specifically relates the Chuang-tzu story to the question of being-with. But does this story not have in Taoism the farther-reaching implication of the universal sympathy which joins together all the things of nature—such as men and fishes? *Being and Time* points out that the nature that "embraces" us, nature then "somewhat in the sense of the Romantic conception of nature," is not "nature as a thing" present-at-hand or ready-to-hand, and thus not the nature that we dominate scientifically or technologically (*SZ* 65, 211). And yet in his lecture from the winter of 1929–30 Heidegger shows that man is separated from other living things by an abyss; according to the "Contributions to Philosophy," nature can be encountered only in the "resonance" to the ringing in us.[16] And so Heidegger does not see man as connected through a universal sympathy with everything that exists; nor is he calling for a return to a primordial immersion in natural nature. Werner Heisenberg, in his lecture "The View of Nature in Contemporary Physics," recalled Chuang-tzu's story of the well-sweep (chapter 12): the old gardener refuses to use the well on the grounds that one who uses machines works mechanistically, and one who works mechanistically acquires a mechanistic heart and loses his harmonious unity with the *tao*. Heisenberg himself thought that the current danger lay in the fact that in the scientific-technological world we are still encountering only ourselves, and encountering things only in the way in which we have incorporated them into the world that we have constructed.[17]

Heidegger corrected this thesis in his essay "The Question of Technology": what we encounter in the world of technology is precisely no longer ourselves, nor the challenge that issues from the world of technology. The meeting of this challenge should lead to the acceptance of technological utilization of things within its limits as a historical task and thus as one possibility among many. We cannot simply go back to untouched nature; even atomic energy is something natural: if its activity in the sun were to cease for even a short period, all life on the earth would be extinguished. The draw-well which Chuang-tzu's gardener rejected as a dead machine is for Heidegger in a different historical situation precisely not a dead machine. Heidegger says of windmills, as semi-automatic, that they are tailored to the winds, and thus mesh with nature and do not simply "set it up" for exploitation. Admittedly Heidegger aligns himself with the poet Johann Peter Hebel in calling for a returning of nature as represented by the Copernican world-view to the "naturalness of nature."[18] This naturalness is nevertheless seen as something historical: the natural world, the everyday, the life-world are not fundamental, but are rather a historically variable product, which in relation to other arrangements can direct us to a new encounter with nature. If Goethe said of Hebel that he wanted to countrify the universe, then Heidegger in looking to the rural life of a past historical epoch calls for a new mode of being-in-the-world as cultivating and dwelling, which in the future must admittedly be totally different from the way it was in times past. In any case the scientific-technological construal of nature must not be allowed to be "touted as the only key to the mystery of the world." Indeed Nishitani goes a step beyond Heidegger when he sees in the explosion of science and technology and the rise of nihilism the task of finding, without polemics from a personalistic standpoint, an immanent meaning even in mechanisms and automatisms. And yet Heidegger is quite far from connecting the regaining of a primordial Greek ground, through the (supposedly) early experience of *phusis,* with the Far Eastern traditions in order to produce a view of man which sees in man only a piece of nature (as Karl Löwith came close to suggesting).

Heidegger sought with Hölderlin, and thereby from a dialogue with the Greeks or a differentiation from them, to achieve a different future. But in contrast with Hölderlin he not only distinguished the Greek from the oriental, but also related the origin of the occidental to the origin that the East Asian world has in Taoism. Heidegger was able, for example, to see in Bremen and Munich, in the collection of Emil Preetorius, Chinese, Japanese, and Korean art. He was since his schooldays a friend of the painter Bissier, who adopted much from the Far East and sought contact with the American painter Tobey (who tried to connect with the East Asian tradition). He showed particular interest in Noh drama and Zen painting. He was thus able to take into account the Taoist conception of art when he gave a lecture in Bremen in 1960 entitled "Image and Word."

The introduction to this talk focused on five texts: "a quotation from Augustine (*Confessions* X, 7 and 8), fragment 112 of Heraclitus, Chuang-tzu's story of the bell-stand (chapter 19), Paul Klee's Jena lecture 'On modern art'—and Heidegger's own couplet, '*Nur Gebild wahrt Gesicht / Doch Gesicht ruht im Gedicht*' (Only images guard the face / Yet the face rests in the poem)." The passage from Augustine stands at the beginning because it is a summation for Europeans of their philosophico-religious heritage. Augustine admonishes us not to see, to hear, to taste, but to turn within; this admonition culminates in the passage that Petrarch, paradoxically, is said to have read on his ascent of Mount Ventoux, which yet gives evidence of a new discovery of the fullness of the world. In memory, which belongs together with anticipation, all things are present in thinking; but their being is thereby related to time (remembering and anticipating), and the question of Being and time dissolves the Greek connection between Being and thinking. Augustine seeks the word in the heart, which is then later understood as the mystical word (X, 3); thus he introduces talk of Being and word rather than Being and time.

This connection between Being, which with its truth belongs to time or the event of appropriation *(Ereignis),* and the word, Heidegger sees addressed in Heraclitus's fragment 112. Heidegger believes that he has found in the word *phusis* a central term of Heraclitus and that this word is to be understood as "arising holding-sway" *(das aufgehende Walten).* Thus he can say with fragment 112 that genuine wisdom consists in saying and doing what is true or unconcealed, and moreover from hearkening to that which arising from itself shows itself *(phusis).* His *Introduction to Metaphysics* also hears in the word "Being" the root *bhu,* which is to be thought of in connection with *phusis* as well as with *fui* and *bin.*[19]

When Heidegger takes the motive impulse for the third part of his talk from the *Chuang-tzu,* he is presuming that people in Bremen have not forgotten that the old Hanseatic town not only became at the end of the nineteenth century the second most important German town for world trade but also absorbed much East Asian art, and with it the elegantly simple thoughts of Taoist wisdom. In choosing the story of the bell-stand Heidegger may appear to confirm that the kind of thinking that he wishes to stimulate through mentioning that Taoism is "aesthetic." But already the conversation with the Japanese visitor in *On the Way to Language* warns against putting East Asian art and experience of the world under the category of the "aesthetic." The "aesthetic" of the European tradition finds in the sensible, according to Heidegger, something non- or suprasensible; but this approach should be abandoned in favor of the experience of the mutual interpenetration of farness and stillness. This interpenetration attracts through hint and gesture and at the same time maintains a distance, thereby conveying a "message" whose language gains its saying from a silence.

As early as the lecture of the summer of 1934, in an abrupt deviation from his stated theme, Heidegger had asked about logic and then elaborated the question deriving from Heraclitus as a question of language. The question of Being and *Logos* or Being and language was then in the subsequent lectures on Hölderlin and on the origin of the work of art conceived more concretely as the question of the truth of Being, which—as well as the Holy, which is above the gods—must be brought to language and into the work. In order to be able to say what a work of art is, Heidegger dismantled, for example, the traditional schema of form and matter (content). Dilthey had already tried to overcome this fundamental distinction in Western philosophy of art and inquired into a form that arises out of matter, and a matter that is always already formed. Corresponding to this "hermeneutic" idea Heidegger had in *Being and Time* conceived understanding *(Verstehen)* as always disposed and disposition *(Befindlichkeit)* as always understanding, and to that extent proceeded at least at first from disposed-understanding articulation, or "discourse" *(Rede)*. He was able to introduce this theme into the Bremen discussion through Chuang-tzu's story of the bell-stand: through long fasting and through concentration and meditation the woodworker becomes able to find in the forest that one tree which is already the bell-stand yet to be made, in such a way that matter and form in this consummate work of art can be completely one.

In this Bremen seminar, however, Heidegger wanted to do more than just break through the traditional religio-metaphysical ideas to those beginnings which he found for the Western tradition in Heraclitus and for the Far East in Taoism. He wanted to follow the trace of this primordial thinking in such a way that it would lead our own time to a new beginning. Therefore he turned to a speech by the painter Paul Klee in which, in June 1924, Klee summed up his experiences as a teacher at the Bauhaus. The painters of our century have articulated in the abstractions of their expressions and constructions those elements that constitute modern art; Klee tried to grasp these elements theoretically as well. His lecture names the measures for line and the play of line, for the weight of light and dark tones, and for color values. The painter can combine these elements into constructions in such a way that one can associate them with something familiar—a plant or a star, for example. If the painter then incorporates something further—such as a vertical standing or horizontal disposition or the attitude of a body swimming—he can then present complex compositions instead of elemental constructions. In these pictures the painter does not depict the visible (nor does he follow traditional iconologies); he rather seeks in the sphere of the visible the key to all possible worlds. Toward the end of the fifties Heidegger wanted to write an epilogue to the *Holzwege* essay on the work of art drawing from Klee's reflections, in order to be able to talk about art in the age of technology.[20] But how could that painter who produced such a "lyrically" toned, fantastically floating, if not remote art, refer us to the task of art in the age of technology? Precisely because Klee does not oppose the scientific-technological advances in nuclear physics, cosmology and evolutionary theory to art, but rather incorporates them into the unlocking of modern art!

Heidegger used to say in conversation that Klee revealed more in his paintings than he was able to say in his theoretical reflections. The theory was too strongly conditioned by a neo-Kantian position (and proceeded too one-sidedly from the formal, in a way that we find also in Conrad Fiedler). When Klee gave his paintings "poetic" titles he was reminding us of another—the decisive—root of his art: of that poetical element in which the finite-fateful or the destined was taken up, in which a limited openness frees itself from sheltering concealment and on the long path to perfection it points to an immanent meaning. Because art has incorporated technological advances in the forming of its structural elements, it can limit these from within: the reminder of the finitude and limitedness of every formulation checks the extravagant proliferation of the scientific-technological approach. The "Enframing" *(Ge-Stell)* of representational and exploitative science and technology, which makes everything into an object and a mere resource, is overcome in the Fourfold *(Geviert),* in which earth and sky, mortals and the holiness of the "divinities" interplay. Only enframing and fourfold together refer to the world. Heidegger himself clarified his couplet on face, picture, and poem from the "cabin booklet" in the summer of 1960 at the conclusion of his Hebel lecture entitled "Sprache und Heimat" (Language and Homeland): "It is only poetical saying that brings the face of the fourfold to shine forth. Poetical saying is what first lets mortals dwell on the earth under the sky before the divinities. Their poetical saying is what first brings forth protection and cultivation, shelter and sanctity [*Hut und Hege, den Hort und die Huld*] for an autochthonous place which can be a resting place in the earthly journey of dwelling man."

Heidegger was able to introduce impulses from the East Asian tradition into his own attempts to awaken reflection. Over a period of decades he observed how his Japanese students sought to reappropriate their own traditions from the perspective of his thinking. He considered the dialogue between Europe and the Far East to be as necessary as it was difficult; he did not want to overlook the element of foreignness that remained in every encounter. There is a world of difference between the life-long dialogues with students and the brief interviews with visitors; nevertheless, a description of one such visit might give some idea as to why Heidegger sought such encounters at all, and how he saw the differences between the traditions but also the commonality in questioning. There is a detailed account of the visit made by the Buddhist monk Bikkhu Maha Mani from Bangkok. This son of a peasant family in Thailand was not only the shining light of his monastery but also a university professor who did not disdain working for the radio as well. Surprisingly, he was granted an interview with Heidegger in front of television cameras; but more significant were the preceding hours spent in Heidegger's house at Zähringen. One might well ask whether the whole spirit of the interview was not perverted by the monk's wanting to talk to "the" German philosopher, since philosophy never lets itself be embodied in an idol. Heidegger was to learn later that the monk and philosophy professor left the order to take up a position with an American television company.[21]

Heidegger said in the conversation that his life's work had been to free us from the prison that we carry with us all our lives—from the overwhelming power of the two thousand years since Plato which distort every conversation through the presuppositions engendered by philosophical systems and doctrines, confessional stipulations and religious schisms, and by educational systems. "We have too much culture!" Not only the Germans, but Europeans in general have no univocal, common, simple relationship to reality and to themselves. This great lack in the Western world is the ground of confused opinions in various areas, and it is clearly also the reason for the turn toward Asia. At the beginning of the thirties the construction of an academic philosophy on the basis of phenomenology no longer satisfied Heidegger; the parties and churches seemed to be failing to provide structures for communal life. Thus in 1933, Heidegger called for a revolution to come from the university, and then for a reflection upon the necessary lengthy transformation from out of Hölderlin. After the catastrophe of Nazism he called for a "new thinking," and he sought to take over the impetus for such a thinking from that spirituality which was still vital in Asia. One might ask to what extent the nostalgic flight away from the chaotic Babel of the contemporary search for meaning played a role here; at any rate in his more detailed characterization of the "new thinking" Heidegger also distinguished between the Western path and that of the East.

The simple and the binding had always been central to Heidegger's thinking when it dealt with the question of Being: the Indo-Germanic languages are informed by "is"-saying, so that the theme of Being came to be the leading and fundamental question in Western philosophy. Especially since the Freiburg inaugural lecture of 1929, "What Is Metaphysics?," Heidegger thought of Being as nothingness in contrast to everything that is. The determination of nihilism through the history of Being of 1944–46 showed that the nothingness of true nihilism is nothing surmountable, but rather, as the mystery, conditions through and through the truth of Being. If the *logos,* which allows this truth to come to language, is characterized by Heraclitus as a gathering to which man must gather himself, then the "new thinking" approaches the realm of contemplation and of mysticism, which leads to the extinguishing of the "I" and the will in favor of the opening up of truth. There nevertheless remains a "difference from the Buddhist doctrine": the West distinguishes man from animals and plants by virtue of his alone having a conscious relation to Being, the ability to (cor)respond to it, and language—all of which determine and attune him as *Da-sein.* At the same time this *Da-sein* is seen as something finite which forces man to "constantly new endeavors." In this respect history—precisely as the breaking through of distorting traditions —is decisive. (In contrast the monk emphasizes: "We know no history. There are only passings of worlds.") From the finitude of *Dasein* and its history comes the consequence that our situation is a definite constellation which we are unable to jump out of directly.

Does this new thinking not lead beyond philosophy into a religious dimension? Heidegger's conversation with the monk runs into difficulties precisely at the point when it comes to talk of the "Holy." Heidegger had been interested in Rudolf Otto's phenomenological philosophy of religion, which appeared in 1917 under the title *Das Heilige* (The Idea of the Holy). But when in the winter of 1920–21 he read *Introduction to the Phenomenology of Religion,* he corrected Otto's picture: religion does not schematize the irrational, in which something numinous comes through, but rather leads actual life historically back to its origin. In this way the formally indicative existential hermeneutics of facticity was able to support the scientific status of a theology which at the same time relates to existential decisions of faith. However, when Heidegger on his departure from Marburg also left behind the concerns of his friend Rudolf Bultmann, he began to speak of the Holy in a new way: Being or its truth can be not only a neutral structural openness, but possibly also that which brings *Dasein* into salvation and thereby shows itself through the unapproachable mystery as the Holy. Heidegger decided not to use the term "religion" for this experience of the Holy because the word comes from the Latin and connotes the authoritative "binding back" to a given revelation. Even in the conversation with the monk the talk of religion serves to effect only a provisional understanding: with talk of the Holy one can hardly think straight away of the beard and aura of the prophets and saints. If talk of the Holy can show what is meant by the religious dimension, precisely such talk still contains difficulties of its own.

The Thai monk understands by religion nothing other than "the sayings of founders." Heidegger responds passionately to this characterization: "Say to him that I hold one thing alone as decisive: to follow the words of the founder. That alone—and neither the systems nor the doctrines and dogmas are important. *Religion is Imitation.*" The young Heidegger had transformed the approach of phenomenological philosophy in as far as he took practical and religious truth along with the theoretical as "truth": he once presented his astonished student Löwith with *The Imitation of Christ,* a book which re-integrated traditional religiosity into practical life. If Eckhart was for Heidegger not only a master of reading but also of living, it was because the latter wanted with his own thinking to direct people to life and to the sphere of praxis and the dimension of the religious. But not only did he read the Gospel of St. John together with his friend Bultmann; in the thirties the hymns of Hölderlin were for him no less than this gospel from the first century a bringing-to-language of the Holy. But can Hölderlin's words still be heard in a time which channels all knowing, behaving, and producing into the struggle for world domination? The philosopher cannot presuppose either this or another theology as given, but must ask whether and in what way a religious dimension belongs to life in the future. Thus Heidegger in his conversation with the monk from Bangkok emphasizes that a new way of thinking is necessary because the question of man cannot be put from the standpoint of religion, and yet in the West the relation of man to the totality of the world is confused. If religion is a "binding back" of man, this has nowadays dissolved in a confusion in which positions and doctrines merely seek to assert themselves. Can thinking again direct man into a simple and binding relationship to the religious dimension of life?

Even Heidegger has difficulty in making his talk of the Holy comprehensible: he attempts it from the direction of "salvation" *(das Heile)* but also builds a bridge to the idea of "harmony."[22] Nobody in the West and in Germany, he says, not without some bitterness, understands his often repeated formulation: "Without the Holy we remain out of touch with the Divine. Without being touched by the Divine the experience of God is not there." The monk thinks he can promise Heidegger that he would find himself understood in Thailand. But does talk of the Holy not remain strange also and especially in the Far East? Nishitani writes (p. 5) that "a few scholars" there have used the idea of "the Holy" for the religious dimension. Yet it is not just a question of a few scholars (above all amongst the successors of Rudolf Otto), but also of Heidegger's own approach. Does this approach allow itself to be connected at all with the Far Eastern traditions? According to the first chapter of the *Pi-yen-lu,* the first patriarch of Zen, Bodhidharma, on being asked by the emperor Wu-ti of the Liang dynasty about the original sense of "holy truth" responded: "Wide open. Nothing Holy!" This indication has a parallel in Heidegger, who in the 1929 essay on the being of ground *(Vom Wesen des Grundes)* characterizes man as a being of distance *(ein Wesen der Ferne),* who may not avoid himself by fleeing back to his idols. To the emperor's question of who it was who was standing before him the patriarch replied: "I don't know." Heidegger too proceeds from the premise that we do not know who we are, and precisely because of that must ask anew in what way a religious dimension belongs to our lives. Perhaps it can be made clear from the perspective of Lao-tzu and the Taoist tradition how Heidegger after the Second World War concerned himself with nothingness, farness and the Holy.[23]

Heidegger's Bremen lectures of December 1949, "Insight into That Which Is," began with the lecture "The Thing," which was then repeated in Munich in June of 1950. Does this hard and fast insistence on the "thing" not exclude that "mystical" relation to nothingness? As a paradigm of the thing a jug is presented. The jug was an ingenious invention of the Neolithic period: while stones break apart in fire, burned clay holds together and brings water to a boil and "magically" transforms a tuber, for example, into something edible. From the first discovery it was a long way to Greek vases or the jugs of modern craftsmanship. Rilke was able—as Heidegger recounts in his Rilke essay in *Holzwege ("Wozu Dichter?" / "What are poets for?")*—to oppose such "grown" *(gewachsen)* things as houses, wells, coats, to the faceless fabrications of technology to such "pseudo-things, life trappings" as were flowing over from America. Heidegger then shows that what is important in a jug is not a "being" that can be abstracted from the jug as a "form," but rather the "emptiness" by virtue of which the jug contains, and in the service of which all form must be usable. With its emptiness, with this nothingness, the jug contains and pours water, or wine. Water and wine are necessary for life; the sacrificial libation can transform the world into something Holy. Thus earth belongs together with heaven, which entices the wine-grape out of the earth; the mortals understand themselves from the dimension of the Holy and the divine. A thing, of which the jug is one, gathers together earth and heaven, divinities and mortals, into their Fourfold (the old root *thing* in the word *Ding* reminds us of this gathering). This view of the jug from the aspect of its emptiness rather than its "being" is supported by chapter 11 of the *Lao-tzu,* which sees the usefulness of the jug in the appropriateness of its containing emptiness: "What we gain is something, yet it is by virtue of Nothing that this can be put to use." Heidegger's subsequent lectures, on the Enframing, the Danger, and the Turning, show how the West pursued the "being" of things, thereby bringing itself for the sake of profit into the Danger of holding on to mere scientific objects and technological products and making even man and God into useful commodities. The way of "being" turns out to be a wrong track, and yet it is not Heidegger's purpose merely to oppose nothingness and emptiness to Being. Rather the Bremen lectures say that Being and nothingness disappear into the "worlding" *(Welten)*, when the thing lets world come near and abide, when world takes place in things, and man renounces all will to the "unconditioned" *(das Unbedingte)*.

Heidegger compares his ground-word *Ereignis* with words such as *tao* and *logos,* and he often remarks that in our word "method" the Greek word for "way" still resonates, but that the insistence on and absolutization of method distort every following of a way and thereby the collecting of oneself for the event of appropriation. It is the development of logic that has inserted itself between way and *logos* on the one hand and event on the other. In order to determine the appropriate place of this logic Heidegger articulates in a number of investigations the "basic principles of thinking" *(Grundsätze des Denkens)*. A contribution that bears this title appears in the *Festschrift* for V. E. von Gebsattel (who looked after Heidegger after his breakdown during the de-Nazification proceedings). Toward the end of this essay he quotes from chapter 28 of the *Lao-tzu:* "He who knows his brightness veils himself in his darkness." This saying of Lao-tzu's is connected with a truth "which everyone knows but yet of which few are capable": "Mortal thinking must let itself down into the dark depths of the well in order to see the star by day." When Heidegger had a star put on his headstone, this showed that he did not mention the "star" on a momentary impulse: while since Plato the sun has been an image for divine reason, which bathes everything in its light without darkness, the star rises alone for us out of darkness and its mysterious depths. But Heidegger seeks in Lao-tzu the trace of the most ancient thoughts only in the service of leading that which determines our history back to its hidden origin. For this one needs an articulation which would bring that which appears to stand firm once again on to its way. Heidegger attempts such an articulation with respect to the "principles of thinking."[24]

It is admittedly surprising that Heidegger speaks of "principles of thinking" rather than of the principle of non-contradiction or the law of excluded middle. These latter principles seek to make thinking conform to proper deductive reasoning. However, with thinking it is not just a question of valid inference, but according to traditional determinations it is also along with the *calculemus* a question of the *distinguamus,* along with the *ars iudicandi* the *ars inveniendi*—and perhaps along with valid inference paradox, too, is significant. In his talk of the principles of thinking Heidegger is evidently following the tradition of German Idealism, which in turn may be seen as standing in the tradition of the logic of Port Royal, which certainly promised an *art de penser*. The idealistic tradition thought itself capable of arriving at a formalization by means of precipitately borrowed mathematical symbols, although the "equal to" sign, for example, conflates the distinction between a predication and an assertion of identity. While for Kant logic was essentially consummated in Aristotle, according to Heidegger's *Introduction to Metaphysics* it had, in spite of Kant and Hegel, "made not a single step of progress in what is essential and primordial" (p. 188). "The only possible step is still only that of unhinging it [namely, as the determinative perspective of the interpretation of Being] from its very *ground*." In fact logic was already in decline in the epoch of idealism, but Heidegger also follows this period of decline insofar as he takes over formalization with the "equal to" sign and seeks a systematization for the principles of identity, non-contradiction and excluded middle (and, in other publications, also for the principle of sufficient reason). Not taken into consideration here is mathematical logic, which has shown in its recent approaches that the principle of non-contradiction may be presupposed for two-valued logic, but not the law of excluded middle.

In contrast one might note that with Hegel thinking ended up in dialectic, and that Hegel hailed contradiction as "the root of all movement and life." Heidegger quotes a similar conception from Novalis, and adduces as an example of a contradiction that is in agreement with itself a line from the poem "In lieblicher Bläue," which is attributed to Hölderlin: "Life is death, and death also a life." Surprisingly, he does not ask whether this view of life and death together in fact asserts a contradiction of the kind that is to be avoided according to the rules of a two-valued logic. It is asserted of Hegel (who, as is well known, placed "method" at the end of his *Logic* and absolutized it) that with his dialectical conception of thinking he paved the way for the technological domination of the world. In this way a line is drawn from this dialectic to the young Marx, who saw world history as that labor in which man generates himself and wins nature for himself. What is left out of account here is that Hegel himself opposed his dialectic to Newtonian physics, that modern physics in its "methodical" character cannot be unified with this dialectic, and that Marx himself later tempered the all-too-extravagant hopes of his early writings. Next to Hegel stands the friend of his youth, Hölderlin, and according to Heidegger the latter offers an alternative in his poem "Andenken" which—"contradictorily" in Heidegger's view—speaks of wine as the "dark light" in the glass. Heidegger supplements this phrase of Hölderlin's with Lao-tzu's line about the wise: "He who knows his brightness veils himself in his darkness." But the "dark light" is contrasted with the explosion of an atomic bomb, which is "brighter than a thousand suns."

What do these juxtapositions of Heidegger's signify? The "dark light" of the red Bordeaux in the glass refers to the southern landscape in which the sun draws the vine out of the earth; Hölderlin in his northern home has with him this fruit of heaven and earth in wine. The wine is dark because it stems from the mystery of the unity of heaven and earth; the wine is light because as a thing it also draws apart heaven and earth into an openness in which life is made possible. Wine as the gift of Dionysos refers to the poets whom Hölderlin connects with the procession of Dionysos who renews and transforms all relationships of life. The "poetical" lets us dwell on this earth because it brings out World as fateful-finite openness from the self-concealing mystery—from the mystery that World opens up at all and is the way it now is. Man, who lives in such a world, is himself a light that must veil itself in the darkness of the mystery. Lao-tzu speaks in chapter 28 of the unity in which male and female, light and dark, glory and shame, are joined together. With the atomic bomb, on the other hand, man by knowingly manipulating technology draws energies from the earth without, in gratitude for what has been granted him, being able to integrate them meaningfully into the limited openness of a liveable world. Brightness, as science and technology spread it across the world, is in its immoderate unleashment self-destructive. But Heidegger in connecting Hölderlin's late poem and Lao-tzu's saying is not advocating a return to a pre-modern and pre-technological world; rather, he wants to bring this contemporary world of ours on to a viable path. The question is whether or not technological advances find their limits in such a way that words and things become possible again, and will let man dwell "poetically."

Heidegger had questioned Being and time, then the truth of Being as dynamic *(Bewegung),* and finally as the way in the underway *(Unterwegs)* and as specific place *(jeweiligen Ort).* Time, as the fulfilled time-play-space and moment-place *(Augenblicks-Stätte)* of the true and the Holy, gains the potential for accepting itself in its currentness and then renouncing itself. Thus time swings into eternity, which is now no longer *aeternitas* or *sempiternitas,* eternal return or eternal will, but the transition that rests in stilled stillness. Heidegger had two lines from chapter 15 of the *Lao-tzu* calligraphed as a decoration for the wall of his study, because these lines characterize the masters who know of the Original-Natural as being opaque like turbulent water: only he who undertakes the way as underway is able to clarify into stillness the turbulence of the water of life, and to engender rest through movement.

II

Heidegger's attempt to translate Lao-tzu constituted an important step on the way along which his thinking was proceeding. Immediately after the publication of *Being and Time* he abandoned phenomenological philosophy because this new grounding of philosophy had become for him a merely "academic" variation on the philosophical tradition. Heidegger now sought to return by way of the history of Being to the ground of the metaphysical tradition and to find a companion for this undertaking of clarification in primordial art and poetry. This undertaking and partnership found itself situated in a world in which the universal technological approach to things subordinated itself to the struggle of the prevalent powers and tendencies towards world domination.

While the first lecture on Hölderlin asked how the poet, like the river Rhine, makes a country inhabitable, the second and third lectures brought the drafts from the period of the Titan hymns into the foreground. Heidegger was reminded by Hölderlin's Ister hymn of his own narrower homeland (the upper Danube valley). The Ister is always on the way; and yet in its movement it also rests: it forms a place within wandering. In mirroring the sun and moon it also bears the heavenly "in mind," bringing heaven and earth, through its receptive emptiness and poverty, into their unity. Even the poet cannot do more. Moreover, after the war Hölderlin was no longer seen in the way Stefan George had represented him immediately after the First World War: as the "cornerstone" of the German future, as the herald of the "New God." Hölderlin was rather heard from the echo that his late, shattering drafts and the "poems of his madness" had found in Trakl. Trakl, before the war claimed him, already saw man as being called to go under; in such detachment the "blueness" of the Holy was to show itself. The war, and also the "cold war," the excesses of the depredation of the earth, of armaments and consumerism, seemed to show in a way that could not be overlooked the madness in which human existence had become enmeshed. The madness *(Wahn-Sinn)* of which Trakl spoke was "to sense otherwise," and thus to render possible a transformation. When in his 1962 lecture "Time and Being" Heidegger presented the guiding questions of his new thinking, he mentioned in a foreword as comparably difficult undertakings Heisenberg's new physics, Trakl's poem "Siebengesang des Todes," and the paintings "Heilige aus einem Fenster" and "Tod und Feuer" from the year of Klee's death.[25] Klee's painting "Death and Fire" (tempera on hessian) depicts a bluish-white skull on a dark glowing red. The image of the modern painter is strongly reminiscent of the Buddhist practice of contemplating skulls. Klee can be put alongside Heisenberg because the painter created ways of art which not only belong to the technological age but also set new limits to its extravagances.

When Lao-tzu saw that his country was declining irrevocably, he left the archive at the court of Chou in order to wander across the border pass. As Heidegger engaged the *Lao-tzu,* he on his side left the archive in which the Western tradition was articulated. The return to the ground of metaphysics was also a way to one's own origin, and yet this origin, which was supposed to have left substance-thinking behind, was in turn understood again as a pre-given, quasi-substantial beginning. If Hölderlin oriented himself in his poetry towards Sophokles, then Sophokles was for him like a far mountain range, unreachable, but which could still suggest the direction of the way. But the first beginning of poetry and thought with the Greeks comes into view in Hölderlin and Heidegger only from the other beginning which is being sought after. When Heidegger begins a dialogue with the East Asian tradition the way to the origin divides into a number of possible ways. Even his own way of thinking *(Denkweg),* which was to take up and transform the way of Western thinking, Heidegger ultimately spoke of as a plurality of ways. And yet there arises the question whether Heraclitus and Lao-tzu are not for Heidegger mere constructs by means of which he articulates his own thinking. Do the thoughts which Heidegger finds in Heraclitus agree with what was once thought on the coast of Asia Minor? The Hölderlin lecture from the winter of 1934–35 traces a line from the power of the "primordial thoughts of Heraclitus" to the "beginning of German philosophy with Meister Eckhart" and then to Hölderlin, Hegel, and Nietzsche.[26] But is Heidegger not reading into the poetical and mythical in Heraclitus the word-mysticism of Eckhart as well as Hölderlin's tying back of philosophy to the poetical and mythical? Heraclitus was early on put in the role of a philosopher of becoming; thus Nietzsche was able to assign him the task of reminding us of the Dionysiac ground of the Apollinian. In his attempt to win back the original ancient ground of tragedy and myth, Nietzsche interpreted Heraclitus' talk of the *aiōn* as if the course of the world after Heraclitus put gods and men into play. When Heidegger speaks of a play "without why" *(ein Spiel "ohne Warum")* the connection with Nietzsche and Eckhart is clear; and yet is he still speaking here of the true Heraclitus? It must be asked similarly whether Heidegger does not also adduce from Lao-tzu only what he himself is seeking. One could ask further: Why Heraclitus and Lao-tzu? Why not Isaiah and Confucius? Why is there talk only of the two-and-a-half thousand years since Heraclitus and Lao-tzu, this most recent moment of our history, and not of the complete history of mankind with the multiplicity of its traditions?

With respect to an existential philosophy of life the young Heidegger had insisted that it make it possible to address the ineffability of dynamic life and existence with its individualized decisions through a hermeneutical articulation. This articulation became in his later works more and more a structure of image-words. Heidegger no longer spoke of the "transcendental horizon," but rather of heaven, which belongs to the earth, of fourfold and clearing *(Lichtung)*, of way and place, of man as the shepherd of Being and the neighbor of death. The images have distinguishable dimensions of meaning that can be articulated, but which are perhaps inexhaustible. Thus Heidegger hears in the word *Ding* the old word *thing* (and so evokes the assistance of etymology). The word *Ereignis* ultimately no longer means an event, but becomes through Herder's way of writing it *Er-äugnis,* but also the "identity" which appropriates Being and man to each other, and thereby lets every thing come into its own. There is already in the essays on Hölderlin's poems a concentration on guiding and basic words. (Hölderlin scholarship has followed Heidegger on this path even when it argued against him in introducing a new scientific approach in the sense of research into fields of synonymous words.) When Heidegger read late Hölderlin from the echo that he had found in Trakl's poems, that dissolution of the traditional structures of meaning came to dominate—in part an effect of Rimbaud's influence on Trakl. The attempt to translate Lao-tzu led Heidegger from the alphabetical languages of the West with their grammar and logic to an ideographic language which uses a character for each word. Now not only were particular image-words emphasized (way, emptiness and expanse, stillness, jug and thing), but the concentration on the individual word was further intensified. Above all Heidegger in his old age devoted a large part of his energy (perhaps the largest part) to those short catchwords and "poems" of which only a few have been published. To concentrate thinking into a meditation upon the simple, and to hold this meditation fast in a poem, is more easily understandable in the light of the East Asian traditions than in terms of, say, Fichte's and Humboldt's sonnets. In China and Japan poems of this kind have a fixed traditional form; such traditions are not, however, valid for Heidegger.

Is Heidegger not abandoning philosophy, and the realm of scholarship altogether, in developing this new way of speaking intended to awaken reflection? As early as the Hölderlin lecture of the winter of 1941–42 he opposes "the fixed apparatus of a science" to listening "to the truth of the heart."[27] From this other "nonscientific" thinking a "transformation" is to proceed "in the face of which all 'revolutions' fall away in the blind helplessness of the unbridled power of a groundless humanity, because such revolutions in turning around simply turn back to and become entangled in the status quo." After the Second World War, in 1946, Heidegger made contact with the psychiatrist Medard Boss (with whom he conducted the

Zollikon seminars for young doctors over the next seventeen years). He later mentioned as a motivation for this contact his hope that his work could, through the mediation of doctors and therapists, "break through the narrowness of academic philosophy and reach much broader circles, for the benefit of a large number of people who are suffering." Does the attempt to translate Lao-tzu throw aside all standards of scholarship? Heidegger "reads" and "translates" the graphemes of a language the spoken words of which he does not understand. But must we not first understand what is really going on when Heidegger speaks and reads as he does? Heidegger demands a language in which it is not primarily a question of univocal concepts and their coherent connection, but rather of images whose meanings are multidimensional and inexhaustible. Heidegger was impressed by the Thai monk because he did not enumerate the viewpoints of the conversation, nor did he proceed in a linear, discursive and analytical way: "For a European would keep saying: 'firstly,' 'then,' 'thirdly' and so forth. But here there is no kind of 'logical progression'; rather, everything comes out of *one* center." Across the various dimensions of meaning every word is connected with every other; the breakthrough to the deeper dimensions transforms thinking and brings it on to a path.[28]

The final sentence of Heidegger's essay "The Thing" reads: "Only what is wrested *(gering)* from World becomes a thing." The sentence can be written in two lines which then rhyme; Heidegger could then use these words as an epithet, as an entry in a visitors' book, for example. If one wants to understand the word *gering* one must think of it in connection with all the dimensions of meaning through which Heidegger moves in his lecture and pulls together in this word. In the *Gering* there should speak the struggling emergence *(Sichherausringen)* out of the "fouring" of the fourfold, and thereby also a flowing forth *(Herausrinnen)*. The *Gering* of earth and heaven, gods and mortals thus becomes the ring (which lets time swing into eternity in what is in Nietzsche another, metaphysical form of thinking). The *Gering* further includes the "ring" of the unity of the fouring, namely the yielding to this unity, but also the *Ringe,* the inconspicuous pliancy of the thing, which mirrors the above unity. The small *(das Geringe)* is also the simple; thereby poverty, in the sense demanded by the mystics, is re-thought in the way suggested by the line from Hölderlin: "Even to the small, great beginning can come."[29]

At a historical ending, which is also to be a transition, Heidegger settles into the beginnings he finds for the West in ancient Greece and for the Far East in Lao-tzu. In ancient Greece the paths of the poet and thinker were yet to diverge. When philosophy arose it would connect with Homeric stories which relate one to the other with respect to a *tertium comparationis.* Thus thinking as a speaking *(Sprechen)* was able to correspond *(entsprechen)* to that *logos* which puts one into the other, and thereby relates everything and even the opposites to the One (by the analogy which was later elaborated as the analogy of Being). Parmenides invokes the Goddess, and so Heidegger in his lecture from the winter of 1942–43 thinks he can show that the *logos* of thinking was initially not opposed to myth but rather belonged together with it. If the Greeks no longer used hieroglyphic writing, but adopted the phonetic alphabet, then words, which had to be composed from letters, became for them conventional signs, with which one could operate. It was then a short step to distinguishing those conclusions in the grammatically elaborated language which are adequate to the rules of logic and assure valid inference. Can such inference, or also the dialectic that developed out of it, ensure "the truth"?

In the Zähringen seminar of 1973, Heidegger emphasized that Heraclitus had taken "the first step in the direction of dialectic" (namely, in the direction of Hegel's dialectic, which strove to surpass the analogy of Being); but dialectic was itself problematic and not a solution to the task assigned to it, and so Parmenides is to be considered deeper and more essential than Heraclitus. And yet Heidegger said of Parmenides that one could not find in him what he (Heidegger) had looked for there for forty years: concealing as the heart-center of all revealing. (Heidegger expressed this opinion in an essay from the winter of 1972–73.) Is there then no trace in the thinking of the Greeks of that clearing for self-concealing which became the theme of Heidegger's thinking? In the 1969 Le Thor seminar Heidegger remarked that the Greeks had had great poetry but had never conceived language "poetically." He quoted as something worth pondering Mallarmé's talk of the "great Homeric aberration."[30] For Heidegger himself, on the other hand, Pindar and Sophokles, and also Hölderlin, Trakl and Klee, show what the "poetical" is. Yet when he connects Hölderlin's talk of the "dark light" with an expression of Laotzu's, he is relativizing the Western tradition and the drama of its aberrations. Is there not a thinking that from the simplicity and smallness of the using of a jug leads to the way of new beginnings of experience? A thinking that does not like the "mysticism" of Meister Eckhart first take the will to unconditionedness out of philosophy and theology in order then to dare the breakthrough to the Godhead through God and to call for the simple dealings with things, and to distinguish the biblical Martha from the "contemplative" Martha?

Heidegger sees himself as "on the way to language" in as far as in the central lecture, "The Way to Language," he dismisses the attempts of Western philosophy and science to engage language. He breaks with Aristotle, who looks at language from the point of view of signs; the voiced sounds are taken as an expression of the psychical *(das Seelische)* and writing as signs for the signs of the sound; in the movement of the psychical are shown the things that are grasped in their "being" by the thought. The relation between *phusis* and *logos* which Heidegger finds in Heraclitus, and then the relation between the *tao* and the jug, both support the attempt to take "language" in the broadest sense of the word as a self-manifesting of things which comes from the mystery that shelters itself back into itself. The sense *(Sinn)* of Being as the transcendental horizon of time, the truth of Being as the time-play-space of the *Ereignis,* the clearing for self-concealing as a place in the underway: these are for Heidegger in the smallness of another beginning only there as a "trace." In conversation with the Japanese guest he says of his own thinking that it has always merely followed a "trace on the way" *(Wegspur);* traces are nevertheless what directed thinking into the realm of its source. Thus the fragment of Anaximander is not only the most ancient saying of Western thought but also a trace. If thinking is related in this way to the trace, then what Heidegger once called "destruction" is taken further. The Rilke essay quotes Hölderlin, who in the poem "Brot und Wein" speaks of "the trace of the gods who have disappeared": Being becomes the trace of the Holy, the Holy the trace of the Godhead. The thinkers who say Being prepare the way for the poetical, so that poets stay on the track of the divine and "trace for related mortals the way to the turning." Also included in the "trace" is that formal intimation which points existents into an existential decision, and yet keeps this decision (a decision of faith, for example) outside itself.[31]

The trace is a small presence of something that is absent. Being as trace is for Heidegger voice and counsel *(Zuspruch),* but not in such a way that the one speaking hears his own voice and encloses himself in presence, but in such a way that the counsel withdraws into the unspoken. The word of Being and of the Holy is a "hint," in which that which is departing presents itself one more time in withdrawing. Being is the look *(Blick),* but also an insight *(Einblick)* into that which is, as a "flash" *(Einblitz),* first as something dazzling and in every case as "dark light." The clearing *(Lichtung)* is no longer to be understood in terms of light, but rather of the openness of a small clearing in an impenetrably dark forest. Must the look and the "face" *(Gesicht)* not be taken up in image and form *(im Bild im Gebilde),* perhaps in writing and inscription? Heidegger clearly takes speaking and writing as equiprimordial: "The word of language sounds and resounds in the spoken word, shines and clears itself in the written image. Sound and writing are certainly something sensible *(Sinnliches),* but the sensible in which a sense or meaning *(Sinn)* sounds and appears."[32] The conclusion of the "Letter on Humanism" says of thinking that it lays furrows in language, but less visible ones than the farmer plows in the field. It is clearly not a case here of comparing thinking and saying with agricultural activity; rather agricultural activity, which makes possible a dwelling on the earth, and language are understood in terms of a common ground. Similarly Hölderlin saw the river Rhine, which makes an entire landscape habitable, in connection with the poet, who allows us to dwell poetically. Do word and image not thereby become "language" as the self-manifestation of the "things" and relationships that comprise being-in-the-world? Heidegger's lecture "What Calls for Thinking?" begins with a phrase from Hölderlin's late hymn "Mnemosyne": "We are a sign, without meaning . . ."

The going, which brings us on to the way, the hand, which puts things to use, the gesture, with which the one who is departing waves once again, the voice, which addresses itself as something not be held on to, the look, which can come to us from image and writing: all of these point to being-in-the-world, in which man is never without things, in which everything worldly is always already a sign in a context. Heidegger does not then proceed to clarify "phenomenologically" to what extent going, hand, hint, voice, look, or the Taoist and the ancient Greek traditions can serve as a guiding thread, what this thread and that one can provide concretely, and how all threads claimed and to be claimed belong together. It is a question of a breakthrough into an original dimension which avoids and surpasses the distortions and entanglements of the historical tradition to which we belong. Husserl's phenomenology, which began as epistemological criticism, remains a variation on the Platonic-Cartesian tradition; and yet the Zähringen seminar of 1973 sees in Husserl's analysis of categorial intuition an attempt to free Being "from its fixation to judgement." Husserl and Parmenides lead to seeing and naming as a "tautological thinking," which as a "phenomenology of the inconspicuous" is a grounding itself upon that "which has let itself be seen by the look."[33]

If Heidegger with this new and daring "thinking" is divorcing himself from philosophy altogether, there still remains the question of whether he is not following a tradition whose paths were not appropriately worked through. Does Heidegger's saying and naming not still stand in the tradition of Plato, which seeks the contemplation of Ideas? What is to be contemplated in Heidegger is certainly, as the self-showing image, no longer separated from the copy (Abbild) of the real and from the painting as the supposed copy of a copy. And yet modern Platonism had already made the idea of the "inner form" fruitful for the philosophy of art. But according to Heidegger contemplation should set one on the way on which the inexhaustible depth of images and their interconnection produce a transformation. The self-sameness which after the catastrophe of nihilism lets itself be experienced as (the event of) appropriation does not bring thinking as seeing together with Being as Idea, but rather sets thinking a task.

In this way hearing and hearkening seem to gain priority in Heidegger. The Anaximander essay speaks of the "dictates" of Being: but in dictates what is heard, and is to be obeyed, ends up in writing. However, the dictated word in Heidegger does not—as in the biblical tradition—attain the power of creation; the "creative" *(Schöpferische)* is only admitted as the drawing forth *(Schöpfen)* from a source whose resources remain unreachable.[34] When the conversation with the Japanese guest takes the hermeneutical in terms of primal announcement, message and commission, then the influences from the religious tradition (which are also named by Heidegger himself) are considerable.

The paths of Heidegger's thinking reflect with various accents various traditions and approaches to phenomena. Correspondingly his usage of words changes again and again: there can be no doubt that *Being and Time* emphasizes the "historicality" of *Da-Sein,* and the work of the thirties renews the emphasis on "history of Being" *(Seins-Geschichte)* and thereby gives prominence to destiny and fate *(Geschick und Schicksal)* in their tragic qualities. But later the *Geschick* of Being is no longer thought of from the standpoint of historicality and fate, but rather from the "sending" *(Schicken)* that sends itself in something and so only gives in withholding itself or "holding to itself." History and destiny have thereby become that *Ge-Schichte* which by virtue of the multi-dimensionality of its structure makes possible the breakthrough to concealed depths. It is precisely the encounter with Lao-tzu that allows talk of various ways to these depths and not merely of the way to a forgotten "origin." In this way the path of thinking can become a plurality of paths. It is true that Heidegger continues to hold to the idea that the concealment in all concealing is, as the "mystery," the "tranquil heart of the clearing" and thus "the place of stillness"; and only from the experience of this stillness could determinations of Being such as "Being as idea" or "as *energeia*" gain their binding power. But must one not also put it the other way around: the experience of this stillness as the center of the new thinking is attained only from various points on a periphery and thereby on various and perhaps incommensurable ways?[35]

On the contrary Heidegger develops, not without one-sidedness, something like a new Chinese prejudice: he is not like Leibniz seeking to derive from the ideographic Chinese language a *characteristica universalis* which with its univocal concepts affords unimpeded inference and calculation; he rather achieves a language and script of images, whose guiding images are openly interwoven with each other across their various dimensions of meaning or "force fields" *(Schwingungsräume).* The title of the Chinese novel *Chin p'ing mei* means, depending on the context, "blossoms in a golden vase" or "beautiful women in a rich house." The decisive thing for thinking is for it to be able to break through from superficial meanings to the depths in order to bring us back on to a way or the underway. However much Heidegger may be in accord with the basic "agricultural" strain of ancient Chinese thinking, he must distinguish himself from more refined traditions such as Zen Buddhism. Forms of Zen practice such as meditation and archery are distinguished by the ultimate incommunicability of the sought-for experience: the transmission of this "art" is a non-transmission; the Zen master can ultimately only direct his students to practice in such a way that the experience suddenly befalls them. In contrast, Heidegger's thinking seems to be more strongly informed by communcability, which leads to the right place in a particular situation and constellation through the explication of what is somewhat superficial, distorting, and endangering. Thinking can also decide to remain in the temporariness of a transitional situation, in order not to force an answer to the questioning and hearing and thereby effect a distortion.

If Heidegger finds the root of thinking, poetry, and art in the "poetical," he also seems to want to conceive an original *poiēsis* from the composing of poetry. In this sense Schelling in the conclusion of his *System of Transcendental Idealism* wanted to lead all modes of knowing, behaving, and producing by way of a "new mythology" back to the "ocean of poesy." For us today hopes of this sort are difficult to entertain since although we grant autonomy to poetry and art, we still see in them something particular which cannot be considered to be also the origin of science and technology, in the sense that Homeric poetry was once the origin of thinking and poetry. Heidegger explicates the ways in which the trace of Being articulates itself in such a way that he finds himself in a position that leads to what should have been avoided—to premature evaluations and polemics.

In wanting to abolish the primacy of "theory" in Western thought, Heidegger fails to ask what the specific contribution of "seeing" is. If one says that the eye is master and the ear slave, it is obvious how "critical" thinking can understand itself primarily as a seeing. The Pythagoreans said that things are numbers, namely forms whose structure is to be grasped by means of abstract mathematical relationships. For Heidegger calculation is in contrast an external putting together that is incapable of leading to a structure. With this not only is the contribution of mathematics misunderstood, but also language and script are seen too much from the perspective of imagistic wholes. One can even show historically and genetically that image and schema are by no means the single origin of script and language; along with them are countability (for example, even already in the signal of a bird-call) or the abstract trace of the steps, wedges, and knots in cuneiform and knot-"writing." When Heidegger contrasts following the way with the grasping of method he fails to rec-

ognize that method, in its abstracting, limits itself to grasping cir-
cumscribed aspects of the real. When he speaks of the age of universal
technology and sees in the technological approach to the world the continuation of metaphysics, it is not made clear that it is precisely the spectacular achievements of science and technology—atomic power and
space flights—that remind man of his finitude.[36] The antagonism between enframing and fourfold improperly absolutizes the methodical and
technological tendency of our behavior in the world, in order to oppose
to it a different thinking as poetry. Thus, in his Athens lecture of April
1967, "The Origin of Art and the Determination of Thinking," Heidegger contrasted the "cybernetic" world-view of "industrial society" with
the poetical nature of art, which in an advisory and enlightening way
directs us into limits. The conclusion of the lecture made reference to Pindar, who speaks of the "word" that determines life "farther out into time
than deeds . . . only when with the favor of the Graces language draws it
out from the depths of the musing heart."[37]

In 1976 Heidegger dedicated the French translation of his book *On the
Way to Language* to René Char with the following sentence: "Is our
beloved Provence the mysteriously invisible bridge from the early
thought of Parmenides to the poetry of Hölderlin?" Provence, which
Heidegger often visited, came closest to him in and through the paintings
of Cézanne: in the last decades of his life Heidegger more and more
related the path that he was following with his thinking to Cézanne's
lonely path. In the twenties, the letters of Van Gogh had opened up space
for the encounter with the artist's paintings; now it was Rilke's letters
about Cézanne which prepared an understanding of the breakthrough
which the French painter had dared to make in his art. Heidegger gave a
lecture for the twentieth anniversary of Rilke's death, which was then
published in *Holzwege*. In November 1947 he read to some acquaintances Rilke's words on Cézanne's work "which no longer had any partial-
ity, no inclinations and preferential fastidiousness, and the smallest component of which was tested on the scales of an infinitely mobile
conscience, and which so incorruptibly drew things together into color
that in a world beyond color they began a new existence without former
memories." Heidegger emphasized, with Rilke, Cézanne's impartiality
which focused on the "thing" without prior evaluations such as "beautiful" or "ugly" or "terrible." The poem "Cézanne," dedicated to René Char
in 1970, asks whether in the painter's later work a path is not revealed
"which leads to the belonging together of poetry and thinking." In the
"realizing" of the painter "the two-fold of presence and what is present
became a unity . . . at the same time distorted, transformed into a mysterious identity." That appropriation is intended which now suddenly as
the identity of Being and thinking entwines the ontological difference

into itself, in that what is present shows itself as what is present or in its presence and becomes a "thing" in the special sense of the word. The poetical "thinking" of art brings things close in giving them distance and unapproachability, and thus the Montagne Sainte Victoire can become (as Heidegger put it) "the Holy mountain." The Athens lecture finds a similar process with the Greeks: from the mystery that truth, World and the Holy happen at all, there appears "in an amazing and at the same time restrained way" in the surrounding Greek light a mountain, an island, a coast, an olive tree, as the root of myth and art.[38]

In following Cézanne on his detour Heidegger was continuing the wandering away from his time that he had begun with Lao-tzu. Was this excursion—as legend has it of Lao-tzu's—forced by the decline of the age and environment, or was it not also an escape from the context of guilt in which the wanderer had become entangled through his own doing and which he was unable to tolerate? Are experiences and motives which must belong to the thinking of our time not being unfairly set aside? The experience of guilt and of evil become also for Meister Eckhart, for Nietzsche, for Lao-tzu, and for Zen Buddhism something of second rank. Someone proposed to Heidegger this sentence from chapter 18 of the *Tao Te Ching* as one of Lao-tzu's incomprehensible teachings: "When the great *tao* falls into disuse, there are humanheartedness and righteousness." However, nothing was closer to Heidegger than this aphorism: for him humanism with its insistence on humanity leads away from the task for which man is needed, and through man's anthropocentrism hinders following a path; the word "right" *(gerecht)* can, as Nietzsche remarked, only too easily mean "revenged" *(gerächt)*. When Paul Celan visited Heidegger in 1967, he wrote in the guest book of the Todtnauberg cabin: "For the cabin book, with a look towards the well-star [the image of the star on the well near the cabin, symbolizing the eternal connection between them], in the hope of an approaching word in the heart." Celan's poem "Todtnauberg" also speaks of this hope; Celan no doubt expected of Heidegger that the hoped-for word would also have accommodated the guilt that stood between the Freiburg Rector of 1933 and the German-Jewish poet. The word "from the depths of the musing heart," of which Heidegger speaks with Pindar, was articulated by Celan from the dimension of the Jewish mystical tradition, which from the experience of persecution and genocide set itself against "evil" and sought "righteousness."[39]

Western mysticism is not a unitary whole but rather multiple—for example, Meister Eckhart's mysticism or Jewish mysticism. The mystical traditions, metaphysics, and Heidegger's path to Cézanne are not only close to each other but also abysmally far apart. In the Far East Lao-tzu is not Confucius; above all one must not immediately presuppose a convergence of the ways of the East and the West. Philosophy can elaborate the world-experiences of the great traditions only when it follows the experiences that are to be had in the various arenas of life. Nor can we presuppose here a simple convergence of basic experiences, for example in the "aesthetic" and "ethical" realms. Heidegger has more than any other European philosopher initiated dialogue between the West and the Far East, and yet he takes up on his path the motives of the great traditions only in such a way that he incorporates them whole into his current point of departure—into the necessity into which his thinking is forced. Today a relatively unified world civilization is being built which is meant to secure the survival of humanity, though it is not that such security could be man's first and last task; in this situation it is imperative to have dialogue between the various traditions. Heidegger has provided a significant stimulus for such dialogue; and yet the task to which he applied himself has not been accomplished, but is being handed down to us as something open-ended.

Translated by Graham Parkes

Notes

1. Cf. Welte's report in Günther Neske's *Erinnerung an Martin Heidegger* (Pfullingen, 1977), p. 249ff.

2. For Heidegger's interest in Eckhart see Hans-Georg Gadamer, *Heideggers Wege* (Tübingen, 1983), p. 131.

3. Heidegger's lecture of summer 1931 is published in *Aristoteles, Metaphysik θ 1–3* (Frankfurt, 1931); see especially p. 46f. Subsequent discussion of Eckhart's development has been controversial. K. Albert, *Meister Eckhart's These vom Sein: Untersuchungen zur Metaphysik des Opus tripartititum* (1976) deals with Eckhart's later work: Being is God. R. Imbach, *Deus est intelligere* (1976) is based on the early *Quaestiones:* God is Knowing. Yet Being and knowing in God are "the same."

4. Bernhard Welte, *Meister Eckhart: Gedanken zu seinen Gedanken* (Freiburg, Basel, Wien, 1979).

5. Keiji Nishitani, *Was Ist Religion?* (Frankfurt, 1982), p. 124f.; *Religion and Nothingness* (Berkeley, Los Angeles, London, 1982), especially p. 64f.

6. Martin Heidegger, *Was Heisst Denken?* (Tübingen, 1954), p. 44; *What Is Called Thinking?* (New York, 1968), p. 105. And *Gelassenheit* (Pfullingen, 1959), p. 36; *Discourse on Thinking* (New York, 1969), p. 63.

7. The proceedings of the symposium "Heidegger and Eastern Thought" are published in *Philosophy East and West* 20, no. 3 (July 1970).

8. For Heidegger's "aesthetic" approach see Chuang-yuan Chang in *Erinnerung an Heidegger*, p. 65f. If the art of China and Japan particularly displays a still beauty and thereby the "aesthetic," one nevertheless finds a distancing from the aesthetic in Buddhism; see, for example, Yoshinori Takeuchi, *Probleme der Versenkung im Ur-Buddhismus* (Leiden, 1972), p. 89f.

9. On Heidegger's predilection for the Chinese and his translation of Lao-tzu see the reports by Hans A. Fischer-Barnicol and Paul Shih-yi Hsiao in *Erinnerung,* pp. 102 and 122f. Heidegger's translations of Lao-tzu have not yet been identified in the *Nachlass* (see Professor Hsiao's essay in the present volume). Heinrich Wiegand Petzet in *Auf einen Stern zugehen: Begegnungen mit Martin Heidegger 1929–76* (Frankfurt, 1983), p. 191, gives a translation of chapter 47 of the *Tao Te Ching* which Heidegger sent to Ernst Jünger; Petzet assumes that the translation is Heidegger's but it is in fact by Jan Ulenbrook.

10. See Martin Heidegger, *Unterwegs zur Sprache* (Pfullingen, 1959), p. 198; *On the Way to Language* (New York, 1971), p. 92.

11. *Identität und Differenz* (Pfullingen, 1957), p. 25; *Identity and Difference* (New York, 1969), p. 36.

12. *Erinnerung,* p. 124 (Hsiao); Petzet, p. 52 (on the de-Nazification proceedings), and p. 227 (on Brecht).

13. "The Thinker as Poet," in Martin Heidegger, *Poetry, Language, Thought,* trans. Albert Hofstadter (New York, 1975).

14. On the Bremen discussion, see Petzet, p. 24; see also *Sein und Zeit,* pp. 122, 188, 263f., 384.

15. On the "ethical" critique of Heidegger see Emmanuel Levinas, *Die Spur des Anderen* (Freiburg/München, 1983), p. 108f.

16. See Heidegger's lectures of 1929–30 in *Die Grundbegriffe der Metaphysik* (Frankfurt, 1983), p. 261f. "Beiträge zur Philosophie" is an unedited work of Heidegger's from the years 1936–38; on the problematic of life in the "Beiträge" see my book, *Der Denkweg Martin Heideggers* (Pfullingen, 1983), p. 257.

17. For Heidegger's criticism of Heisenberg see *Vorträge und Aufsätze* (Pfullingen, 1954), p. 35; "On the Question of Technology," in *On the Question of Technology and Other Essays,* trans. William Lovitt (New York, 1967).

18. The Hebel lecture is reprinted in Heidegger, *Aus der Erfahrung des Denkens 1910–76* (Frankfurt, 1983), p. 133ff. and especially 144 ff.

19. See Petzet, pp. 65, 175f. On fragment 112 of Heraclitus, see Heidegger and Fink, *Heraklit* (Frankfurt, 1979), p. 248; see also *Einführung in die Metaphysik* (Tübingen, 1953), p. 54f.; *An Introduction to Metaphysics* (New Haven and London, 1977), p. 70f.

20. See *Aus der Erfahrung des Denkens,* p. 155ff. and especially 180. Petzet also reports (p. 154ff.) that Heidegger wanted to add "a second part" dealing with Klee to the essay on the work of art.

21. See Petzet, p. 175ff. and especially 183, 185, 188–190.

22. Since Plato, reason through "harmony" makes the world a work of art; Schleiermacher's *Reden über die Religion* also ascribes harmony to the universe as well as to the religious mediator, but dissolves the ancient conception of harmony into the intuition and feeling of religion. Heidegger may, however, be thinking of translations of Zen Buddhist writings, which understand harmony as "grace of the spirit" and "stillness": see, for example, D. T. Suzuki, *Zen and Japanese Culture* (Princeton, 1970).

23. On the "religious dimension," see my book, *Heidegger und die hermeneutische Philosophie* (Freiburg/München, 1983), p. 353ff.

24. See Heidegger, "Grundsätze des Denkens," in *Jahrbuch fur Psychologie und Psychotherapie* 6 (1958), pp. 33–41.

25. See Heidegger, *Zur Sache des Denkens* (Tübingen, 1969), p. 1. See Nishitani, p. 105f., who also offers a comparison with T. S. Eliot's "The Waste Land" in which the dead flow across London Bridge. On Heidegger's interest in Klee see

my book *Die Frage nach der Kunst: von Hegel zu Heidegger* (Freiburg/München, 1984).

26. Heidegger, *Hölderlins Hymnen "Germanien" und "Der Rhein"* (Frankfurt, 1980), p. 133f.

27. See Heidegger, *Hölderlins Hymme "Andenken"* (Frankfurt, 1982), pp. 93, 108.

28. *Erinnerung an Martin Heidegger,* p. 31 (Boss); Petzet, p. 184.

29. See Petzet, p. 80; Heidegger, *Erläuterungen zu Hölderlin's Dichtung* (Frankfurt, 1971; 4th, expanded ed.), p. 171.

30. See Heidegger, *Vier Seminare* (Frankfurt, 1977), pp. 74, 133, 138. Certainly the alternative which Heidegger proposes to logic and dialectic is neither the only nor the most appropriate one; I myself have drawn attention to the tradition of the *Topik;* see "Topik und Philosophie" in *Topik,* ed. D. Brever and H. Schanze (München, 1981), pp. 95–123.

31. See *Unterwegs zur Sprache,* pp. 131–137; *On the Way to Language,* pp. 37, 41. *Holzwege* (Frankfurt, 1950), pp. 150f., 340; *Early Greek Thinking,* trans. David Krell and Frank Capuzzi (New York, 1975), p. 54.

32. See *Aus der Erfahrung des Denkens,* pp. 150, 209. Jacques Derrida has taken up Heidegger's hints in as far as he combines structuralist motivations with an emphasis on "difference" and the "dead point" in time from Levinas. But the way in which Derrida speaks of the voice is quite different from Heidegger's, since Derrida proceeds from the premise that we hear our own voice and thus enclose ourselves in "presence."

33. See *Vier Seminare,* pp. 115, 137.

34. *Holzwege,* pp. 303, 340.

35. See *Zur Sache des Denkens,* pp. 8f., 75.

36. Oskar Becker has in his works elaborated this distancing from Heidegger's starting point; see my essay "Hermeneutische und mantische Phänomenologie," in *Heidegger: Perspektiven zur Deutung seines Werks,* ed. O. Pöggeler (Köln/Berlin, 1969), pp. 321–357.

37. See the reprint of Heidegger's Athens Lecture, "Distanz und Nähe," in *Festschrift für Walter Biemel,* ed. P. Jaeger and R. Lüthe (Würzburg, 1983), pp. 11–22.

38. See *Vier Seminare,* p. 149; Petzet, p. 150f.; *Aus der Erfahrung des Denkens,* p. 223; *Distanz und Nähe,* p. 14.

39. See Petzet, p. 122; *Erinnerung,* p. 122f.; see also my lecture "Mystische Elemente im Denken Heideggers und im Dichten Celans," in *Zeitwende 53* (1982), pp. 65–92; also in *Mystik ohne Gott?,* ed. W. Böhme (Karlsruhe, 1982), pp. 32–59.

Joan Stambaugh

Heidegger, Taoism, and the Question of Metaphysics

The two themes in Heidegger I would like to talk about that seem to me to have a definite Taoist flavor are those of Way *(Weg)* and releasement *(Gelassenheit)*. In the course of inquiry into these themes, it will become increasingly clear that they are almost impossible to separate. Nevertheless, I shall attempt to start with the Way as the more basic theme that determines or attunes releasement. Strictly speaking, the two are not concepts belonging to metaphysical thought; they are themes of post-metaphysical or non-metaphysical reflection. The question of the relation of both Heidegger and Taoism to metaphysics will be taken up briefly at the end of this paper. If we were to consider these two themes in a traditional metaphysical manner, the Way would represent the objective side of a relationship and releasement would represent the subjective side. We want to try to understand that and also how neither Heidegger nor Taoism does this.

Way (Weg, tao). In contrast to releasement, which has implicit precursors in *Being and Time* but really is developed only in Heidegger's later thought, the theme of the Way is explicitly present in *Being and Time* and runs throughout all of Heidegger's writings. Thus, in *Being and Time* we are told that *Dasein* is always underway and that standing and remaining are only limit cases of this directional "underway." And at the very conclusion of the book Heidegger states: "One must seek a *way* of illuminating the fundamental question of ontology and then *go* this way. Whether this is the *sole* or *right* way can be decided only *after one has gone along it.*"[1] The central importance of the way and being underway or on the way stands out in the titles of at least three subsequent works: *Woodpaths, On the Way to Language,* and *The Fieldpath.* One thinks also of *Wegmarken,* a volume reprinting many works.

Unlike Lao-tzu who begins by saying that the Way or *tao* that can be told of (literally, that can be wayed) is not the eternal *tao,* Heidegger has a good deal to say about the Way. What finally could not be told of for Heidegger was Being. In the foreword to the collection of essays entitled *Holzwege* or *Woodpaths*, we read:

> Wood is an old name for forest. In the wood are paths that mostly wind along until they end quite suddenly in an impenetrable thicket.
> They are called "woodpaths."
> Each goes its peculiar way, but in the same forest. Often it seems as though one were identical to another. Yet is only seems so. Woodcutters and foresters are familiar with these paths. They know what it means "to be on a woodpath."[2]

As D. F. Krell points out in his general introduction to the anthology *Basic Writings*, the meaning of the colloquial German expression, "to be on a woodpath," does not coincide with the philosophical meaning Heidegger gives the phrase. The popular expression means to be on the wrong track, to be on a path that doesn't go anywhere. This popular meaning finds its way into the title of the French translation of *Holzwege: Chemins qui ne mènent nulle part*, ways that lead nowhere. Now we could say that woodpaths do lead somewhere or other, but where they lead us is somehow incidental. The function of woodpaths, which the woodcutters leave behind them as they cut and gather wood, is not to lead someone from one point to another; rather, the path is almost a necessary byproduct of the woodcutter's activity. For those of us non-woodcutters walking in the forest, we don't know where the woodpaths are leading and if our primary aim were to arrive at some fixed destination in the shortest amount of time, we wouldn't be on a woodpath. Thus, the *philosophical* meaning of being on a woodpath is not so much that it doesn't go anywhere but that the meaning of being on it is not to arrive at a known or predetermined destination. One does not necessarily know at the outset where one is going. For Heidegger, woodpaths express the fact that thinking is thoroughly and essentially questioning, a questioning not to be stilled or "solved" by any answer, a questioning that cannot calculate in advance the direction in which it will be led, let alone the destination at which it will arrive.

We need to ask what Heidegger means by "way." Following his own tactic and that of many thinkers before him, we might best begin by saying what way does *not* mean for him. First of all, he brings his own conception of way into sharp contrast with the way or method (*methodos*, way) of the sciences.

> To the modern mind, whose ideas about everything are punched out in the die presses of technical-scientific calculation, the object of knowledge is part of the method. And method follows what is in fact the utmost corruption and degeneration of a way.

For reflective thinking, on the contrary, the way belongs in what we here call the country or region. Speaking allusively, the region is that which regions, is the clearing that sets free, where all that is cleared and freed, and all that conceals itself, together attain open freedom. The freeing and sheltering character of this region lies in this way-making movement which yields those ways that belong to the region.[3]

The topic of the sciences and in general of technology is far too vast to go into here and is, moreover, not essential to this inquiry. Suffice it to say that Heidegger's conception of way has nothing to do with the uncanny and threatening usurpation of the objects of knowledge by the calculative procedures and methods of technology that, as Heidegger says, represent the utmost corruption and degeneration of what he means by way.

If, then, it has essentially nothing to do with scientific and technological method, what kind of way is Heidegger talking about? Two other possible conceptions remain to be discussed and ultimately rejected. The first is the obvious, literal meaning of a way or path leading from one place to another. Although most of the connotations belonging to this conception are inappropriate for what Heidegger is after, the "literal" meaning of way is very germane to what he is saying and is not to be sacrificed in favor of some kind of abstract symbolism. The Way is not to be taken in an abstract, symbolic sense, a literal path standing for some kind of royal road to the Absolute. This would be sheer metaphysics. The whole schema of something concrete and sensuous symbolizing something abstract and nonsensuous very definitely belongs to a metaphysical kind of thinking that Heidegger always sought to avoid, particularly in his work on the Pre-Socratics and the poets. Thus, we are to retain something of the "literal" meaning of a path. But, in keeping with Heidegger's whole constant polemic against *Vorhandenheit,* against objective presence, presence at hand, a way for him is not something lying there all finished, leading from one point in the parameters of space to another. Heidegger's understanding of space, and later of time when he gains some distance from his earlier, fundamentally Kantian conception, is quite close to the Taoist conception. I shall have something to say on this and some other points of similarity between Heidegger and Taoism in my concluding remarks on the question of metaphysics.

For Heidegger, the way is of such a nature that it originates with the movement of walking on it. Strictly speaking, one could almost say that the way *is* this movement.

Thinking itself is a way. We respond to the way only by remaining under-way. . . . We must get on the way, that is, must take the steps by which alone the way becomes a way. The way of thinking cannot be traced from somewhere to somewhere like a well-worn rut, nor does it at all exist as such in any place. Only when we walk it, and in no other fashion, only, that is, by thoughtful questioning, are we on the move on the way. This movement is what allows the way to come forward.[4]

At least two things are striking here. First of all, the way is not already there for us to follow, but comes into being as we go along it. Since it is not already stretched out in space, this also means that it has no initial point of departure and no final goal. Besides stressing the fact that it doesn't lead anywhere, one should also emphasize that it doesn't begin anywhere either. We are always already underway and remain so as long as we dwell on earth.

Secondly, the way is essentially a way of *thinking*. This points forward to our imminent discussion of releasement and can form a sort of transition to it. We had remarked at the beginning that way and releasement would be difficult, if not impossible, to separate. If the way is a way of thinking, does this not mean that we produce the way, that the way is something subjective? I shall come back to this second point about the way of thinking after discussing the first point further.

Perhaps the most fundamental characteristic of Heidegger's way is that it allows us to *reach* something, to reach something not as a final goal to be possessed, but as an ongoing reach*ing* that belongs to what it reaches.

> Within language as Saying there is present something like a way or path. What is a way? A way allows us to reach something.[5]

The way allows us as we listen to attain language and thus belong to Saying. We are able to attain language only because we already belong to Saying. What is it that the way allows us to reach here? For Heidegger, the term Saying points to the way in which we respond to what happens. Saying is not simply linguistic; it includes poetic and artistic kinds of human response as well as silence. Saying is a kind of showing what happens. What happens is Appropriation, the primordial relation, the belonging-together of man and Being. This relation, thought by Heidegger under both aspects of identity and difference, is more fundamental than the "elements" in it. The elements, man and Being, don't constitute the relation; the relation constitutes the elements.

It is the way which is the "how" of the happening of Appropriation. The way is how Appropriation does what it does, better expressed, lets happen by making its own, appropriating.

> The way to language belongs to Saying determined by Appropriation. Within this way, which belongs to the reality of language, the peculiar property of language is concealed. The way is appropriating.[6]

This passage leads us right into the heart of Heidegger's later thinking. The central themes of Appropriation, language, and Saying are now brought into relation with the way. The passage continues and introduces a further qualification of the way that seems to be Heidegger's utmost effort to make an initially somewhat indeterminate thought, the way, as concrete as possible.

> To clear a way, for instance across a snow-covered field, is in the Alemannic-Swabian dialect still called *wëgen* even today. This verb, used transitively, means: to form a way and, forming it, to keep it ready. Way-making understood in this sense no longer means to move something up or down a path that is already there. It means to bring the way . . . forth first of all, and thus to *be* the way.[7]

The totality of what Heidegger has to say about the way gets crystallized in this word from the Alemannic-Swabian dialect, *Bewëgung*. Without the umlaut, the word is the common designation for movement. Peter Hertz translates it as way-making. Literally, it means waying. To try once more to place it in relation to Appropriation, language, and Saying, we might try to say that way-making is how Appropriation (the belonging-together of man and Being) appropriates by bringing Saying to language, to unconcealment.

I would like to note that in the following passage Heidegger's turning (which could be expressed here as the turning from man on the way to Being to Being on the way to man) is very clearly stated with regard to language.

> Appropriation appropriates man to its own usage. Showing as appropriating thus transpires and Appropriation is the way-making for Saying to come to language. This way-making puts language (the essence of language) as language (Saying) into language (into the sounded word). When we speak of the way to language now, we no longer mean only or primarily the progression of our thinking as it reflects on language. The way to language has become transformed along the way. From human activity it has shifted to the appropriating nature of language. But it is only to us and only with regard to ourselves that the change of the way to language appears as a shift which has taken place only now. In truth, the way to language has its unique region within the essence of language itself. But this means also: the way to language as we first had it in mind does not become invalid; it becomes possible and necessary only in virtue of the true way which is the appropriating, needful way-making. For, since the being of language, as Saying that shows, rests on Appropriation which makes us humans over to the *releasement* in which we can listen freely, therefore the way-making of Saying into speech first opens up for us paths along which our thinking can pursue the authentic way to language.
>
> The formula for the way: to bring language *qua* language to speech, no

longer merely contains a directive for us who are thinking about language, but says the *forma,* the *Gestalt,* in which the essence or language that rests in Appropriation makes its way [literally, "ways itself, moves"].[8]

Stated as simply as possible, what Heidegger wants us to do is to stop representing language as a system of information and begin to reflect. To reflect *(sinnen)* means for him not the absolute reflection of German Idealism (the bending and shining back into itself of absolute Spirit), but entering into the movement of waying. This could tie in nicely with the literal meaning of the English word "experience" which means to go through.

Finally, in the lecture series entitled *What Calls for Thinking,* Heidegger ruminates on the meaning of the word "call" *(heissen)* and brings calling into relation with the way.

> In the widest sense, "to call" means to set in motion, to get something underway—which may be done in a gentle and therefore unobtrusive manner, and in fact is most readily done that way. In the older Greek version of the New Testament, Matthew 8:18, we find: "Seeing a large crowd around him, he called to them to go to the other side." *(Idōn de ho Iēsous ochlon peri auton ekeleusen apelthein eis to peran.)* The Greek verb *keleuein* properly means to get something on the road, to get it underway. The Greek noun *keleuthos* means way. And that the old word "to call" means not so much a command as a letting-reach, that therefore the "call" has an assonance of helpfulness and complaisance, is shown by the fact that the same word in Sanskrit still means something like "to invite."
>
> The meaning of the word "call" which we have described is thus not altogether unfamiliar to us. It still is unaccustomed as we encounter it in the question "what is called thinking—what does call for it?" When we hear that question, the meaning of "call" in the sense of "instruct, demand, allow to reach, get on the way, convey, provide with a way" does not immediately occur to us.[9]

The last passage to be quoted that speaks of the way is the one where Heidegger has the most to say explicitly about *tao* itself.

> The word "way" probably is an ancient primary word that speaks to the reflective mind of man. The key word in Laotse's poetic thinking is *Tao,* which "properly speaking" means way. But because we are prone to think of "way" superficially, as a stretch connecting two places, our word "way" has all too rashly been considered unfit to name what *Tao* says. *Tao* is then translated as reason, mind, *raison,* meaning, *logos.*
>
> Yet *Tao* could be the way that gives all ways, the very source of our power to think what reason, mind, meaning, *logos* properly mean to say—properly, by their proper nature. Perhaps the mystery of mysteries of thoughtful Saying conceals itself in the word "way," *Tao,* if only we will let these names return to what they leave unspoken, if only we are capable of this, to allow

them to do so. Perhaps the enigmatic power of today's reign of method also, and indeed preeminently, stems from the fact that the methods, notwithstanding their efficiency, are after all merely the runoff of a great hidden stream which moves all things along and makes way for everything. All is way.[10]

Surely the terms supposed to "translate" *tao* that Heidegger mentions here are woefully inadequate, if not outright distortions. Heidegger's main point seems to be that *tao* is the *source* of what we call reason and mind, and which we *assume we understand.* This is somewhat analogous to thinking Being as a being. We fail to think the source; more stringently, perhaps, it fails to "think" us.

We turn back now to the second point we made about way, that it is a way of *thinking.* This will lead us into the second theme of our essay, releasement. To put this back into Heidegger's own language, if the *tao* belongs more on the "Being" side of the belonging-together *(Ereignis)* of man and Being, then releasement belongs more on the side of man, although it is nothing that he does or accomplishes. To anticipate, we could say tentatively that thinking is a kind of "waying" through which the Way, *Tao,* comes to presence.

In an essay interpreting a poem from Trakl, Heidegger discusses the word for madness *(Wahnsinn),* saying that a madman has a different mind or way of sensing from other people; not that he has a mind filled with senseless delusions, but he senses differently. Then Heidegger tells us that *Sinnan,* sensing, originally meant to travel, to strive after . . . to take a certain direction; the Indo-Germanic root *sent* and *set* means "way."[11] Thus, to sense, or, in Heidegger's special use of the term, to think, means precisely to be on the way. In answer to our previous question whether the fact that the way was a way of thinking meant that the way was something produced by us, and thus totally subjective, we can now say that thinking, sensing, being on the way is about as far removed from subjectivity as you can get. The change from all subjectivistic reifying representational thinking to the kind of thinking or sensing Heidegger is trying to convey occurs through releasement *(Gelassenheit).* The Taoist equivalent for releasement is, of course, *wu wei* (at times perhaps best rendered as "non-interference").

Now, *Gelassenheit,* or releasement, is, of course, not a term originating with Heidegger, but is, for example, a central term in Meister Eckhart. It even has a kind of precursor in the Stoic conception of *apatheia,* a term designating freedom from strong and turbulent emotions. *Gelassenheit* is often translated as detachment, which can be misleading if it implies mere indifference, an attitude of not caring about anything. In order to distance his own conception from this negative one, Heidegger states that releasement lies outside the distinction of activity and passivity.[12] It definitely has nothing to do with willing and yet it is not just a passive doing nothing. Heidegger characterizes *Gelassenheit* as a kind of waiting. In contrast to expecting, which has an object, which is an expecting something, waiting does not have to have an object and is closer to a keeping oneself *open* without having anything definite in mind. Heidegger is here in an area where there is nothing spectacular, nothing excitingly or dramatically metaphysical to say. The phenomenon is so simple that it eludes us. Instead of being describable in terms of what one is doing or supposed to do, *Gelassenheit* means rather to *stop* doing all the things we constantly do. One is reminded of Nietzsche's poem "Sils-Maria":

> Hier sass ich wartend, wartend,—doch auf nichts,
> jenseits von Gut und Böse, bald des Lichts
> geniessend, bald des Schattens, ganz nur Spiel,
> ganz See, ganz Mittag,
> ganz Zeit ohne Ziel.

> Here I sat waiting, waiting—yet for nothing,
> beyond good and evil, sometimes enjoying light,
> sometimes shadow, completely only play,
> completely lake, completely noon,
> completely time without goal.

Like the way, *Gelassenheit* has some roots in *Being and Time*, for example, when Heidegger speaks of *letting* the real Self act. Less obvious, but certainly equally important, is his emphasis on resolve *(Entschlossenheit)* which he uses in the unusual, literal sense of being unlocked, of being open for something. In later works, the conception of letting-be is quite prevalent. The root of the word *Gelassenheit* is *lassen*, letting, allowing; it is a conception that becomes more and more central in Heidegger's later works.

Heidegger moves this word specifically into a *philosophical* framework, that is, he is not talking so much about the way we should lead our everyday lives as about what the philosopher should stop doing in order to get out of metaphysics. There are three things the philosopher should "let go of": (1) the subject-object dichotomy where the human being becomes an ego and things become objects for that ego; (2) and (3) he should desist from representing the relation of *Gelassenheit* to what it lets be, for example, that which regions *(die Gegnet)* as (a) any kind of causal connection *(Wirkungszusammenhang)* and as (b) a horizonal-transcendental connection. The statement that the relation of *Gelassenheit* to that which regions cannot be thought of as any kind of causal connection means that the relation cannot be thought as an ontic one. The statement that the relation of *Gelassenheit* to that which regions cannot be thought of as a horizonal-transcendental connection means that the relation cannot be thought as an ontological one. With this, Heidegger has left behind one of the most fundamental distinctions, not only in *Being and Time,* but throughout all his writings, the distinction ontic/ontological, beings/Being, the ontological difference. *Gelassenheit* simply enables us to step out of the realm of that distinction.

We might briefly consider the relation of *Gelassenheit* to the will before going on to see its relation to thinking. In other words, seeing what it is that Heidegger wants us to let go of will bring us closer to the kind of thinking that may be able to lead us back to the direction of Being. For Heidegger, the will is perhaps the most insidious ingredient of metaphysics culminating in the will to will, or technology. The delicate question of what it is we are "doing" in *Gelassenheit* if we are not willing and are also not totally passively idle leads Heidegger to speak of *Gelassenheit* as

> the release of oneself from transcendental re-presentation and so a relinquishing of the willing of a horizon. Such relinquishing no longer stems from a willing, except that the occasion for releasing oneself to belonging to that which regions requires a trace of willing. This trace, however, vanishes while releasing oneself and is completely extinguished in releasement.[13]

This is tricky business. But anyone familiar with any kind of meditation will recognize what Heidegger is trying to deal with here. We cannot will not to will, will to relax, calm down or be enlightened, and yet we won't get there by doing nothing at all. We can't simply drop into the lap of Being. Here Heidegger brings in another word to intimate the kind of "doing" he has in mind. The word is *Inständigkeit,* indwelling, and points to the same phenomenon designated by perdurance *(Austrag).* This phenomenon is related to the kind of thinking Heidegger calls *Andenken.* It is a kind of waiting, not a passive waiting, but a very attentive, intense one. Perhaps as not too apt examples we could cite the solo musician who is about to begin his recital, collecting and gathering himself in an intense concentration, a centering; or even a baseball player at bat as he waits for the pitch. One could adduce many such examples. Each one would fall short and fail in one way or another, but perhaps they could point us in the right direction. *Inständigkeit* or perdurance is a kind of intensely receptive sticking something through, sticking it out, perhaps something akin to what we do when we try to recall something we have forgotten. It reminds me of what the Buddhist thinker Dōgen called "sustained exertion." A kind of non-willing (not unwilling) *exertion* distances *Inständigkeit* from all flabby passivity. To use the more familiar word, when we endure something, we are not willing it, but we are not passive either. What we endure could be either something greatly painful or greatly joyful. Even the way we read a great and important

book could be characterized by *Gelassenheit* and *Inständigkeit*. If I read
the book in an unfocused way, I will only get a diffuse picture of it. I must
have something in mind I want to find, the way I read when I am going to
teach or write something on the book; and yet I must be open and receptive to something of which I perhaps have no idea.

A final mundane "example" might be found in the phrase "I am growing carrots and peas." There is no way on earth that I can grow carrots
and peas or anything else; all I can do is *let* them grow by providing the
proper conditions of water, good soil, and so on.

The concluding section of this essay will concentrate on the question
of metaphysics and of Heidegger's and Taoism's relation to it. I shall be
asking to what extent Heidegger, who started out wanting to do fundamental ontology, succeeded in extricating himself from metaphysics. I
shall contend that Taoism was never metaphysical at all, at least not in
Heidegger's sense of that term. Of course, it all depends on how you
define metaphysics, so perhaps it is best to begin with that. One of my
main intents will be to show that the way out of metaphysics does not
lead back to some kind of naive empiricism, nor can it lead "beyond"
metaphysics which would again be a sort of super-metaphysics, or, better, a hyper-metaphysics. Heidegger's phrase is to step back out of metaphysics, leaving it as it is.

Heidegger's definition of metaphysics is clear and univocal. Metaphysics begins with the separation of essence and existence, of the "what" and
the "that." This occurs explicitly with Plato. Nietzsche saw this separation occurring in Plato as the separation of the true world from the
apparent world, the world of Being (the Forms) from the world of
becoming. Heidegger defines essence as what is possible and what makes
possible. If there is going to be a tree, treeness makes that actual tree possible; the tree becomes a tree by participating in treeness. The actually
existing tree is then the real, reality. Essence thus has to do with possibility, existence with reality.

This is undoubtedly Heidegger's fundamental conception of metaphysics. This conception later broadens to what he calls onto-theo-logic.
Christian Wolff, a contemporary of Leibniz, had divided metaphysics
into general metaphysics and special metaphysics. General metaphysics
was the equivalent of ontology, the science of being; special metaphysics
was then divided into three sectors: rational psychology, dealing with the
soul; rational cosmology, dealing with the world; and rational theology,
dealing with God. Heidegger takes the entire content of general and special metaphysics and gives it the label of onto-theo-logic, the logic of
being and of God. Metaphysics thinks the Being of beings as *summum
ens* and *causa sui,* as the highest being and as the cause of itself.

The whole of metaphysics with its separation of essence and existence belongs on one side of another, more fundamental division: the ontological difference, the difference between Being and beings. The separation of essence and existence occurs within the realm of beings; it is not applicable to the division of Being and beings. The significance of the ontological difference in Heidegger's later works is not without some ambiguity. He is trying to work his way out of a metaphysically tainted conception of the ontological difference to a conception more appropriate to his direction of the step back out of metaphysics. In at least one of his latest formulations (in one of the Le Thor seminars), the enterprise of the ontological difference is said to be ultimately untenable.[14]

We shall try to characterize briefly as best we can Heidegger's way out of metaphysics and where it led him. In conclusion, we shall then make a few general remarks about a basic compatibility of this realm of thinking with that of Taoism. More we cannot do within the scope of this essay. The topic is vast, and we have barely scratched the surface.

For starters, the title of the essay, "Overcoming Metaphysics," is somewhat misleading. It sounds as if we, we human beings, were able, if we wanted to and decided to, to set about getting rid of metaphysics by surmounting or transcending it to a "higher" point of view or position. Heidegger often used the far less common word for overcoming, *Verwindung,* to indicate that we cannot simply do away with metaphysics by our own efforts; rather, we can learn to live with it by not paying excessive heed to it or getting obsessed with surmounting it. Basically, Heidegger is saying that metaphysics is where we *are* right now, the reality oppressing us in the form of the will to will, of framing, of the essence of technology. To think that we can change this by some kind of *fiat* is a sheer pipedream. All attempts at overcoming anything, not just metaphysics, are inextricably caught in the fatal net of this will to will, of the *Ge-stell* (framing). Metaphysics is with us, and there is no way that we can assert with any degree of certainty that it won't stay with us. The wish for this degree of certainty is itself already a consequence of the modern gestalt of metaphysics, the Cartesian desire for clarity and certainty, for an unshakable foundation *(fundamentum inconcussum).*

Basically, there is nothing whatever we can "do"; the doing is part of the problem, if not its source. All "doing" is itself metaphysical; it is a kind of production that finds the epitome of its expression in Karl Marx. "If one believes that thinking is capable of changing the place of man, this still represents thinking in accordance with the model of production."[15] No wonder when asked in the *Spiegel* interview what philosophy could do to save us in our present situation, Heidegger answered quite simply: nothing. His much-touted statement that only a god can save us is only another way of saying the same thing.

Put as succinctly as possible, Heidegger is waiting for, is attentive to, the possibility of a shift from the history of metaphysics as the history of the Being of beings to the entry into Being as Being, which has no history, certainly not in the metaphysical sense in which Heidegger has interpreted philosophy from Plato to Nietzsche. This leaves him with the non-metaphysical "experiences" (I avoid the term "concept"), partially prefigured and even present in *Being and Time,* of *Lichtung* (opening, clearing, unconcealedness, "truth"), *Ereignis* (Appropriation, belonging-together) to which belongs difference (no longer the metaphysically thought ontological difference, but the *perdurance* [*Austrag*] of the difference between Being and beings) and, in slightly different contexts, the fourfold *(das Geviert)* of earth and heaven, immortals and mortals.

To sum up, apart from the two fundamental thoughts of the Way and releasement which I have attempted to touch upon in this essay, there are other more pervasive, less easily specifiable non-metaphysical affinities between the later Heidegger and Taoism which I would state as follows:

1. Taoism is basically outside the Aristotelian categories of predication (example: *yin* and *yang* cannot be pinned down either as substances or as forces); Heidegger is trying to move outside of them (example: Being is certainly not a noun, a being or thing; but saying that it is a verb, an activity or process, doesn't solve much either). Similarly, the genus-species classification is lacking in Taoism and is rejected by Heidegger.

2. There is no emphasis on causality. Instead of a succession of phenomena in the relation of cause and effect, Taoism sees rather changes of aspect; Heidegger moves from the "why" of things to their "because" (Silesius' poem: "The rose is without a why; it blooms because it blooms").

3. Thinking is neither representational nor abstractly conceptual nor calculative. A correlate of this kind of thinking (*Andenken,* thinking *toward,* in the direction of something instead of representing it as something over against us—ob-ject) is that space and time are not thought in terms of parameters and measurement. Again, in Taoism they never were, and Heidegger always distanced himself from the outset from looking at the world in terms of objective presence or presence at hand *(Vorhandenheit),* reifying objects in Newtonian container-space and conceiving time as the Aristotelian series of now-points.

These points are all so interconnected that they can barely be discussed in isolation. Finally, the *tao* has been described, I think rather aptly, as "the rhythm of the space-time structure," as "an uncircumscribed power ruling the totality of perceptible givens, itself remaining inaccessible to any specific actualization."[16] This is not exactly Heidegger's language, but surely the true spirit of his thought.

Notes

1. *Sein und Zeit* (Tübingen: Niemeyer, 1953), p. 437. My translation.
2. Quoted in *Basic Writings,* ed. D. F. Krell (New York: Harper and Row, 1977), p. 34.
3. *On the Way to Language,* trans. Peter D. Hertz (New York: Harper and Row, 1971), p. 91, with minor changes.
4. *Ibid.,* p. 126.
5. *Ibid.*
6. *Ibid.,* p. 129.
7. *Ibid.*
8. *Ibid.,* p. 130.
9. *What Is Called Thinking,* trans. Fred D. Wieck and J. Glenn Gray (New York: Harper and Row, 1968), p. 117.
10. *On the Way to Language,* p. 92.
11. *Ibid.,* p. 53. Omitted from the English translation, as are many of the passages dealing exclusively with the etymology of the German.
12. *Discourse on Thinking,* trans. John M. Anderson and E. Hans Freund (New York: Harper and Row, 1966), p. 61.
13. *Ibid.,* pp. 79–80.
14. *On Time and Being,* trans. Joan Stambaugh (New York: Harper and Row, 1972), p. 40.
15. *Vier Seminare* (Frankfurt am Main: Klostermann, 1977), p. 128.
16. Marcel Granet, *La Pensée Chinoise* (Paris: La Renaissance du Livre, 1934).

Paul Shih-yi Hsiao

Heidegger and Our Translation of the *Tao Te Ching*

I learned of Heidegger's interest in translating the *Tao Te Ching* of Lao-tzu in the spring of 1946, on our meeting in the Holzmarktplatz in Freiburg. At that time he suggested to me that we collaborate in the summer on translating the *Tao Te Ching* into German in his cabin at Todtnauberg, since only in the summer would he have a break from his work. I agreed gladly, being convinced that Lao-tzu's ideas would contribute to the reflections of the German people, and indeed of the Western world, after the disastrous World War. Unfortunately we did not complete the project, but I nevertheless have the impression that the work exerted a significant influence on Heidegger. Heidegger himself once said to a German friend that through this engagement with Lao-tzu along with Confucius and Mencius he had learned more of the East.

I

I first made Heidegger's acquaintance in 1942. After completing my degree in psychology and Chinese philosophy in Peiping, I went to Milan to pursue my studies further. There, accustomed to the Scholastic rigor at the University of the Sacro Cuore, I became acquainted with a no less rigorous discipline and a new depth of thought. I was permitted to attend Heidegger's seminars as an auditor. Now and then I handed him parts of my translation of the *Tao Te Ching* into Italian,[1] which Benedetto Croce had recommended that I publish. Presumably Heidegger found something in my translation that he had not found in others, or else he would not have suggested that we collaborate on a translation into German.

On 27 November 1944, the beauty of the city of Freiburg im Breisgau, the scenic capital of the Black Forest region, was destroyed by an air raid. The air raid was unexpected, since Freiburg was supposed to have been declared exempt. Twelve hours beforehand many animals and people became uneasy. Particularly strange was the behavior of an enormous duck in the city park, which for almost twelve hours quacked and flapped around wildly. One is generally inclined to think that wild animals have premonitions of natural catastrophes, prompted by certain atmospheric changes "in the air." But air raids are not natural catastrophes, but actions decided upon and directed by human beings. The monument to the duck by the lake in the Freiburg city park (bearing the inscription: God's creature laments, accuses, and warns) offers food for thought not only for parapsychologists but also, I believe, for philosophers.

I mention these impressions from my years in Freiburg because I repeatedly discussed them in my conversations with Heidegger. For I had the same experience as many other Asians: in my attempts to understand Heidegger's ideas, I had first to learn why his thinking was so difficult for many of his Western contemporaries to understand, or appeared so sensational. What he "brought to language" has frequently been said similarly in the thinking of the Far East. For example, temporality has always been understood differently in China than in the West. For us the duck does not need any paranormal powers: everything is connected with everything else, and in each moment there is concealed the entire past and also the open future.

In the midst of the destroyed old part of the town, with debris still surrounding the cathedral, I met Heidegger again for the first time after the war in the Holzmarktplatz, a central point in the city of Freiburg. All visitors admire the cathedral there with its beautifully impressive steeple. It is held to be the most beautiful steeple of all the Gothic cathedrals in Europe. We Chinese also find it beautiful, although not in the same way as Westerners do. We are accustomed to simple, Romanesque-looking ancestor-temples and imperial palaces, and so find this Gothic structure somewhat lacking in proportion, impressive but not harmonious. Only one who has known the piety, the yearning, and the awe for the divine loftiness of Gothic man is able to understand this magnificent structure. But now, in 1946, the city still lay devastated; nevertheless, we were glad to be there, still alive. Many of our acquaintances and friends were resuming their former activities; others had given up their lives on the battlefield, in captivity or beneath the ruins. Yet we were by no means carefree. My return to China to take up a teaching post was still uncertain. Heidegger was still undergoing the de-Nazification proceedings, which could often be unpleasant, bureaucratically formal, and full of malicious resourcefulness.

"Mr. Hsiao, what would you say if people made two contradictory assertions about the same piece of writing of yours?" Heidegger surprised me with this sudden and somewhat provocative question. "How is it possible? The Nazis said of a section of my book *Being and Time:* 'Herr Heidegger, from what you have written in your book here it is clear that you are not Aryan.' And now your allies, the French, have presented me with the same passage and said: 'Herr Heidegger, from what you have written in your book here it is clear that you are a Nazi.' You see, Mr. Hsiao, what different effects the same passage from the same book can produce. What do you say to that?"

I was dismayed, and could hardly dream that the Europeans could misunderstand their own languages in such a way. My confusion stemmed in part from the widespread misunderstandings of Heidegger's past. Everyone knew that in 1933 to 1934 Heidegger had been Rector of the Albert-Ludwig University in Freiburg; but he soon retired from this unfortunate position. Yet from what time was he no longer in agreement with the ideology and practices of the Nazis? And how could it have been at all possible that he wanted to collaborate with them? Without really knowing, I had assumed it as evident that Heidegger must have been not only a "hanger on" but a fully fledged National Socialist, or else he would never have become Rector in 1933. And how was one to imagine that—a Heidegger as a "hanger-on"?

I found the disappointment of Gabriel Marcel, who had greatly revered Heidegger, comprehensible. When I visited him in Paris during the sixties Marcel said to me that the philosophical world's admiration for Heidegger would have doubled if after the war he had not maintained his stubborn silence and had said something about his behavior in 1933. This also gave me some inhibitions about our collaboration. It was not until after his death that I learned that Heidegger had already ten years previously said in the *Der Spiegel* interview that he had been Rector for only ten months. Here Heidegger shows his wisdom and greatness!

In short, I stood there opposite Heidegger in the Holzmarktplatz with very mixed emotions. Yet at the same time I felt considerable empathy: Heidegger was obviously suffering an injustice—one does not need to know the passage from *Being and Time* to be able to say with conviction that either the Nazis or the Allies must be wrong. Indeed if those responsible on either side were likewise pseudo-philosophers, they could all very well be wrong. The content of the passage had no doubt nothing to do with the accusations; that both accusers were innocent is not possible. It is a pity that I did not at that time ask Heidegger which passage was at issue.

Admittedly, after the war, China was (as a Chinese expression puts it: "with burned head and wounded brow") a pitiable victor, in reality only a "half-Ally," even if belonging to the "four great powers" in the world. (France had at that time been left behind a little to the left.) In spite of this I now stood before Heidegger with something of the calm pride of the victor—even if at the same time a slightly restless conscience, since I saw clearly how unfairly and foolishly Heidegger had been treated. And with that, the spirit and strength to fight against injustice rose within me.

This was in a sense normal for a Chinese: like most Chinese I had in my youth read many novels about robbers and stories of knights and heroes. Whether robbers or heroes, they all fought against injustice: while the heroes did not rob, the robbers robbed only from the rich for the benefit of the poor. And so the Chinese generally have the need—in which they take great joy—to rebel against wrongs, and especially in the interests of others.

In actuality I was at that moment unable to do anything at all for Heidegger. Although I was a "half-Ally," I was still under the jurisdiction of the French military. I was unable to treat the officers in charge as schoolboys, even though many of them, like those in charge in other occupied zones, deserved it. As the victors they were unable to free themselves from the bad influences of soldiery, no matter how much they professed to be crusaders for democracy and humanitarianism.

In my confusion some consoling words of Mencius (372–289 B.C.), the greatest Confucian after Confucius (551–479 B.C.), occurred to me. "Professor Heidegger, you ask me what I say to the statements of the Nazis and the Allies. I can only give you a Chinese answer. I find that the surely false interpretations of the Nazis and the Allies attest to the same thing: in the future one must study your philosophy more assiduously and carefully. If it is understood properly, it will have great relevance for the future. Mencius said: 'If heaven wants to impose a difficult task on someone, it first fills his heart and will with bitterness, rots his sinew and bones, starves his frame, imposes great poverty upon his body, and confounds his undertakings, so that his heart will be inspired, his nature stimulated and his deficiencies remedied. . . . From all these things we learn that life arises out of anxiety and care, misery and privation; and that death on the other hand is the product of comforts and pleasure.' "

Heidegger appeared to be quite moved by this quotation. We did not subsequently talk further about this topic. It was at this same meeting that he proposed translating the *Lao-tzu* together. I agreed to the proposal with joy.

II

As soon as the summer semester finished, we met regularly every Saturday in his cabin on top of Todtnauberg. Our working together provided an opportunity to counteract injustice somewhat. A friend had gladly put a motorcycle at my disposal so that it would not be commandeered.

Moreover, as a "half-Ally" I received every week a priceless package full of all kinds of good things which were otherwise impossible to obtain in Germany: coffee, cocoa, noodles, sausage, butter, cigarettes, and so forth. These we shared. Also the roads to Todtnauberg were very difficult, and there was no public transportation. Mrs. Heidegger was concerned to preserve her husband's time for his intellectual work, and so tried herself to buy everything in town and bring it back to the cabin. Now I was in a position partially to relieve her of this burden. Twenty years later the farmer with whom I sometimes parked my precious Puch 200 told Heidegger with astonishment of this "Chinaman" who used to come up in those days, and who even knew how to ride a motorcycle.

At first our task of translation proceeded from the *Lao-tzu* text of Chiang-Hsi-Chang,[2] which was compiled from a comparison of over eighty-four ancient texts and could be regarded provisionally as the critical edition. We did not consult other translations and commentaries, since we wanted to offer a commentary on the *Tao Te Ching* from Lao-tzu's own thought as far as possible.

First we worked on the chapters concerning the *tao,* which seemed to be the hardest and the most important. Because of the very thorough nature of Heidegger's thinking, we had only worked on eight of eighty-one chapters by the end of the summer. According to the insightful observation of his friend Hans Fischer-Barnicol on a personal visit, Heidegger was "a timid, very shy person. Not only modest in the conventional sense, but one who listened in a remarkable way, very attentive to what the other person had to say, humble. . . . Committed to thinking, and, it seemed to me, most people did not want to come without any thoughts before the presence of these eyes—these truly remarkable, astonishing eyes that listened rather than looked. Even though the nature of Heidegger's humor was not clear to me, these eyes were able to laugh."[3]

At the end of an entire summer only a tenth of the work had been completed. Presumably we would have finished in a decade or so, or perhaps somewhat sooner, since the other chapters are not nearly as obscure, and Heidegger would not have needed to question me so penetratingly and trenchantly, fixing me with that listening, inquiring gaze. Now I understand Heidegger's saying, "for questioning is the piety of thinking."[4] And it is this piety of thinking that drove Heinrich Buhr so forcefully into his engagement with the younger generation.[5]

We wanted to continue our work the following summer. In the interim I was invited to give my first lecture at the University on the topic of "the encounter between China and the West." Upon this followed numerous invitations to lecture throughout Germany, also during the summer. I had to decide: should I continue this significant collaboration with Heidegger or accede to these other requests? Heidegger's *Lao-tzu* translation with me would cause a sensation in the world of philosophy. On the other hand my lectures could afford the German people, who had suffered various injustices and privations, some kind of solace, especially through the words of General Chiang Kai-shek. In contrast with the Allies in Germany, he considered the Japanese people innocent and even spoke against reparations. For according to him the decisiveness of the era of peace lies in "whether we are capable of guiding the enemy so skilfully and well that he repents in his heart and becomes an advocate of peace."[6] On the other hand—and I have to admit this—I could not during our work together get free from a slight anxiety that Heidegger's notes might perhaps go beyond what is called for in a translation. As an interpreter and mediator this tendency unsettled me.

Heidegger had essentially inquired—and asked penetratingly, tirelessly, and mercilessly—about every imaginable context of meaning in the mysterious interplay of the symbolic relations within the text. Only the complete constellation of meanings was sufficient for him to dare to determine the outline of a form of thought capable of rendering the multilayered meaning of the Chinese text into Western language in a clear and comprehensible way.

Aside from a brief communication from October of 1947 (see below), in which he wrote two lines from chapter fifteen, Heidegger unfortunately did not give me any more attempts at translation. So there remains only that the hope that his notes from the *Nachlass* may come to light during my lifetime. After the summer of 1946 we did not resume our collaboration on the *Lao-tzu* translation. Once, during the sixties, when a friend with whom I went to visit Heidegger mentioned *Lao-tzu,* he pointed his index finger at me somewhat excitedly, but at the same time with a smile, and said: "But it was he who didn't want to do it." I smiled too, from embarrassment.

III

Although the eight chapters of the *Tao Te Ching* are only a small portion, they exerted a significant influence on Heidegger. In a presentation of his lecture on "Technology and the Turning" in the Paulus-Kirche in Freiburg, Heidegger said with reference to contemporary ways of thinking: "God can in the light of causality sink to the level of a cause, a *causa efficiens.*" Then he added something to the effect that: "If you want to prove God's existence by way of any of the traditional proofs, whether ontological, cosmological, teleological, ethical, and so on, you thereby belittle Him, since God is something like the *tao,* which is ineffable." It would be a "sin," I now think, to demote God to the status of *causa efficiens,* and a major deficiency of certain contemporary thinkers or scholars, who call themselves philosophers but do not like to think, or else are in the wrong place, as a Chinese proverb puts it: "Sitting at the bottom of a deep well one yet expects to see the entire sky."

After the lecture I heard a simple housewife make the following remark: "Who says that Heidegger is difficult to understand? I am no philosopher, but I understood sixty to seventy percent of his lecture!" I also found the lecture clear, but one had to listen attentively and retain the major points and above all the newly explained words; otherwise misunderstandings could arise.

One day an industrialist friend of mine forced me to take him up to the cabin on Todtnauberg. He wanted to persuade Heidegger to give a lecture to a select circle of distinguished people. Heidegger declined because he did not have time. We happened to learn that he had also declined the invitation of his good Spanish friend José Ortega y Gasset. I later heard that he was afraid that instead of engaging in dialogue he would have to conduct a monologue, for most Spaniards do not like to converse in German.

My industrialist friend did not want to miss the golden opportunity to continue the conversation: "Herr Professor and honorable master, you now want to translate Lao-tzu, but as a European I find Lao-tzu in many ways incomprehensible. Some examples: 'When the great *tao* is abandoned there is humanity and rectitude' (ch. 18). 'If an army is strong, it will destroy itself. If a tree is strong, it will break itself' (ch. 76). 'The sage empties his self and his self is preserved. Is this so because he has no thought of self? Because of this he is able to fulfil himself' (ch. 7). Why do the Chinese speak this way?" I felt as if I too was being addressed and so, after waiting a little, I said: "Because the Chinese of that time did not know Aristotelian logic." "Thank God that they didn't," Heidegger remarked spontaneously. Heidegger was certainly not against logic, but was opposed to its misuse, to the tendency towards rationalism. In fact Lao-tzu's dictum in chapter seven was ultimately misunderstood by a well-known European sinologist, as if Lao-tzu were the greatest egoist in the history of the human race; as if the sage wished precisely to consummate his ego; or as if Lao-tzu were glorifying by this dictum the slyness and craftiness of the sage. In fact Lao-tzu's dictum comes close to Augustine's saying: "Love, and do what you will."

Heidegger rarely talked of religious questions in conversation. Once I visited with Lady Yau-Wan-Shan, a well-known Buddhist artist from Hong Kong. She wanted to hear his opinion of religion. But Heidegger said to her: "The greatest failing in our world is the laziness of thinking." For a Buddhist this was a totally religious response.

Profound thinking was indeed for Heidegger a spontaneous tendency of living. Admittedly, in my translation of the *Lao-tzu* into Italian I had not dared, nor even thought of daring, to go beyond what literally stood in the text. The two lines from chapter 15, literally translated, run: "Who can, settling the muddy, gradually make it clear? Who can, stirring the tranquil, gradually bring it to life?" But Heidegger thought this through farther, in saying that clarifying finally brings something to light, and subtle motion in the tranquil and still can bring something into being.

Heidegger asked me to write out these two lines in Chinese as decorative calligraphy. I inscribed these two lines of eight characters each on such parchment as was then available; "the *tao* of heaven," which is not in the text, I wrote as a decorative device in the middle. I gave a careful etymological explanation of all the characters, so that he could grasp everything in detail. The Heideggerian version again shows the depths of his thinking.

In our translation we tried not to concentrate too much on the details in order to have time for the authentic text. Otherwise we could have opened up a number of questions after the first chapter—for example, the "person" of *tao,* which probably did not interest Lao-tzu at all; *tao* as the overcoming of immanence and transcendence; nothingness in Taoism, Buddhism, Christianity, and in Heidegger himself; ways of thinking in Lao-tzu and Heidegger; the border between philosophy and mysticism, and so forth.

IV

The well-known scholar Chao-Yi from the time of the emperor Chien-Lung (1736–95) in the Ch'ing dynasty once said that a person is not to be judged until the lid of the coffin is closed. Many people now would agree that it is still too early to judge Heidegger. As far as a European ranking in the "history of philosophy" is concerned, that may well be right. In my opinion the inhibitions vis-à-vis Heidegger come from (mostly unacknowledged) fright in the face of the depth of his thinking. We do not hesitate to be thankful, because in precisely these profound questions we may—perhaps for the first time in a long time—again discover ourselves, and our own questions and questionability.

That is what I shall never forget: the enormous earnestness of his questioning. Often with a look, he would wordlessly inquire further; asking always after deeper understanding. May Westerners then learn from Heidegger to inquire after the truth with such integrity, openness, and perseverance as has been handed down to us Asians—"for questioning is the piety of thinking."

Translated by Graham Parkes

Notes

1. *Il Tao-Te-King di Laotse, Prima Traduzione da un testo critico cinese* (Bari: Laterza & Figli, 1941).

2. Chiang-Hsi-Chang, *Lao-Tse-Chiao-Ku* (Shanghai, 1937).

3. Hans A. Fischer-Barnicol, "Spiegelungen—Vermittelungen," in *Erinnerung an Martin Heidegger* (Pfullingen: Neske, 1977), p. 88.

4. Martin Heidegger, *Die Technik und die Kehre* (Pfullingen: Neske, 1978), p. 36.

5. Heinrich Buhr and Erika Reichle, "Der Weltliche Theolog, Vor der Gemeinde als vor dem lieben Gott," in *Erinnerung an Martin Heidegger.*

6. "Responsibility for Peace," speech by Chiang Kai-shek, translated with a commentary by Paul S.-Y. Hsiao, in *Die Gegenwart,* nos. 1–2 (January 1946).

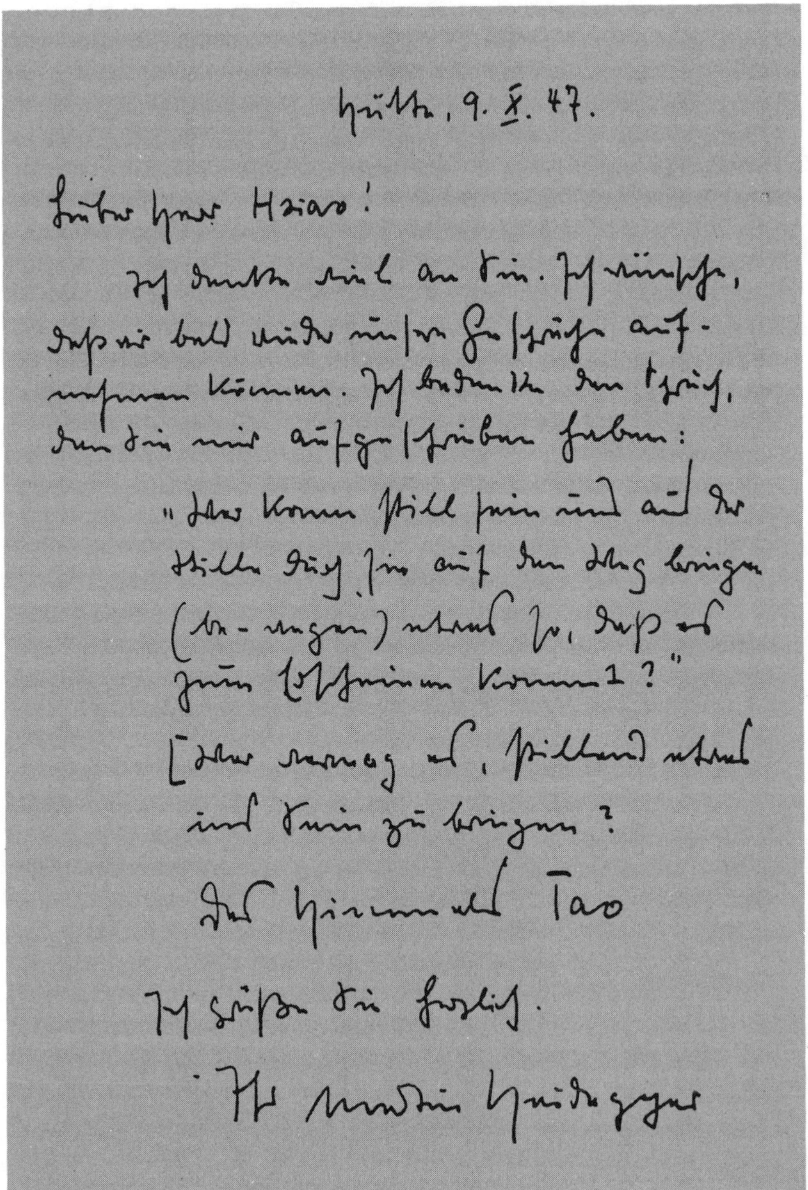

Hütte. 9.X.47

Lieber Herr Hsiao!

Ich denke viel an Sie, und wünsche dass wir bald wieder unsere Gespräche auf-
nehmen können. Ich bedenke den Spruch, den Sie mir aufgeschrieben haben:

"Wer kann still sein und aus der Stille durch sie auf den Weg bringen (be-
wegen) etwas so, dass es zum Erscheinen kommt?"

[Wer vermag es, stillend etwas so ins Sein zu bringen?
Des Himmels Tao.

Ich grüsse Sie herzlich.

Ihr,
    Martin Heidegger

The Cabin. October 9, 1947

Dear Mr. Hsiao,

I think of you often, and hope that we can resume our conversations again
soon. I think of the passage that you wrote out for me:

"Who can be still and out of stillness and through it move something on to the
Way so that it comes to shine forth?"

[Who is able through making still to bring something into Being?
The *tao* of heaven.

With kind regards.

Yours,
    Martin Heidegger

Graham Parkes

Thoughts on the Way:
Being and Time via Lao-Chuang

phusis kruptesthai philei
Heraclitus

— PROLOGUE

Time: Evening of October 9, 1930; after Heidegger's public lecture
            "On the Essence of Truth"
Place: The house of a Mr. Kellner, in Bremen, north Germany
Topic: Whether one can truly put oneself in another's place
Occasion: An impasse in the discussion

HEIDEGGER [*turning suddenly to the host*]:
    Herr Kellner—would you please bring me the *Allegories of
Chuang-tzu?* I should like to read something from them.

    [*Mr. Kellner leaves the room and reappears with a copy of the
    Martin Buber edition*[1]]

HEIDEGGER [*turning to chapter 17*]:
    Chuang-tzu and Hui Shih were standing on the bridge above
the Hao river.
    "Look at the minnows swimming around," said Chuang-tzu.
"That's how fish are happy."
    "You aren't a fish," said Hui Shih. "So how do you know the
fish are happy?"
    "You aren't me, so how do you know that I don't know the fish
are happy?"
    "Not being you, I don't know about you. But I do know that
you're not a fish, and so you can't know the fish are happy."
    "Let's go back to your initial question. When you said '*How* do
you know the fish are happy?' you asked me the question already
knowing that I knew. I knew it from my own happiness at being
up above the Hao."

105

[*Later*]

MR. PETZET [*aside*]:

> With his interpretation of this story Heidegger is unexpectedly
> getting through better than with his difficult lecture, which to
> many people still remains obscure. Whoever is still in the dark
> about the essence of truth, reflection on this Chinese tale will
> show him Heidegger's position on it.[2]

٭   ٭   ٭

HEIDEGGER:

> *The essence of truth is freedom.* . . . Freedom reveals itself as the
> letting-be of beings . . . as letting oneself into what-is.
>
> "On the Essence of Truth"[3]

Introduction

> *Being and Time* is a *way* and not a shelter. Whoever
> cannot walk should not take refuge in it. A way, not
> "the" way, which never exists in philosophy.
> Heidegger, *Schelling* (1936)

Heidegger did not publish the text of his enigmatic lecture on the essence
of truth until 1943. Three years later he spent the summer working with
Dr. Hsiao from Taiwan on a translation of parts of the *Lao-tzu*.[4] But it is
not until the late fifties that he makes any reference to Taoism in print. In
the lecture "The Principle of Identity" he mentions "the Chinese *tao*" in
the same breath as the (Presocratic) Greek *logos*.[5] Two years later, in
Underway to Language (1959), in which he gives the first and only
account of his engagement with philosophers from Japan, he offers a
brief discussion of the idea of "Tao" in "the poetic thinking of Lao-tzu."[6]
Professor Chang Chung-yuan reports that when he visited Heidegger in
Freiburg in 1972, the latter produced a German translation of the
Chuang-tzu about which he was eager to ask questions and engage in discussion.[7]

What were the grounds for Heidegger's interest, stretching over almost
half a century, in a philosophy as apparently alien to Western thought as
Taoism? Can we find any predisposing factors, and any elements in
Heidegger's thinking prior to his contact with Taoist ideas that would
suggest a "pre-established harmony" between them? And what would be
the point of engaging in a comparison of the two philosophies? *Harmo-
niē aphanēs phanerēs kreittōn,* says Heraclitus. The hidden harmony is
deeper, the invisible connection stronger, the inconspicuous correspondence more interesting, than the apparent. The parallels between Heidegger's later work and Taoist ideas are so striking that they have already

prompted comment.[8] The concern here will be rather with *Sein und Zeit,* where the areas of similarity are obscure and—assuming that its writing antedates the author's contact with Chinese thought—where influence is unlikely.[9]

Such a comparison points up some hitherto overlooked themes in Heidegger's early work that have a remarkably Taoist tone to them, rendering comprehensible why he should soon have found Taoism and Zen so congenial. It may also bring into relief some features that are only vaguely limned in the texts of the Taoist thinkers. Counter to the tendency of some of the secondary literature to exaggerate the differences between Heidegger's early and late work, a tendency exacerbated by viewing only the later writings as poetical and in harmony with Asian ideas, the present comparison will support Heidegger's assertions of the essential unity of his thought throughout its many phases. Above all, parallels demonstrated between his early, "pre-contact" work and a non- and anti-metaphysical philosophy from a totally different historical and cultural situation lend considerable weight to Heidegger's claim to have succeeded in overcoming the Western metaphysical tradition.

A reading of Heidegger's and the Taoists' texts together makes apparent the extent to which, in philosophy, the form of what is presented constitutes the content. A foundational paradigm of content's being embodied in form is the Platonic dialogue. Had Plato wished to convey "his philosophy," in the sense of setting forth his ideas about the nature of reality, he would have written discursive treatises. Because he was more concerned with prompting people to question for themselves, with inducing them to follow and make the *way* of thinking (which Heidegger calls *Denkweg* and the Taoists *tao*), to undergo the experience of going over the same topics again and again, of mis-taking highways for by-ways, of losing track of the way altogether, ending up—amazed—in cul-de-sacs and blind alleys through following at the heels of that Protean guide and master of the *aporia,* Socrates: he wrote dialogues. And given that Plato consistently wrote himself out of these dialogues, the question arises: what is his position? Where do we find his own views? To say that they are expressed in the speeches of Socrates is too simplistic. Many of the views expressed by interlocutors other than Socrates are eminently reasonable for a person to hold at that stage of inquiry—and some are surely views that Plato himself once held. To the extent that there is such a thing as Plato's position on a certain topic at a certain stage of his thinking, it is to be found *between* (one of Heidegger's favorite prepositions) that of Socrates and those of the other participants in the conversation, generated out of the tension of the opposing views presented.

Although discursive prose is not entirely inappropriate for writing on the early Heidegger alone, a comparison with the writings of Lao-

Chuang calls for a somewhat different form. Some kind of dialogue would be apposite, since Heidegger published two of his most fascinating pieces in the form of dialogues—and one might have expected more, in view of his predilection for spoken dialogue as a medium of instruction.[10] Further, the perspectivism of Taoist philosophy makes the dialogue an appropriate medium of explication, especially since the *Chuang-tzu* consists largely of conversations and altercations. However, dialogue need not be overtly dramatic, as in Plato. The interlocutors in what follows are not *dramatis* but rather *cogitatoris personae,* representing tendencies within a single individual—and especially within one engaged in thinking about Heidegger and comparative philosophy. The different voices, which will be distinguished typographically, represent less differing positions than different attitudes or perspectives on certain issues common to the Taoists and Heidegger.

二 DIALOGUE

Fragmentary Beginnings

Although everything happens according to the *logos,*
men behave as though they do not understand it, both
before they have heard it and after hearing it.
                                                         Heraclitus 1

My words are very easy to understand and put into
practice, yet no one in the world can understand or put
them into practice.

                                                         Lao-tzu 70

It is for good reason that Heidegger mentions the *tao* in the same breath as the Presocratic *logos.* A major ground for his openness to Taoist ideas is his becoming attuned early on to reading comparable texts in the form of fragments from the Presocratics. Of particular relevance in this context would be the writings of Heraclitus, the Western thinker closest in spirit to Taoism, and to whom Heidegger ascribes the deepest understanding of Being.[11] The texts of the two great Taoist classics, though written somewhat later than the fragments, occupy a place in the history of East Asian thinking comparable to that of Heraclitus's work in the West. The impact of Lao-Chuang was of course initially much greater, giving rise to one of the foremost schools of Chinese philosophy, and subsequently constituting a major force in the development of Zen Buddhism. Some of Heraclitus's ideas entered the Western mainstream through Plato, though they were largely overwhelmed by the latter's grander metaphysical concerns. Heraclitus continued, however, to be a fascinating figure exerting a mysterious and appropriately intermittent and sporadic influence throughout the development of Western thought, until Hegel's treatment (of the Presocratics in general) ended a period of relative neglect. Since then, interest in him has been further reanimated by Nietzsche and Heidegger—not to mention the numerous poets who have been inspired by the fecundity of the fragments.

The form of Heraclitus' text is especially congruent with that of Lao-tzu's, both being woven from pregnant utterances couched in an archaic language rich in allusive power and interspersed with lacunae of obscurity. Though the patchwork of the *Tao Te Ching* may have a somewhat more cohesive unity, a greater proportion of the fragments of Heraclitus come from a single hand than the verses attributed to Lao-tzu. But stylistically they are remarkably similar in their blending of the arcane and the oracular, the gnomic and the poetical. [12]

*Granted some elective affinity between Lao-Chuang and Heraclitus, there is nevertheless something perverse about comparing the two major classics of Taoist thought, with their inimitably terse and poetic styles, with—of all of Heidegger's works—*Sein und Zeit. *The prose of SZ, though hardly as hard on the reading ear as the English translation,* Being and Time, *is somewhat ponderous and far from poetical. [13] In contrast to the "book of five thousand characters" (as the* Lao-tzu *is sometimes called), which must rank amongst the most profound of the world's short philosophical texts, and to the episodic and fragmentary texture of the* Chuang-tzu, *the length and architectonic complexity of SZ are formidable.*

In the attempt to highlight "Taoist" ideas in Heidegger's masterwork, the writing of which antedates not only his contact with Asian philosophy but also his more prolonged meditations on the thought of Heraclitus and Parmenides and Anaximander, the following reading will indeed have to wrestle constantly with the book's distinctly un-Taoist style. There will be a constant tension between the effort of sober exegesis of a hard and serious text and the temptation to escape to the later Heidegger, where language is granted far freer play and the resonances with Taoist ideas are clearly audible. As the interpretation is pulled away from close textual analysis it may do occasional violence to the text. But given Heidegger's idea that ontological interpretation and the analysis of Dasein must essentially be acts of "violence" *(Gewaltsamkeit)*, [14] it is remarkable how little violence SZ has elicited from interpreters in this present age of deconstruction (of which the idea of *Destruktion* in SZ is a precursor). And for a text that happens to take the hammer as a paradigm of things we encounter in our everyday dealings with the world, a wrench or two here and there won't hurt.

The first and major task is to engage in a fairly close reading of part A (secs.

14–18) of the third chapter of *SZ*, which establishes several themes crucial to the development of the text as a whole. The arguments of these sections also adumbrate the primary topics of our comparison: those of nature, utility, uselessness, nothing and death—and the possibility of authentic existence. The epilogue will entertain a few of these themes with reference to the works of the "middle period."

The Nature of Nature

> Even the phenomenon of "Nature" in the sense of the
> Romantic conception of nature can be grasped ontologi-
> cally only from the conception of world.
>
> *SZ 65*

> Man models himself on earth, earth on heaven, heaven
> on the way, and the way on what is naturally so.
>
> *Lao-tzu 25*

One of Heidegger's major criticisms of traditional Western ontology is that it overlooks what he calls "the worldness of the world" *(die Weltlichkeit der Welt)*, what it is about worlds that makes them worlds. The task of the third chapter of *SZ* is to remedy this deficiency by an analysis of the phenomenon of *Welt* by way of an examination of the being of the everyday *Umwelt* (environment). Heidegger begins by remarking that traditional ontology has taken as its primary theme "things of nature" rather than "things invested with value" (63).

It is precisely Heidegger's treatment of this issue in his early work that threatens to derail the comparison with Taoism. A salient feature of SZ *is that it gives remarkably short shrift to the world of nature. The entire analysis of the phenomenon of "world," and the concomitant criticism of traditional ontology, is based on the notion of* Zuhandenheit *("to-hand-ness").*[15] *Heidegger's phenomenology of the ways we customarily relate to things in the world simply assumes that we treat them as "to-hand"* (zuhanden), *viewing them from the perspective of utility, and relating to them in terms of what we can* do *with them.*

The Taoist view—on the conventional understanding of Taoism—could be characterized by the injunction: "Be natural."[16] *A central dictum in Taoism speaks of the unity of man and nature* (t'ien jen ho yi), *suggesting that man's problems stem in great measure from his becoming separated from* t'ien. *To bring his being into harmony with* tao, *man should re-align himself with the way of heaven, the* tao *of* t'ien, *natural* tao. *A comparable understanding of nature is totally lacking in Heidegger—at least in the early work. Moreover, Taoism is so radically against anthropocentrism and so roundly condemns the utilitarian perspective that Chuang-tzu in particular is renowned for his extolling of "the usefulness of being useless." The Taoist would consider SZ to be informed by a hopelessly utilitarian and instrumental view of man's essential being, and would discern in the text a program justifying the violation of the earth in the name of technology. One might even say that Heidegger's misdirected zeal over certain political issues in the early thirties was prefigured by his excessive enthusiasm several years earlier concerning the possibilities of modern technology.*

From another perspective, Heidegger's ideas about the phenomenon of world can be seen as an extreme literalization of Kant's attitude toward (knowing rather than utilizing) nature as expressed in the preface to the second edition of the Critique of Pure Reason *(B xiii), where he writes that human reason*

> *must not allow itself to be kept, as it were, in nature's leading strings, but must itself show the way . . . constraining nature to give answer to questions of reason's own determining. . . . Reason . . . must approach nature . . . in the character of an appointed judge who compels the witnesses to answer questions he himself has formulated.*

In the language of SZ: Dasein projects in advance a world, a horizon of possibility in terms of which things can make sense to us and thus appear as things. And this is for the most part a horizon of utility.

It is true that by the time of the essays of the mid-forties Heidegger had turned things around (a consequence of the famous Kehre*) and developed a view that was less anthropocentric. In the later work, the appropriate attitude toward the "thingness of the thing" is to let it suggest to us the best mode of approach. If we refrain from projecting a human horizon of world as the context or background against which to encounter things, we realize that things in a way generate their own worlds, and it is through those atmospheres that we should approach them. That is all quite harmonious with Taoism—but the later texts can hardly be adduced to show that Heidegger was pursuing these lines of thought prior to the "turning."*

To return to the topic of nature: it is hardly discussed at all in SZ. Hildegard Feick's Index lists only ten pages on which the term occurs.[17] *Moreover, the section for* die Natur *is entitled: "Nature as disclosed in for-sight (als umsichtig entdeckte) or as theoretically known," which corresponds to Heidegger's characterization of being-in-the-world as concern for beings in the world as to-hand and on-hand. Even authentic Dasein, the being for whom "its own being is an issue," relates to things in terms of their utility—as indeed it must, if it is to continue being. In general, for the Heidegger of SZ, nature is merely "discovered along with" the disclosure of the world of factical Dasein, and is thereby seen as something on- or to-hand.*

If we look at the text, we see that Heidegger first broaches the topic of nature at the beginning of chapter three, just before introducing the ideas of *Zuhanden-* and *Vorhandenheit*. The aim of the chapter is to elucidate the phenomenon of world, by considering the being of beings within the world:

> Beings within the world are things, things of nature *(Natur-dinge)* and things "invested with value" *("wertbehaftete" Dinge)*. The thingness *(Dinglichkeit)* of these things becomes a problem; and insofar as the thingness of the latter depends upon nature-thingness, the being of things of nature, nature as such, is the primary theme. The fundamental character of things of nature, of substances, is substantiality. (63)

This is Heidegger's account of the viewpoint of traditional ontology, and an approach which he thinks can never on its own disclose the phenomenon of world. He is critical of the tendency to interpret this phenomenon on the basis of nature as determined by the natural sciences, which is already to see things in a particular and restricted perspective: "Dasein can discover beings as nature only in a definite mode of its being-in-the-world. This knowing *(Erkennen)* has the character of a definite de-worlding *(Entweltlichung)* of the world" (65). The "definite mode" he has in mind is presumably the taking of nature as something on-hand.

From Pen to Hammer

> To-handness is the ontological-categorical definition of what-is, as it is "in itself."
> *SZ* 71

The next mention of nature occurs five pages later; but within these pages Heidegger introduces five key ideas—those of *Zeug, Verweisung, Zuhandenheit, Umsicht,* and *Vorhandenheit*—which are relevant to our topic. He calls what we immediately encounter in our everyday dealings with things *Zeug* (68), a word so basic in German that it is almost impossible to translate, especially since it occurs in a variety of compounds.[18] He gives as examples writing utensils *(Schreibzeug),* sewing equipment *(Nähzeug),* tools *(Werkzeug,* literally: "work-thing"), vehicles *(Fahrzeug:* "travel-thing") and measuring instruments *(Mess-zeug).* *Zeug* basically means "things" or "stuff," and in Heidegger's usage more specifically "something for such-and-such an activity or use." The primary feature of *Zeug* is that there is never just one of it: "Ein *Zeug 'ist'* strenggenommen *nie.*" A piece of equipment can be what it is only with reference *(Verweisung)* to other equipment: "writing materials, pen, ink, paper, blotting pad, desk, lamp, furniture, windows, doors, the room." The context is primary: these items do not present themselves individually and then make up a totality; rather, the room as a whole is what we immediately experience—and not "in a geometrically spatial sense, but as a 'living-utensil' *(Wohnzeug)*" (68).

This theme corresponds to the Taoist insistence that any thing is what it is only in relation to other things, that a particular is entirely dependent on its context. In fact Chuang-tzu makes this point with specific reference to the idea of utility, in terms similar to those Heidegger uses to describe *Verweisung,* emphasizing that usefulness is nothing absolute but is always relative to a context. In the "Autumn Floods" chapter, Jo of the North Sea says: "A battering ram is good for smashing down a wall, but not for stopping up a hole, which is to say that it is a tool with a special use" (ch. 17, IC 146–147). In the language of *SZ,* the battering ram is "something . . . in order to" destroy a city wall; it has a "reference" to the entire relational matrix of sieges and fortifications. In filling a small hole the battering ram would be—because of its great mass, which suits it ideally for demolishing something firm—with respect to something fluid entirely useless.

This "relational dependence" of usefulness is made even clearer by the realization that what is useful depends for its utility on what is not being used. This point is exemplified by a passage from the Outer Chapters which invites us to contemplate our relationship to the earth, the ground on which we stand and walk. Chuang-tzu is speaking to Hui Shih:

> "In all the immensity of heaven and earth, a man uses no more than is room for his feet. If recognizing this we were to dig away the ground around his feet all the way down to the Underworld, would it still be useful to the man?"
>
> "It would be useless."
>
> "Then it is plain that the useless does serve a use."
>
> (Ch. 26, IC 100; cf. ch. 3, IC 62)

A piece of ground does not *an sich* support anything (at least not anything locomotive); the abyss is, as in Nietzsche, always already "there." It provides support only in relation to something to-hand—in this case: to-foot—that is not being used, but offers the *possibility* of being used. Thus Heidegger characterizes the "in-itselfness" *(An-sich-sein)* of the to-hand as being founded upon the phenomenon of world. An implement has its possibilities only as long as it participates in a relational matrix.

That passage from *SZ* in which Heidegger coins the neologism *Wohnzeug* is reminiscent, by the way, of one of the few discussions of "equipment" in the *Lao-tzu* (chapter 11), which makes the point that a room can be used as a "living-utensil" only if it includes emptiness in the form of space between the walls, and within them in the form of windows and doors.

Let us not be carried away by notions of emptiness until we have understood the more prosaic reality of pens and paper. There is a danger of reading into these sections of SZ *something (or nothing) that is simply not there. In characterizing the way of being of tools or equipment Heidegger is doing precisely that: he is not making a universal ontological statement about the ultimate nature of things.*

But he nevertheless does want us to see the thing of use as a paradigm for things in general—especially since the purpose of his discussion here is to elucidate the phenomenon of world.

And if we continue to follow this elucidation, it will lead us back to our original topic: nature.

The scene changes from study to workshop, as Heidegger goes on to argue that no mere observation of a hammer, nor theoretical contemplation of it, can lead to a genuine understanding of its being.[19] Its "to-handness" can be appreciated only if we grasp the hammer in its being by picking it up and using it. "Hammering itself discovers the specific 'handiness' *(Händlichkeit)* of the hammer. The way of being of *Zeug* is *Zuhandenheit*" (69). Heidegger calls the hammer's "to-handness" its *An-sich-sein*, its "being-in-itself": we shall return shortly to the paradox (which has generally gone unnoticed) generated by this unusual use of *An-sich-sein*. In dealing with things as to-hand we see them in the context of a network of "in-order-to's" *(Um-zu)*—the pen is something "in-order-to" make marks on paper—and so Heidegger calls this kind of vision *Umsicht,* or "for-sight."[20] Having stressed that for-sight does not grasp the being of what is to-hand explicitly in any kind of thematized understanding, and that we most fully understand its being by handling it, Heidegger then remarks on its most peculiar feature—namely, that when a thing of use is optimally fulfilling its function it *withdraws.* "What is peculiar about what is immediately to-hand is that it simultaneously withdraws in its to-handness, just in order to be properly to-hand."[21]

Back to Nature

Nature is itself a being which we encounter within the world and is discoverable in various ways and on various levels.

> *SZ* 63

Heidegger goes on to remark on another feature of our dealings with things as to-hand: that our attention is directed not so much to the tool itself as to the work we are engaged in. For example: when writing, our attention is focused not on the pen but rather on the-words-appearing-on-the-page. He points out that the work always carries with it a reference to a further possible use, to other people as possible users—and also to nature. "Through using tools 'nature' is also discovered, 'nature' in the sense of natural products" (70).

He goes on to distinguish three possible ways in which things of nature can be encountered.

> But nature must not be understood here as what is merely on-hand—nor as the power of nature (die Naturmacht). The wood is forest, the mountain is quarry, the river water power, the wind is wind "in the sails". . . . It is possible not to see the being [of nature] as to-hand, and to discover and determine it simply in its pure on-handness (Vorhandenheit). This cognizance of nature misses it as something which "stirs and strives," overwhelms us, captivates us as landscape. The plants of the botanist are not the flowers of the hedgerow, the geographically determined "source" of a river is not the "spring in the ground."

It is clear from this passage that Vorhandenheit and Zuhandenheit do not refer to two set classes of things but rather to two different ways in which things can be encountered. A hammer can be to-hand or on-hand, depending on the mode of our concern with it—practical or theoretical. And the same is true of a tree, or the wind, or any other natural phenomenon, depending on whether our concern is to utilize it or investigate it scientifically. (For example: a botanist who does pull-ups from the bough of a tree on his day off is treating it as Zeug, as something for exercising with, taking it as something to-hand, rather than in his usual working mode as something on-hand.)

However, the passage implies that there is a third way of relating to things of nature, which is to understand them—the flowers of the hedgerow and the source in the ground—as manifestations of the "power of nature." Heidegger goes on to talk about how "environing nature" (Umweltnatur) is disclosed, though not explicitly as such, in our dealings with various kinds of Zeug, and then immediately embarks upon a discussion of Zuhandenheit without saying anything more about the third possible way of treating things of nature (71).

He mentions this third possible mode of being only once again, in a similarly off-hand manner, at the beginning of the section entitled "Reality and Care": "The nature which 'surrounds' us . . . does not, however, display the mode of being of the to-hand or the on-hand in the sense of 'the thingliness of nature' " (211). But again the theme is left undeveloped and disappears, the subsequent references to nature having to do with the traditional ontological and scientific understanding of the natural world.[22]

There is, however, a long and rather cryptic footnote in one of the 1929 essays which contains a further reference to nature. There Heidegger warns specifically against "[interpreting] being-in-the-world as commerce with things of use (Umgang mit den Gebrauchsdingen),"[23] and continues:

> But if in the . . . analysis of Dasein nature is apparently missing—not only nature as an object of the natural sciences but also nature in an original sense (cf. SZ 65f)—, there are reasons for this. The decisive thing is that nature lets itself be encountered neither in the surroundings of the environment (im Umkreis der Umwelt) nor primarily as something to which we relate (wozu wir uns verhalten).

> Nature is originally manifest in Dasein in as far as the latter exists as disposed-
> attuned *(befindlich-gestimmt) in the midst of* what-is. . . . [It is only in the] full con-
> cept of care *(Sorge)* . . . that the *basis* for the *problem* of nature can be attained.

Heidegger forgoes an investigation into "nature as an object of the natural sciences" (as something "on-hand") because his concern is on a deeper ontological plane—with that projected horizon which determines in advance whether
we see a given being as a natural thing, a possible tool or resource, an object of
scientific study, or whatever. "Nature in an original sense" presumably corresponds to what was called "the power of nature" in *SZ*.[24] The next couple of
sentences make it clear why the scientific or instrumental perspectives cannot
see nature "in the original sense"—because it manifests *inside* us as much as
outside. And yet, unfortunately, the analysis in *SZ* of *Stimmung* (mood) as an
"attunement" of our being-(t)here[25] that is neither internal nor external gives
no examples related to nature.

Such a study of the ways in which natural (including meteorological
and physiological) phenomena condition the clearing of our being-here
would be well worth while. Presumably the third possible attitude
toward nature, being neither practical nor theoretical, is primarily aesthetic. Whereas to deal with manufactured things as to-hand is to disclose them as they are *in themselves (an sich)*, to relate to natural things
only as on/to-hand is not to discover "nature in an original sense," is to
fail to appreciate the "power of nature." It is indeed disappointing that
Heidegger failed to elaborate on the third way, in view of the misinterpre-
tations that have arisen as a result of overlooking the two cursory mentions of it in *SZ*. He does, however, describe the appropriate attitude
toward things of nature (and in general) in the essay from 1935 "On the
Origin of the Work of Art."[26]

Uses of the Useless

> "Now this talk of yours is big but useless, dismissed by
> everyone alike."
> > Hui Shih to Chuang-tzu

> Philosophy is not knowledge which one . . . could
> apply and calculate the usefulness of. However, what is
> useless can still be a true power.
> > *Introduction to Metaphysics*

*This talk about utility needs to be tempered by the consideration that one
of the major thrusts of the Taoists' attack against anthropocentrism is a
repudiation of the utilitarian view of the world. They are wary of most
forms of discriminative consciousness, holding the value judgements that
issue from them to be inherently one-sided and therefore distorting; but*

they particularly abhor the division of things into the instrumental cate-
gories of the useful and the useless. Along with the exhortation to a cre-
ative engagement with nature is their rather idiosyncratic praise of use-
lessness.

The theme is exemplified in the Inner Chapters *primarily in stories*
concerning things of nature (including human beings) which reach an
advanced age precisely through not being good for anything. Of trees
that are useful to human beings Chuang-tzu says: "So they do not last out
the years Heaven assigned them, but die in mid-journey under the axe.
That is the trouble with being stuff which is good for something" (ch. 4,
IC 74). In the same chapter, Carpenter Shih encounters the gigantic old
oak at the earth altar, and says of it: "This wood is wretched timber, use-
less for anything; that's why it's been able to grow so old." But shortly
afterwards the holy oak appears to him in a dream and says: "Supposing
that I had been useful, would I have had the opportunity to grow so big?
You and I are both things . . . and the good-for-nothing man who is soon
to die, what does he know of the good-for-nothing tree?"[27] Even grant-
ing Heidegger a kind of mitigated instrumentalist position, Chuang-tzu's
emphasis on the "usefulness of being useless" is too prominent to allow a
comparison on this topic to be viable.

It is true that one doesn't find in early Heidegger a corresponding
praise of usefulness *per se,* but he does appreciate the usefulness of the
unusable—at least for the task of a phenomenology of "everydayness."
And in fact we have just reached the point in the text where Heidegger
takes up precisely that issue.

At the beginning of section 16 Heidegger reminds us that the point of his
investigation of things to-hand was to help elucidate the phenomenon of world.
He had left himself (and us) in the *aporia* of trying to grasp the being of the
hammer by using it—and then experiencing its withdrawal as soon as one starts.
One is reminded of the Taoist dictum (*Lao-tzu* 64): "He who grasps, loses it."
As a way out, Heidegger points our attention to three ways in which the
Weltmässigkeit of the environment (*Umwelt*) announces itself: "conspicuous-
ness" (*Auffälligkeit*), where a tool is unusable or a particular material unsuitable
for the job; "obtrusiveness" (*Aufdringlichkeit*), in which the work is obstructed
when a needed tool is missing; and "obstinacy" (*Aufsässigkeit*), where a tool is
not unusable or missing but is irremovably "there" and in the way (73–74).

(There comes to mind here an example—which Heidegger, being an
oenophile, would appreciate—of a situation in which all three features come
together. At a picnic on a hot summer's day we take out the carefully chilled
bottle of wine—only to find that we've left the corkscrew at home. The cork,
having been rendered un-to-hand, announces itself as conspicuously immovable

without the obtrusively absent corkscrew; while the unopenable bottle stands there as obstinately and tantalizingly un-to-hand—or, even more so, un-to-mouth. To push the cork *into* the bottle is a solution about which Heidegger would probably hesitate longer than Chuang-tzu.)

Owing, then, to the peculiar tendency of what is to-hand to withdraw, for us to become aware of its being it must "in a certain way [lose] its to-handness." There has to be "a disturbance of reference *(Verweisung)*" (74), "a *breach* in the relational context disclosed by our for-sight" (75). These gaps, disturbances and interruptions in our ongoing dealings with things serve to illuminate the context in which all this activity has been taking place—and the phenomenon of world thereby "announces itself."

To this extent the idea of unusability serves a function in Heidegger comparable to the role of uselessness in *Chuang-tzu,* insofar as it makes us pull back and contemplate the surrounding context and thereby lets us see the perspective of utility *as* a perspective. This kind of consideration counters the tendency to exaggerate the differences between Heidegger and Chuang-tzu by making the latter look overly "anti-" and the former overly "pro-instrumentalist." There are, of course, from the thing's point of view, definite disadvantages in being potential *Zeug* or "[good] for something." But for the Taoists the problem is less with the standpoint of utility *per se* than with getting stuck in any single perspective. And surely Heidegger, with his emphasis on the "multi-dimensionality" of Being, would, just as much as Chuang-tzu, pray with Blake that we be kept from "single vision and Newton's sleep."

The issue is exemplified amusingly in the exchange between Chuang-tzu and Hui Shih concerning the large gourds the latter has been given. He ends up in frustration smashing them to pieces because they are too unwieldy to be used as water containers or dippers—"because they were useless" (ch. 1, *IC* 47). Chuang-tzu's response is that Hui Shih has been stupid in failing to see that he could have "[made] them into those big bottles swimmers tie to their waists and [gone] floating away over the Yangtse and the Lakes." The point is not that the perspective of utility is inherently pernicious; the anecdote rather points up our tendency to become fixated in calculating and utilitarian modes of relating to things, rather than conducting ourselves "with a full view of heaven." And even within the perspective of utility our vision tends, like Hui Shih's, to be too narrow, our "for-sight" too short: being taken in by the customary ways of understanding things we become blind to their myriad possibilities. Because Hui Shih was fixated on putting the gourds to their conventional use by putting water in them, he could not see his way to putting himself on them and getting into the water instead.

Finally, if we look at the language Heidegger uses to talk about our relations to things to-hand, we'll find that it's much less aggressive than our objector's neo-Kantian paraphrase (in terms of laying down in advance how things can be encountered) suggested.

The contrast between early and late Heidegger, between the supposedly aggressive instrumentality of SZ and the serene releasement *(Gelassenheit)* of the later writings, is indeed generally overdrawn—as we can appreciate if we go on to look at section 18.

Inquiring after the worldness of the world, Heidegger asks: "How can world let things be encountered? . . . What we encounter within the world has been . . . freed in its being for concernful for-sight *(ist für die besorgende Umsicht . . . in seinem Sein freigegeben)*. . . . What does this prior freeing *(Freigabe)* amount to?" (83). This freeing, or release, takes place through *bewendenlassen* (letting be involved), which he characterizes as "to let something to-hand *be so-and-so (Zuhandenes so und so sein lassen) as* it already is and *so that* it can be so" (84). The double *so* here is significant: for-sight lets things be what they already are *and* as they can also be. Through the prior freeing of a being for being to-hand we help it come into its own. This is not a one-sided operation in which we unilaterally impose our will on things, but rather a reciprocal interaction. In forging a piece of metal into a knife, for example, the metalworker realizes a certain potential of that metal for sharpness, a potential it could never realize on its own. But the success of the work depends in advance on certain properties of the metal itself—since no amount of working on wood could ever achieve such sharpness.

It is true that at the root of the complex network of interconnections among things to-hand there is the ultimate *Worum-willen* ("for-the-sake-of-which") which informs the entire structure—namely, our concern for our own welfare. This means that we naturally look at things in the light of our concern for our own being, and so always "let things be encountered as to-hand" (86). That, for Heidegger, is simply a fact—Wittgenstein would say "form"—of life.

A Short Handnote

> "Not too slow, not too fast; I feel it in the hand and
> respond from the heart, the mouth cannot put it into
> words, there's a knack in it somewhere which I cannot
> convey to my son."
>
> *Chuang-tzu* 13

In line with the Taoist emphasis on being-in-the-world without being taken in by it, the models the *Chuang-tzu* offers of people who are on to the *tao* are not sage-hermits who spend their lives meditating in isolation from the world, but are often artisans and craftsmen and others who have attained consummate mastery of certain psycho-physical skills—

most of whom work primarily with their hands.[28] Manual dexterity, smooth, graceful, and effortlessly responsive, is a sign that one's power *(te)* has become fully integrated. The idea behind many Taoist stories is that if one can disconnect discursive thought and respond from the wisdom of the body, the hands will do their own kind of thinking.

In the early forties, as he became more concerned with the idea of *Denken,* Heidegger alluded to its relations to the hand by calling genuine thinking a *Handeln,* or activity. He soon began to refer to thinking as a *Hand-Werk,* a craft—but literally a work of the hand.[29] Thinking with the hands rather than with the brain consists for Heidegger in the hand's "reaching and receiving, holding and carrying, pointing and gesturing." It is not surprising that he also mentions the hand's drawing *(zeichnen),* given his admiration for artists such as Cézanne and Klee for their thoughtful renderings of things and (their) Being.[30]

"The gestures of the hand pervade the whole of language and in fact most purely when man speaks in being silent." Heidegger surely has in mind here not only a language of gesture,[31] but also the thinking that takes place in writing, the silent movements of the hand over the page. In writing, if one is fortunate to receive a block of inspiration, he then has to work somewhat as a carpenter works wood. From a rough draft the careful writer will make numerous passes over it as with a plane, smoothing out the rough surfaces and shaping the form of the whole.[32]

It is true that Heidegger did not develop this theme until the later work; but if one looks at *SZ* "chirologically" one sees that a thinking of the hand, though not explicitly called such, runs throughout the text—in the descriptions of our everyday dealings with things as *zuhanden.* Not that our everyday activity is on a par with the accomplished Taoist's, but perhaps authentic dealings with things, as described below, could be.

Some Ado about Nothing

> It is a world of words to the end of it,
> In which nothing solid is its solid self.
> Wallace Stevens[33]

The exchange between Chuang-tzu and Hui Shih about digging away the ground around where one is standing illustrated the usefulness of the unused (in Heideggerian terms, the dependence of utility on possibility). A related theme in Taoism is the interdependence of utility and emptiness, or nothing *(wu).*[34] Chapter 11 of the *Lao-tzu* presents three kinds of thing: a cartwheel, a jug and a room; and in each case the point is to show that these implements are only "to-hand" on the basis of an emptiness, a nothing, where there is a breach in the fullness of the material. "Thus what we gain is Something, yet it is by virtue of Nothing that this can be put to use." Were there no hub at the center of the wheel, there could be no rotation; were there no hollow within the jug, it could not hold anything; and were there no openings in the walls in the form of windows and a door, neither light nor occupants could enter the room.

These verses offer in a way the inverse perspective on utility from the analysis in *SZ*. There the implement can be what it is only insofar as it stands out against a surrounding horizon of World; in *Lao-tzu* the thing can function only on the basis of an emptiness *within* the implement itself. But in both cases the realization of a particular emptiness, lack, or non-being within the world conduces to a realization of the Nothing that is the ultimate (un-)ground of everything. Heidegger was later to write of a jug in a manner reminiscent of—and probably influenced by—Lao-tzu, in the 1950 essay "Das Ding" (The Thing).[35] In both cases the jug (or wheel, or room) is to be taken as an image for the human being: were there in us no emptiness, we would not be able to be, as human beings, here (or there). In fact Heidegger remarked on the thing's intimating its own nothingness as early as 1935:

> Beings cannot, however, throw off the question-able thing about them that whatever they are and how they are—they also could *not* be. This possibility is not something we . . . merely add in thought, but the being itself announces this possibility, announces itself as the being in [the possibility].
>
> (*EM* 22, *IM* 29)

Let us go back for a moment to Heidegger's discussion of the breakdown of our dealings with things to-hand. When something to-hand is missing, there opens up "a *breach* in the relational context disclosed by our for-sight. For-sight falls into emptiness . . ." (75). This is the first intimation of Nothing in *SZ*. Since in our everyday activity our concern is not with the implements themselves but with the work they are being used for, it is only when something goes wrong that the relational context which conditions and makes all such activity possible comes to light. Only through a break can we see the World—as that which conditions in advance all "what-for's," "in-order-to's" and other implemental relationships. This totality of the relational context, the world, is itself no thing: it is neither to-hand nor on-hand; but only thanks to this empty horizon can any implement, or thing, be what it is. But in "everydayness" we tend to lose ourselves in beings and fail to attend to that which lets them be—to the empty horizon of World, the background of Nothing against which every being presents itself as *not* nothing, i.e., as something.

(This is the subject of the question with which *Introduction to Metaphysics* opens: "Why is there anything at all and not rather nothing?" Why? To what end? What's the use of it all? The answer, insofar as there is one, would be: No reason, no ground—simply, World. Heidegger re-reads the principle of sufficient reason with an idiosyncratic change of emphasis: *Nihil* est *sine ratione*—nothing *is* without ground.)

We don't encounter anything corresponding to the emptiness revealed through this break again until the sixth chapter of Division One, in the section that describes how *Angst* discloses "nothingness, i.e., the world as such" (187).

> *Now* there *is a key phenomenon in Heidegger to which nothing—or perhaps one should say, rather, "not anything"—in Taoism corresponds.* Angst *plays a pivotal role in SZ in the transition to authentic existence as described in Division Two. There is no trace of existential anxiety and the related phenomena of constriction and weird uncanniness* (Unheimlichkeit) *in the writings of Lao-Chuang. The abyss* (yüan) *of tao and the emptiness of nothing are contemplated with a calm serenity that is far from "the terror of the abyss"* (der Schrecken des Abgrundes) *of which the later Heidegger so eloquently speaks.* [36]

There does appear to be a major discrepancy there, a difference in tone and quality of affect. But when we look to the underlying views of the self which Heidegger and the Taoists inherit from their respective traditions, it may turn out to be more a difference in degree than in the nature of the (understanding of the) self itself. Both cultures began with a sense of the self's open participation in the world, of a dynamic process of flowing and permeable boundaries. Shortly before the emergence of Taoism, the self had apparently begun to coagulate, as it were, around a core of self-interest. So that Confucius, in a spirit similar to that which moved Socrates, had to exhort his fellow men to "overcome the self" *(k'o chi)* by ignoring prospects of profit and gain, honor and reputation, and re-open the self, through the observant practice of sacred ritual *(li)*, to the matrix of relationships in which it essentially inheres. In the same vein the Taoists speak of "forgetting the self" *(wang chi)*, such that "the utmost man has no self" *(Chuang-tzu* 1).

While Socrates similarly abhorred self-interest and considerations of personal profit, power, and fame as motives for action, the resulting dynamics of the self were different—consisting in a gathering of the rational soul into itself so that it would not suffer dissolution after separation from the body at death. The idea of the self as substance persisted as a central tenet of the Platonic/Christian tradition, culminating in the extreme coagulation of the *res cogitans* around the center of the ego in the philosophy of Descartes—and in the absolute separation of this substance from the radically different substance *(res extensa)* comprising the world. In spite of Nietzsche's attacks on the substantial conception of the self and his attempts to crack the hardened husk of the "atomic" soul-coagulate, the idea of self which Heidegger was faced with was still far harder to "destruct" and far more abysmally separated from the world than that which confronted the Taoists. Hence the *Angst* when the center fails to hold and the construct begins to fall apart.

But the degree of proneness to Angst *has to do not only with different understandings of the self but also with a concomitant difference in their understandings of the world. For the ancient Chinese the question of the possible meaninglessness of the cosmos simply never arises: the cosmos is inherently invested with meaning. There may be dispute amongst various schools as to the nature of its meaning, but—for the Taoists at least—the cosmos is an ordered whole. Not patterned from without by transcendent* archai, *nor heading purposively towards a pre-existent* telos, *but informed from within by the patterning they call* tao.

The cosmic situation in which post-Copernican Western man finds himself after "the death of God" is indeed more alienating than the situation of the Chou dynasty Chinese. The collapse of a structure that had given meaning to existence for over two thousand years was bound to occasion considerable psychical and spiritual turmoil.

However, there is another side to the picture. The passage in which Heidegger speaks of the terror of the abyss reads:

> The clear courage for genuine anxiety guarantees the mysterious possibility of the experience of Being. For close by genuine anxiety as the terror of the abyss dwells awe. This clears and protects that realm of human being within which man dwells at home in the enduring.

The point he is making here is that *Angst,* as anxiety in the face of the abyss, and *Scheu,* as awe and wonder at there being *anything* at all, are two aspects of the same phenomenon. In the major discussion of *Angst* in the entire corpus (in "What Is Metaphysics?") the encounter with nothing is said to be pervaded by "a strange kind of peace" and "a spellbound calm."[37] But even though the terrifying side is not evident in Taoism, what *Angst* reveals does—as we shall see shortly—have a counterpart.

It might help to establish that point if we first take a quick look at the salient points from the discussion of *Angst* in *SZ*. That will also help us to appreciate better the analogy between the breakdowns described in section 16, in which breaches in the fabric of interconnections of things to-hand reveal what they are *for,* and the breakdown *par excellence* that is *Angst,* in which all our relations to things in the world are ruptured.

We learn from Heidegger's description in section 40 that "what anxiety is about is not anything within the world . . . nothing of what is to- and on-hand"; and he speaks of the "obstinacy *(Aufsässigkeit)* of the Nothing and Nowhere within the world" that presses upon us in *Angst* (186), which turns out to be "the *possibility* of what is to-hand at all, that is: the world itself" (187). The "nothing of what is to-hand *(dieses Nichts des Zuhandenen)*" is grounded in "the world as such," "the world as world," or—as he puts it in the second discussion of *Angst,* in Division Two—"the nothing of the world *(das Nichts der Welt)*" (343).

In this more global breakdown, things recede from us, and the hitherto unnoticed background (the empty horizon of World) comes to the fore and lets us see what it is all for: nothing. The full realization is then that the nothing of the world is also the nothing of the self. Wallace Stevens has expressed something like this in "A Primitive Like an Orb":

> With these they celebrate the central poem, . . .
> Until the used-to earth and sky, and the tree
> And cloud, the used-to tree and used-to cloud,
> Lose the old uses that they made of them,
> And they: these men, and earth and sky, inform
> Each other by sharp informations, sharp,
> Free knowledges, secreted until then,
> Breaches of that which held them fast. It is
> As if the central poem became the world . . .

The Issue of Death

> Which of us is able to think of nothingness as the head,
> of life as the spine, of death as the rump? . . . He shall
> be my friend.
>
> > *Chuang-tzu 6*
>
> For Hades and Dionysos are the same.
>
> > Heraclitus 15

Heidegger makes the connection between *Angst* and death in the Second Division, revealing the nothingness of world to be—since "Dasein *is* its world"—the nothingness of the self. His understanding of death as a constant presence within life rather than a state beyond and opposed to life is close to the Taoists'. Just as Heidegger emphasizes that "*our sight is too short* if life is made the problem *and then also occasionally* death is considered" (316), so Lao-tzu remarks that "it is because people set too much store by life that they treat death lightly" (ch. 75).

But at first glance the Taoist perspective on death appears quite different from Heidegger's. Death is not a major theme in the Tao Te Ching, *and most of the references to it there have to do primarily with literal, biological death. Lao-tzu has heard tell of "one who excels in safeguarding his own life . . . for [whom] there is no realm of death" (ch. 50); and one gets the general impression from the work that the sage has identified himself with* tao *in such a way that the encounter with death is of little moment. The issue figures more prominently in* Chuang-tzu, *and Angus*

Graham has remarked upon "the ecsatic, rhapsodic tone" in which Chuang-tzu writes on the topic (IC 23). As in Lao-tzu, *the prospect of death loses its terror because the individual has identified with the larger cycles of change which pattern the cosmos, and is thereby able to move into death as simply the next transformation in the endless series of cycles that constitute* tao.

In SZ *on the other hand, the encounter with death in* Angst *and the appropriate response of total openness to that nothing of the self are crucial for both an existential and ontological understanding of our being here. The tones of the treatments are quite different: the Taoists' informed by a serenity tinged with wonder, a grave matter-of-factness tempered by traces of exultation at the prospect of the next transformation;* Heidegger's *weighted heavily towards* Angst *and grim resoluteness in the face of the abyss.*

When death is faced with equanimity there are several possible background conditions. At one end of the spectrum, death has hardly become an issue, since the person's individuality is not yet sufficiently differentiated from the social group—as in the case of members of so-called "primitive" societies, for example. The prospect of death is terrifying only to the ego, to that part of the self which has come to experience itself as an entity separated from the world. To the extent that one is identified with the deeper layer of the self which is implicated in the procession of the generations, the prospect of individual death has less import—since there is no reason to suppose that the annihilation of whatever self there is will have any effect on the larger process in which it participates.

At the other extreme is an equanimity based on a belief in the immortality of the soul. In this case (of which the Socrates of the *Phaedo* would be a paradigm) the individual withdraws from the world of the senses, dis-identifies with the body, and identifies with the highest functions of the rational soul, which are universal and transpersonal. In the first instance there is no problem because the self is insufficiently concentred to be self-aware, and in the second because it is so powerfully concentrated that dissolution appears impossible. Since for both Heidegger and Chuang-tzu there is already an awareness of the self, the question is whether either of their views involves a regression to a state of "primitive" non-self-awareness, a simple acceptance of annihilation, a belief in transcendence and individual survival, or some further alternative.

There seems to be a difference between the Lao-tzu *and* Chuang-tzu *on this point. The Taoists' emphasis on spontaneity and their praise of primordial naturalness might suggest that their ideal involves a total immersion in purely natural processes and a regression to a stage of quasi-prim-*

itive participation in the world, and some passages in Lao-tzu *which advocate "returning to the root" and reverting to "the uncarved block" reinforce this impression. Under these circumstances death would not be an issue, because there is not sufficient self-awareness or extension of consciousness beyond the present moment. On the other hand, the predominance of Taoist imagery about wandering above and beyond the dust and grime of worldly affairs and their concern with not being bound by things (especially evident in* Chuang-tzu, *ch. 6), taken together with the passages that seem to suggest that* tao *is at least in part transcendent to the world, inclines one to ascribe the Taoists' equanimity in the face of death to their having transcended the realm of life and death. Neither alternative, however, would characterize Heidegger's position.*

That is true. But even though there is a sense in which both Chuang-tzu and Plato view death as a transformation, their understandings are essentially different. In Taoism the movement of transformation is the opposite of the Platonic one: rather than concentering the soul in preparation for the ascent to unity with the Absolute, one de- and ex-centers the self to allow it to merge in all directions with the formlessness of *tao*. To the extent that *tao* is "transcendent" it is transcendent to the individual as a particular, but it is wholly immanent in the world if we include in that the history of the race. And to the extent that the Taoists advocate detachment from the dust and grime of the world, this is to be understood as only a necessary stage on the way to a reintegration with it. The "true man" *(chen jen)* has gone beyond mere unconscious participation in the world and also beyond transcendent detachment from it. He has reintegrated himself with the processes of change in such a way as to become "the helper of heaven" *(hsiang t'ien)*. He is one "in whom neither heaven nor man is the victor," who participates in the world-process with full awareness of its macrocosmic dimensions, "[opening] things up to the light of heaven."[38] If one insists on applying the categories of transcendence and immanence, one would have to characterize the Taoist position as one of "transcendence-*in*-immanence." There is after all something paradoxical about Chuang-tzu's position on death, which Graham sums up well when he writes that Chuang-tzu "seems to foresee the end of his individuality as an event which is both an obliteration and an opening out of consciousness" (*IC* 23).

Thus the Taoist attitude toward death, which helps one "forget" the self and allow it consciously to identify with the macrocosm, may not be so different from Heidegger's existential conception of death as possibility. But rather than go further into this vast topic, let us focus on what kind of transformation of our dealings with things is effected by the confrontation with death.[39]

Authentic Use

To find,
Not to impose, not to have reasoned at all,
Out of nothing to have come on major weather,
It is possible, possible, possible. It must
Be possible.

Wallace Stevens

An obstacle remains in the course of comparison concerning the incompatibility between Heidegger's insistence that authentic existence continues to relate to things as to-hand and the Taoist idea of wu wei. This idea of "doing nothing" or "non-interfering activity" appears to involve a broadening of one's perspective(s) so that one is able to see things in "the full light of heaven," and a forgetting of the self in such a way that one is open(ed) to respond to the movements of tao *by spontaneously realizing one's own particular* te, *or natural potential. Such a process seems quite foreign to the emphasis in* SZ *on grim resoluteness and self-assertion.*

In the account of authentic existence in *SZ* Heidegger twice speaks of "letting the ownmost self act through one *(in sich handeln lassen)*."[40] One does this by letting the self "shatter itself against death," so as to "give death the possibility of assuming power *(Macht)* over the existence of Dasein."[41] This idea corresponds to the Taoist notion that if one can "empty out" the self, then *tao* will naturally work (and play) through one in the form of "the daemonic" *(shen)* or, more generally, as "power" *(te)*. Angus Graham's commentary on a passage from chapter 4 of Chuang-tzu describes this phenomenon in terms remarkably similar to Heidegger's: "Then the self dissolves. . . . The agent of his actions is no longer the man but Heaven working through him, yet paradoxically . . . in discovering a deeper self he becomes for the first time truly the agent" (*IC* 69).

One of the factors which appear to vitiate the comparison with Taoism is in fact an artifact of the English translation of *SZ*. Macquarrie and Robinson's choice of "resoluteness" for *Entschlossenheit* gives a misleadingly subjectivistic or "will-full" impression of what authentic existence is about. A better word for that essential precondition for authentic relations with things would be "openedness." Heidegger constantly plays the term off against *Erschlossenheit* (disclosedness), describing *Entschlossenheit* as the authentic mode of the disclosedness of being-(t)here.[42] He makes it clear, however, that this openedness, far from distancing us from the everyday world, rather "brings the self precisely into the current concernful being with what is to-hand" (298). The difference between such openedness and the "average" disclosedness is that the guiding *Umsicht* has a far wider temporal and spatial range. He calls such an

"opened being with what is to-hand" in the current situation "the active let-
ting-be-encountered *(das handelnde Begegnenlassen)* of what is *present* in the
environment," and "the undistorted letting-be-involved of that which in acting
it grasps *(dessen, was sie handelnd ergreift)*" (326).

The key term here is "undistorted" *(unverstellt)*. Heidegger's view is that in
general our perceptions and conceptions of things are conditioned by *das Man,*
by "the way things have been publicly interpreted" (sec. 27). The culture has
already set up the structures of meaningfulness and laid down in advance what
and how things are. Thus, our everyday dealings with things are grounded in a
Worum-willen (for-the-sake-of) that is inauthentic—usually in something equivalent to "for-the-sake-of-staying-alive." However, the ultimate *Worum-willen*
includes our uttermost possibility—death.

In inauthentic existence our understanding "projects itself upon what we are
concerned with, upon what is feasible, urgent, indispensable in the business of
everyday activity" (337). Understood temporally, we "come back to ourselves" from the things (to-hand) with which we are concerned—rather than
from our "ownmost, irrelatable being-able-to-be" (337), which is the nothingness of our death. Authentic being-toward things to-hand operates in the
"moment" *(Augenblick),* which is deeper and broader than the present "now."
"In openedness the present is not only brought back from its dispersal into the
immediate objects of concern, but is held in the future and past too" (338).
Heidegger then uses what is in the context of *SZ* an unusual word to characterize the authentic relation to things to-hand as experienced in the moment:
Entrückung, or "rapture." The term "moment" refers to "the opened, but *held
in openedness,* rapture of being-(t)here by the possibilities and circumstances
of the situation." The idea of rapture is the more passive counterpart to the
more active *ekstases* of temporality: to talk of "the raptures of future, past and
present" (350) is to balance the ways in which we "stand out from" ourselves
toward those horizons by pointing up the ways in which we are "transported"
by them.

The closest thing we find to an explicit account in *SZ* of authentic dealings
with things to-hand is in section 69(a). Heidegger begins by emphasizing again
that authentic existence is still concerned with producing and using things to-
hand (352). He reiterates that there is never some *one* thing to-hand but always
a multiplicity of things to-hand in a context: the fact that one tool can be
present and another, related one be missing underscores their belonging
together.[43] This time around, in tracing the structural relationships involved in
using tools Heidegger stresses the temporal aspects of "letting things be
involved": that we are always "ahead of" ourselves in dealing with what is to-
hand, allowing the "what-for" *(wozu)* to guide our present activity, and at the
same time retaining a sense of how the work has been going up till now and also
of the present context. He goes on to say that " 'authentic' wholehearted
dealing with things . . . dwells neither with the work nor with the tool, nor

with both together" (354)—presumably since our awareness at all times pervades all three horizons of temporality.

This suggests that in authentic dealings with things to-hand we see through the network of equipmental relationships to the ultimate *Worum-willen* which gives them meaning—the empty horizon of World and death. With one eye on Nothing, an ear open for the voice of stillness, and one foot always already in the grave, we let the hand be guided by the power of Being. So that when he says that "In order to be able—'lost' in the world of equipment—'really' to go to work and get busy, the self must forget itself" (354), he is speaking on two levels, referring both to the dissipation of the self into the world of its concern and to authentic dealings with things. In the latter, however, forgetting the self means opening it up to allow one's actions to be guided by the authentic self, which, itself nothing, is one with the nothing of world.

Technology versus Ecology

> If one takes everyday ideas as the sole measure of
> things, then philosophy is always something crazy
> (*etwas Verrücktes*). . . . It constantly brings about a
> shifting (*Verrückung*) of standpoints and levels. In phi-
> losophy one often doesn't know for long periods of time
> where one's head is.
>
> *The Question about the Thing*

Granted that authentic existence as described in SZ is less aggressively manipulative—involving more "freeing" and "letting" and "releasing"— than it might first appear, the issue of technology in relation to ecology still seems to force the parallels of the comparison apart. There are numerous passages in the Taoist texts describing a primeval condition of mankind living in simple harmony with the world of nature, and advocating a return to such a condition. Chapter 80 of the Lao-tzu *paints the (admittedly somewhat extreme) picture of a society in which people own such things as ships and carts—but make no use of them. In the first three Outer Chapters of* Chuang-tzu *we find praise of a primal Utopia conjoined with a vigorous repudiation of technology and numerous denunciations of man's interference with the course of nature. And then there is the famous episode (ch. 12) concerning the old gardener who contemptuously dismisses the idea of using a well-sweep—an ecologically respectable and respectful implement if ever there was one—as a substitute for laboriously watering his garden by hand.*

The story of the well-sweep is at first puzzling, since the gardener's rejection of such a benign labor-saving device seems uncharacteristically rigid and narrow—if he represents the Taoist position. However, a careful reading of the story makes it clear that the gardener's objection is to the frame of mind that gives rise to calculating dealings with things, and which the use of technology in turn encourages, rather than to the products *per se* of this way of thinking.[44]

But the important thing to understand is that the thrust of the technological examples in these chapters is primarily metaphorical. As Angus Graham puts it: "[The Primitivist] objects to people wanting to manipulate human nature as the potter moulds clay rather than to the potter himself" (*IC* 186). As long as we don't take these examples literally, the attitude of *Chuang-tzu* toward technology does not appear especially negative (though its products are not treated with any great enthusiasm either).

Correspondingly, on the Heideggerian view, to take things as to-hand is not necessarily to manipulate or mis-handle them. It is quite possible to take advantage of the power of nature in a way that is quite compatible with the Taoists' *wu wei*. In making use of the wind to propel a sailboat, for example, or of water to drive a mill-wheel, we can contribute to the wind's and water's being what they are "in themselves." (The paradoxical nature of the *an sich* again.) In making responsible use of fire or in using a tree for shade, we can, by bringing forth their appropriate possibilities, reveal those elements more fully in their being.

Heidegger would no doubt want to go further and say that the felling of trees for lumber to build a cabin could still be an instance of authentic use of the wood. The question is at what point the use of a natural thing as *Zeug* in such a way as to realize its possibilities with respect to human concerns begins to impinge overly on the unfolding of its possibilities when left to itself. Clearly the deforestation of an area of beautiful trees in order to mass-produce ugly furniture is something even the most social-utility-minded Heideggerian would not condone. At the other extreme there is no doubt that Heidegger would applaud a woodworker who himself seeks and finds the perfect tree for the chair he has in mind, and then proceeds to fashion it with thoughtful hands that respond to the uniqueness of the wood, so that its hidden beauty may shine forth to the fullest. One is tempted to say not just that the woodworker has helped the tree to become more fully itself, but has actually helped it to become *more* than itself.

There is a story along these lines in the *Chuang-tzu* about the woodworker Ch'ing, whose bellstand was so beautiful as to be "daemonic" (ch. 19, *IC* 135). After going into the forest to "observe the nature of the wood as heaven makes it grow," he waits for "a complete vision of the bellstand" before picking his tree and going to work. He is sufficiently open to the daemonic to be able to describe his working the wood as

"joining heaven's to what is heaven's"—by allowing the *te* in him, his natural ability, to respond to the *te* in the wood, its natural potential. It is
characteristic, incidentally, of Taoism to prize especially a craft in which
careful *subtraction* rather than skilful composition is the art.

Chuang-tzu's view of the instrumental approach toward things can be
summed up by citing a remark from one of the stories concerning
Chuang-tzu himself (ch. 20, IC 121). After commenting on the advan-
tages to a tree of its not being good for timber, Chuang-tzu, later the
same day, on being asked which of two geese should be killed for dinner,
replies: "The one that can't cackle." On being pressed by a disciple to say
what his position really is, he responds: "I should be inclined to settle
midway between being good for something and good for nothing." This
corresponds to the attitude towards technology recommended later by
Heidegger in *Gelassenheit:* "the simultaneous Yes and No to the world of
technology."[45] However, the story finishes by suggesting that even more
important than "[settling] midway between being good for something
and good for nothing" is to loosen ones ties to things altogether by
"[refusing] to be turned into a thing by things."

This admonition suggests a final interesting parallel between Heidegger and Chuang-tzu. The latter plays on the noun *"wu,"* for "thing," by
using it as a verb, "to thing" (*IC* 185). Graham brings together a number
of passages in which Chuang-tzu talks of "thinging things" under the
heading "Self-Alienation," and compares the idea with Hegel's notion of
alienation and the tendency of people to "turn themselves into things by
becoming identified with their possessions." The comparison with Hegel
is illuminating, but even more so is the parallel with a major theme in *SZ*
—namely, that (existentially speaking) we misunderstand ourselves by
"falling into" the things in the world with which we are concerned, and
(ontologically) the Western metaphysical tradition has misunderstood the
nature of human being by interpreting it as a being on a par with other
beings, as something *vorhanden,* or on-hand.

Chuang-tzu asks: "If you treat things as things and are not made into a
thing by things [literally: 'thinged by things'], how can you be tied by
involvements?" (ch. 20, IC 121 and 185). Put in Heideggerian terms: "If
you let things (to-hand) be involved in the context of the ultimate possibility of nothingness, and allow your own nothingness to keep you from
understanding yourself as something either on- or to-hand, how can you
be taken in *(benommen)* by things in the world?" Correspondingly,
Chuang-tzu's "What things things is not itself a thing" (ch. 22, IC 164)
would elicit immediate assent from Heidegger. It is true that it is not until
the later Heidegger that we hear talk of "things thinging"; but it was not
long after *SZ* that he began to say that "world worlds" *(die Welt weltet)*
and "nothing nothings" *(das Nichts nichtet).*[46]

三 EPILOGUE

Poetry is the subject of the poem,
From this the poem issues and
To this returns. Between the two,
Between issue and return, there is
An absence in reality,
Things as they are. Or so we say.
Wallace Stevens

The Chalk Is Flightier than the Hammer

[The scene is Lecture Room 5 at the University of Freiburg, at the start of the summer semester of 1935. The course is entitled "Introduction to Metaphysics," and the early lectures begin by considering the difference between Something and Nothing.[47]]

HEIDEGGER [*turning from the blackboard, a piece of chalk concealed in his left hand*]:
    What is needed is, without being seduced by over-hasty theories, to experience in whatever is closest things as they are. This piece of chalk here is an extended, relatively hard, gray-white thing with a definite form, and in and with all that a thing to write with.

[*Places the chalk on the lectern*]

Just as certainly as it belongs to this thing to be lying here, it belongs to it as much to be able to be not here and not so large. The possibility [*Möglichkeit*] of being drawn along the blackboard and being used up is nothing that we merely add to the thing in thought. It itself as this being is in this possibility, otherwise it would not be a piece of chalk as a writing instrument [*Schreibzeug*].

STUDENT B [*aside*]:
    This must correspond to the being "in-itself" [*an-sich-sein*] of what is to-hand, in the account in *SZ*.

HEIDEGGER [*goes to the board and writes the word* Möglichkeit]:
    Correspondingly, every being has in various ways this potential [*dieses Mögliche*] to it. This potential belongs to the chalk. It itself has a definite appropriateness for a definite use in itself. . . .

[*Holds the chalk up between forefinger and thumb*]

Our question should now first open up what-is [*das Seiende*] in its wavering between Notbeing and Being. Insofar as what-is withstands the uttermost possibility of Notbeing, it itself stands in Being and yet has never thereby overtaken and overcome the possibility of Notbeing.

STUDENT A [*aside*]:

Didn't Lao-tzu say that something and nothing produce one another, and that it's by virtue of nothing that something can be put to use?

*   *   *

[Six months later Heidegger is teaching a course on Kant's *Critique of Pure Reason,* in which this early lecture is devoted to a more general consideration of what a thing is. He is discussing space and time, since what appears to make a thing the particular thing that it is, what seems to make it "this one," is that it occupies a particular place at a particular time.][48]

HEIDEGGER:

Initially we have the impression that space and time are in some sense "external" to things. Or is this impression deceptive?

[*Picks up a piece of chalk from the lectern*]

Let us take a closer look! This piece of chalk: Space—or rather the space of this classroom—lies around this thing . . . This piece of chalk, we say, takes up a particular space; the space taken up is bordered by the outer surface of the chalk. Outer surface? Surface? The piece of chalk is itself extended; there is space not only around it but at it, or even in it; only this space is occupied, filled up.

[*Places it back on the lectern*]

The chalk itself consists inside of space; we even say [in German], it takes *in* [*ein,* "up"] space, encloses it by its outer surface as its inside. Space is thus not a merely external frame for the chalk. But what does inside mean here? How does the inside of the chalk look? Let us see. We'll break the piece of chalk in two.

[*Picks it up and breaks it in half*]

STUDENT B [*aside*]:

Is this the right way to go about it, I wonder? Didn't he suggest in his lecture on the work of art the other day that any way of approaching things that perpetrates an "assault" [*Überfall*] on them is bound to fail?[49]

HEIDEGGER:

Are we now at the inside? Just as before we're outside again; nothing has changed. The pieces of chalk are somewhat smaller; but whether they're larger or smaller makes no difference now. The surfaces at the break are not as smooth as the rest of the outer surface; but that is also unimportant. The moment we wanted to open the chalk up by breaking it into pieces, it already closed itself off, and we can continue this process until the whole chalk has become a little heap of dust.

STUDENT B [*aside*]:

So that's what he meant in the other lecture by speaking of the mere thing's "holding itself back" [*Sichzurückhalten*] and being essentially "off-putting and closed off" [*das Befremdende und Verschlossene im Wesen des Dinges*].[50]

STUDENT C [*who has been leafing through his copy of* Sein und Zeit, *stops at page 69 and reads to himself*]:

"What is peculiar about what is immediately to-hand is that it simultaneously withdraws in its to-handness, just in order to be properly to-hand." I'm beginning to understand what he means by saying that a primary feature of what is to-hand is "self-withholding non-outgoingness" [*das ansichhaltende Nichtheraus-treten*] (SZ 75). But now he seems to be extending this notion to apply to *all* things.

HEIDEGGER:

[We] were unable to find the space we were looking for inside the chalk, the space which belongs to the chalk itself. But perhaps we weren't quick enough. Let's try breaking the piece of chalk once again!

[*Repeats the routine*]

So where on earth does the inside of the chalk begin, and where does the outside stop?

Earth and World (from Chalk to Rock)

[The scene is a lecture hall in Frankfurt; the date: November 1936; the topic: "The Work [of Art] and Truth."][51]

HEIDEGGER:

The Greek temple [as a work of art] opens up a world [*Welt*] and sets this back on to the earth [*Erde*]. . . . Through the open-ing up of a world, all things receive their time and pace, their farness and distance, their breadth and narrowness. . . . The earth is the forthcoming-sheltering . . . the unimpressionable tireless-indefatigable . . . the essentially self-closing . . . which withdraws from any attempt to open it up and holds itself constantly closed.

STUDENT A:

Given Professor Heidegger's background, it's likely that the roots of these ideas of world and earth are in Presocratic thought and Greek myth; certainly the idea of world has become more concrete than it was in *SZ*. But I wonder whether he's been reading Wilhelm's translation of the *I Ching*, since *Welt* and *Erde* are strikingly similar to the primal powers represented by the primary trigrams of *yang* and *yin* lines respectively: *ch'ien*, "the creative," associated with the openness of heaven, and *k'un*, "the receptive," associated with the darkness of the earth.[52]

HEIDEGGER:

What is the earth, that it thus attains what is unconcealed? The stone is heavy and manifests its weight. But while its weight weighs on us, it at the same time refuses any penetration into it.

[Proceeds to ponder the heaviness of the stone as he did the space within the chalk in the earlier lecture]

STUDENT C [*aside*]:

So we have the same situation as with trying to comprehend the being of what is to-hand. Contemplate the hammer in a detached and objective manner and you'll never grasp it in its being. Pick it up and hammer with it and it withdraws. Feel the weight of the stone in your palm and its heaviness remains somehow mysterious. Try to get to the inside of it by smashing it and the fragments pose the same enigma—plus you've lost the stone. Put it on the scales and you can no longer feel the weight. Subject it to molecular analysis and you lose the stone again. There seems to be a certain "earthiness" to all things, from hammers to rocks.

HEIDEGGER:

The earth thus lets every penetration shatter against it. It lets every merely calculative pushiness turn into a destroying.

STUDENT D:

This reminds me of a discussion I heard recently between Werner Heisenberg and Niels Bohr on the topic of "complementarity." One of them pointed out the impossibility of determining the position of every atom in a cell without killing the cell.[53] Heisenberg's "uncertainty principle" suggests that the exclusively *yang* power of "world" is unable unequivocally to open up the secrets of the *yin* power of "earth." And it seems that Heidegger is advocating something close to what Chuang-tzu calls the "ultimate *yin* [which unravels things]" approach for when the going gets tough and the inquiry deep (*Chuang-tzu* ch. 3, IC 62–63).

HEIDEGGER:
All things of the earth, and earth itself as a whole, flow together in reciprocal harmony. But this confluence is not a blurring. Here flows the stream—resting in itself—of distinguishing, which distinguishes everything present in its presence. Thus there is in each of the self-enclosing things a similar not-knowing-itself.[54]

STUDENT D:
This is rather uncharacteristic language for Professor Heidegger. It sounds a lot like Taoism—with overtones of Chinese Buddhism—in which the oneness of all things similarly maintains distinction within non-difference. It's in chapter two, I think, that Chuang-tzu says something to the effect that "The Way interchanges [apparently opposite] things and deems them one. . . . All things, whether forming or dissolving, in reverting interchange and are deemed to be one."

HEIDEGGER:
World and earth are essentially different from one another and yet are never separated. . . . The world as the self-opening tolerates no being closed off. But the earth inclines as the sheltering to envelop and encompass world within itself. The opposition of world and earth is a contention [*Streit*] . . . [which is different from] discord and dispute.[55]

STUDENT F [*aside*]:
I keep being reminded of Nietzsche's distinction between the forces of the Apollinian and the Dionysian in *The Birth of Tragedy*. Taken as very general perspectives on the world, or world views, or projections which create worlds, the Apollinian attitude, with its penchant for openness and distance and light, seems analogous to the power of world, while the Dionysian, with its more feminine darkness and closeness and blurring of borders, would correspond to the power of earth.

HEIDEGGER:
The contention is not a rift [*Riss*] as in the tearing open of a mere gap, but is rather the interiority of the belonging-to-one-

another of the contenders. This rift draws the opponents together
into the origin of their unity from a single ground. . . . The *Riss*
does not let the opponents burst apart, but brings the opposition
of measure and border into a unitary outline [*Umriss*].

STUDENT A [*looking at the* t'ai chi *symbol he has been drawing in his
notebook*]:

Since *Riss* means "line" as well as "rift," it
could also refer to the line between the *yin*
and *yang* in the *t'ai chi* symbol and the outline [*Umriss*] bounding them. And since
Heidegger further characterizes the *Riss* as
the image of the primordial contention of
truth as the opposition between revelation
and concealment, it would correspond to
tao as the "single ground" of the origin of
the unity of *yin* and *yang*.[56]

HEIDEGGER:

[The issue of truth could not even come up] if the unconcealment of what-is had not exposed us to that clearing into which all
beings stand and from which they withdraw. . . .

This clearing . . . this open middle is not surrounded by what-
is, but the illuminating middle itself surrounds—like Nothing,
which we hardly know—all that is.

Every being that is encountered maintains this strangely ambiguous presence, in that it always simultaneously holds itself back in
concealment. . . .

In this way, self-concealing Being is illuminated.[57]

LAO-TZU:

The Way is empty, yet use will not drain it.
Deep, it is like the ancestor of the myriad things.
Abysmal, it only seems as if it were there.
I do not know whose son it is.
It images the forefather of the Gods.[58]

CHUANG-TZU:

The myriad things have somewhere from which they grow but no
one sees the root, somewhere from which they come forth but no
one sees the gate. Men all honor what wit knows, but none
knows how to know by depending on what his wits do not know;
may that not be called the supreme uncertainty?[59]

STUDENT A [*waking up after having dozed off briefly*]:
It seems as if I was just sitting at the feet of a Chinese sage.
Something to do with the myriad things' entering into and with-
drawing from unconcealment?

[*Looks down at his notebook where someone has transcribed a
few lines from the* Chuang-tzu]

"While we dream we do not know that we are dreaming, and in
the middle of a dream interpret a dream within it; not until we
wake do we know that we were dreaming. Only at the ultimate
awakening shall we know that this is the ultimate dream."[60]

Was I just dreaming that I was listening to Lao-Chuang? Or is
this all Professor Heidegger's dream? Or shall I wake up to find
I'm a butterfly dreaming it was in a lecture theatre? Is *this* what
Chuang-tzu means by "the transformations of things"?

Notes

The present form of this essay is the latest in a series of transformations. It was
first written in German and presented under the title "Laotse, Tschuangtse, und
der frühe Heidegger" at a meeting of Die Gesellschaft für die Erforschung der
gegenwärtigen Philosophie in Kyoto in June of 1983. After being revised and
translated into Japanese, it appeared in the journal *Risō*, no. 608 (Tokyo, January 1984), under the title "Haidegga to Rō-Sō shisō: mu no yō, sono kanōsei wo
megutte." An expanded English version, "Intimations of Taoist Ideas in Early
Heidegger," was published in *The Journal of Chinese Philosophy,* vol. 11, no. 4
(1984). The core ideas remain more or less the same in this latest essay, though
since they are developed here with reference to different parts of the texts and in a
different form, there is little overlap.

The epigraph from Heraclitus is from (Diels-Kranz) fragment 123: "[The true]
Being/nature [of things] loves to hide."

1. Martin Buber (hrsg.), *Reden und Gleichnisse des Tschuang-Tse* (Leipzig:
Insel Verlag, 1921), p. 62. The translation has been slightly modified in the light
of the translation by A. C. Graham—see below, note 4—p. 123.

2. The scenario is based on the account given by Heinrich Wiegand Petzet in
Günther Neske (ed.), *Erinnerung an Martin Heidegger* (Pfullingen: Neske,
1977), pp. 183–184, and in his book *Auf einen Stern zugehen* (Frankfurt: 1983),
p. 24.

3. *"Vom Wesen der Wahrheit,"* in *Wegmarken* (Frankfurt: Klostermann,
1967), pp. 81–83; D. F. Krell (ed.), *Martin Heidegger: Basic Writings* (New
York: Harper and Row, 1977), pp. 125–127.

4. The *Tao Te Ching,* attributed to Lao-tzu, is the better known of the two
great works of philosophical Taoism, the other being the anthology known as the
Chuang-tzu. For the former I have used the translation by D. C. Lau, *Lao Tzu:
Tao Te Ching* (Penguin Books, 1963), and also Ch'en Ku-ying, *Lao Tzu: Text,
Notes and Comments,* translated by Rhett W. Young and Roger T. Ames (San

Francisco: Chinese Materials Center, 1977). A revised translation by Professor Lau, based on the Ma Wang Tui manuscripts, has been published recently in a bilingual edition under the same title (Hong Kong: Chinese University Press, 1982). In quoting from *Chuang-tzu* I shall refer to the chapter number and also to the partial translation by A. C. Graham, *Chuang-tzu: The Inner Chapters* (London: George Allen and Unwin, 1981), henceforth abbreviated as *IC* followed by the page number. Professor Graham's seems to me the philosophically most insightful of the extant translations, and is furnished with an illuminating commentary. It also has the great virtue of retaining intact the crazy patchwork texture of the text, rather than distorting it by smoothing it out into a seamless whole.

Both the *Chuang-tzu* and the *Lao-tzu* are anthologies compiled by a succession of editors. The traditional view used to be that Lao-tzu was an older contemporary of Confucius, but Professor Lau argues convincingly in appendix 1 of his translation that it is doubtful whether Lao-tzu was in fact a historical person at all, and that the text probably dates from as late as the third century B.C. Of the thirty-three extant chapters of the *Chuang-tzu*, which appear to date from the fourth, third and second centuries B.C., the first seven, known as the "Inner Chapters," are thought to come from the same hand—that of Chuang Chou (Chuang-tzu), who flourished probably around the end of the fourth century B.C.

5. *Identität und Differenz* (Pfullingen: Neske, 1957), p. 25; *Identity and Difference* (New York: Harper and Row, 1969), p. 36.

6. *Unterwegs zur Sprache* (Pfullingen: Neske, 1959), p. 198; *On the Way to Language* (New York: Harper and Row, 1971), p. 92.

7. Chang Chung-yuan, "The Philosophy of Taoism according to Chuang Tzu," *Philosophy East and West* 27, no. 4 (1977).

8. Chang Chung-yuan has done the most work on the comparison with Taoism—though he focuses almost exclusively on the later Heidegger: see, in particular, *Tao: A New Way of Thinking* (New York: Harper and Row, 1975), and *Creativity and Taoism* (New York: Harper and Row, 1970). There is, however, the danger in working exclusively with the later writings that their poetic style, because it admits of freer interpretations, also allows greater possibility of distortion in the interests of comparison.

9. Since nobody has yet looked at the work of the middle period from the comparative point of view, the epilogue will play with excerpts from works published shortly after *SZ*, up to the second book on Kant, *Die Frage nach dem Ding* (Tübingen: Niemeyer, 1962), which is based on lectures given in the winter semester 1935–36 (English translation by W. B. Barton and Vera Deutsch, *What Is a Thing?* [Chicago: Regnery, 1967]).

Buber's edition of *Chuang-tzu* was published in 1921, so Heidegger could have read it before authoring *SZ*. However, given how wary he was of assimilating philosophical influences—and especially in the case of a philosophy couched in a language so alien to his mother tongue—any comparable themes discovered in the works of the few years following his first exposure to Asian thought will still be of significance.

10. "Zur Erörterung der Gelassenheit: Aus einem Feldgspräch über das Denken" (1945), in *Gelassenheit* (Pfullingen: Neske, 1959), and "Aus einem Gespräch von der Sprache" (1954) in *Unterwegs zur Sprache;* English translations in John M. Anderson and E. Hans Freund (trs.), *Discourse on Thinking* (New York: Harper and Row, 1966), and *On the Way to Language*. Both dialogues were based on actual conversations, but were considerably re-worked by

Heidegger. The Heraclitus seminars conducted with Eugen Fink *(Heraklit)* were published in the form of a dialogue but are closer to transcripts than something written by Heidegger himself.

In the *Vorbemerkung* to *Einführung in die Metaphysik* Heidegger writes (presumably without having said it): "What has been spoken no longer speaks in what has been printed." *Einführung in die Metaphysik* (Tübingen: Niemeyer, 1953); *An Introduction to Metaphysics,* trans. Ralph Manheim (New Haven: Yale University Press, 1959)—hereafter abbreviated as *EM* and *IM* respectively.

11. A comparison of the ideas of Heraclitus and Lao-Chuang would be a fascinating study in its own right. For a sketch of fruitful areas of comparison between Taoism and a late Western scion of Heraclitus, Nietzsche, see Graham Parkes, "The Wandering Dance: *Chuang-tzu* and *Zarathustra,*" *Philosophy East and West* 29, no. 3 (1983).

12. Heidegger's intuition that the *logos* of Heraclitus and the *tao* are comparable is on the mark—and to examine the similarities between the two ideas could be an illuminating instance of explicating *obscurum per obscurius.* The fragments concerning the cyclical transformations of the cosmic elements have obvious counterparts in Taoist cosmology, and Heraclitus' understanding of the mutual interdependence of opposites and the relativity of all perspectives harmonizes closely with the thought of *Chuang-tzu.* A thorough comparison would examine the deeper implications of such comparable utterances as the following (the numbers of Heraclitus' fragments are preceded by H, and the chapters of *Chuang-tzu* and *Lao-tzu* by C and L respectively): H50, C1; H102, C2; H111, L2; H88, C6; H61, C18; H103, C17/27; H40, L81; L40.

13. The language of *SZ* is undeniably innovative, though few of the neologisms are elegant. The text is characterized by a multitude of subtle interconnections and word plays, some but by no means all of which have been pointed out by Macquarrie and Robinson in their footnotes. The language also has powerful "body" which has gone largely unnoticed by commentators.

14. *Sein und Zeit* (Tübingen: Niemeyer, 1967), p. 311; *Being and Time,* trans. John Macquarrie and Edward Robinson (New York: Harper and Row, 1962), p. 359. Cf. also *SZ* 327: "Acts of violence are in this field not capriciousness but rather a necessity grounded in the issue itself."

References to *SZ* will be given hereafter in the body of the text simply by way of the page number (the pagination of the German edition is given in the margins of the Macquarrie and Robinson translation). All translations from the German are mine.

15. The terms *das Zuhandene* and *das Vorhandene* defy elegant translation. In an attempt to preserve something of the simple similarity of these terms they will be rendered as "[what is] to-hand" and "on-hand" respectively. Heidegger emphasizes in his use of *das Vorhandene,* which is a common word in German, the connotation of "objective" or "neutral presence," whereas he uses *das Zuhandene* so much as a technical term that it comes close to being a neologism. In both cases it is important to retain the "hand" of the original German in view of the philosophical import of the somatic metaphors in *SZ.*

16. The problem of the natural in Taoism is compounded by the fact that there is no single term in Taoist vocabulary that corresponds exactly to our word "nature" in the sense of the natural world. The one that comes closest is *t'ien,* or "heaven"—especially when it occurs in the compound *t'ien ti,* meaning "heaven-and-earth." Two relevant terms that are distinctively Taoist are *chen,* meaning "genuine, authentic, true," and *tzu jan,* meaning "spontaneous activity" or, more literally, "self so-ing."

17. Hildegard Feick, *Index zu Heideggers "Sein und Zeit"* (Tübingen: Niemeyer, 1968), p. 63. (Omits one of the more important references—*SZ* 362.)

18. Macquarrie and Robinson opt for "equipment," which has the advantage that it catches the primary feature of *Zeug* which is that there is no such thing as "a" single, isolated "equipment."

19. It is not clear why Heidegger changes his example from writing utensils to hammers, since he could make all the same points about handiness, and make them more vividly, with reference to his immediate activity of using a pen to write the text of *SZ*. Perhaps Nietzsche's enterprise (made explicit in the preface to *Twilight of the Idols*) of "philosophizing with a hammer" is a subliminal influence here—though his penchant for percussing idols with a hammer "as with a tuning fork" is exercised in the workshop of traditional philosophical ideas and ideals.

20. Heidegger repeatedly remarks that most of our everyday activities are carried out without any theoretical reflection or thematized understanding, but rather in the light of a "pre-ontological understanding" based on *Umsicht*. While Macquarrie and Robinson's choice of "circumspection" for *Umsicht* has the virtue of being a straightforward translation of the German word, it fails to reflect the distinctive meaning Heidegger gives to the term. They are right to note that "Heidegger is taking advantage of the fact that the prefix *'um'* may mean 'around' or 'in order to' " (footnote 2 on p. 98 of *Being and Time*). Heidegger does want to emphasize that *Umsicht* involves peripheral rather than sharply focused vision (and in this sense it corresponds to the "soft focus" and global appreciation of the entire situation that is the precondition for Taoist spontaneity). But, especially when talking about inauthentic everydayness, he lays much more stress on the meaning "in order to"—to emphasize that in the light of *Umsicht* we see and understand things in terms of what they are "for." For this reason "for-sight" would be an appropriate translation (even though the German word is not a neologism), especially if we can hear in it an overtone of the understanding of future possibilities. Far from conveying a sense of circumspection, the term suggests a certain confidence in dealing with things that is grounded in our pre-ontological familiarity with how they work. As long as the hammering is going well, one's hand can pick up more nails without one's having to look over at the can in which they are stored.

21. *Das Eigentümliche des zunächst Zuhandenen ist es, in seiner Zuhandenheit sich gleichsam zurückzuziehen, um gerade eigentlich zuhanden zu sein* (*SZ* 69). This is reminiscent of Chuang-tzu's remark that "When one has the proper shoes one forgets one's feet" (ch. 19).

22. Toward the end of the book Heidegger takes up the topic (in the passage overlooked by Feick) of the *a priori* "mathematical projection of nature" that is the prerequisite for modern scientific discovery—a theme he was to develop fully in the second book on Kant in 1935–36.

23. "Vom Wesen des Grundes," in *Wegmarken*, p. 51; *The Essence of Reasons,* trans. Terrence Malik (Evanston: Northwestern University Press, 1969), pp. 80–83.

24. The particular passage Heidegger is referring to on *SZ* 65 says that even the "Romantic conception of nature" must be understood on the basis of the concept of world. Be that as it may, it is nevertheless strange—in view of the traditional interest in nature on the part of German philosophers from Kant through the *Naturphilosophen* and up to Schopenhauer and Nietzsche—that Heidegger discusses it so little in *SZ*. This would have been more understandable had he been an insensitive city-dweller; but his love of living close to the land is well known—and evident from the content of his later essays.

25. There is a danger in the common (and well-justified) practice of leaving the term *Dasein* untranslated, that the reader may simply mouth the German term, forgetting that *Dasein* is always mine, yours, ours. While *Dasein* is an ordinary word for "existence," Heidegger made it into such a special term that there is some justification for rendering it by the written neologism "being-(t)here." While not a particularly attractive word to look at (and difficult to pronounce), it has the advantage of conveying the ambiguity of the German primal syllable *da,* which means both "here" and "there." To write "being-(t)here" and say "being here and there" invites us to hear the "here" and "there" both spatially and temporally: "here/now" (anywhere) and "there/then" (any other time—future or past).

26. "Der Ursprung des Kunstwerkes," in *Holzwege* (Frankfurt: Klostermann, 1972)—subsequent references will be abbreviated *UK* and followed by the page number in *Holzwege;* "The Origin of the Work of Art," in *Poetry, Language, Thought,* trans. Albert Hofstadter (New York: Harper and Row, 1975)—hereafter *OWA.* Any impression that the proper attitude toward things is merely technological is quickly dispelled by this essay, a major concern of which is to describe a way of relating to things that is quite different from taking them as to- or on-hand. The work of art, whose essential nature cannot be appreciated if it is taken as an implement or an object of scientific investigation, is to be seen here as a paradigm of things in general. The "Epilogue" will point up the distinctly Taoist tone to what, for Heidegger, is the appropriate attitude to the work and the thing.

27. *IC* 73. There are four passages about useless trees in chapter 4 (*IC* 72–75), one at the end of ch. 1 (*IC* 47), and another in ch. 20 (*IC* 121).

28. Aside from the well-known story of Cook Ting, the adept carver of oxes, in the Inner Chapters (ch. 3, *IC* 63), there is the wheelwright Pien of chapter 13 (*IC* 139–140), the buckle forger in chapter 22 (*IC* 139), and the stories of numerous woodworkers and other artisans collected in chapter 19 (*IC* 135–138). Several consummate swimmers—the human counterpart to the many fish that swim through the *Chuang-tzu*—play roles as models for our behavior. (Heidegger would no doubt want to include skillful skiers.)

29. "Nachwort zu: 'Was Ist Metaphysik?',", in *Wegmarken,* p. 106; *Was Heisst Denken?* (Tübingen: Niemeyer, 1954), p. 51; *What is Called Thinking?,* trans. J. Glenn Gray (New York: Harper and Row, 1968), p. 16. This is *besinnendes* as opposed to *rechnendes Denken,* sensitive and meditative rather than calculative thinking. This is comparable to the distinction in *Chuang-tzu* between *lun,* a kind of "sorting" which "evens things out" rather than ranks, and *pien,* which denotes the kind of thinking that discriminates between opposites and weighs alternative courses of action. (See Graham's discussion of these two in *IC* 12.)

30. See Otto Pöggeler's discussion of Heidegger's interest in these artists, *supra;* and see also his book, *Die Frage nach der Kunst: von Hegel zu Heidegger* (Freiburg/München: Alber, 1984).

31. See David Levin's discussion of *mudra, infra.*

32. This suggestion may appear to contradict Heidegger's saying in almost the next breath, then writing on the next page, that "Sokrates is the purest thinker of the West. Therefore he wrote nothing" (*Was Heisst Denken?,* pp. 51–52; *What Is Called Thinking?,* pp. 16–17).

33. "Description without Place." Wallace Stevens apparently knew little about Heidegger and less about Taoism. However, sometimes he simply seems to say it better than anybody else.

34. Emptiness—whether of things, the self, or of *tao*—is a major theme in

Taoism; see Graham Parkes, "Intimations of Taoist Ideas in Early Heidegger," *The Journal of Chinese Philosophy* 11, no. 4 (1984).

35. "Das Ding," in *Vorträge und Aufsätze* (Pfullingen: Neske, 1967); "The Thing," in *Poetry, Language, Thought*—hereafter *PLT*).

36. "Nachwort zu: 'Was Ist Metaphysik?'," in *Wegmarken*, p. 103. While there are no extended discussions of death in later Heidegger, the topic retains a central position: as "the shrine of nothingess" death is still our sole access to Being itself (*VA* 177; *PLT* 200). The only substantial treatment in the later work is in the essay on Rilke, "Wozu Dichter?," where Heidegger elaborates a position aligned with Rilke's, regarding "Death and the realm of the dead [as belonging] to the totality of beings as its other side" (*Holzwege*, p. 279; *PLT* 124).

37. "*Was Ist Metaphysik?*" (Frankfurt: Klostermann, 1981), pp. 32–34; *Basic Writings*, pp. 102–105.

38. Ch. 19, *IC* 182; ch. 6, *IC* 85; ch. 2, *IC* 52.

39. For an explication of Heidegger's position on death (quite compatible with Taoism's) see Graham Parkes, "Heidegger on Death: The Force of *Angst*," forthcoming.

40. *SZ* 288 and 295. It is significant that the word Heidegger chooses for the operation of the authentic self *(handeln)* has "hand" as its root.

41. *SZ* 385 and 310. The only mention of "joy" *(Freude)* in *SZ* occurs, significantly, in this context of giving death power over one's existence (310). Heidegger speaks later of the necessity of letting death become powerful in one's being *(den Tod in sich mächtig werden [lassen])* so that one can experience one's fate historically (384).

42. *SZ* 297. At the same time he characterizes the disclosedness of world as "the release *(Freigabe)* of the current involvement-totality of what is to-hand."

43. This time Heidegger presses the point home by playing on the word *zu,* "[in order] to": "This simply shows that what is to-hand belongs *to* something else to-hand *(Darin aber bekundet sich die Zugehörigkeit des gerade Zuhandenen zu einem anderen)*" (353).

44. As Angus Graham remarks: "The 'Primitivist' writer is unrepresentative, as we imply by giving him that name" (*IC* 185). Cf. his comments on the well-sweep story (*IC* 186), and also Otto Pöggeler's discussion of it, *supra*.

45. This "simultaneous Yes and No" actually constitutes "releasement towards things *(Gelassenheit zu den Dingen)*" (*Gelassenheit*, p. 23; *Discourse on Thinking*, p. 54).

46. In "The Origin of the Work of Art" and "What Is Metaphysics?" respectively.

47. The year 1935–36 was a particularly productive one for Heidegger. The lecture notes from two courses from that year were published as two of his best books, *Einführung in die Metaphysik* and *Die Frage nach dem Ding*, and lectures given outside the university during that period were published as his most extended meditation on the work of art, "Der Ursprung des Kunstwerkes." Heidegger's words are taken from *EM* 23, *IM* 30.

48. For the rest of this section Heidegger's words are taken from *FD* 14–16.

49. *UK* 14–21, *OWA* 25–32.

50. *UK* 21, *OWA* 32.

51. All Heidegger's words from here on are taken from the second and third sections of *UK*.

52. Richard Wilhelm (tr.), *I Ging: Das Buch der Wandlungen* (Düsseldorf/Köln: Diederichs, 1970). Wilhelm's translation of the *I Ching* with commentary

was first published in 1923. The translation of his translation by Cary F. Baynes, *I Ching: The Book of Changes* (Princeton: Bollingen Series, 1967), has become the definitive edition in English.

The distinction between *Erde* and *Welt* also corresponds to Schelling's distinction between *Grund* and *Existenz* (ground and existence) as articulated in his essay on Human Freedom (1809). Heidegger devoted a semester's course to lectures on this text in 1936, which have been published as *Schellings Abhandlung über das Wesen der menschlichen Freiheit* (Tübingen: Niemeyer, 1971). The reciprocal relationship between *Grund* and *Existenz* together with a number of related ideas in Schelling's essay have a remarkably Taoist tone to them, independently of Heidegger's interpretation. An interesting comparison of Schelling's thought with Taoism and T'ien-t'ai Buddhism can be found in Bruno Petzold, *Die Quintessenz der T'ien-T'ai-(Tendai-)Lehre,* edited by Horst Hammitzsch (Wiesbaden: Harrassowitz, 1982).

53. Heisenberg recounts a conversation from the early thirties in which Bohr says, "In principle, we could probably measure the position of every atom in a cell, thought hardly without killing the living cell in the process. What we would know in the end would be the arrangement of the atoms in a dead cell, not a living one" (Werner Heisenberg, *Physics and Beyond* [New York: Harper and Row, 1972], p. 111). It is interesting that in another conversation with Bohr the following year Heisenberg mentions the Chinese idea of *tao* (p. 136).

54. *So ist in jedem der sich verschliessenden Dinge das gleiche Sich-nicht-Kennen* (*UK* 36, *OWA* 47). The final phrase is ambiguous. Albert Hofstadter takes the *Sich* as plural rather than singular, and so translates it: "the same not-knowing-of-one-another." While this reading is grammatically possible, it seems to go against the sense of "reciprocal harmony" just mentioned. Things have sufficient self-enclosing tendencies to keep them from merging into total undifferentiation —but presumably could not flow together in reciprocal harmony if they did not know each other at all.

55. *Streit* is difficult to translate here, since Heidegger specifically dispels connotations of "strife" and "struggle." He probably has in mind Heraclitus' notion of *polemos*—since he mentions fragment 53 earlier in the essay (*UK* 32, *OWA* 43) —which has in any case a very Taoist ring to it.

56. The comparison *Welt/Erde* and *yang/yin* prompts a further reflection. Just as the latter are so primordial that they operate as powers in the human psyche as well as in the cosmos as a whole, so world and earth might also be thought of in regard to the distinction between consciousness and the unconscious in depth psychology.

57. *Dergestalt ist das sichverbergende Sein gelichtet* (*UK* 44, *OWA* 56).

58. *Tao Te Ching,* ch. 4.

59. *Chuang-tzu* 25, *IC* 102.

60. *Chuang-tzu* 2, *IC* 59–60.

Keiji Nishitani

Reflections on Two Addresses
by Martin Heidegger

I

With the encounter of East and West proceeding in all fields of human activity at a surprisingly rapid tempo, mutual understanding is, needless to say, one of the most important tasks facing mankind today. Among the many difficulties lying hidden along the way of this task, the greatest appears when, trying to penetrate in some degree the inner thought, feelings and purposes of our copartners, we find words and concepts, the inevitable vehicles of this communication, rising up time and again to bar the way.

In that region near the innermost core of the mind, in the region of things spritual, the above-mentioned difficulty becomes almost insurmountable. It is especially so in the case of encounter between world-religions, such as Buddhism and Christianity, where the differences between the religious faiths, residing in the innermost mental core of both sides, are concerned. In each of them, their own faith or insight has long been formulated into creed and authoritatively laid down as dogma predominating over all that men think, feel or will, so that people become firmly convinced of their own opinions and come to have great confidence in themselves. Often their conviction and self-confidence are armored by sharp analysis and subtle dialectics which are developed in dogmatics. In short, the religious faith or insight is translated into words and concepts, and these give birth to dogma and dogmatics, which, in turn, serve to confirm that faith or insight. Here is a process in which faith is brought closer and closer to itself, thereby becoming more firm and more self-confirmed, and thus more enclosed within itself. Such is the process that occurs in most cases within the innermost mind in religious thinking, and therein arises the extreme difficulty of mutual understanding between minds of different religious faiths.

145

Of course, dogmatics has not always been narrowly enclosed by dogma. By the very causes that make the establishment of dogmatics necessary (the needs, for instance, of defending the dogma against criticism from without), religion is compelled to accept from philosophy as many concepts and theories as are useful to its purposes. Dogmatics comes in this way to contain elements which make a dialogue with "outsiders" possible; it becomes in this way more or less open-minded and is enabled to exist as an open system. But however open-minded it may become, even when its system is made as open as possible, so long as it remains dogmatics, that is, so long as it stands on an exclusively closed basis of faith and dogma, it can never avert the above-mentioned procedure: it must produce, in all its own efforts to become "open," a means to confirm itself alone. And thus, as it becomes more "open," it must become all the more firmly closed. It is compelled to return to its original enclosure, making futile all its "openness." It thus betrays itself, and allows mutual understanding to remain despairingly difficult.

But however hard it may be, in order to pave the way to mutual understanding, we must descend to the region of faith and dogma, where the aforementioned extreme difficulty appears; because that region is, after all, the deepest plane mankind has yet attained in his long history. The encounter of East and West cannot be ultimate as long as it does not plumb that region where resides the marrow of the mind of men. But, as we have seen, this region is at the same time the very place where the most troublesome *aporia* arises to thwart mutual understanding. The encounter cannot truly take place there, for on that plane (of faith and dogma) even a world-religion, however open it may be within its own confines, still remains closed against any other world-religion. And between two closed systems there can only be collision, not an encounter in any true sense.

We should, therefore, after once arriving at the plane of faith and dogma, break through it and search beyond it on some deeper plane for the possibility of encounter and mutual understanding in a true sense; an entirely new plane, where perhaps the innermost core of man's mind, as we usually understand it, should also be broken through. We are standing today before a trenchant requirement; to transcend our innermost spiritual forms and norms, the rigid framework of dogma and dogmatics. This requirement is a trenchant one, because it calls upon us to return to our basic "self" beyond all dogma, to strip ourselves once and for all of those fixed forms and norms enclosing our thoughts, feelings and volitions within ready made and seemingly eternal frames. It calls upon us to return to the most basic plane where man is solely man or is merely a son of man, no more, no less, where he is thoroughly bare, bare-headed, bare-backed, bare-handed and bare-footed, but where he can bare his innermost heart as well. It is as if we were demanded to walk bare-footed the city of "the variegated cow" as Nietzsche called it,—a world multi-colored with miscellaneous forms. However hard it may be, to descend in ourselves to such a basic plane seems necessary in order to prepare the open place for the true encounter in question.

But granted that such a procedure is today necessary, can we find in the actual world any clue at all for making the realization of that procedure possible? If so, what is it and where can we find it?

Now, that possibility seems to be comprised in no other than basic historical circumstance, which at present is necessitating an encounter of Buddhism and Christianity. I mean by this the situation in which now the whole world is rapidly becoming one world. Today, in almost all fields of human life, in industrial, economical and political activities, and in the arts, morality and philosophy, the one world is more and more emerging as the stage of their plays. There is no need to speak in this regard of science and technology. Their new inventions are making communication easier and speedier between distant parts of the globe. They are bringing at the same time, by their essential character of "objectivity," the minds of all peoples on to a common plane of thought and intention. They are the main actors in the drama of the emergence of the one world, necessitating the encounter of various cultures and religions.

This general current has been able to arise only through the process of "secularization," the process in which various sorts of man's activites have become emancipated one by one from the ban of religious dogma and dogmatics that have long commanded them. Today religion, with its dogma and dogmatics, stands aloof in the world, encased in itself, the sole exception to the world's general trend. In such a situation, the only possible way of a true encounter and mutual understanding of East and West in the most basic locus of human existence—in the innermost kernel of man's mind, heretofore shackled by dogma and dogmatics—seems to be discovered solely through candid self-exposure to the deep complexities of the actual world and by grasping therein some new point of departure. That would mean, in truth, to delve into the basis of existence itself through and through until we reach the hidden source; the source, in which originates the present emergence of the one world with its thorough and universal secularization of human life, and from which are arising now all sorts of social "progress" through the rapid development of science and technology, as well as the devastation of traditional culture progressing side by side with the "progress" of modern civilization. To expose oneself candidly to this situation of the actual world would then signify that we, everyone of us, become in the most simple and radical sense a "son of man" who has nowhere to lay his head. The word "simple" here means being a "son of man" stripped of all his traditional forms and norms, or, as expressed above, a "bare" man; the word "radical" means to be a "son of man" to whom all religious dogma and dogmatics would be the holes of foxes or nests of birds which he has *not*. Today no real encounter with Jesus seems to become possible without a descent to the deepest plane of our existence, on which everyone of us has nowhere to lay his head and is "homeless." Today "man should," as Bonhoeffer has said, "live in the presence of God, as if there were no God." On that plane alone can we become qualified for the commencement of the quest for the way to exist truly in the emerging one world and thus qualified to search for a way of true encounter between East and West.

II

In his speech "Ansprache zum Heimatabend," delivered in 1961 in Messkirch, the place of his birth, Heidegger begins with the problem of the *Heimat* ("home" in the sense of native place). In our age of modern technology, we are, he thinks, essentially reduced to the state of home-lessness. By television and radio, for instance, we are continually trans-ported abroad, although we think of ourselves always to be at home. We live in truth amidst *das Unheimische* (the un-"home"-like). Heidegger speaks then of *das Unheimliche* (the uncanny) that reigns in the sphere of *das Unheimische,* haunts man wandering there, and draws him into the state of homelessness *(Heimatlosigkeit)*. What then will man be like in the future? Heidegger says, "Perhaps man is settling into homelessness. Perhaps the connection with the *Heimat* is vanishing from the existence of modern man." But he then continues, "Perhaps, however, in the midst also of the pressing *Unheimische* a new relation to the *Heimische* is being prepared." What does he mean by this? Within our constant escape into something new, newer and newest, there lurks a deep boredom *(Lange-weile),* in which time hangs heavy upon us; this boredom floats within the abysses of existence like a fog driven to and fro. In this boredom is concealed a home-sickness. Boredom is the veil of the home-sickness, which is a longing for the home, a drive towards the home. In the midst of homelessness, there occurs a drive towards the home. The fact that man is perpetually on the way of escape into the *Unheimische* indicates the presence of an impelling drive to the *Heimat,* which is none other than home-sickness. Perhaps deep boredom is the hidden, unconfessed drive to the *Heimat,* the drive which we thrust away and yet are unable to evade. In the depression of the hidden home-sickness, the home presents itself with more pressure upon us than anywhere else. There-fore, Heidegger says further: "Thus in all un-home-like things the home we seek, although veiled, yet comes to us." Because it comes to touch us in such a form again and again, we should go out to meet it. But how? In such a way that we are willing to preserve that, whence we have come. Right in the midst of that homelessness which, lurking in the future, comes to haunt us at present, we can find a way to the place of our origination. That place, the home, is no other than what "sustains us in the core of our existence *(was uns im Kern unseres Daseins trägt)*." Stepping forward into the future to meet it, we tread backward towards it. Thus alone can we preserve home in the midst of our homelessness.

Buddhism also knew, from its beginning, this homelessness. Moreover, the Buddha and his disciples chose voluntarily the life of the homeless. In order to emancipate themselves thoroughly from this world with its suffering, from the transitoriness of all things and the birth and death of their own being, they made up their minds to sever all threads of attachment. This was a turn-about similar to that stated above: the turnabout consisting of the return to the "son of man" in its simple and radical sense. The Buddha said, "Hear ye who have ears; give up thine own faith *(saddhā)*." While the teachers of the *Upanishads* gathered around them only limited groups of men who accepted some definite faith, the Buddha broke that limit, established a universal standpoint and preached to all kinds of men. He went down to the basis of human existence prior to any sort of "home." There, he then transcended all attachments, became completed and was emancipated into the great repose called nirvana. He became the Awakened One; he became "the knower of all," "the conqueror of all," and "the one who knows himself."

This awakening, this attainment of repose in the midst of transitoriness, can mean a way of discovering the home in the immediate midst of homelessness, as is also pointed out by Heidegger. Of course, this does not signify an escape from this world to some other world. The transcendence of this world was compared, to be sure, to an escape from a burning house, but the true meaning of it lies in becoming truly awakened, in becoming the awakened one, or in awakening to the true Self. Nirvana signifies living as an awakened one (as the Awakened One) in this world, that is to say, to "live" in the true sense. Apart from this "life," the "other world" could be only a world of fancy conceived by a man remaining attached to this world; it cannot be our "home."

Needless to say, the above-stated way of awakening in the Buddha was afterwards inherited and developed in Mahayana Buddhism. It would here suffice to be reminded of the famous phrase in the sayings of Rinzai: "not to leave one's house, while being on the way" and "not to be on the way, while leaving one's house." In Pure Land Buddhism, the Pure Land used to be called "the home." In this case also, the concept of the "home" is essentially connected with awakening of the Amida Buddha, although it has assumed the character of the other world in the devout aspirations of the converts.

The vocation of Buddhists today is two-sided. On the one side, a Buddhist must seek, amidst the uncanny homelessness of the present technological age, amidst the wide-spread situation of man's estrangement from himself, the way back to his *Heimat* or, as Heidegger has put it, to that which sustains man in the core of his existence. On the other side, he must strive to recover, in and through the same situation of estrangement, his own authentic way of awakening and to revive Buddhism for the present age. This effort is at the same time an effort to shed all ready-made dogmas and dogmatics, because the above said situation of estrangement acts as a cathartic fire for Buddhism as well as for other religions. As the Buddhistic way of awakening itself signifies the return to and repose in the *Heimat,* it is clear that these two sides are united in one and the same task.

Christianity also is certainly burdened today with the same task of indicating the way home to a wandering mankind. Man, in becoming a wanderer, can be said essentially to have become self-indebted, and his deliverance from that debt is now the common task of all potent religions. This task is the debt with which religions today are saddled for the sake of mankind.

Thus far, we have tried to take up, in regard to Heidegger's first address, the most fundamental point that seems to be in contact with Buddhism, which may help somewhat the mutual understanding of East and West.

III

In a second address delivered in his home town in 1964, "Über Abraham a Santa Clara," instead of expressing his own thought, Heidegger speaks of a seventeenth century preacher, who had also been a pupil of the school of Messkirch. The drastic speeches here quoted of this vigorous Catholic preacher contain words which might deeply impress Buddhists. For instance, he speaks of the mass deaths of a plague in Vienna, "I have seen that Death is a mower, who cuts down with his scythe not only the low clover but also the high growing grass. I have seen that Death is a gardener, who breaks to pieces not only the violets clinging to earth but also the high ascending larkspurs . . . I have seen that Death is a thunderbolt, that hits not only the transparent straw-huts but also the most translucent houses of monarchs." What he goes on to say is especially interesting: "I have seen *Leiber* (bodies of living beings), not *Leiber*; I will say *Körper* (material bodies), not *Körper*; I will say bones, not bones; I will say dust, not dust; I will say the Nothingness *(das Nichts)* of the crowned kaisers and monarchs." But the most interesting is the phrase which is quoted next; "man—this five foot long Nothingness."

Heidegger comments on this passage, a passage poignant and humorous at the same time: "The very contradiction between the Nothingness and the length of five feet tells the truth, that earthly magnitude and the emptiness of its meaning belong together." To men of Zen, however, this phrase may sound almost like Zen. But Zen would then contrive further to turn the interpretation advocated by most Christians, including, perhaps, Abraham a Santa Clara himself. This turn-about would be made possible by breaking through the Nothingness here mentioned and by opening beyond it a still deeper dimension of the Nothingness, namely that of the Buddhist *Śūnyatā,* as it is curtly stated in the basic Mahayana thesis, "Form is no other than Emptiness; Emptiness is no other than Form." (We may also say "things" instead of "Form.")

Here, a turn-about must necessarily occur. Standing on this new dimension, Zen approaches the same phrases, "man—this five foot long Nothingness," from the opposite direction, so that it is now taken up in a wholly new light, the accent being put on the "five foot long" instead of the "Nothingness." It would then be possible to come back from the length of five feet to dust, not dust; I will say bones, not bones; I will say corpses, not corpses; I will say living bodies with flesh and blood. The "five foot long Nothingness" is, as such, a five foot long living body.

Jōshū, the Chinese Zen master of the ninth century, when asked, "Is there Buddha-nature in a dog?" answered, "None (Nothingness)." This is a well known kōan. The Nothingness in this answer does not mean, of course, that which is conceived of merely as something opposite to Being. It lies beyond the alternative of "to be" and "not to be." Therefore Jōshū could on another occasion answer, "There is (Being)," to the same question. Whether in the case of "None" or in that of "Being," we must not remain on the dimension of the alternatives, where both termini are taken up merely as words or concepts and drawn into logical or semantical interpretations. When the words "Being" or "Nothingness" are presented from the dimension beyond duality, by someone, say Jōshū, who stands existentially on that dimension, then we ought at the same time to fix our eyes on the one who is there speaking. We must pay attention to the whole of the actual occasion, or, rather, to the togetherness in the whole: to that whole consisting of the chance theme, "a dog" for example, the words spoken, ourselves who just are listening, and especially the speaker himself. Jōshū, the speaker on that occasion, standing beyond all alternatives, embodies absolute freedom and can give to the dog or rob it of its essential "Being" (namely the Buddha-nature inherent to it) as he likes. This Jōshū, embodying absolute freedom, exists in his five foot long body side by side with all other bodies and sits near the questioning monk and, also perhaps, near the dog in question. He looks at them, hears the question and speaks the words of answer. He is there, and where he is, there is also the place whence his words come, with which he bestows or takes back "Being" freely: the place whence the Being of a dog originates, and its two foot long Nothingness; the place, whence the Buddha-nature in all living beings comes forth and whence even all Buddhas originate—the above-mentioned *Heimat.* The same one, Jōshū, whose body is sitting there on a chair, is at the same time nowhere; he is the very "Nowhere," *Śūnyatā* (Nothingness) making the place of his Being, whence come also his words of answer. In this Nowhere he is absolutely free. And in this absolute freedom he is everywhere. He is, on the occasion above mentioned, there, where the dog is. He is wholly together "with" it, even while sitting next to it.

All of this together expresses the state of *satori.*

We have above quoted Heidegger's comment to the phrase "man—this five foot Nothingness." He asserts that in the very togetherness of the contradictory factors, the Nothingness and the five foot length, the truth becomes manifest: the truth of the togetherness of earthly magnitude and the emptiness of its meaning. We cannot see clearly, at least from this address alone, the thorough implication he gave here to the words, "truth" and "together." He, too, may have interpreted the phrase along the line of usual interpretation; namely to the effect of the meaninglessness of earthly things, of *vanitas vanitatis.* Heidegger says, however, in another part of this address, "There awoke in the second half of the seventeenth century a new spirit of creative affirmation and formation of the world *(schöpferische Weltbejahung und Weltgestaltung),*—the spirit of the Baroque." It may be then not altogether impossible to sense this new spirit behind the above mentioned phrase. We may be able to attribute some positive meaning to the gathering of those contradictory factors. Heidegger's saying about the "truth" of their togetherness may be interpreted as hinting not only at a negative truth but rather more at a positive one. Howsoever it may be, Zen at any rate can take the phrase as expressing a positive truth about man's essential mode of being.

The spirit of world-affirmation, man's positive attitude to the world, seems to be found in its full manifestation in another quote from Abraham a Santa Clara: "A man who dies before he dies, does not die when he dies." Heidegger comments on this sentence that it brings forward a decisive thought. This sentence would not sound strange if it had come from the mouth of a man of Zen. In fact, the same thought, in literally the same mode of expression, has been pronounced, we suppose, by a great number of Zen teachers. There is, for instance, a well-known Japanese *waka* of Shidō Bunan, a Zen master of the seventeenth century: "Become a dead man, remaining alive; become thoroughly dead; then do what you like, according to your own mind; all your works then are good." The first part of the poem: "To become a dead man, remaining alive," is an exhortation toward the Great Death as it is called in Zen. The latter part indicates the mode of man's being in *satori,* a life of work, absolutely free. The poem expresses that the way to *satori* is through the Great Death.

In the above-mentioned saying of the Christian preacher the spirit of creative world-affirmation through Death is breathing, it seems to me, as lively as in the poem of the Zen teacher. It might be in this sense that Heidegger found in this sayng a decisive thought. That was certainly the reason that we have dared in our interpretation to attribute a positive meaning to the phrase, "man—this five foot Nothingness."

IV

Finally, Heidegger remarks on the following profoundly poetic saying of the preacher: "Come here, you silver-white swans, who are rowing about on the water with your wings, in defiance of snow." He says, "Everyone knows that snow melts in the water and disappears. Swans, on the contrary, preserve a 'pure' whiteness with their very feathers. They thus carry the snow on, so to speak, over the waters. Swimming, they prevent the snow from sinking into the waters. The movement of the white swans on the waters is an image of the permanence in the most transitory things *(das Unvergängliche im Vergänglichsten).*" This reminds us of some similar poetical metaphors that are familiar in Zen; as "A white horse enters the flowering reeds" or "The thousand mountains covered with snow, why is a solitary peak not white?" We can at first sight hardly discriminate a white horse, trotting through the broad shallows covered with white reedflowers; there being only one color. It is difficult to search for it. But after a time, as our eyes get accustomed to the scene, the figure of the horse gradually becomes discernible and stands out conspicuously in the one color; like that "silver-whiteness" of the swans who defy the snow and its whiteness. From the ground of one color, emerges something which is equally colored, yet distinguishable from all other things; something solely different in the midst of the indifference of all. The above-mentioned metaphor of a "solitary peak" remaining unwhitened amidst the snow-covered thousand mountains is, therefore, an indication of the mode of being as in the metaphor of the white horse, only seen from the opposite side.

Both sides—the one white color, on the one hand, and the silver-whiteness of the swan or the figure of the white horse standing out in prominence within the reedflowers, on the other hand—or, in terms of philosophical categories, the side of oneness and the side of otherness, and likewise the side of indifference, identity, universality and that of difference, distinctiveness, singularity—are equally essential. Although the latter side "defies" the former and stands in contradiction to it, the otherness being the negation of the oneness, the difference the negation of the indifference, it must have in the former the ground that sustains it; it can only subsist, as a relief, by standing out in prominence within its own ground. The latter must, at the same time, "preserve" *(bewahren)* the former, elevating it to a higher plane, as swans preserve with their snowcovered wings "a pure whiteness." The whiteness of the snow appears on the swan's wings as shining silver-whiteness. The whiteness of the snow appears here in a truer degree of itself than is found in itself. It appears in its own ultimate reality, that is, as a "pure" whiteness. This silver-whiteness belongs, however, not only to the snow, as its heightened true color; it is also the color of the swans and also belongs to them. It is they that preserve, through their very swimming, the snow and prevent it from disappearing in the waters. "The movement of the white swans on the waters is an image of the permanence in the most transitory things." Isn't it also an expression of the spirit of the world-affirmation? Isn't it permissible to view this movement of the white swans as an image of a man who "dies before he dies and does not die when he dies?" If so, we could see here also an attitude deeply similar to that of Zen. But, although it is too hasty to say here "yes," the words of Abraham a Santa Clara and Heidegger's commentary on them are certainly moving, without their knowing of it, in the neighborhood of Zen and contain various points of contact with it.

The second speech can conduce especially to genuine contact between Christianity and Zen Buddhism, while the first implies a valuable suggestion as to the basic plane on which the encounter of Eastern and Western thought in general ought to occur.

Yasuo Yuasa

The Encounter of
Modern Japanese Philosophy
with Heidegger

It was on May 26, 1976, that Heidegger passed away. The news reached Japan on the following day. That night during the commentary hour of an NHK television program, the well-known newscaster Isomura mourned his death and recounted the philosopher's achievements, which started with *Being and Time*. At the end Isomura added that "a West German television station devoted only ten seconds to reporting this philosopher's death." For some reason this left an impression on me. I wondered if in the contemporary German intellectual world the name Heidegger had already faded from memory. No, it would seem rather that the contemporary intellectual situation of the world has itself dashed ahead into economic, scientific, and technological developments, leaving philosophy behind. The most essential event for man and philosophy is not talked about aloud in public. Heidegger's way of life in his later years, in which he chose to be a hermit off in a corner of the world, might perhaps be the path of destiny that contemporary philosophy itself ought to persevere in. It is an age of misfortune when, as in the fascist period before the war, an ideology, philosophically armed, is talked about aloud. It is also an age of misfortune when philosophy is completely forgotten. Heidegger lived and persevered through those two ages of misfortune and passed away.

There is probably general agreement that among philosophers in the contemporary world Heidegger has left the greatest as well as the most continuous influence on philosophy in Japan. Sartre gained popularity after World War Two, but his influence skidded somewhat on movements in journalism. In the following, I would like to offer my thoughts on the encounter of modern Japanese philosophy with Heidegger, first introducing the reader to modern Japanese philosophy and then taking up two philosophers, Kiyoshi Miki and Tetsurō Watsuji, as illustrative of this encounter. I have chosen these two philosophers because they attempted to go beyond Heidegger's philosophy in their own unique ways in spite of their having been strongly influenced by him. Much research has been published on Heidegger's philosophy and his works are still studied as texts in the philosophy departments in Japanese universities.

I. The Kyoto School

In Japan the period after 1868 (the Meiji Restoration) is called "modern" because at that time the feudal samurai period ended and the country began to accept wholly Western cultures. In philosophy there was first a strong influence from England, but then around the turn of the century German thought became more influential. One reason for this was the political situation at the time. Japan chose Germany, which was then the undeveloped capitalistic country in Europe, as a model for modernization. At about this time, many Europeans and Americans gained positions in various fields such as law, economics, and scientific technology. They were invited by the Japanese government and given a high stipend.

In 1893, Raphael von Köbel (1848–1923) was invited by the Japanese government and became a philosophy teacher at Tokyo Imperial University. Köbel had studied philosophy at the universities of Jena and Heidelberg after having studied piano under Rubinstein at Moscow Music Conservatory. He lectured on, among other things, Greek philosophy, the history of Christianity, and Kant's philosophy. His refined personality and artistic sensitivity attracted brilliant Japanese students pursuing philosophy. The well-known ones among them were Seiichi Hatano (1877–1950), Hajime Tanabe (1885–1962), Tetsurō Watsuji (1889–1960), and Shūzō Kuki (1888–1941).

These students yearned after Germany as the Mecca of philosophy. Japanese students often visited the southwestern universities in Germany, with the University of Heidelberg as the center. At that time Rickert and Windelband of the Southwest German school were best known in Japan. Hatano went to Germany in 1904 to study under Rickert and Windelband. He first introduced to Japan the Southwest school's philosophy of value. Since he was a Christian, he developed under the influence of Plotinus and Kant a unique philosophy of religion in his later years in the work entitled *Time and Eternity (Toki to Eien)*.

Hatano's system is comprised of three stages: the natural life, the cultural life, and the religious life. The natural life takes place in a world where self and others are opposed to, and compete with, each other. This implicitly indicates the standpoint of existential philosophy. Hatano apparently felt that the claims of existentialism, which dominated the philosophical world after Heidegger, were "shameless." It was a philosophy which did not know the dignity of the Kantian moral personality and the spirit of Eastern propriety. Hatano himself was a refined gentleman. He showed a disgust for Kierkegaard, commenting that the latter was "the fellow who doesn't know whether he is talking about himself or about others." Accordingly, Hatano overcame the natural life. The cultural life takes the order of the world as the object of aesthetic observation. This is represented by the spirit of Greek *theōria*. At its summit is established a mysticism represented by Plotinus and Eckhart. Furthermore, the self *qua* subject *(shutai)*, after becoming nothing in a mystical experience, gains a spiritual rebirth vis-à-vis God who is the absolute other. Therein a personalistic community is formed, based upon love of the self and others. The religious life for Hatano is like Kant's "realm of ends" with psycho-spiritual *(shinrei)* characteristics analogous to the community of saints *(communio sanctorum)*. This is how Hatano rejected existentialism. Hatano's three stages of life somewhat resembled Kierkegaard's three spheres of existence—that is, the aesthetic, the ethical, and the religious. For Hatano, Heidegger and existentialism were enemies which had defeated the Neo-Kantianism to which he had devoted himself in his youth. Like a Japanese samurai he sought revenge on his masters' enemies while according them a certain respect.

Hajime Tanabe went to the University of Freiburg in 1922 and studied under Husserl and Heidegger. Since at the time his interests were in the epistemology of mathematical and natural science, he was strongly influenced by Kant's philosophy, and his influence from Heidegger is relatively small. Tanabe had a side to him which was sensitive to the social movements of the time. Consequently, after returning to Japan, he began, under the influence of Hegel, to have an interest in the problem of the state and its people. His philosophy is called "the logic of species" *(shu no ronri)*. The term "species" is borrowed from the tripartite classificatory system in biology of genus, species, and individual. It also corresponds to the middle term between the generic (universal) concept and the particular. The modern Western view of man, as can be seen in the ideology of democracy, takes individual, personal dignity as its point of departure, and immediately goes on to establish it as a universal principle. This is used as a foundation for establishing the state and society. However, the state and society in actuality are always established with the specificity (species) of the people and race as their foundation. Therefore, the ideal for the state, even though it may start with the personal dignity of the individual, contradicts and opposes the specificity of species as its antithesis. Universality, which synthesizes the dialectical opposites and goes beyond them, cannot be found in a state like democracy, which takes as its principle abstract universals. It can be found only in the state that actualizes what Hegel called "concrete universals."

Although it is not clear what kind of political form a state like this would take, Tanabe hoped to give to Japan a new philosophical ideal different from that of various modern Western states. Behind thoughts like this one can discern Tanabe's feeling as a Japanese that the Asian peoples had not been properly treated in the first half of the twentieth century. Thus, he was deeply saddened by the defeat of Japan. After the war Tanabe led a hermit-like life.

His philosophy in his later years aimed for a universal love which synthesizes Christian love and Buddhist *karuṇā,* or compassion. Universal love is awakened through a spiritual resurrection arising from facing death. By taking the problem of death as the pivotal theme of his philosophy, Tanabe approached Heidegger to a certain extent. However, Heidegger's ontology was for Tanabe still essentially an ontology of life since it lacked an eternal love transcending death. As such, it had not reached the ontology of death. The phrase that Tanabe cherished in his later years was "to remember [one's] death" *(memento mori).* Behind this one can discern his sense of the misery of war, and especially the feeling that takes the atomic bomb in Hiroshima as a symbol for the contemporary spiritual crisis.

Shūzō Kuki was called Baron Kuki because of his aristocratic origins. He spent an elegant life as a researcher in Europe for over eight years beginning in 1921. He studied at the universities of Heidelburg, Freiburg, and Marburg under Rickert, Husserl, and Heidegger, respectively. Among the three, however, his strongest interest was Heidegger. Since Kuki's major interest was French philosophy, he soon moved to Paris and studied under Bergson. During that time, he learned French from a young French student. This student was Jean-Paul Sartre. Although it is probably not known outside Japan, it was Kuki who instilled in Sartre an interest in Heidegger's philosophy. After returning to his country Kuki received a position at Kyoto Imperial University.

His work *The Problem of Contingency (Gūzensei no Mondai)* was written under the influence of Heidegger. While living in Europe, Kuki discovered himself existing in a "white" society as a single "yellow" man and felt that he was a being who lacked necessity. Based on this experience, this work attempts to investigate the contingent in its internal structure. Another well-known work by Kuki is *The Structure of Iki (Iki no Kōzō).* It attempts to analyze the unique Japanese aesthetic consciousness of *iki* by means of a phenomenological-hermeneutical method. Kuki was a philosopher with a unique personality and acumen, but unfortunately he died prematurely.

All of the foregoing—Hatano, Tanabe, and Kuki—had had in one way or another a connection with Heidegger and existential philosophy. Through them, one can catch a glimpse of the impact that Heidegger's philosophy had on modern Japanese philosophy. These three philosophers were all professors at Kyoto Imperial University. The gathering of well-known philosophers in the 1930s at this university gave rise to the name "the Kyoto school." The one who was regarded as the central figure in the school was Kitarō Nishida (1870–1945). Nishida did not go to Europe to study, nor did he have an association with Heidegger; it would therefore deviate a little from our present theme to deal with him.[1]

II. Kiyoshi Miki—Existential Anxiety and Contemporary Politics

Kiyoshi Miki studied at Kyoto Imperial University under Nishida, Hatano, and Tanabe and then went to Germany in 1922, where he first studied at Heidelberg under Rickert. The following fall he moved to Marburg and studied under Heidegger for about a year. He moved to Marburg because, learning of Heidegger's reputation, he wanted to receive instruction from him in person. A story recounted in Miki's *A Journey of My Readings (Dokusho Henreki)* recalls vividly how Heidegger was received in Germany at the time. Heidegger was then thirty-two and Miki twenty-six. Both teacher and student were young, and their future destinies were not known to them. *Being and Time* was not yet published.

> After moving to Marburg and studying under Professor Heidegger I was absorbed in reading with deep sympathy Hölderlin, Nietzsche, Kierkegaard, and Dostoevsky. Hölderlin was then influencing the intellectual/spiritual atmosphere among German youth. Heidegger's philosophy was an expression of "postwar anxiety." Later, Heidegger dealt with literature through Hölderlin (*Hölderlin and the Essence of Poetry*, 1936). . . . Germany at the time was in total spiritual anxiety. While I thought the popularity of Hölderlin was rising, persons like Gandhi were also welcome. We could also discern from outside the tendency of students to divide into left wing and right wing. The philosophy of Professor Heidegger itself could be seen as an expression of this anxiety. His philosophy sprang from the prevailing atmosphere of the popularity of Nietzsche, Kierkegaard, and Hölderlin. This was the reason that Heidegger attracted overwhelming popularity among young students.[2]

After completing his studies in Germany, Miki headed for France. He read Pascal at his boarding house in Paris and later remarked that "while thinking about the *Pensées*, I felt that what I learned from Professor Heidegger was given life." Accordingly, he wrote in Paris *A Study of Man in Pascal (Pasukaru niokeru Ningen no Kenkyū*, 1926). This book took in advance the analytic of *Dasein* developed in *Being and Time*, which was to be published in the following year, and superimposed it on Pascal.

Miki's first work was thus published prior to the publication of *Being and Time*. He must have comprehended and absorbed Heidegger's philosophy in lectures and through conversations. He took his first step as a philosopher by appropriating Heidegger's philosophy as his own. However, no sooner did he return to Japan in 1925 than he started swiftly moving towards Marxism. He surprised the public by publishing a new interpretation of Marxism with Heidegger's existential philosophy as its base. The period was that of approaching economic depression and ideological confusions on the eve of fascism. Miki's fresh interpretation elicited a great response in literary circles, making him overnight a central figure in the world of the critics. On the other hand, he was severely criticized by orthodox Marxists for illegitimately bringing in bourgeois philosophy. He then undertook the intellectual task of synthesizing existentialism and Marxism. This theme was proposed by Sartre after World War Two, but Miki was already tackling this issue twenty years earlier. As the so-called structural crisis of capitalism was being heralded because of the world-wide economic depression, the two phrases "existential anxiety" and "socialistic revolution" began to work as stimulants, captivating the minds of the younger generation in Japan. The Japanese secret police, in close surveillance of the movements of the younger intelligentsia, began arresting communists and socialists while controlling sympathizers. Miki was also detained in prison for a brief period in 1930. Triggered by this incident, he resigned from the university and started playing an active role in the contemporary literary scene.

I shall pursue a little further Miki's attitude towards Heidegger and reserve for later a summary of his philosophy. In the essay "Heidegger's Ontology," written in 1930, he commented upon the fundamental attitude of Heidegger's philosophy, saying that it was a project "returning from that which is Greek to what is originally Christian." That which is Greek is an attitude of grasping the eternal essence of things in accordance with *logos* or reason. The contemporary representative is Husserl. Behind Husserl lurks the tradition of the philosophy of reason since Descartes. In contrast, Heidegger interprets that which is eschatological, or in other words, man's life in light of death as the end of life. Thus the man he speaks of, that is, *Dasein,* is Christian man. The forerunners of Heidegger are Augustine, Pascal, and Kierkegaard. Miki goes on to criticize Heidegger by contending that his philosophy cannot be "contemporary" because his *Dasein* remains in the standpoint of individual subjective life without a social aspect. One can, however, recognize "something new" in Heidegger's philosophy as a criticism of modern reason. Miki's central concern is, on the one hand, directed towards the irrational which lurks at the base of anxiety in life, and on the other hand, it is directed towards the movements of history and society which go beyond the individual. With respect to the former, he sympathized with Heidegger, but in respect to the latter, he felt a dissatisfaction. The discrepancy between Heidegger's and Miki's concerns is clearly manifest here.

It is probably worthwhile to add a word or two from our present standpoint about Miki's comment in this essay that the essence of Heidegger's philosophy is Christian and anti-Greek. Since we know that Heidegger later moved more towards the Greek after World War Two and separated himself from the Christian tradition, Miki's criticism was premature. But insofar as Heidegger in his early period is concerned, we should recognize that Miki's interpretation is correct. What Miki failed to perceive, however, was the point where Heidegger's most fundamental concern was centered on philosophy and history. Granted, it is probably true that in the early period "existential anxiety" for Heidegger was an important concern where he saw it coinciding with the "postwar anxiety." But from that time on Heidegger's essential concern could be seen as directed towards the origins of European spirituality in the distant past rather than towards contemporary Europe. Heidegger opens *Being and Time* with a quotation from Plato's *Sophist*. This could not be a predilection for mere display of erudition. It would seem that Heidegger is the type who approaches a view of the movements of the history and society indirectly through the spiritual tradition of the classics. This is seen from his demonstrated acumen in freely and freshly interpreting the philosophical classics. This is unlike Miki and Sartre, who were engaged in thinking in the face of immediate social movements. In short, one of Heidegger's fundamental concerns, concealed at the base of his ontology, was to gain a fresh grasp of the two traditions that formed the backbone of European spirituality. He did this by tracing Christianity and Greek philosophy back to their origins. The issue of the destiny of contemporary Europe cannot be rightly questioned except through the mediation of that distant past. The problem lies not in modern spirituality but in the origins of European spirituality itself. This kind of concern is indicated to a certain extent in the announced plan of *Being and Time*. In this sense, Heidegger's eyes were directed towards the past, towards things old, towards origins. In contrast, Miki's eyes were directed towards the contemporary, towards the new. It was unfortunate that Miki failed to perceive what Heidegger was seeing. Such a misunderstanding was not Miki's alone; it was also a difference that separated Heidegger from Sartre, as was made manifest after World War Two in "The Letter on Humanism" *(Brief über den "Humanismus")*.

Miki wrote a short piece called "Heidegger and the Destiny of Philosophy" when Heidegger's support for the Nazis was reported in 1933. This deals with Heidegger's inaugural speech as Rector Magnificus, "The Self-assertion of the German University." While commenting that Heidegger's position was approaching Nietzsche's, particularly his idea of *amor fati,* Miki was critical and warned of its danger: "Heidegger seems to be seeking a principle for the nationalistic unity of Germany in blood, earth and destiny—in the realm of pathos, in which there is no discernible objective principle."

Heidegger's association with Nazism was an episode that is deeply troubling. The tragedy of Heidegger was born when the purely academic person was all of a sudden drawn into the earthly vortex of politics. In terms of his philosophical orientation, his Achilles heel lay in his being a critic of modern rationalism. What interested me in reading the interview in the magazine *Der Spiegel,* published after Heidegger's death, was his own comment on "The Self-assertion of the German University." He says that he was absorbed in Presocratic philosophy. According to him, "The Self-assertion of the German University" was to be juxtaposed also with the Nazis' politicization of science *(politische Wissenschaft).* To bring out an ancient philosophy of the distant past in dealing with the upheaval of contemporary political situations is idle nonsense for the political man who intends to control by power the immediately real world. However, for a philosopher it is not meaningless to cast a reflective eye upon Western history and scholarship while viewing the political crisis in contemporary Europe.

The present author feels, although this is slightly different from Heidegger's view, that the remote cause of the spiritual crisis which has become manifest in contemporary Europe might lurk in the Western history of *epistēmē* prior to the modern period. It would seem that at present this issue has not yet been clearly answered, even though the ideological assessment of Nazism has been completed. *Being and Time* is a book filled with contradictions, for on the surface its language creates an atmosphere of modernity, while at its base it unfolds a vast perspective that questions the historical origins of Western intellectual history.

It was not clear in Miki's criticisms of his teacher how he felt about "the destiny of philosophy." In the piece "A Recollection of Professor Heidegger," written in 1939, Miki notes while recollecting the days when he studied under Heidegger at Marburg that he was struck with a sense of wonder at finding a great many literary works in Heidegger's study. He offers at the end of this piece the following thought:

> At one time, upon becoming Rector Magnificus at the University of Freiburg, he entertained the view expressed in "The Self-assertion of the German University." He soon resigned from this position, perhaps because his association with the Nazis did not go well. I hear that he is lecturing on the philosophy of art these days. Recalling that in Japan many people escaped to the philosophy of art when the oppression against Marxists became severe, I sense Professor Heidegger's present state of mind and am led to ponder generally the relationship between philosophy and politics.[3]

It was the period when World War Two had already been proclaimed, and on the Asian continent the Sino-Japanese war was dragging on. Miki was already over forty years old and had begun to feel the shadow of politics and the imminence of war. This is the last reference Miki made to the man Heidegger.

Miki's attitude in dealing with Heidegger shows the typical pattern which the younger Japanese intelligentsia displayed in approaching existential philosophy. The sympathy and frustration shown by Miki towards Heidegger's philosophy were expressed in an amplified fashion in the response that the younger Japanese generation showed towards the political and social situation after the defeat in the war. That is, on the one hand, they were interested in the nonrational anxiety fundamentally inherent in human nature. On the other hand, they took the attitude of discovering a challenge in the political situation where people's lives were oppressed. A truly human way of life lies in the pursuit of actual truth *(shinjitsu)* in both one's inner and outer world. Therein we can find a reason why Sartre's claim that "existentialism is a humanism" gained explosive popularity after the war. Although this sort of response was a tendency common to the advanced nations of Europe and America, after the seventies Sartre's popularity dwindled. This is not because we have found an answer. It simply means that the crisis has become chronic. We probably cannot expect an answer from politics.

How did Miki as a philosopher engage this problem? His central concept, which from the beginning remained consistent throughout his thinking, was the concept of "fundamental experience" *(kiso keiken)*, seen in the preface to *A Study of Man in Pascal*. It corresponds to Dilthey's "life" *(Leben)* or Heidegger's "mode of being of *Dasein*." The reason that Miki designates it as *fundamental* experience is because it exists at the foundation of rationality, that is, *logos,* and supports the latter's activities while giving it birth. In Miki's view, both Dilthey and Heidegger took rationality too lightly and overemphasized only irrational pathos. In the field of fundamental experience, the anxiety of irrational pathos is like a whirlpool. However, insofar as man is a being with *logos,* one should not separate rationality and pathos. One must discover a pathos where the *logos* is found, and see that pathos is the womb and foundation which give birth to *logos.* And also one must discover the *logos* where the pathos is found. Miki says that the hermeneutical task or duty of the philosopher is to clarify the *logos* at which the pathos aims and where the pathos wells up.

The essay "The Anthropological Form of Marxism" *(Marukusushugi no Ningengakuteki Keitai)* is a project which attempted to discover the "fundamental experience" of Marxism. Marxism is usually taken to be a political ideology. However, at its base is a philosophical anthropology that supports its ideology. It portrays an image of intellectual man with a definite *logos* in his possession. Consequently, a philosopher should clarify the anthropology of Marxism while discovering a pathos in the fundamental experience of Marxists. Miki tried to discover its pathos in the existential view of man as expressed in *Being and Time*. His interpretation, like that of Sartre, indicates a tendency to synthesize Marxism and existentialism, based on humanism.

Miki attempted to apply this kind of view in forming a methodological theory for understanding history. In *The Philosophy of History* (*Rekishi Tetsugaku*, 1932) he distinguishes three kinds of history. The first is history *qua* actual event, which he calls a history *qua* being *(sonzai)*. The second is history *qua* discourse *(rogosu)*, which is the description of events. The third is history *qua* lived event *(jijitsu)*. The term *jijitsu* corresponds to the German word *Tatsache* and means the "matter" *(Sache)* as an action *(Tat)*. This is a fundamental experience that gives birth to actual history, the concept corresponding to Dilthey's "life" or to Heidegger's *Dasein*. In looking at past history, we must seek a clue in history *qua logos* (the description of events). History *qua logos* copies history *qua* being (events). In addition, at its base lurks human lived experience *(Tatsache)* which has given birth to the history that the philosophy of history questions. The dialectic which has so far been considered as the sole method for the philosophy of history has dealt simply with the form of changes in history *qua* being which have surfaced in history. It stops at a horizontal dialectic that remains on the ontic *(ontisch)* dimension. We are in need of a vertical dialectic that discovers the human "fact" which produces history. Miki says this would be a true ontological *(ontologisch)* dialectic mediating *logos* and pathos. Such thinking comes close to Dilthey's epistemology of history as seen in light of Heidegger. Yet, on the other hand, progressive scholars supportive of Miki consider it a theoretical deepening of the historical consciousness of Marxism. Miki's philosophy of history, however, reminds the present author of a method which somewhat parallels E. H. Erikson's psycho-history, although the sophisticated terminologies favored in German philosophy obscure Miki's intent.

Miki used the concept of *jijitsu* in place of Dilthey's "life" or Heidegger's *Dasein*. This is because he emphasized the human action *(Tat)* that produces history. He criticized Dilthey's and Heidegger's views of man as emphasizing the subjective, affective aspect, and failing to grasp sufficiently the aspect of action that engages the world. Miki attempted to overcome Heidegger's philosophy by means of a standpoint in which man in a historical situation creates a new logos through his action. However, one would hesitate to claim that Miki built a unique philosophical system. His concern for the Japanese political situation during the wars did not afford him time to absorb himself in speculative thinking. From the Sino-Japanese war until the Pacific War, he was conceiving an ideology that hoped for cooperation among the Asian peoples. He insisted that it must be a "cooperationalism" *(kyōdōshugi)* that goes beyond liberalism, Marxism, totalitarianism and nationalism. However, the rapid change in contemporary politics shattered his philosophical dream. Towards the end of the war he was arrested by the police, which had turned hysterical. He died in prison in September 1945 when American soldiers began appearing in Tokyo.

Miki's thought in his later years indicates an approach towards Nishida's philosophy. His idea that emotions *qua* pathos are discovered at the base of the action that produces history approximates Nishida's idea of "acting-intuition." The world is *Sache* (event) in *Tat* (human action), which the passions for life engender. Miki attempted to deepen his thinking in a large work entitled *The Logic of Imagination (Kōsōryoku no Ronri)*, but this work remained unfinished. Along with this work, he was at the same time deepening his concern for the religious world. After his death an unfinished manuscript dealing with Shinran, a famous medieval Japanese Buddhist, was discovered. The Pure Land school that Shinran inaugurated in Japan was the faith long held in Miki's family.

III. Tetsurō Watsuji—Nature and Mores

Tetsurō Watsuji was older than Miki by eight years and was the same age as Heidegger. He studied under Kōbel at Tokyo Imperial University. From an early date he studied Kierkegaard and Nietzsche, and he became the first person to introduce existential philosophy to Japan. In his youth he had a deep interest in literature, intending to become a writer. The writer he most respected is Sōseki Natsume, who was well known as a humanistic writer. Inspired also by Tenshin Okakura, who brought Oriental art to the Boston Museum, he developed an interest in the old Japanese arts. The essay *Pilgrimage to Ancient Temples (Koji Junrei, 1919)*, which was published while he was young, is the record of a journey around the old temples in Nara. He won a large audience from this work. After becoming a philosopher, he initially chose as major themes for his research the Eastern cultural traditions. This culminated in such works as *Ancient Japanese Culture (Nippon Kodai Bunka, 1920)* and *Early Buddhism—A Practical Philosophy (Genshibukkyō no Jissentetsugaku, 1927)*. Although he also demonstrated excellent ability as a scholar of Western philosophy, he thought his goal was to build a philosophy which represented Japan. He obtained a chair as Professor of Ethics at Kyoto Imperial University in 1925.

Watsuji headed for Europe from the port of Yokohama as a passenger on the N.Y.K. line in the spring of 1927, five years later than Miki's visit to Europe. Crossing the Indian Ocean and the Mediterranean Sea to Marseilles was over a month's voyage by boat. Although it might seem dreamlike today with the development of air travel, Europe at that time for the islands in the Far East was an *El Dorado,* illusively shining in the far distant clouds.

I mention here Watsuji's voyage because the experience of this journey served as an occasion for him to write the well-known work *Climates and Cultures: A Philosophical Study (Fudō: Ningengakuteki Kōsatsu,* 1935). He classified the climates of the southern Eurasian continent into three types. One is the monsoon zone, which covers India through Southeast Asia. The second is the desert zone of western Asia, with Arabia as its center. The third is the meadow zone of Europe. What he felt particularly impressed with was the contrast between the monsoon and the desert zones. Nature in the former brims with invigorating life, while in the latter it is composed of lifeless rocks and sand. Two completely different cultures were developed. Doesn't this phenomenon have some relation to the climatic differences? Watsuji contrasts here the Buddhist and Hindu cosmologies with the Judeo-Christian and Islamic ones. Pantheistic polytheism, charged with affective character, was developed in the foremer, while in the latter an absolute monotheism which demands a strong will and strict morality was developed. What is the reason for this difference? Nature in the monsoon zone nurtures plant and animal life through heat and the abundance of rain. From this is born a receptive life-style that accepts the blessings of nature, which is great and alive. Nature can become violent, causing floods and droughts, but if these are tolerated it soon returns to its former state. From this comes the Eastern world-view which accepts the destiny of life while receiving salvation from the gods by extolling them. In contrast, nature in the desert bestows death upon those who would sit around and wait. Man in this zone must actively overcome nature so as to possess his life. This calls for a strict morality through which one obeys the will of an absolute god that transcends nature. Watsuji thought that in this lies a historical "womb" for the aggressiveness of ego-consciousness which is seen in the tradition of Western spiritual history.

Watsuji visited Europe in 1927, the year *Being and Time* was published. Its publication was then having an impact upon the philosophical world in Europe. He recalls his impression of the book in the following passage in which his experience of the voyage, which had been embodied in *Fūdo,* seeps through the narration.

> It was in the early summer of 1927, when I was reading Heidegger's *Sein und Zeit* in Berlin, that I first came to reflect on the problem of climate. I found myself intrigued by the attempt to treat the structure of man's existence in terms of time but I found it hard to see why, when time was thus made to play a part in the structure of subjective existence, at the same juncture space also was not postulated as part of the basic structure of existence.

Indeed it would be a mistake to allege that space is never taken into account in Heidegger's thinking, for *lebendige Natur* was given fresh life by the German Romantics, yet even so it tended to be obscured in the strong glare to which time was exposed. I perceived that herein lay the limitation of Heidegger's work, for time not linked with space is not time in the true sense, and Heidegger stopped short at this point because his *Dasein* was the *Dasein* of the individual only. He treated human existence in the world as being the existence of an individual *(hito)*. From the standpoint of the dual structure—both individual and social—of human existence, he did not advance beyond an abstraction of a single aspect. But it is only when human existence is treated in terms of its concrete duality that time and space are linked and that history also (which never appears fully in Heidegger) is first revealed in its true guise. And at the same time the connection between history and climate becomes evident.[4]

When reading this account, I sense the subtlety of a "personal encounter." Miki met Heidegger when he was twenty-six. A personal encounter during one's youth, with its overbrimming sensitivity, provides a direction to one's life. Watsuji, however, was close to forty, and had already secured social status. An important point is that Watsuji was already aware, in his own way, of what Eastern spirituality was through his research on ancient Japanese culture and early Buddhism. It is due to this fact that he could immediately point out the "limitation" of *Being and Time* without becoming captive of the ineffably alluring tone of the work. Had it been Watsuji at the time when he was studying Nietzsche and Kierkegaard, he would have been enthused, probably wholeheartedly, by Heidegger's philosophy.

Watsuji remarks in the final chapters of *Fūdo* that there is a difference in culture due to "place" *(tokoro)* as well as a difference due to time. At the base of history and culture lie climate and nature. This is self-evident, for example, if we observe the difference in character between the Eastern arts and Western arts. Watsuji questions here the philosophy of history represented by Hegel and Marx. Hegel said that the history of human civilization begins in the East and is perfected in the West, just like the movement of the sun. Such a simple developmental theory goes counter to the actuality of the contemporary world. Histories and cultures develop with multifaceted directions and modes. The mode of development of the European civilization is only one of them. It is an error, Watsuji contends, to judge the essence of history and culture for all peoples by using European civilization as a measuring standard. It is easy to discern here Watsuji's pride and awareness as an Asian.

Watsuji's idea of seeing the problem of climate at the foundation of history reminds me of the view of history held by the school of Annales *(l'École d'Annales)* which has recently flourished in France. The theory of this school starts primarily with the study of medieval European history. It regards as important the world-view which is linked to the natural environment, mores, and life-style of the populace, all of which lurks at the bottom layer of history. Originally the Japanese term *fūdo* does not simply refer to "climate" as a natural phenomenon. It also means the life-style and mores which are intrinsically molded by climate. In the tradition of Western thinking patterns, culture and the arts are human made, and nature and culture are opposed to each other. However, the Eastern arts do not oppose nature, as can be seen in the Japanese garden and brush painting, both of which were influenced by Zen Buddhism. Rather, culture is interfused with nature, and the invisible life latent in nature is brought to pure expression. Consequently, history which is a product of human life cannot be assessed without taking climate *(fūdo)* into consideration. History and nature, like man's mind and body, are in an inseparable relationship. However, since Watsuji sought a methodology for his philosophy of *fūdo* in Husserl's phenomenological method, he failed to indicate clearly its theoretical ground.

After returning from Europe, Watsuji published numerous books dealing with Japanese cultural history and the history of Western philosophy. He also began writing his major theoretical work, the *Ethics (Rinrigaku)*. This book shows us a unique encounter with Heidegger's philosophy, which I shall deal with later. Watsuji moved to Tokyo Imperial University in 1934 (for this reason, he is not counted as a member of the Kyoto school). Then in 1937, the Sino-Japanese war broke out. Watsuji felt a certain anxiety about the future of Japan. But he was not a pacifist; he believed in the justness of his country. Since his youth he had been regarded as a conservative intellectual. He was known for his hatred of Marxism, and he had always been attacked by progressive right-wing intellectuals.

When the Pacific War broke out, he believed that it was a just war that would liberate the oppressed races in Asia. One pamphlet he wrote during the war preached the sacredness of the emperor, based upon Japanese Shinto and the way of the samurai. It claimed that the core of the national character of the United States is an animal instinct that seeks speed and thrills. He believed that Eastern spiritual strength in the end would surpass the material strength of the West. (Robert Bellah has written an interesting article about this pamphlet, contrasting it with Ruth Benedict's *The Chrysanthemum and the Sword*.)[5] After the war, the American Occupational Headquarters issued a directive banishing the nationalists, and Watsuji barely escaped expulsion from the university because of this pamphlet.

Watsuji believed that in the contemporary age the Japanese were a people with a special historical mission. The mission was to overthrow the world order controlled by the imperialistic Western powers. Just as Hegel believed that the power of the absolute spirit dominating history lies in the Prussian state, so Watsuji believed in the providence that guides and leads Japan. Consequently, Japan's defeat was a severe shock to him. He had to reconcile himself to the fact that the historical mission of Japan in the contemporary age had ended in failure. (However, Japan's defeat ironically brought about the independence of Asian peoples one after another. The "cunning of reason" *(List der Vernunft)* of which Hegel spoke, as controlling history, had punished Japanese militarism while allowing in a certain sense for her historical mission.) Nevertheless, after Japan's defeat in the war Watsuji never stopped protesting against the speeches made by the left wing, which maliciously criticized Japanese history and its cultural tradition. In opposition to the criticisms launched by progressive intellectuals and journalists against the emperor, he insisted that the Japanese cultural tradition and the existence of the emperor could be harmonized with democracy. In his later years he avoided association with journalism, and devoted himself exclusively to scholarly research.

The *Ethics* (1937–40), Watsuji's three-volume *magnum opus,* was strongly influenced by *Being and Time.* He says that ethics is an ontology of man—that is, an ontological analysis of man. However, Watsuji, like Miki, ignored Heidegger's later works. Also, his system differs completely in substance from Heidegger's thought, in spite of the fact that he employs a seemingly Heideggerian terminology. This tendency was also detectable in *Fūdo.* There are two major points on which Watsuji criticizes Heidegger. The first is that Heidegger treated the mode of being-in-the-world only from the aspect of temporality and took lightly the aspect of spatiality. The second is that *Dasein* is grasped with an emphasis on its individuality and without sufficiently considering the social relationship between the self and others. Underlying these two points, which are intrinsically related, runs Watsuji's strong Eastern sensitivity.

Watsuji first of all sees the social human relationship as one of "betweenness" *(aidagara).* The Japanese term *aidagara* expresses the character of various human relationships, whether they be intimate or distant. The term *aida* (between) means a spatial distance that separates one thing from another. At the foundation of social human relationships is natural space. This is an application of the idea from *Fūdo,* where space-consciousness is regarded as more important than time-consciousness. A person *(ningen)* for Watsuji is a tie in the social network found in life-space.

Based upon the meaning of the term *ningen* in Japanese, Watsuji offers the following explanation of human existence *(ningen sonzai).* The Japanese term *ningen* is comprised of two Chinese characters. These designate "man" *(nin)* and "between" *(gen* or *aida)*, and they are used in either singular or plural form. Following this, Watsuji argues that man's life can exist only in the "betweenness," which is its foundation. (Furthermore, at the foundation of "betweenness" is found spatiality.) This view of man, we might note, inherits the East Asian tradition of Confucian ethics. Insofar as his mode of behavior is concerned, a person *(ningen)* is determined a priori by his position within the social hierarchy. Needless to say, Watsuji rejects the status distinctions of the feudal period. The social network of human relationships, however, is always found in any period. When the individual rebels against the order of the whole, though he may be granted independence for a while, he has to return to the network of the social order. Otherwise man cannot go on living. Watsuji's view of man was once criticized as being an Eastern conservatism. Strangely enough, however, it reminds me of the new view of man held by structuralism after Lévi-Strauss—a view that has begun to replace existentialism.

For his methodology Watsuji used Dilthey's hermeneutics and Heidegger's ontology. By interpreting the unique usage of Japanese terms, he skillfully deployed their implications as philosophical concepts. This is an influence from Dilthey's methodology and from Heidegger's skillful use of terminology. Watsuji's attitude towards Heidegger is in some ways unique. As has already been noted, Watsuji calls his philosophy (his ethics) "human ontology." Yet, it does not have as its purpose a pursuit of the meaning of Being itself, as Heidegger attempted. It is closer in substance to an anthropology which employs the hermeneutical method. In the case of Heidegger, the two possible modes of being of *Dasein* are everydayness and authentic existence. For him, the state in which one lives with others in everyday life (that is, the mode of being of *das Man*) means nothing but the fact of living habitually in the midst of rumor, curiosity, and ambiguity. By becoming aware of the anxiety latent at the base of everydayness, and thereby facing one's death, a passage to authentic existence is opened up, which enables one to pursue the being of the authentic self. Contrary to Heidegger, Watsuji does not consider the standpoint of existence meaningful. He takes as the objective expression of the mode of human existence the standards of behavior such as customs and morality, or generally the mores, that control and restrict the everyday life-space. Consequently, hermeneutics can clarify the essence of human nature via these objective expressions by analyzing their implications. Individual consciousness and the anxiety of death are meaningless, for the individual disappears in death, while the social network as the mode of human existence continues to exist.

Watsuji's ethics, accordingly, does not start with the analysis of an individual's moral consciousness, as is done in the tradition of Western ethics. It starts first with the two-person community of husband and wife, since if there were no relationship between man and woman, no life could be born. Here the Western view, which creates a dualism between spirit and flesh, love and sexuality, is rejected. The personality is not a mere spirit but a spirit that is concretized in the body. This is because the possibility of human life exists only in *space,* and for this the body is the indispensable precondition. From the two-person community families are formed, and from the family units are formed the regional community. This develops further into the economic system. On top of the economic system are various cultural communities (participating in scholarship, art, and religion). Human existence grows in this manner as a pyramid-shaped hierarchical system. The apex of the pyramid is the state. Religion for Watsuji is a phenomenon belonging to the cultural level and axiologically inferior to the state. This view is biased by the historical condition that Shintoism, which is the old religion indigenous to Japan, has not expanded outside the Japanese people.

In this manner, Watsuji's ethics deals only with mores as the standard operative in the actually existing social network. No fundamental principle of moral law or transcendental ideal is considered, as the Western reader would expect from ethics. I too feel that Watsuji's ethics is inadequate in this respect, but I must point out that it is indicative of the Eastern attitude of thinking in Watsuji. Watsuji does not distinguish *ens morale* and *ens physicum.* Life always displays an inseparable union between nature and mores, just as climate and history, nature and culture, and body and mind are not separate in the everyday life-world.

Watsuji calls the highest principle in his philosophy *śūnyatā* (emptiness). This concept is borrowed from Mahayana Buddhism, particularly from Nāgārjuna. When viewed methodologically, the process of inference used in bringing out this concept is not clear in Watsuji. This concept reminds me of either Hegel's absolute spirit or Nishida's *basho* (literally, "place") vis-à-vis absolute Nothing. All human lives have come to be, by emanating from the source of "emptiness," and they return there. He says all the distinctions disappear therein. This seems to be a philosophical conceptualization of pantheistic nature. Spinoza was one of the philosophers that Watsuji held in high regard.

IV. Conclusion—A Turn from Temporal to Spatial Life

I would like to offer here my opinion on the problematics that have emerged from the encounter of modern Japanese philosophy with Heidegger.

As has been pointed out earlier, there is a strong tendency in Watsuji to regard spatiality as primary in viewing human experience and modes of

life. Nishida's concept of *basho* points to the experience of an inner transcendence that lurks potentially in the ground of the life-space as the
basho vis-à-vis Being. Also, Watsuji's concept of "betweenness" is of the
social network inseparably tied with natural space. The issue of temporality is secondary. We might surmise, from the fact that these two
were intimately familiar with Eastern cultural traditions, that discoverable at the base of the Eastern philosophical tradition is the idea of space-
consciousness as more important than time-consciousness. To put it conversely, there is a tendency in the Western philosophical tradition to
regard time-consciousness as more important than space-consciousness,
and therein to locate the core of ego-consciousness. Herein lies one of the
historical reasons for this difference in sensitivity between East and West.

In the contemporary period, the tendency to regard temporality as
more important and spatiality as less important is clearly restored in
Bergson's philosophy. Bergson considered the most immediate experiential state given to consciousness to be an experience of lived time as pure
duration. In Bergson's case, the form of spatial experience arises from the
habitual inertia into which the intellect is liable to fall and in which one
cannot find the essence of life. Heidegger, after Bergson, resurrected the
theory of time again as the central theme of contemporary philosophy.
Viewed in this manner, we can see that Miki's opinion was correct in
judging that the view of man at the foundation of *Being and Time* is in
the tradition of the Christian thought pattern which is still alive in the
contemporary period. It was with this view of man that Watsuji's extreme
sensitivity as an Easterner felt discordant. The essence of life lies where
one is embraced by the brimming rhythm of life of natural space, just as
Watsuji grasped it intuitively in *Fūdo*.

Jung says that the traditional Eastern spirit is introverted in contrast to
the traditional Western spirit, which is extraverted. The extraverted attitude finds the focal point of one's personal character in an ego-consciousness that confronts and controls the external world. In contrast, the
introverted attitude tends to withdraw into itself before intending the
things in the external world. Jung says that the focal point of one's ego-
consciousness in the Eastern person lies not in the ego, but in the interiority of the unconscious. Nishida's absolute Nothing is the emanation of
the transcendental power that moves the ego from behind. The individual's ego-consciousness in the thought of Watsuji is a kind of appearance.
What is truly real is the activity of the transcendental "emptiness." The
fundamental principle is always found in the process of transcending
towards the interiority of consciousness, going behind everyday consciousness. When we superimpose the structure of the inner world on the
being of things in the external world, the world-space and the universe
become a gigantic psycho-spiritual body of life; and time becomes the
shadow of eternity.

Here we must consider the relationship between Heidegger's early and later philosophies. The analytic of *Dasein* in *Being and Time* is fundamental ontology, which questions the meaning of the Being of beings. This supplies a passage to where we must take up *general ontology*, which questions the meaning of the Being of *all* beings, including beings other than humans. Heidegger's later philosophy aimed at this goal. In the process of moving from fundamental ontology to general ontology, there is the difficulty of the so-called "turn" *(Kehre)*. As I see it, the "turn" seems to mean a turn from temporal life to spatial life. Temporality as *Dasein*'s mode of being-in-the-world contains the structure of *geworfener Entwurf* (thrown projection). That is, man as *Dasein* experiences the world as a world by holding at hand the past and future. What is important in this respect is *Entwurf* (projection)—that is, an attitude of *actively* intending a future. For, as with Husserl's transcendental subjectivity, *Dasein actively* bestows the experience of consciousness with meaning and constitutes it as the world. Sartre interpreted Heidegger by assuming such a standpoint. However, if we were to turn from the Being of man as a "being-in-the-world" and to cast off such a mode of Being, we would have to shift our emphasis to the thrownness *(Geworfenheit)* of life. The anxiety of life is the relating of oneself introspectively to one's state that has been thrown into the world. *Geworfenheit* will no longer mean the temporal holding of the past, but will come to bear a new meaning as the *fundamental passivity* of the being of the self in the world. That is, the self is *thrown* into the world-space. We intend a certain future only because we hold at hand a definite past, but when one faces one's death, one can no longer hold one's future. The need to hold the past then also disappears. Only then do we become aware, in a fresh perspective, of the fact that one's life has been thrown into the world originally, without any necessity and without any reason. The meaning of the being of *Dasein* cannot yield, in the face of one's death, any meaning from the human perspective. But, if this meaning can be clarified in some manner, we must start our thinking from the fact that the existence of life becomes possible only as a life thrown into the world-space.

Being and Time is a book that has been misinterpreted ever since its publication. People have always understood it anthropocentrically: Miki, Watsuji, Sartre, and Jaspers are no exception. But if it is correct to understand Heidegger's "turn" in the above manner, then the reason Heidegger rejected existentialism becomes self-evident. The fundamental task for Heidegger was how to break through the anthropocentrism in the fundamental ontology of the early period. If the meaning of *Sein* in its ultimate sense can be questioned, *Zuhandenes* (things ready-to-hand), and *Vorhandenes* (present-at-hand) must equally be *Seindes* (beings) for *Sein* (Being). The fundamental goal of Heidegger's philosophy was to open up this kind of new horizon. Consequently, the goal for the path of his thinking, if seen in light of the turn from the earlier period to the later period, was to stand on the horizon that overcomes the Christian tradition in which man had been grasped as "the image of God," and in terms of the recognition of "the superiority of man over nature." Moreover, Heidegger sensed that the thinking pattern of "man as superior to nature" had already begun surfacing in Plato and Aristotle, wherein we can probably find the reason why his concern shifted to the Presocratic Greeks.

Might not the contemporary West be able to find a new path for dialogue with the traditions of thought outside the Western world only by questioning the distant origin of its historical destiny as Heidegger had attempted? Heidegger's "light of Being" is the voiceless voice of something that is revealed in silence through the mysteries of living nature. I feel that the life which anticipates a light from the darkness beyond, while pricking the ears to the voice, shows something in common with the Eastern way of life which inhabits the great earth with all that is *(sattva)*. I wonder whether a new path for a dialogue with the East may be opened by journeying into the extreme North of Western spirituality. We cannot hear an answer from this philosopher, Heidegger.

Translated by Monte Hull and S. Nagatomo

Notes

1. I have already offered my interpretation of Nishida in the first part of *Shintai—Tōyōteki Shinshinron no Kokoromi* (The Body: Towards an Eastern Mind-Body Theory) (Tokyo: Sōbunsha, 1976).

2. Kiyoshi Miki, *Dokusho Henreki* (A Journey of My Readings), in *Miki Kiyoshi Zenshū* (Collected Works of Miki Kiyoshi), vol. 1 (Tokyo: Iwanami Shoten, 1966–68), pp. 369ff.

3. Kiyoshi Miki, "Haiddegeru Kyōju no Omoide" (A Recollection of Professor Heidegger), in *Collected Works*, 17:274ff.

4. Tetsurō Watsuji, *Climates and Culture—A Philosophical Study*, tr. Geoffrey Bownas (Tokyo: Kokuseido Press, 1971), preface.

5. Robert N. Bellah, "Japan's Cultural Identity: Some Reflections on the Work of Watsuji Tetsurō," in *Hito to Shisō* (Man and Thought), ed. Y. Yuasa (Tokyo: Sanichi Shobo, 1973).

Akihiro Takeichi

On the Origin of Nihilism—
In View of the Problem of
Technology and Karma

I

The fundamental form of European philosophy is metaphysics, which Aristotle called "first philosophy." First philosophy is "the study of being as such" as well as a "theoretical investigation of the primary origin and cause." It would seem that these two different definitions are merged by positing the eternal unmoved mover which, as pure form, is the purpose of all beings and their movements. In this regard, God *qua* eternal unmoved mover is not simply the highest being *(das Seiendste)*, but can serve as the primary origin of all beings by being the ultimate purpose and thereby the good. That is, because this being assumed the character-istic of the good, Aristotle was able to unify two definitions, "the study of being as such" and "the theoretical investigation of the primary origin and cause," by positing the Divine which is after all only a being in spite of being the highest.

However, this notion had already been established as a central feature of Western metaphysics when Plato sought the ultimate source of being in the idea of the good, which is the idea of all ideas. This character became all the more dominant from the medieval age onward when the Christian God with its ethico-religious character of love and justice was introduced into philosophy.

II

Consequently, when Nietzsche exclaimed "God is dead," this did not sim-ply mean the death of the Christian God. It also meant a collapse of the god of metaphysics, that is, the ultimate good posited as beyond all beings and as bestowing purpose and order to the totality of beings. Nietzsche refers to this death of God by saying, "The ultimate value is deprived of its value." This, he claims, is the essence of European nihilism. According to this interpretation, the death of God as the collapse of the metaphysical world is interpreted in terms of value, which is a modern perspective. As a result, prior to his death God is already deprived of his beingness *(Seiendheit)* as the highest being, and thus he becomes simply a "value" which is appropriate for something.

Two important problems emerge from this. One is that God is relativized by the interpretation in terms of value, as we have just seen. Value is value insofar as it bears a value for something in a given circumstance. This "something," as in "for something," is generally speaking a human subject. To use Nietzsche's expression, it is "life" or "will." Consequently, God came to be regarded as a value for life, that is, a condition for the will. A condition is appropriate as a condition only in a given circumstance. Therefore, God cannot but die in a circumstance where the condition, God, is inappropriate and valueless for life.

What is the circumstance that has rendered the condition, God, valueless for life? It is the invasion of nihilism. But to respond in this manner is tautological insofar as we interpret the essence of nihilism as the death of God and the devaluation of the highest value. Thus, in seeking the origin of nihilism the answer to this question should be sought by determining the intrinsic cause of life itself which has rendered God, the condition for life, valueless.

But is this kind of search not already a thinking within a nihilistic circumstance? For insofar as we question the intrinsic cause of the appropriateness or inappropriateness of God regarded as the condition of life, God is not regarded as necessary for the life in essence. Therefore, life becomes primary, and God becomes a secondary being whose existence or non-existence does not in the final analysis matter. However, to disclose life as the principle of positing God means that the Western metaphysical system in which the highest good was regarded as the origin of Being collapsed in Nietzsche. Moreover, it means that the principle supportive of such a system is laid bare. That is, the essence of Being itself was presented for the first time by Nietzsche in terms of will, which posited the highest value as God and so itself transcends the perspective of value. This means that Aristotle's "study of being as such" came to be carried out for the first time in its true sense.

III

Because "the will to power" is a principle for positing values, it can also be a principle for overthrowing old values. This overthrowing leads old values to valuelessness. This means nihilism. To use Nietzsche's words, it is a "most extreme nihilism." However, this "most extreme nihilism," so long as its transvaluation is executed consciously with the principle for positing new values, is at the same time no longer nihilism. The will to power posits all beings as beings, which are newly valued. Accordingly, beings are no longer nothingness, and therefore nihilism is overcome.

It is said that nihilism is overcome in Nietzsche. But has it really been overcome? Passive nihilism which is the deprivation of all values can at the same time be transformed into active nihilism. This is simply because it gains a principle for positing new values while overthrowing all old ones. Insofar as the will to power as this principle is the essence of Being, nihilism is after all nothing but a phenomenal fact; it is only a superficial, negative, and temporal aspect of "life" (will) which develops as a whole while repeating the process of generation-extinction. But is nihilism nothing but a phenomenon to this extent? Can life or will, conceived of as the basis of this phenomenon, remain indifferent to nihilism without being subverted by it? Why does will have to posit value at all? We said that will or life, but not God, is presupposed as the primary Being in Nietzsche. But on what ground is this presupposition established?

Will constantly posits value, and by positing the condition for itself, will secures itself. This means that for will to be will it needs to posit itself (and thereby it maintains and enhances itself) by constantly positing an object. That is to say, to secure itself in this manner is the essence of will. The positing of an object for will is at the same time the giving of a ground for will's independent existence. Will, insofar as it is will, always needs to ground itself by positing a thing other than itself. This means that will itself lacks a ground; the basis of will is groundless. That its ground is nothing urges will toward positing values constantly.

We said earlier that Nietzsche regarded God as value prior to killing him, and that this was nothing other than nihilism. Now we must consider "nothingness" as the "origin of nihilism" which thrusted this thought of Nietzsche's from its depth. This "nothingness" lurks as the base of the will to power, which is itself the principle for the positing of all new values and so for overcoming nihilism. It would seem that this nothingness lurking at the base of the will to power was experienced by Nietzsche as the abyss of the eternal recurrence. But, since nothingness was experienced as that very eternal recurrence, this nothingness was incorporated within the will to power by the will to power itself in the manner of "I willed! I will! And I shall will!" Thereby, nothingness is affirmed and is transformed into an objective being for will. Conversely, the will to power, which lacks a ground and hence must be constantly securing itself, comes to be endowed by means of the eternal recurrence with a ground that is eternity and necessity. Consequently, the nothingness lurking in the will to power (though such a nothingness is primordial nothingness as the ground of the world, insofar as the will to power is the essence of Being) was not thoroughly thought out in Nietzsche in its relation to the nothingness of nihilism as the essential form of history.

To get a little ahead of ourselves, we could say that nothingness, as the ground of the world, is in this respect, the nothingness of the "original nihilism" which Heidegger considered the essence of nihilism. Therefore, from this point on, we should like to reflect upon Heidegger's definition of nihilism and then move on to consider whether or not his definition can really reach the "origin" of nihilism.

IV

The essay which best shows Heidegger's thinking on nihilism is "The Determination of Nihilism in terms of the History of Being" ("Die seinsgeschichtliche Bestimmung des Nihilismus"), which is contained in the second volume of *Nietzsche*. The title straightforwardly expresses the character of Heidegger's interpretation of nihilism. That is, nihilism has to do with nothing (*nihil*-ism), and he intends to determine it in terms of the history of Being.

First, to determine nihilism by way of the history of Being is to determine it in relation to the history of metaphysics, insofar as "metaphysics has so far been the sole history of Being which can be surveyed." That is, it does not mean to determine nihilism as a psychological phenomenon, nor to analyze it politically or sociologically, nor to deal with it ethically as a problematic of morality. But rather this approach thinks of nihilism as a phenomenon bearing the essence of metaphysics as "the study of being as such."

Secondly, if, judging from the above, metaphysics has an essential bearing on nihilism, we might say that the question that questions being as such in metaphysics, that is, the question about the Being of beings, is shown to have an essential bearing on nothingness.

Heidegger asserts in many places that the question of Being in metaphysics is the question about the Being of beings, and furthermore, it is a question questioning Being from the viewpoint of beings. In such a questioning the truth of Being itself, says Heidegger, is left out, and with respect to Being itself it is nothing *(es ist mit dem Sein nichts)*. In contrast, Heidegger insists that his own questioning of Being is the question of Being itself, that is, the question about the truth of Being.

One might very well object that this sort of distinction, in which Being itself is nothing in the question of metaphysics while Heidegger questions Being itself, is meaningless unless the substance of each question is shown. In response to such an objection one needs to point out, as Heidegger has done, the fundamental structure of the oblivion of Being throughout the history of Western metaphysics, so that it can be demonstrated that the content of the metaphysical question is questioned in the absence of the truth of Being itself. But even if one carries out the questioning as Heidegger actually did, that is, if one criticizes Western philosophical thinking as the oblivion of Being, placing Heidegger's standpoint of the thinking of Being itself on one side and Western philosophy as the standpoint of the oblivion of Being on the other, this would simply be in the end an external critique of traditional Western philosophy. Most criticisms of Heidegger defend the position of traditional philosophy, interpreting Heidegger's position in this manner.

However, an understanding of Heidegger's thought (with respect to his critique of metaphysics), which criticisms like this involve, in fact betrays a fundamental misunderstanding of Heidegger's thinking. Such a view assumes that something like Being itself is or can be thought in its pure form in Heidegger's thinking, while on the other hand Being itself is absent from metaphysical thinking. This sort of scheme of understanding is in the final analysis nothing but the method of cognition of metaphysics, which has not changed since ancient times. It is the method of placing on the one hand a pure thinking of the truth of the absolute and on the other hand an incomplete knowledge of the finite world.

But if we look at Heidegger's own thinking without distorting it through this sort of schema of traditional metaphysics, it is actually quite different. There is no denying that Being itself is questioned in his thinking, but this Being itself is nothing like an absolute or *causa sui*. Rather "that it belongs to the truth of Being that Being never essentially presents itself without beings."[1] That is, Being discloses itself *(lichtet sich)* in beings and it is nothing other than this disclosure. Accordingly, although metaphysics is endowed with the truth of beings and Being itself is absent in this openness *(Offenheit)* of beings, we must recognize that Being itself is essentially present as that very absence in metaphysics. The openness of Being is at the same time the concealment *(Verborgenheit)* of Being, and the truth of Being emerges only as the untruth *(Unwahrheit)* of Being.

Therefore, if we designate as "nihilism" the essence of metaphysics which is opened up as the truth of the Being of beings, and in which the truth of Being itself is "nothing" *(nihil)*, then this nothingness of nihilism is not simply derived from the knowledge of finite beings, but it belongs to the essence of Being itself. Conversely, we must grant that Being as absence must be the essence of nihilism.[2]

V

All nihilistic phenomena, or nihilism in the ordinary sense, are derived from the essence of nihilism which we have just discussed. Metaphysics seeks the Being of beings, that is, beingness *(Seiendheit),* in place of Being itself *qua* absence, and "only beings" exercise "sole authority." For example, all the beings in the world of today are brought into the destiny of Being which is "modern technology" appearing in the final perfected stage of the history of Being, and they are set up as that which is useful. The world is replete with these "useful" beings.

However, since a being is recognized as a being only insofar as it is useful, it cannot maintain its own steady beingness through itself. Once it loses its usefulness, it will be thrown away. Not only that, if people get tired of it after a certain passage of time, it will be re-made even though it may still be useful. People do not expect a work of architecture to have an everlasting solidity. A building is constructed in such a way that it can be easily demolished in the future. To be "built and scrapped" is the destiny of beings in the contemporary age. That something is a being is only a provisional, temporary appearance.

So, the contemporary world is replete everywhere with beings, and, no doubt, beings are exercising sole authority, but actually this fact itself is realized on the basis of the essential nihility of beings. We must recognize that the origin of the flood of beings in the contemporary world is nothing but this nihility of beings itself. For this reason, the various nihilistic phenomena in the contemporary world are the other side of the inundation of beings. (For example, we can think of the excess of commercial art in contrast to the absence of essential art.)

Thus, beings, to the degree that they exist in the contemporary age, are supported by nihility, but Being which has been concealed through the flood of beings is presented in this very nihility as concealed Being. That is, the essence of "original nihilism," that is, the absence of Being itself, is disclosed in the nihility that negates beings unlimitedly and in their basis.

It would seem that the preceding is Heidegger's definition by way of the "history of Being" which is given to the essence of nihilism and to the nihilistic phenomena derived therefrom. Going one step further, we must ask what is the "origin" from which the essence of nihilism is derived. To respond to this question, we must think out further the absence of Being, which Heidegger has thought of as the essence of nihilism.

VI

As has been noted, absence belongs to the essence of Being itself, and since nihilism is *the* essential mode of the history of Being, "the truth of Being has remained hidden from metaphysics throughout its history from Anaximander to Nietzsche."[3] But this can be restated by saying that the truth of Being has been kept essentially concealed, and for this reason metaphysics from Anaximander to Nietzsche was able to blossom. That is, the absence of the truth of Being and the blossoming of the truth of beings which is metaphysics are two sides of the same thing. The oblivion of the truth of Being is not a result of a deficiency in metaphysical thinking, but was an essential and necessary consequence for metaphysics, which is the truth of beings, the revealing *(Entbergung)* and the unconcealment *(Unverborgenheit)* of beings.

Accordingly, it would seem that one of the ways to investigate the origin from which the essence of nihilism as the absence or concealment of Being is derived is to inquire into how the revealing of beings, inseparable from the absence of Being, is realized. No doubt, one can think of investigating the origin of concealment *(Verborgenheit)* from the concealment itself, but insofar as it is an investigation by means of language whose essence is to express, such an alternative is not viable. Rather, the path we should follow lies nowhere else than in guarding *(wahren)* to the end the concealment *qua* concealment. Thus it should not end up that "in the emerging of unconcealment what is essential to it, namely concealment, be lost, and moreover in favor of that which is unconcealed, which appears as what is."[4] In guarding the concealment, we must clarify how the unconcealment is realized, that is, how the unconcealment breaks through the concealment, thereby disclosing beings and (at the same time) concealing the concealment itself. That is, we must clarify how the truth of beings brings about the oblivion of Being and the oblivion of this oblivion.

If the unconcealment of beings and the essence of nihilism, which is the concealment of Being, are two sides of the same thing, then the destiny of Being as the essence of technology, in which nihilism culminates, is also the time when beings are completely revealed. In fact, all beings, as has been seen, are exposed in the world of contemporary technology in broad daylight throughout the world. And what are thereby exposed are taken up one after another as that which is useful in some manner or another. However, the destiny of technology, or to use Heidegger's terminology, "enframing" *(Gestell),* is not the destiny of Being which has just now started, but "has been dominant, though in a concealed form, from ancient times."[5] The function of setting up in "enframing" *(Gestell)* is derived from the function of setting up in *poiēsis* in ancient times. The functions of these settings up are essentially related, because they are both revealing *(Entbergung).*[6] Moreover, the meaning of *thesis* (setting up) functions in a concealed way in the term *phusis,* which is the primordial word expressing Being.[7] Heidegger characterizes it as follows: "*Phusis* is *thesis:* to lay something before one, to place it, to produce and bring it forth, namely into presence *(Anwesen)*."[8]

Seen in this manner, insofar as Being is Being, or insofar as Being is the revealing, it essentially has the function of "setting up." Therefore, the destiny of Being as "enframing" is the destiny originally determined insofar as Being is Being. "Enframing is the Being itself."[9] When "enframing" can be traced back to the primordial essence of Being, the concealment of Being itself, which is inseparable from the derivation of "enframing," is traced back to the primordial essence of Being also. However, from where are derived the functions of "setting up" and "revealing" which are "the same"[10] as the concealment?

"Enframing" is referred to as "making" *(Machenschaft)* in the lectures of Heidegger's middle period[11] and indicates the gathered totality of human creation and doing. If we interpret the function of "setting up" as the original sense of revealing, it corresponds to the "projection of world" *(Weltenwurf)* in *Being and Time* which makes it possible in advance for beings to be. However, Heidegger does not question why "projection of world," "making," and "revealing" emerge. Insofar as one remains within the standpoint of phenomenological description, one cannot go beyond asserting that Being always is only as revealing and that man is that which constantly acts and carries out the projection of world. This is nothing other than the fundamental fact of Being and man. If the unconcealment of beings is fundamental, then the concealment of Being, which is inseparable from it and which is the essence of nihilism, also turns out to be a fundamental fact. Consequently, it seems that one can only assert that nihilism is a fact of experience in the most profound sense.

If the essence of nihilism is manifest in the contemporary world as the fundamental nihility of beings, the contemporary period is the age when the oblivion of the truth of Being is thoroughly complete. And at the same time, it is also the age when the concealment of the truth of Being is exposed without any longer being obscured by the unconcealment of beings. When the concealment is experienced as concealment, it becomes possible to question the way to mitigate in some manner the violence of the destiny of technology which is the extreme form of the revealing of beings.

Incidentally, the fundamental nihility of beings in light of Buddhism is "all that is, is transitory" *(shogyō mujō)*. Buddhism teaches that "all that is, is transitory" is the true aspect of the world and claims that the enlightened awareness of this is transformed immediately into Nirvanic awareness of tranquility. In contrast, if we think of enlightened awareness in Heidegger or in the destiny of Western metaphysics, it must be thought to be achieved through the process of history, and moreover, at the very time when the oblivion of Being, though preventing such an awareness, reaches its maximum limit. At this moment the oblivion of Being turns round.

However, there must also be in Buddhism an ideal that one is prevented from this enlightened awareness, with his eyes enchanted only by beings rather than by the truth of Being. This brings us to the idea of *gō* (karma), the discussion of which will shed some light on the question with which we have been concerned, that is, the origin of the revealing, and thus, the origin of nihilism.

VII

The term *gō* is a Japanese translation of the Sanskrit word *karma* and means "making" *(zōsa)*. That is, it means to "make and act" *(gyō; saṃskāra)*. If it is correct to understand *gyō*, which is the second element of the formula of twelve-fold causation *(engi; pratītya-samutpāda)*, as *karma*,[12] then it means to "make by gathering." "Gathering" is a gathering of all indirect and direct causes *(innen; hetu-pratyaya)*. All things are realized by virtue of various harmonious combinations of direct and indirect causes. This requires something to gather all the direct and indirect causes: this is *gō*, or karma. The substance of karma is understood in early Buddhism to be "intention" *(shi)*, the "function of will."[13] Seen in this manner, karma can be understood as the function of will that gathers all things in order for beings to be. This corresponds to what Heidegger called the revealing of beings, although the former is formed with a volitional aspect.

Where does karma thus understood come from? The origin of karma is the concealment of truth, as it is said that "to make and act" *(gyō; saṃskāra)* is due to "absolute ignorance" *(mumyō; avidyā)*. Just as the concealment of Being engenders the revealing of beings in Heidegger, so the concealment of truth which is absolute ignorance emerges outwardly as karma. According to early Buddhist sutras, absolute ignorance is always juxtaposed with craving *(katsuai)*. Craving is insatiable "ego-desire," as in, for example, a thirsty person ceaselessly drinking water. Consequently, karma generated by absolute ignorance, that is, the essence of the function of will that reveals beings, can be understood as ceaseless ego-desire.

The idea of karma is further deepened in Mahayana Buddhism, especially in the thought of Shinran (1173–1262) in Japan. We have just said that the essence of karma is ego-desire. However, this does not mean that the "I" performs karmic action. Whether the present "I" does good or evil is dependent upon past karma *(shukugō; pūrva-karma)*.[14] The moral standpoint based upon the self-power *(jiriki)* is completely denied in the statement that "it is not because my mind (heart) is good that I do not kill." This means that all of one's existence is dependent upon past karma, that past karma determines all of one's present and future actions. However, the past, in which everything is determined before-hand, is no longer an aspect of time which is past, but is eternal. Past karma is an eternal fact without beginning or end. That is, past karma exists along with ignorance in an inseparable oneness with the existence of man. Past karma and absolute ignorance are, as it were, the funda-mental fact for human existence. This corresponds to the very same fun-damental fact that both the concealment of Being and the revealing of beings are equiprimordial.

As seen in the foregoing, past karma has ego-desire as its essence. Accordingly, if past karma is the fundamental fact for human existence, it means that we must carry on our shoulders ego-desire as the essence of our self, even though we have not chosen it ourselves. We must always live according to it. We are endlessly driven by our ego-desire, through which we constantly end up committing ourselves to something. This is our life. However, whatever we commit ourselves to, whether good or evil, is not our doing. It is brought about by our past karma, which is ego-desire.

Heidegger's investigation of the essence of technology does not at-tempt to define technology by placing man in the center in such a way as to regard technology either as a means for an end or as a tool for man's action. Rather, he regards the essence of technology as the function of truth that reveals beings, and through which all beings including man are set up. Consequently, the essence of technology thus conceived is not that which is "made by man,"[15] that is, it is not technical. Rather, it has "a transcendental character" which is unmanipulatable by man, tools, or machines produced by man. It claims man and thereby controls him. Because man always listens to the calling of this claim, he goes around ceaselessly so as to set up all beings as useful.

Seen in this manner, we must recognize that karma and the essence of technology are fundamentally functions of the same thing. In other words, karma or technology means ceaseless human action without beginning or end. An action in this sense has emanated from eons ago up to the present through the fountain of absolute ignorance (the conceal-ment of Being) accompanying the flood of (essentially nihilistic) beings, and thereby has formed the essence of history. This I take to be the ulti-mate origin of nihilism.

VIII

Finally, I would like to offer briefly my thoughts concerning how we should deal with the destiny of nihilism. As we have observed, the reveal-ing of beings (Enframing) or karma has generated history *qua* nihilism. However, insofar as revealing and karma are the eternal essence of human life and Being, their denial is a rejection of life and Being as such.

That is, the origin of nihilism is Being and life as such. But if we do not somehow reject nihilism, it leads to the destruction of Being and life. Either alternative means death. This is, no doubt, an inescapable predicament. How do we break through it?

One must shatter the delusion of beings which dominates the contemporary period by seeing thoroughly into the fundamental nihility which runs at the bottom of the stream of beings. Thereby one must bring karma, which brought forth this stream of beings, to self-awareness *(jikaku)* as "one's own sin of karmic action" which originated in the beginningless past. One must existentially bring to self-awareness the fact that Being is immediately "danger" and life is immediately "sin." The origin of ignorance or nihilism will not be transformed fundamentally until each of us carries out this "self-awareness." Only then, it would seem, can the "Enframing" and "karma" be housed within a quiet and calm light. However, the self-awareness that would bring about a transformation of world history cannot be attained through a half-hearted reflection on sin. Every one in his or her own self-awareness must realize that he or she is the most sinful being in the world. The phrase expressing such a self-awareness is "When I carefully consider the Vow *(gan, seigan)* which Amida brought forth after five kalpas' contemplation *(goko shiyui),* I find that it was solely for me, Shinran, alone!"

Translated by Monte Hull and S. Nagatomo

Notes

1. Martin Heidegger, *Was Ist Metaphysik?,* 6th ed. (Tübingen: Niemeyer, 1981), p. 41.
2. Heidegger, *Nietzsche II* (Pfullingen: Neske, 1961), p. 356.
3. Heidegger, *Was Ist Metaphysik?,* p. 10.
4. *Ibid.,* p. 11.
5. Cf. Heidegger, *Einblick in das, was ist* (1949).
6. Heidegger, *Vorträge und Aufsätze* (Pfullingen: Neske, 1967), pp. 28, 38.
7. Cf. Heidegger, *Einblick in das, was ist.*
8. Heidegger, *Vorträge und Aufsätze,* p. 49.
9. Cf. Heidegger, *Einblick in das, was ist.*
10. Heidegger, *Vorträge und Aufsätze,* pp. 270–272.
11. Heidegger, *Einführung in die Metaphysik* (Tübingen: Niemeyer, 1953), p. 122.
12. Kazuya Funabashi, *Gō no kenkyū* (Study of Karma) (Kyoto: Hozokan, 1952), p. 13.
13. *Ibid.,* p. 38.
14. I have learned much on the interpretation of *shukugō* (Karmic determination) from Yoshifumi Ueda's *Bukkyō ni okeru gō no shisō* (The Thought of Karma in Buddhism).
15. Heidegger, *Vorträge und Aufsätze,* p. 26.

Kōhei Mizoguchi

An Interpretation of Heidegger's Bremen Lectures: Towards a Dialogue with His Later Thought

The positive reception of Heidegger's philosophy in Japan can be roughly divided into two types. The first focuses entirely on the earlier period of Heidegger's thought, as does the great majority of Europeans who appreciate his philosophy. The other views the later Heidegger as of extremely positive value, and tries to reinterpret his early period from this latter standpoint, as Heidegger himself does. This tendency in Japan is probably due less to a desire to follow Heidegger himself very closely than to a recognition of an affinity with Oriental thought, and especially with Zen Buddhism, in the later Heidegger. This evaluation is largely attributable to the Kyoto School established by Kitarō Nishida, who tried to universalize and rationally explain his Zen Buddhist experiences through his encounters with Western philosophy.

The European philosophy which Kitarō Nishida critically confronted and assimilated was extremely broad-ranging, but Nishida only had occasion to learn of Heidegger's early thought, and therefore he could not help but be critical of Heidegger's failure to escape from what he perceived as a subjectivistic locus.[1] This position of Nishida's was intensified by his coinage of the term "the logic of place" in his later years, wherein he anticipates Heidegger's "turning" *(Kehre)* and goes beyond him, reaching the standpoint of "absolute nothingness" (which for Nishida is also absolute realism and absolute objectivism, transcending the polar opposition of subject and object). Nishida's "absolute nothingness" goes beyond the standpoint of Hegelian abstraction *(Idee)*; it is a philosophy of fundamental place, which lets things be the self-limitation of this place, and which accepts the reality of things as they are, established from that basic standpoint. According to this philosophy, the working of the self-limitation of "place" is at the same time the self-consciousness of the historically grounded human self having a concrete physical body.

If we may be allowed a comparison, the thought of absolute nothingness, as far as its form is concerned, has the character of a synthesis of
the "topological" thought of the later Heidegger and the "existential"
thought of the early Heidegger. Thus the Kyoto School, which tries to
follow the tradition of Nishida, naturally esteems very highly the topological thought of Heidegger after his turning. In addition to structural
similarities, of course, the existence of common terms and elements also
plays an important role in making possible the dialogue between these
two different traditions. But at the same time, the danger of lapsing into
subjectivity (or losing our objectivity) always lurks within the posture of
such a cross-philosophical dialogue. This danger increases in the philosophies of Nishida and Heidegger, which are both grounded in basic experience, and also try to go beyond the usual styles of thinking and forms of
expression. To retain our objectivity, therefore, we must always be conscious of their differences. This should be a fundamental precondition of
our mental attitude towards the appeal of any foreign philosophical tradition, and serve to shock us out of preconceptions which might otherwise lead us into subjectivism. With these provisos in mind, then, this
essay will attempt to interpret Heidegger's Bremen lectures, *Einblick in
das was ist* (1949), which both express the fruits of his middle period and
serve as an approach to his later thought.

Heidegger gave four successive lectures under the above title: "The
Thing" *(Das Ding),* "The Enframing" *(Das Gestell),* "The Danger" *(Die
Gefahr),* and "The Turning" *(Die Kehre).* Taken as a whole, these lectures
connect the shift from the "being-historical thought" *(seinsgeschichtliches Denken)* of his middle period with the notion of "Event" *(Ereignis)*
which is central to his later thought. To put it a little differently, these lectures suggest certain relations between Heidegger's topological-transcen-
dental side and his being-historical side, which constitute the most difficult problem in understanding both Heidegger and his appraisals by the
Kyoto School. While Nishida and the later Heidegger show some similarities in their topological and transcendental standpoints, there is a discrepancy between their views on the historicity of thinking itself, most
visible in their specific critical analysis of the contemporary historical
world. For Heidegger, the modern technical world is analyzed and characterized concretely as the Enframing, which is a privative form of the
coming-to-pass *(Geschehen)* of Being itself, and this analysis comes from
his being-historical thought and his topological investigations. Nishida
also treats the world as a concrete historical bodily presence. But even if
he formally emphasizes the historical world, since he sees history in an
abstract and formalistic view as the "self-limitation of absolute presence,"
he fails to look specifically at historical periods and analyze them. The
presence or absence of this critical analysis will not ultimately be due to

whether they treat history as a central issue, but to how radically historically grounded they see themselves as being. I want to focus on this problem of the historicity of thought as one of the noteworthy differences
between us and Heidegger. In the following interpretation, I shall treat
the problem of the historicity of thought as a problem of the relationships
between Event *(Ereignis)* and Enframing *(Gestell)*. In particular, I shall
focus on an analysis of the internal structure of Heidegger's thought, as
an attempt to lay the groundwork for a concrete philosophical dialogue.

I

The overall title of the lecture series which we are considering here,
"Insight into that which is" *(Einblick in das was ist),* is itself significant.
This title has a double meaning, which suggests the twofold nature of the
lectures' contents. First of all, "that which is" signifies the things which
exist and present themselves to us. But of course it does not just refer
only to the various things and events before our eyes. As Heidegger says,
"Without Being . . . all beings would remain without being."[2] Thus,
beings have to be seen from the perspective of Being. Moreover, we must
take the relative pronoun "which" *(was),* following Heidegger's technical
vocabulary, as referring to the active expression of essence *(Wesen).* Then
"that which is" expresses the "belonging together" *(Zusammengehörig-
keit)* of Being itself and the particular things which are for us within it.
"Being could not come to presence without beings."[3] So "Insight into that
which is" implies firstly the investigation into and thinking about the
coming-to-presence of Being, in terms of beings that are proximally
present. Heidegger treats the primary mode of the being of beings in
terms of technology *(Technik).* Enframing *(Gestell),* in turn, refers to the
destiny *(Geschick)* of Being which controls in and through the form of
technology. If we follow the structure of being-historical thought, then
the things which are must be taken from the assembling *(versammelnde)*
presence of history, and thus Enframing is understood as the ultimate
completion or fulfilment of metaphysics, the collective state of Western
traditional metaphysical essence. In this sense, for Heidegger, the interpretation of the present period and of historical thought becomes one. So
"Insight into that which is" is firstly an inquiry into technology, namely a
philosophical investigation of the nature of technology, or Enframing.

If Heidegger's thought had stopped at the standpoint of the traditional
ontological questions, "Insight into that which is" might have finished
with the question concerning technology. This is because ontological
issues tend to take as their central theme the study of the being of beings;
their enterprise begins and ends there. In fact, the system of ontological-
metaphysical inquiry treats truth as fixed and static, overlooking the

ever-changing reciprocity between truth and the being of the people who are inquiring into it. As far as the being of truth is concerned, the being of the inquirer is not necessarily essential to the being of truth itself. However, for thinking which takes as its basis the dynamic reciprocity of truth and the "historical" *(geschehende)* being of its inquirers, truth becomes something whose appearance *(Erscheinen)* is dynamically modified through that reciprocity with existence.[4] Therefore a philosophy which looks into the essence of technology, witnesses or experiences the essential modifications of Being as it is presented to human beings, within the belonging together of human beings and Being *(Zusammengehören von Mensch und Sein),*[5] which in other terms is the mutual reciprocity of thinking and truth. It is here that the relative pronoun "which" *(was)* in his title takes on the secondary meanings of an active verb. The philosophy which would look into the essence of technology—that which is—by experiencing the presence of that essence, gains the possibility of witnessing a new world different from that technology. In this sense the "that which is" *(was ist)* no longer signifies the modern technological way of being, but the coming-to-presence *(Wesen)* of the new, modified world. This modification of the world does not of course mean a change in the subjective perspective of beings. The entire mutual interrelationship between Being and beings undergoes a revolution. In my view, "that which is" means in Heidegger "what truly is," and this means "what essentially is" *(was west),* and that is the essential being *(Wesen)* of another new and authentic world as Event *(Ereignis).*

It is true that at the end of his lectures, Heidegger himself views "that which is" as the presence of Being itself.[6] But even Being itself is not something independent of beings, but refers to the whole, including both elements in their belonging together. If that were not the case, Being itself would, Heidegger emphasizes, again become something structurally similar to a metaphysical substance. We must also interpret from this perspective his position that the thing has no special elemental status in the Fourfold *(Geviert),* when he develops the Fourfold in his lecture "The Thing."

Heidegger takes this changing world (it is still a potential world) as the world in which things themselves each express their own peculiar characteristics *(dingen).* It is a presence (worlding) of the world itself in which the four elements of earth and heaven, mortals and divinities, are constantly and reciprocally reverting *(enteignen),* particularized into their individual being, and at the same time unified *(vereignen)* in their nature —a world of mirror-play *(Spiegel-Spiel).* He calls this world the Fourfold, and these kinds of happenings "Event" *(Ereignis).*[7] Thus this "Insight into that which is" is a philosophical inquiry into things, and things as they come to express themselves as things. But if we take the modifications of this world as the movement of Being itself, then an "Insight" *(Einblick)* does not simply mean an insight from the human side. Rather, it refers primarily to a "flash" *(Einblitz)* of the whole turning of affairs.[8] Thus "Insight into that which is" is also "The Turning" *(Die Kehre)*.

Especially in this case, the relationships between Enframing and Fourfold are not clear and distinct, but harbor problems. While both can be seen as the presence of Being itself, Enframing should be taken primarily in terms of a refusal of the world as the neglect of the thing *(die Verweigerung von Welt als die Verwahrlosung des Dinges)*.[9] On the other hand, the Fourfold, as the preserver of Being *(Wahrnis des Seins)*, is also regarded as the truth of the presence of Being *(Wahrheit des Wesens von Sein)*. Fourfold and Enframing are not similar *(das Gleiche)*, but are the same *(das Selbe)*. Yet in another place, Heidegger calls Enframing the prelude *(Vorspiel)* of Event.[10] Furthermore, the world as Fourfold is never a single mode of Being. Here, we once again confront the distinction between authenticity and inauthenticity from *Being and Time,* and the eschatological dimension of Heidegger's middle and later periods. Whether Heidegger's thought can contribute to modern philosophy depends largely on how we interpret this relation between Fourfold and Enframing.

Thus "Insight into that which is" comprises first "The Enframing," then "The Thing," and then "The Turning." What is then the relation of these to the remaining lecture, "The Danger" *(Die Gefahr)*? If we follow Heidegger, the Danger means the essence, coming-to-presence itself, of Enframing, which is the essence of technology. Heidegger tries to explain this curious relationship between the Danger and Enframing from the Old High German etymological root *fara,* which connotes both urging forward and exposing to danger. Leaving aside the accuracy of this derivation, we can explain the essence of the dominant function of the setting *(Stellen)* within "Enframing" as urging *(Nachstellen),* and that urging as Danger (gathering of urgings). At the same time, the extremity of Danger which we feel within the word we read as "Danger" points to a peculiar privative "hiddenness" *(Verborgenheit)* in the nature of Being itself. The Danger also expresses the coming to presence of hiddenness which is a fundamental tendency of Being itself. "Enframing comes to presence as Danger."[11] Therefore Enframing, as the Being of beings, refers to the present unhiddenness *(Unverborgenheit)* of beings which are.

Then "The Danger" refers to the coming-to-presence of Being itself which withdraws itself by conferring Enframing, namely the experience of the coming-to-presence of Being itself in the period in which Enframing dominates. In other words, "The Danger" comes to refer to a constellation of hiddenness and unhiddenness as a whole, or the simultaneous presence of both elements. From another perspective, if we can say that Being itself can turn, then Being itself can turn in that constellation. This is the terminus of the correlative circular movement of thought and experience itself (both of which progress from technology to Enframing). It expresses the extreme experience of Being itself, under the domination of technology. Here we have the conclusion and gathering of the workings of the being-historical thought *(seinsgeschichtliches Denken)* which Heidegger had carried out through his middle period. So "The Danger" is "The Turning" from "The Enframing" to "The Thing," and that which gives form to the point of contact of that move. The locus of this movement, which is given form and opened by the Danger, is the one and only place where we can treat the problem of the relations of Enframing and Fourfold. It is here that the experience of the domination of Enframing, as oblivion of Being, as distress, and as pain[12] *(Seinsvergessenheit, Not, Schmerz),* comes to take on a definite meaning, because this experience first proclaims the possibility of the modification of the world. Thus Heidegger's lectures on "Insight into that which is" are formulated on the necessary internal relations of each lecture, and as a whole, they point to one "occurrence" of Being—or in Heidegger's words, the Event.

Now as we noted before, these lectures occur in the order: "The Thing," "The Enframing," "The Danger," and "The Turning." But if we follow the above interpretation, considering their internal relations, the lecture on "The Thing" ought to come last. Then why is it put first? For the time being, we can think of two reasons. One is based on the peculiarly cyclical nature of Heidegger's thought, on the insight that "Primordial *(anfänglich)* earliness shows itself to man only at the end."[13] Thus the world of Event presented in "The Thing" is at once the last element and the earliest origin, and so is placed at the beginning as the origin. The second point is a problem of methodology which is essentially related to the first issue. In order to accomplish the fore-project *(Vorentwurf)* in terms of the hermeneutic circle, "The Thing" is placed first and so gives from the start to the subsequently developed thought a horizon which becomes a locus where the thought is achieved, and can later serve as a criterion. In this case, too, that which is placed first can also be placed last.

As has been often pointed out, the world of the Fourfold as Event articulated and developed in "The Thing" is a Presocratic Greek world dominated by myth *(muthos),* and is thus the oldest and earliest world. But Heidegger's philosophy does not assert simply its recurrence. If we follow being-historical thought, the oldest things endure in hidden form and are gathered even into the present age, as having been *(Gewesen).* For Heidegger, the oldest thing is at once the beginning and therefore the origin *(Anfang und Ursprung).* Those ancient origins which are now hidden are in fact the truth of Being itself. So if we want to think about the truth of Being, we first have to recollect the past *(das Gewesene)* itself. That is at the same time not only the oldest of things, but when we think about it, it must become the first thing to stand in our memories. In other words, we have to "pre-think" *(Vordenken)* against the arrival of the earliest origins again in the future. Heidegger writes: "Recollecting the past is pre-thinking into that which is unthought and should be thought. Thinking is recollecting pre-thinking *(Denken ist andenkendes Vordenken)*."[14] Thus the position of "The Thing" as the first lecture is most significant.

There arises here another confusing problem. Even if the world of Event is based upon the past, as long as it is pre-thought to be in the future, then it is no more than a possible world and not the real world of experience and actual occurrences. Moreover, the object of this kind of thinking has the danger of becoming merely a kind of thought-construction or idea. In one dialogue Heidegger mentions the arrival of Event as follows: "I don't know if this will ever happen or not! But within the essence of technology, I see the first glimmer *(Vorschein)* of a much deeper mystery, of what I call the 'Event'."[15] Does it suffice that we treat this as simply another case of Heidegger's often-touted prophetic personality? If we take Heidegger as being merely prophetic here, then we learn nothing from this statement, for there is no ultimate conclusion nor universal theory of Being within this view of his forward-looking thought of Event. Rather, it is precisely at this point that we find the most basic characteristic of Heidegger's perpetual inquiry into "that which must be thought." We may say that this is the integrity of Heidegger's thinking. Thus an interpretation which over-emphasizes the notion of Event is in danger of mistaking the basic direction of his thought. It is here that we see the decisive gap between Heidegger, who follows the process and direction of historical thought, and Nishida, who tries to draw out all reality based on a dialectical theory from absolute nothingness as the ultimate ground. Heidegger tries to ground the forward-looking character of his thought in a historical process. Therefore it is more appropriate to take his thought as the unification of the present, the future, and the past, based on the entirety of his "Insight into that which is." This entails a re-examination of the meaning of the lecture "The Thing" in its relation to the whole, from the standpoints of the cyclical nature of his thought and the structure of the hermeneutic circle.

II

The ontological hermeneutic circle, as presented in *Being and Time,* must be taken for the basic and necessary structure of human thought of which the basis is the mutual interdependence or correlativity between historical existence itself and the object of thought.[16] In the working of the hermeneutic circle, a fore-project takes over the past as legacy, and is revised through concrete interpretation and then concretely articulated. If we apply this kind of structure to the present case, then the world of the Fourfold presented in "The Thing" covertly plays the role of fore-project for Heidegger's thought, and as a criterial horizon, through a concrete interpretation of the present world as Enframing it itself becomes concretized, resulting in a new expression of the world of Event.

The world of the Fourfold as Event is not simply a world prophetically anticipated, rather it is the criterial horizon for the ontological interpretation in a broad sense of the present technological world. This may be recognized at several points. For example, only by using the world of Event as a criterion can we perceive the deficiencies of previous Western metaphysical systems which return into Enframing: "oblivion of Being," "neglect of the thing," the loss of true closeness *(Nähe)* in "uniform distance" *(das gleichformig Abstandslose)*.[17]

The being-historical thinking of Heidegger's middle period had continually seen that kind of negative, privative structure within the history of Western metaphysics, and thus tried to interpret and accomplish the fore-project of Event by making this Event a criterion and clue. This fore-project of Event was already made within a limited realm and covertly through Heidegger's turning. Of course this is not something concrete or thematized from the beginning; it shows its concrete form first through the process of circular practice.

Moreover, the criterial characteristics of the Fourfold go so far as to take the privative characteristics of Enframing as the coming-to-presence of Being itself. For example, this can be seen in the case of "The Question Concerning Technology" *(Die Frage nach der Technik)*. In this treatise, Enframing is regarded not only as the coming-to-presence of Being itself, but also as a derivative of the producing and exhibiting *(Her- und Darstellen)* seen in the ancient Greek *technē*.[18] For there is a similarity between Enframing and the revealing *(Entbergen)* as bringing-forth *(Hervorbringen)* seen in *technē*. Thus we can interpret the present world of technology as the working of the revealing of Being. On this point as well, the world of the ancient Greeks again functions as a fore-projected criterion for drawing out an interpretation of Heidegger. But in this case, the world of the Fourfold as Event which takes ancient Greece as its model is again the recurrent conclusion reached through a hermeneutic circle. Here we have to reflect more closely on that circular structure.

The horizon of meanings *(Sinnhorizont)* which bears the role of the fore-project in the movement of the hermeneutic circle does not exist independently in itself, nor is it derived or invented purely from thought. If we follow the thought of the earlier Heidegger and of other hermeneutic philosophies, the horizon of meanings originates and is derived dialogically from the past as history which already forms its present basis.[19] In this regard, insofar as Heidegger tries to take over the ancient Greek experience of Being as the true past, that Greek experience becomes the criterion and the fore-project underlying all interpretation of Being. But the situation is not so simple when the problem concerns the ontological horizon of meanings itself, since the ontological horizon of meanings has already been transmitted in some form or another from the past, before meeting with the past clearly and thematically. Gadamer calls this transmitted horizon of meanings "prejudice" (Vormeinung).[20] Here the horizon of meanings itself as prejudice is already a historical past condition, upon which the thematic engagement with the past can for the first time take place, and based on which dialogical circle a modified horizon of meanings becomes possible. The immediate past horizon of meanings, as "prejudice," is the primarily transmitted horizon of meanings of the present period, but it is not necessarily either self-conscious nor are its origins clearly discerned. Rather, it is because those origins are unknown that that prejudice wields its power.

But when Heidegger started down the road towards the question of Being in Being and Time, the first problem he encountered, in trying to clarify its meaning and origins, was the ontological horizon of meanings as just this prejudice. He did not start his analysis from the authenticity of Dasein, but rather from "everydayness." This shows that he took the prevalent prejudice for the fundamental reality, and therefore for the basic issue. Now if we want to look at prejudice for what it is, and treat it as a new problem of its own, then we need a new horizon that is not under the sway of prejudice. Again following the ideas of hermeneutic philosophy, that new horizon must be formed out of the dialogical interaction of prejudice and tradition. In Heidegger's case, the formation of a new horizon of meanings whereby to take prejudice for itself does not come immediately out of the encounter with the tradition of ancient Greece. Ever since Being and Time, the early Greek experiences of Being were a leading thread to which Heidegger continually referred.

This is not to say that the form and expression of ancient Greek experience directly guided all the concepts and analysis of Being and Time. Rather, what first contributed to forming the horizon of prejudice was traditional Western metaphysics, which he later was to characterize as privation—especially the philosophy of the eighteenth century onwards —which had already confronted and criticized such traditional metaphysics from a limited realm. (We may consider, among others, the names of Kant, Hegel, Nietzsche, Dilthey, and Husserl in particular.) But it is Heidegger's horizon that becomes a problem again in terms of its prejudices; it is here that the clear and dialogical encounter with ancient

Greece first takes place. Thereafter, within this encounter, prevalent prejudice and traditional Western metaphysics, which help form the horizon by which that powerful Greek tradition is interpreted, become a single great historical prejudice.

What does all of this clarify? First, insofar as we continue to have a limited perspective on the structure of the hermeneutic circle, then the new horizon formed from Heidegger's central encounter with ancient Greece must be formed from a dialogical encounter between Greece and the (later Western) metaphysical tradition as the prevalent prejudice. So of course we cannot call this new horizon objectively and historically equivalent to the ancient Greek experience of Being. Heidegger himself achieves "the effort to think through original thinking more originally,"[21] and recognizes this point when he calls that which must come "the other beginning" *(der andere Anfang)*. Secondly, the newly-formed horizon becomes a criterial horizon for the interpretation of both ancient Greek experience and the traditional and currently predominant interpretations of Being; but insofar as this new horizon is formed from a kind of fusion in the encounter with these two traditions, we cannot imagine that either will be completely adequate for a self-interpretation of this new horizon as a whole.

To put it a little differently, it is not the case that of the two—the ancient Greek experience and the predominant modern interpretations of Being—one would become a standard of truth, and the other merely a derivative. So, we cannot take the Fourfold of ancient Greek experience presented in "The Thing" as referring simply either to Heidegger's "protection of the truth of Being," nor to a unique form of the coming-to-presence of the world itself (worlding), nor to the expression of that which is awaited in the future. Rather, the fore-projected horizon leading Heidegger is not yet adequately and concretely articulated. So the world of the Fourfold as Event presented in "The Thing," even if it appears to take the final form of a fore-project itself, in the movement of the hermeneutic circle, is nevertheless in its basic nature something different. Nor can we say that the world of the Fourfold is a criterion by which the Enframing comes to be interpreted. As Heidegger tried to express their relations above, both are identical in their revealing *(Entbergen)*, and with respect to the coming-to-presence of Being, not equivalent but the same. At the same time, Enframing is the privation of the Fourfold, and the "luminescence of things to come." But these complicated expressions show us rather that their relations are not yet adequately experienced or understood. Heidegger could not achieve a dialogue synthetically fusing the classical Greek experience of Being and the traditional Western metaphysics which presently wields power in our prejudices; he was not able adequately to structure a horizon of meanings fusing the two. If that were possible, then from the viewpoint of the Fourfold, Enframing would be something other than mere privation; it would be given a concrete basis. Similarly, the world of the Fourfold would be locatable within the united whole of the present Enframing and the Fourfold and not need to be based in some future state separate from the present.

If we can make the comparison here, Nishida's standpoint of "absolute nothingness" tries to combine at one stroke both authenticity and inauthenticity, by locating it in the self-development of the dialectical self-determination of absolute nothingness. While this move of Nishida's philosophy bypasses metaphysics in its traditional sense, by grounding everything at once in absolute nothingness, it retains the metaphysical character of affirming everything in its hierarchic order of Being. Conversely, everthing is ultimately reduced to the absolute presence of absolute nothingness, by which it takes on a trans-historical position. Certainly Nishida himself thinks of the historical world as "the self-determination of the absolute present," and "immanence as transcendence."[22] But the specific historical contents of that self-determination are the focus of the world and neglected within "unlimited creativity." Even if the philosophy of absolute nothingness talks about historical determination, it fails to look at itself within that context. The world of technology which appears privative to Heidegger is indiscriminately given a positive evaluation as the active intuition of absolute nothingness in Nishida's philosophy.[23]

By contrast, because he wants to ground his thought in history and to avoid placing the authentic Event within a transcendentally absolute present, Heidegger tries to base his thought on the historical future. We do not have time to examine the implications of these differences here, but if we limit ourselves to Heidegger's side, we might make the following conjectures. The fore-project guiding Heidegger's thought may best be sought within the "and" linking Enframing and the Fourfold—and the domain opened up through their relationship might provide for the first time a criterion for interpretation. It is perhaps this question which covertly guided Heidegger's thinking on this issue.

Contrary to our original intentions, we have here abandoned the standpoint of looking at "Insight into that which is" as a complete movement of the hermeneutic circle for which "The Thing" is both fore-project and result. The lectures in their entirety constitute an attempt at a dialogue between current prejudices and ancient Greek experience, in the progressive pursuit of the formulation of a new horizon of Being. From this perspective, "The Danger" and "The Turning" express the hidden points of contact in the dialogue between "The Thing" and "The Enframing." This also sheds light on the role and position of the world of the Fourfold as Event, which are full of mysteries uninterpretable at a glance. Heidegger's pre-thinking is not towards the world of the Four-fold, but rather towards the unifying and fusing dialogue of Greek and modern thought hinted at in the "and" linking the Fourfold and En-framing.

Based on this understanding of the internal relations and the overall meaning of these complicated lectures, we can gain a better perspective on our own activities of interpretation. There has been hardly any work done on the internal criticism of Heidegger's idea of Event, which is cen-tral to his later thinking, nor of his lectures on "Insight into that which is" taken together—except for the work of Otto Pöggeler. This may be partly due to the fact that these lectures were not published as a whole, but more importantly to the fact that his thinking about Event takes a form which hardly admits of any criticism. That difficulty of criticism rests rather in our own tendency to view Heidegger's thought on Event as his ultimate teaching. If so, then the way to the idea of Event is closed to us, insofar as any approaches to Event are not indicated by Heidegger except through the "Turning of Being" and the "Leap" *(Sprung)*. For by what kinds of criteria, in what way can we criticize a philosophy of something we have never even approached, much less experienced?

At this point, we can simply point out certain questions which arise. If the thought of Event originates in the dialogue with Greek philosophy and takes ancient Greece as its model, is it not always something progres-sively self-determined, and not the ultimate conclusion of Heidegger's philosophy, nor adequate to express the entire domain of his problem? If this question is appropriate, then it gives us another chance and indeed a sounder ground upon which critically to re-examine the dialogue which Heidegger is conducting. Such a critical re-examination would start, not from a one-sided use of ancient Greece as a criterion, but from the possi-bility of the fusion of the Greek experience with the present horizon of meanings. Then we come to wonder whether it is necessary for the present horizon of meanings to include a dialogue with ancient Greece—or, to put it differently, whether the "dialogue with ancient Greece" itself is not already one of Heidegger's prejudices, which needs to be reconsid-ered. The possibility of this criticism in turn prepares the way for the dia-logue with Nishida's philosophy.

Translated by Carl Becker

Notes

1. Cf. *Nishida Kitarō Zenshū* (The Complete Works of Nishida Kitarō) (Tokyo: Iwanami Shoten, 1965–66), 10:406.

2. Martin Heidegger, *Was Ist Metaphysik?*, 9th ed. (Frankfurt: Klostermann, 1965), *Nachwort*, p. 46.

3. *Ibid.*

4. We can see how the ideas of the appearance of truth in the twentieth century are influenced by Hegel's *Phänomenologie des Geistes;* see H. Rombach, *Leben des Geistes* (Freiburg i. Br., 1977), p. 302.

5. Cf. Heidegger, *Identität und Differenz* (Pfullingen: Neske, 1957), p. 17.

6. Heidegger, *Die Technik und die Kehre* (Pfullingen: Neske, 1962), p. 43 (abbreviated as *TK* below).

7. Heidegger, *Vorträge und Aufsätze,* vol. 2 (Pfullingen: Neske, 1967), p. 52f. (abbreviated as *VA* below).

8. *TK*, p. 43f.

9. *TK*, p. 46f.

10. This is from *Identität und Differenz*, p. 25; in other contexts Heidegger uses the expressions *Vor-Schein* and *Vor-Erscheinung*. Cf. Heidegger, *Vier Seminare* (Frankfurt: Klostermann, 1977), p. 105; also R. Wisser, *Martin Heidegger im Gespräch* (Freiburg/München, 1970), p. 73.

11. *TK*, p. 37.

12. Cf. *TK*, p. 38; and also Heidegger, *Nietzsche II* (Pfullingen: Neske, 1961), p. 391f. Concerning *Schmerz*, cf. Heidegger, *Unterwegs zur Sprache* (Pfullingen: Neske, 1965), p. 27.

13. *VA*, 1: 22.

14. Heidegger, *Der Satz vom Grund* (Pfullingen: Neske, 1965), p. 159. Concerning *Vordenken*, cf. *Identität und Differenz*, p. 30.

15. R. Wisser, *Martin Heidegger im Gespräch*, p. 73.

16. Cf. Heidegger, *Sein und Zeit*, 10th ed. (Tübingen: Niemeyer, 1963), p. 148ff.

17. *VA*, 2:38.

18. *VA*, 1:13, 20.

19. Cf. H. G. Gadamer, *Wahrheit und Methode*, 4th ed. (Tübingen: Mohr, 1975), p. 250ff. *(Grundzüge einer Theorie der hermeneutischen Erfahrung)*.

20. *Ibid.*

21. *VA*, 1:22.

22. *Nishida Kitarō Zenshū*, 11:442.

23. *Ibid.*, 10:353.

Tetsuaki Kotoh

Language and Silence:
Self-Inquiry in Heidegger and Zen

I. The Question of the Existence of the Self

Our existence is thrown into total darkness. No matter how much our insights may illuminate it, darkness not only obscures the path we have come along and where we are heading for, but also casts shadows over our everyday life. If we are thrown into this world and are to be taken away from it without knowing why, this means that we exist as merely ephemeral and lack an ultimate goal. It is impossible to think that there are necessary reasons for human existence, which happens to be born on a small planet in the dark universe for such a short period of time in the vast history of the planet. Such a circumstance is not different at all from that of ants in the field. This absolute lack of ground constitutes the abysmal darkness of human existence. At the bottom of our existence is total nothingness which repels any kind of reasoning from the human perspective.

However, awareness of the darkness of existence is extremely rare. We are busy in everyday life, and if we instinctively sense anxiety in facing the darkness of existence we nevertheless usually manage to forget or avoid the abysmal aspect of our being. The structure of our everyday lives is informed by a double concealment: oblivion of the darkness of existence and escape from one's self. We ground our existence in numerous purposes which we think necessary for carrying out actual life. "Customs" or "habit" would be a name for this. Thus, the everyday self dozes comfortably in the peacefulness of existence, of which only the surface is comprehended.

There would be no problem if one could go through life in such pleasant somnolence without ever realizing its darkness. However, it is possible to share the tragic astonishment expressed by Kūkai in *Hizō Hōyaku:* "It is dark at the very beginning of one's birth and is still dark at the very end of one's death." Human beings do not only exist but are also capable of conscious rumination about existence—which constitutes both our dignity and misery. Once a crack starts to open up in a life which runs along the tracks of custom, the dark abyss begins to threaten our existence. Human beings are not sufficiently cunning to be able to conceal their true selves to the end; nor are they strong enough to endure such darkness.

This is the very reason why, from the beginning, philosophy and religion have sought a way of being in which one interrupts the somnolence of everyday life, becomes aware of its darkness, acknowledges and illuminates this darkness, and rests with a peaceful mind. Illuminating and acknowledging life and death is the ultimate concern for Buddhism. Such inquiry into the self is what is urged by the "Know yourself!" of Socrates, and is the essence of conversion in Christianity whereby one reaches the state spoken of in Galatians in which "it is not I who lives, but Jesus Christ who lives in me." There is no more urgent or basic concern for a human being than the conversion by which the everyday self becomes aware of its self-concealment, returns to the dark bottom of life and seeks a solid place in which to reside peacefully. However, self-transformation does not mean that the self changes to another self, but that the self whose true existence is concealed returns to the non-vacillating self, and in this sense means the birth of the true self.

There is a variety of ways of self-inquiry. It is possible to look at it as a change in the way one relates to others or to society, or as a change in total world-view. This could even be studied from a psychological or neurophysiological perspective. In this paper I shall treat the problem from the perspective of language. To explain why I take this perspective, I must touch upon "the linguisticality of human experience of the world," as discussed by Heidegger and his successor Gadamer. Since the idea of the primacy of language is more prominent in Gadamer's thought, I shall present it with reference to his work, though I shall end by suggesting that he ultimately misunderstands Heidegger's thoughts on language.

II. The Linguisticality of Human Experience

In response to Heidegger's later thought, in which the emphasis on language is expressed in the famous dicta, "Language is the house of Being" and "Language speaks,"[1] Gadamer develops his theory of the "linguisticality of human experience of the world." "The linguisticality of human experience" means that "the human relationship to the world is absolutely and fundamentally linguistic" (*WM* 45; *TM* 432–433). The question whether or not pre-linguistic experience can be described is not the issue; it is rather that the existence of any pre-linguistic state is denied.

Gadamer's contention is that "coming to language" *(Zur-Sprache-Kommen)* constitutes a universal ontological structure and, therefore, all that can be understood is language (*WM* 450; *TM* 431–432). Normally, the propositional statement is considered to be the level at which language first emerges; but, according to Gadamer, possible objects of propositional expressions, preceding propositions, are included in the horizon of the world (*WM* 426; *TM* 408). This means that even a perspective independent of language, such as the "pure transcendental subjectivity of the self" in Kant and Husserl, cannot escape involvement with a linguistic community and so cannot be posited at the ground of language as the subjective restriction which makes language possible and valid (*WM* 330; *TM* 311). In other words, language has invaded the transcendental domain as an *a priori* restriction that enables the world to emerge. Language in this sense has to be distinguished from linguistic phenomena (phonetic letters and forms of their representation) which are found alongside other beings within the world already constructed by language. Further, this function of language pervades not only linguistic phenomena but also the structure of all possible objects. An abysmal unconsciousness or self-oblivion which "presents the world and itself disappears" envelops language perceived as "a particular and unique process of life" *(Lebensvorgang)* (*WM* 422; *TM* 404), which enables the objectification of everything without itself becoming an object.

How does the linguisticality of experience gain its foundation? Gadamer argues that experience is essentially understanding, and that understanding and interpretation *(Auslegung)* are essentially intertwined (*WM* 377; *TM* 361). "The internal twining" means that "conceptualization is internally woven into all possible understanding," in other words, "linguistic formulation" resides tacitly as the "historical sediment of meanings" (*WM* 380f; *TM* 364f). Behind this is the claim that "language is the universal medium in which understanding itself realizes itself. Its mode of realization is interpretation" (*WM* 367; *TM* 350). What constitutes the basis of Gadamer's thought is the thorough study of the historicality of human beings, and he connects this "belonging-to-history" with Heidegger's elucidation of "the structure of pre-predicative understanding."

Human beings are constantly thrown into finite circumstances formed by historical conditions, and these historical circumstances delimit their cognition and experiences. Historical tradition is formed by the interaction of "my past and not-my-past" and it involves "pre-concepts or pre-judgements" which have become an historically active reality in our existence beyond our will and actions. Understanding does not follow tradition blindly. It includes existential possibilities of the future which apply to and vitalize the past (tradition), and it integrates these into the present circumstances (*WM* 290; *TM* 274). Therefore, tradition does not wither but continues to live as a determinant which opens up new understanding. Though restricted by tradition, understanding is a creative process which vitalizes it. As in Heidegger, understanding becomes further articulated in linguistic interpretation.

Gadamer claims that the linguisticality of experience exhausts all possible experience. His argument for this rests on a combination of Heidegger's articulation of the "as-structure" of experience with the historicality of experience. An extensive network of linguistic meaning-associations, which, sedimented historically, is the linguistic community in which we were raised through acquiring a language, forms the tacit perspective (world horizon) or ground for beliefs which have not yet been thematized. This network serves as the source of fore-seeing and of the as-structure of experience. Language constitutes a "medium" (*Mitte*—*WM* 432; *TM* 414) between people and the world through representing *(darstellen)* the world for human beings. Human being as being-in-the-world is a being *in* language.

Why language is a guide to self-inquiry has become clear: it provides the encompassing perspective for all inquiry into the self. However, the question is whether this means that everything can be reduced to language. Can the entire reality of our being be grasped from the level of language? I shall not for the time being attempt to answer this interesting question in contemporary philosophy that has experienced "the linguistic turn." What I do want to say is that until one situates the approach to the question of self-transformation within the realm of linguistic phenomena it will not be possible adequately to illuminate the internal relationship between the reality of the self and language. Self-transformation can then be described as a process in which the normal relationship between language and reality breaks down into silence, and language then revives through such silence. It is only at the level of the everyday self that language as self-evident presupposition restricts our experience of the world. The true relationship between self and language is restored when the framework of everyday language breaks down to let silence emerge and give rise to creative language. This intimate relationship between language and the ground of self (silence), which is central to Heidegger's thinking about language, is something Gadamer fails to recognize. Furthermore, this emphasis on silence distinguishes Heidegger from the mainstream Western tradition, which makes *logos* central, and also brings him close to oriental thinking based on silence.

III. The Collapse of Everyday Language

A major theme in *Being and Time* is that everyday *Dasein* suffers from "loss of self" *(Selbstverlorenheit)* through "evaporating" *(Aufgehen)* into the world of its concern. *Dasein* allows itself to be absorbed into *das Man,* the impersonal, collective "one"—and a major factor here is language in its aspect of *Gerede,* "idle talk" or "chatter." As *Gerede* language, rather than functioning as a medium, closes *Dasein* off from the world and from itself, and provides comfort and security by giving everything out as unmysterious and self-evident. In this capacity, language is, admittedly, necessary for carrying out the business of everyday life, but one should not be misled into thinking that it thereby discloses the world as it is. This becomes clear when language as *Gerede* collapses and is no longer viable.

Various things can trigger the awakening from the everyday self—incurable disease, the death of a loved one, the realization of one's own death, and so on. What is common to these triggers is a negative understanding such as loss of perspective or collapse of a value system, and the resulting feeling of insecurity and despair. In Nietzsche's words, "We lose the center of gravity which has enabled us to live. For a while we lose all sense of direction." (*Will to Power,* sec. 30) Existential questions like Kierkegaard's—"Where am I? Who am I? How have I come here? What is this world called 'the world'? Who has brought me here and left me here?"—surge forcefully forth.

These are not the ephemeral questions of a weak soul, but derive from the very structure of human beings, who are able to reflect upon their own existence and to try to seek reasons and meaning for it. In everyday life, the purposes of practical life have been substituted for the reasons for human existence. When the meaning-relations of everyday language collapse as a whole, one is thrown into an incomprehensible chaos of phenomena without meaning. When the ultimate meaning of life fails, what one sees is mere nothingness which repels any attempt at rationalization. Language is unable to grasp such a bare reality. The world becomes disconnected from language and floats by itself. "Our entire foundation cracks and the earth opens up into abysses" (Pascal, *Pensées* 72). The experience of *Angst* is so oppressively heavy that one is unable to speak.

IV. The Authentic Self and the Creation of Language

The experience of the abysmal nature of our being, of the nothingness at its ground, is not necessarily terrifying, as long as one has the appropriate attitude. From the perspective of Zen (and something similar is true for Heidegger) the experience of the abysmal nothingness of the self and the world is the starting point for "salvation." In Dōgen's words: "One who falls to the ground gets up with the help of it" *(Shōbōgenzō).* For Zen, one who realizes the "suchness" *(tathāta)* or "Buddha-nature" of all things may be called "the true person who exists everywhere and nowhere." In the "Birth and Death" fascicle of the *Shōbōgenzō,* Dōgen writes: "When one lets go and forgets both body and mind, throws them into the Buddha's house, lets things happen from the side of the Buddha, following along with them, one would not force things or strive to expend one's mind—and thus one leaves behind the world of birth and death and becomes a Buddha." Here, beyond the concerns of life and death, there opens up a condition in which one's true self is freely based on no-ground.

In such a condition there is no split between the world and the one who observes it. "The mountains and waters of this very moment" *(nikon no sansui)* are at the same time "the presence of the Way of the ancient enlightened ones" *(kobutsu no dō genjō).* The true self is not separated from the world but has become one with it; there is neither subject nor object. What opens up within the horizon where subject and object are not yet separated is the state where experiences remain as they are without being judged (Nishida's "pure experience"). There the world, which had hitherto been rigidified by linguistic segmentation, gradually becomes fluid, thereby dissolving the boundaries created by segmentation. The shapes of things which have been sharply distinguished from each other subtly lose their sharp definition, and with the elimination of distinct boundaries things come mutually to interpenetrate each other. What now comes to the fore is "spontaneous arising" *(jinen shōki),* in which things inherently arise and open up the field of cosmic mutual interpenetration, and which is itself Nothing, without segmentation, and one with itself. This entire *Ekstase* is "pure experience."

The Zen tradition offers many examples of such "pure experience": "samadhi in perception" *(chikaku zammai),* "seeing color / forms, the self is enlightened" *(ken shiki myō shin),* "hearing sound the Way is realized" *(mon shō go dō).* These expressions come from Zen masters' attaining enlightenment through seeing a flower, hearing a pebble strike bamboo, and so on. This state is also described in Dōgen's poem: "Since there is no mind in me, when I hear the sound of raindrops from the eave, the raindrop is myself." The raindrop is me because at bottom there opens up another dimension—spontaneous arising—in which we are of the same "element." There is no mystery in this state; it is rather that we are facing reality as it is. However, this reality is totally different from reality as ordinarily experienced, since it is perceived without the overlay of everyday language. In the former state, life is experienced as transparently condensed combustion. The moment of combustion is pure silence beyond where language is exhausted. There the primordial reality of the world, which cannot be reached by language, keeps silently boiling up.

The language of the true self emerges from this silence. It arises from and is nourished by silence to become something which expresses this silence. Silence is also a feature of the experience of nihilism, in which one realizes the inadequacy and unreliability of ordinary language in describing the reality that is beyond it. In the case of nihilism silence is experienced "negatively" in the severing of the thread connecting language with reality. Such silence is a dead silence which rejects linguistic articulation. However, for the true self silence is an echo of true reality, and it becomes the positive ground for the production of a language to describe the world. Kūkai calls this level of true reality "esoteric language" or "esoteric mantra," which Mahāvairocana (*dainichi nyorai* in Japanese—a *mana*-like life-energy which pervades the totality of nature) speaks in the silence of nothingness. Mahāvairocana is the working of spontaneous arising (which one might compare with Heidegger's *Ereignis*) which is the ground of the world without aspects or segmentations and makes possible the arising of all phenomena. Spontaneous arising, the genuine state without segmentation or differentiation, the source of all existence, is entirely hidden by ordinary language with its definitions of reality and its segmentation by means of standard constants.

Kūkai says: "With ordinary people the true perception of true nature is prevented by "obscuring fantasies" *(mumei mōsō)*. What he means by "obscuring fantasies" must be this ordinary language as a network of standardized invariables. The very language which was acquired to describe the world has concealed it and has confined the everyday self into a life run by habit and inertia. However, the true self, by returning to silence as the pure manifestation of reality, joins with the flow of spontaneous arising's silent segmentation, and for the first time encounters the original segmentation which begins to create the worlds of individual things. The pulse in the silence of the original segmentation, which is audible in the world's beginning to produce its original meaning, is Kūkai's "esoteric language." This is not of course a physical sound that can be acoustically perceived, but is rather what Dōgen calls the "expounding of impermanence" *(mujō seppō)*, which should be heard "through the entire embodied self" *(tsū shin sho)*, or what Kūkai calls "the expounding of *dharmakāya*" *(hosshin seppō)* or "the conversation language of *dharmakāya*" *(hosshin dango)*. This can be considered as the original phenomenon (original segmentation of beings) which transcends language—corresponding to Heidegger's "echo of silence" *(Geläut der Stille)*. The original segmentation of beings that is esoteric language wells up within the silence of the true self. As Kūkai says in *The Meanings of Sound, Word and Reality (Shōji Jissō Gi):* "Sound resounds through the five great things, there is language throughout the ten realms, everything in the six dusts is text." This echo of the silence of the original segmentation of beings, which can be called "cosmic language," flows out wondrously into the arena in which people live. This silence cuts into and explodes the network of ordinary language which has degenerated into mannerism. At the same time it restructures and modifies previous meanings in such a way as to create a new form of language. Ordinary language can thus be constantly questioned and nourished by silence and be reborn as a language capable of describing the life-breath of silence. The thread which was cut between reality and language is then retied through this silence. Silence is the source of language.

V. Heidegger and the Echo of Silence

It is possible to gain a better sense of Heidegger's thinking about language, which has not been fully understood so far, if we consider it in the light of the Eastern ideas about language, silence, and esoteric language discussed earlier. Furthermore, Heidegger's philosophical analysis, being relatively systematic and quite rigorous, can help to clarify the idea of the realm of silence, the Eastern descriptions of which have been primordially mystical in nature. Heidegger has clearly affirmed the fundamental role of language in constituting the world and our experience. Language is not "the means to portray what already lies before one," but rather it "grants presence—that is Being—wherein something appears as existent" (*US* 227; *WL* 146). Since language is "the house of Being," one reaches Being by constantly going through this house. "Whenever we go to the well, or walk through the wood, we are always already going through the word 'fountain' and the word 'wood,' even though we are not saying these words or thinking of anything linguistic" (*Hw* 286; *PLT* 132). In saying this, Heidegger means that language is correlative with experience of the world. "Phenomena in the world occur simultaneously with the occurrence of language"; and "the world exists only where words exist" (*EH* 35ff). It is obvious that such a view, which could be misunderstood as a theory of the absolute primacy of language, has influenced Gadamer's view of language (*WM* 461; *TM* 443).

However, the central perspective in Heidegger's thought is that of viewing language in relation to Being—that is, questioning why language can be "the presencing of Being" through returning to the truth of Being which constitutes the origin of language. Regarding the unhiddenness of Being, he says: "This does not mean that we depend on what unhiddenness says, but that everything that is said already requires the domain of unhiddenness. Only where unhiddenness reigns can something be said, be seen, be indicated and be heard." In other words, we stand in between Being and language, "two principles which attract each other at the same time repel each other" (*EH* 43), and we try to find the way to the true nature of language where Being "itself comes to language" (*EH* 74).

What stands in between language and the truth of Being (the source of language) "what has not yet attained birth (Old High German *giberan*)" is not language but silence (*US* 55)—"blazing insight" trembling in "the incandescence of sacred lightning" (*EH* 67; *WL* 186). This means that the basic phenomenon which Heidegger attempted to reveal is the movement whereby language issues from and is supported by "the echo of silence" which is heard and followed within "the silence of stillness" (*Schweigen der Stille—US* 67), and that this movement is a basic current which flows through not only his theory of language but also through his thinking in general. The extent to which Heidegger's thinking on this topic is consonant with the Eastern ideas discussed in the previous section should now be obvious.

Section 34 of *Being and Time,* which Heidegger later called "quite sparse . . . too short" (*US* 137; *WL* 41–42), already suggests the origin of language. In these chapters the way of being of language is defined as *Rede* (discourse). *Rede* is "the articulation of the disposed *(befindlich)* intelligibility *(Verständlichkeit)* of being-in-the-world according to its significance" (*SZ* 162). Heidegger's early theory of language, developed through *Rede,* comprises the following three points: (1) the function of *Rede* is to articulate in terms of linguistic meaning our understanding of being-in-the-world and to make it possible to see it. *Rede* is the basic factor in disclosing the present "there" *(Da)* of being-in-the-world. (2) However, both disposition *(Befindlichkeit)* and understanding *(Verstehen)* participate in the structuring of disclosedness. (3) What is essential in Heidegger's theory of *Rede* is the fact that language is grounded in Dasein. Heidegger distinguishes meaning *(Sinn)* and significance *(Bedeutung)*. *Bedeutung* (what is articulated by *Rede*) is preceded by already-projected meaning as something which is possible prior to linguistic articulation; that is, *Rede* is post-articulation of Dasein. This does not mean that Dasein is dependent on language but that language has its roots within Dasein. In other words, language appears based on being-in-the-world as historical existence and is cultivated and defined there. After the so-called turning *(Kehre),* corresponding to Dasein's being seen from the perspective of the destiny of Being as the *Da des Seins,* the true being of language is vividly characterized as an echo or response to "the soundless voice of Being." Language, which functions in the disclosing of world, considers the world (and the clearing of Being—*Lichtung des Seins)* as its own hidden source for appearing. It can be born for the first time only by responding to *(Entsprechen)* the calling *(Anspruch)* of the soundless voice of Being. Even though the openness of Being eventually manifests as language, it is itself the source of language and as such is not under our control. Language makes sense because it has its origin in the "soundless voice of Being," which precedes and continues to accompany language, and without which language cannot say a word. Therefore, Heidegger says that "according to the essence of the history of Being, language is the house of Being which arises from and is structured by Being" (*US* 79). Just as a wave is always a sway of the ocean, language is "language of Being" (*US* 119).

However, this does not mean that the truth of Being quickly and at once becomes language. Being disappears the minute we thought it appeared *(An-und-Abwesen)*. The truth of Being is not like "a fixed stage where the curtain is left open" but appears from within in active tension where it constantly breaks out into openness. In order to correspond accurately to our original reality which appears as a duality of revelation and concealment, what is needed is a sharpened "preparedness" which becomes aware of the hiding of the constantly escaping Being and which looks from the "mystery" *(Geheimnis)* to the "hidden source." This awakened readiness is silence—a place of no language—and is a place of stillness (*SD* 75). Heidegger spoke earlier of the way in which anxiety silences speech and is "one of the essential places of speechlessness in the sense of the terror that attunes man into the abyss of nothingness" (*WM?* 32 and 51). And later, in a different metaphor, he spoke later of "looking at aspects of the invisible" (*US* 73).

It will lead to the mistake of focusing too much on language, as Gadamer did, if one fails to place the "stillness of silence" (*EH* 66) at the center of Heidegger's theory of the relationship between language and Being. It is silence that hears the echo of stillness which constitutes the essence and origin of language. It is not *logos* but silence as "basic mood/voice" *(Grundstimme)* that encounters the wonder of the presencing of Being, being attuned *(gestimmt)* by the silent voice *(lautlose Stimme)* of Being and responding *(abstimmen)* from it (*EH* 74). Therefore, the echo of stillness which can be heard within this silence, even though it is the source of language (*Ursprache—EH* 40) which moves language from its ground and supports it, is not in itself "something linguistic." The echo of stillness is the silent *logos* of the ancient origin beyond the particular features of everyday-level language, such as history, society, or communication, and is "an original announcement" (*Urkunde—US* 267; *WL* 135) of the world-reality which can exist purely only inside the silence which does not yet allow the invasion of linguistic articulation. The echo of stillness should be distinguished from the articulation by "the language of historical human being" (*IM* 50) which resulted from it. And, therefore, no matter how genuine a word may be, generated as the echo of stillness, it is not itself linguistic, and it is impossible to articulate exhaustively the echo of stillness, which can live purely only in silence. Silence which belongs and listens to the echo of stillness clings endlessly to the language which corresponds to the truth of Being both at the beginning and in its phenomenological process. In this sense, the true nature of language is characterized as "not saying and at the same time saying" or "silent indication" *(Erschweigen)* (N 471f).

If philosophy is to grasp the phenomenon itself, if it is to crystallize into living language the primordial phenomenon by "exploding already-existing meaning," rather than by organizing "a chaotic world" into an "already acquired system of meaning," then it does not follow that philosophical thinking must necessarily consider language as ultimate and regulate everything in accordance with language. Rather, one should step into the circle of language and experience which are vitally and intensely tied together, and listen belongingly *(gehören)* to the sound of silence which constantly emanates from the depths of the indescribable, and continue to let this be the source of one's own language.

Translated by Setsuko Aihara and Graham Parkes

Note

1. Martin Heidegger, *Basic Writings,* p. 193, and *Poetry, Language, Thought,* p. 190.

Subsequent references will be cited in the body of the text by means of the following abbreviations followed by the page number:

BW *Martin Heidegger: Basic Writings,* ed. David F. Krell (New York: Harper and Row, 1977)

EH Heidegger, *Erläuterungen zu Hölderlins Dichtung* (Frankfurt: Klostermann, 1951)

Hw Heidegger, *Holzwege* (Frankfurt: Klostermann, 1972)

IM Heidegger, *An Introduction to Metaphysics,* trans. Ralph Manheim (New Haven: Yale University Press, 1959)

N Heidegger, *Nietzsche I* (Pfullingen: Neske, 1961)

PLT Heidegger, *Poetry, Language, Thought,* trans. Albert Hofstadter (New York: Harper and Row, 1975)

SD Heidegger, *Zur Sache des Denkens* (Tübingen: Niemeyer, 1969)

SZ Heidegger, *Sein und Zeit* (Tübingen: Niemeyer, 1967)

TM Hans-Georg Gadamer, *Truth and Method* (New York: Seabury, 1975)

US Heidegger, *Unterwegs zur Sprache* (Pfullingen: Neske, 1959)

WL Heidegger, *On the Way to Language* (New York: Harper and Row, 1971)

WM Gadamer, *Wahrheit und Methode* (Tübingen: J. C. B. Mohr, 1960)

WM? Heidegger, *Was Ist Metaphysik?* (Frankfurt: Klostermann, 1981)

Graham Parkes

Afterwords—Language

The only extended engagement with Asian philosophy in Heidegger's published works is the "Dialogue on Language between a Japanese and an Inquirer" of 1954 (published in *On the Way to Language*), and although this work has been mentioned in one or two of the preceding essays, a few words more about it may be in place. The original title is significant: "Aus einem Gespräch von der Sprache zwischen einem Japaner und einem Fragenden." The assonance between the words *Gespräch* and *Sprache* intimates a close connection between the conversation and its concern. More important is that the conversation is not *über* but "von *der Sprache*": the *von* is ambiguous and suggests that the conversation is as much (or more) *from* or by language as it is about it. The interlocutors strive to avoid speaking *about* language, trying rather to let the conversation be led by and issue from out of the essential being of language itself *(vom Wesen der Sprache her)*.

The tone of "the questioner"—sounds like Heidegger himself, on the track of Being—is from the beginning not overly optimistic. If language is "the house of Being," then European and East Asian thinkers presumably dwell in very different houses, and "a dialogue from house to house thus remains almost impossible."[1] Heidegger has pondered the being of language as deeply as any other thinker, and yet he has his questioner admit near the beginning: "I do not yet see whether what I am trying to think as the essence of language is *also* adequate to the nature of East Asian language . . ." (G 94, E 8). This expressed concern distinguishes Heidegger's reflections on the nature of language from those of his predecessors, deepening his discourse away from the tradition of taking into account only the Indo-European languages.

Later in the conversation the questioner reiterates that "for East Asian and European peoples the *essential being* of language (*das Sprach*wesen)

213

remains something completely different." He then asks his guest: "What does the Japanese world understand by language? Asked even more cautiously: Do you have in your language a word for what we call language? If not, how do you experience what with us is called language?" (G 113, E 23). The stage directions here prescribe a long silence during which the Japanese reflects upon the questions. If he says no, there is no such word, he may not be able to think about language as we understand it. Eventually he replies that there is indeed such a Japanese word—but without saying what it is. The suspense is maintained until close to the end of the dialogue: the conversation veers off on a detour of over twenty pages before coming back to the point.

The word in question turns out—to the disappointment of some, perhaps, who may have been expecting something more exotic—to be the usual Japanese word for language: *kotoba*. The second of the two characters which comprise this word, *ba*, means "leaves," or "petals." There is an interesting temporal element to this character, which may have intrigued Heidegger, in that one of its components is *se*, which means "world, generation, age, era." But it is the *koto*, according to the Japanese guest, that is the difficult thing to determine—although the task is made easier by the conversers' having already spent a great deal of time and effort pondering the term *iki*. They eventually agree to render *iki*—in patently Heideggerian language—as "the pure delight of the calling stillness," and the Japanese suggests that *koto* can then be characterized as "that which itself gives delight, which uniquely in each unrepeatable moment comes to shine in the fulness of its grace" (G 142, E 45).

Shortly thereafter, the guest calls *koto* the source of the interplay between *iro* and *kū*. These two are the Japanese readings of the Chinese *se* and *k'ung*, which are in turn translations of the Sanskrit *rupa* and *śūnyatā*. These are the Buddhist terms for beings, or existents (what Heidegger would call *das Seiende*), and nothing, or emptiness *(das Nichts)*. *Kotoba* as language would thus be "the leaves/petals that stem from *koto* [understood as the source of beings and nothingness]." The questioner is delighted with this, calling it "a wondrous word, inexhaustible by thinking," adding that it means something other than do our Western, "metaphysical" names for language (G 144, E 47). This delight is echoed in a lecture from four years later, in which Heidegger meditates at some length on a stanza of a hymn in which Hölderlin calls language "the flower of the mouth," and remarks that "In language the earth blossoms towards the bloom of the sky" (G 206, E 99). *Kotoba* can also be understood as "the flower of the mouth," since it shares with its counterparts in European languages a reference to the mouth and speech. Read pictographically, the character for *koto* shows a mouth with sound issuing from it, and the Chinese-based reading of it is *gen*, meaning "speech." On the Western side, our word "language" and its cognates in the Romance languages come from the Latin *lingua,* meaning "tongue," the Greek *glōssa* means "tongue" as well as "language," and the German *Sprache* comes from *sprechen,* "to speak."

However, something strange is happening here: there seems to be a step missing, some premise suppressed. There is no inherent connection between *iki* and *koto,* and the interlocutors have not established one. How do they get from the speaking mouth to the source from which arise existents and emptiness? How does the Japanese *koto* avoid being subverted by metaphysics—which dichotomizes language into two components, a sensible (spoken or written word) and a suprasensible (meaning) —the way our Western tongues are? It cannot be simply because *ba* denotes tangible issues in the form of petals and leaves rather than some suprasensible, ideal meaning. One speaks in Japanese of *koto no ha* as well as of *kotoba,* and some etymologies suggest that the *ha* was originally a different character, *hashi* (Chinese reading: *tan*), a remarkable graph meaning both end and origin—edge or border—beginning and end. So language would be the ending origins, or original edges, first blooms from the source of beings and nothing.

There is something behind the *koto* that is the link. It is a central idea in Confucian thought that to speak is tantamount to *to do,* that saying is action in the fullest sense. This, like many other Confucian ideas, carries over to the Japanese tradition and manifests in the fact that *koto* meaning "speech" was originally the same word—in *manyōgana,* the ancient phonetic use of Chinese characters—as *koto* (Chinese reading: *ji*), meaning "matter" in the sense of "affair" or "circumstance"—a nonsubstantial "thing" spoken by language. With this meaning in mind we can appreciate the questioner's frequently expressed delight at the idea of language's being the petals that blossom from the source of beings and nothing. *Koto* can now be understood as *die* Sache *des Denkens*[2]—a frequent locution in the later Heidegger, and one that is difficult to translate. Perhaps "the *matter* of thinking" in the sense of "topic," "subject," or "theme" will do—as long as one does not understand "matter" in the purely physical sense. Language as *koto* would then be that "thing" which calls for thinking, the matter at hand as one plies the craft of thought, and from which words (cor)respondingly issue as spontaneously as the petals of a flower unfold.

If the flowers unfold somewhat differently in the East and the West, perfect translation from one language to the other will not always be possible. However, the difficulty of translation obtains also within each individual tradition: just as certain ideas in Plato stubbornly defy translation and have to be read in the original Greek, so there may be ideas in ancient Asian philosophies which cannot be adequately expressed even in the corresponding modern languages—let alone in languages of the Indo-European family. But the impossibility of complete translation does not necessarily rule out communication altogether—especially if both sides learn the other's language. Because the Western and East Asian houses of Being are set apart does not mean that dialogue is as close to impossible as Heidegger's questioner fears. Houses stand on ground, just as leaves and petals stem from roots in the earth. And one can, with time and effort, come to feel at home in another house.

Notes

1. Martin Heidegger, *Unterwegs zur Sprache* (Pfullingen: Neske, 1959), p. 90; *On the Way to Language,* trans. Peter D. Hertz (New York: Harper and Row, 1971), p. 5. The translations of Heidegger's German are my own, and I shall refer to the German original and the English translation by the abbreviations G and E respectively, followed by the page number.

2. *Die Sache* has been an important idea in modern German philosophy—and especially in phenomenology. Hegel uses it to denote the proper object of philosophy as *Wissenschaft* in the Preface to *The Phenomenology of Spirit,* and it is the watchword of Husserl's famous call: *"Zu den Sachen selbst!"* The importance of the term for Heidegger is evidenced by the title of one of the last works he published: *Zur Sache des Denkens.*

Hwa Yol Jung

Heidegger's Way with
Sinitic Thinking

> Only connect!
> —E. M. Forster

> By "way," or "how," we mean something other than
> manner or mode. "Way" here means melody, the ring
> and tone, which is not just a matter of how the saying
> sounds. The way or how of the saying is the tone from
> which and to which what is said is attuned.
> —Martin Heidegger

I

The influence of Heidegger on twentieth-century thought has been immense, pervasive, and immeasurable. The German critical theorist Jürgen Habermas, though he was by no means totally sympathetic to Heidegger's thought, once summarily acknowledged him as the most influential thinker since Hegel. Heidegger's intention is to deconstruct or subvert the hegemony of the metaphysical or logocentric tradition of the West from Plato to Nietzsche. By deconstruction, Heidegger means a critical procedure in which the accepted concepts are traced back to their sources for the sake of reconstruction. This deconstructive thought poses challenges for an epoch that has experienced the planetarization of Western science and technology, that is, the global domination of what Heidegger himself calls "calculative thinking." Of course, there has been a long German tradition in the comparative study of intercultural thematics from Humboldt and Herder to Forke. Since Leibniz, however, there has never, I think, been a mood of Oriental *étrangisme* in philosophy more favorable than the one engendered by Heidegger. According to the legendary report by William Barrett of Heidegger's reaction to reading D. T. Suzuki, Heidegger remarked that he was trying to say exactly what Suzuki had said in his writings on Zen. And it is Japan—Suzuki's birthplace—that has been most receptive to Heidegger's philosophy in Asia.[1] In fact, Heidegger's famous "Conversation on Language" (1953–54) was occasioned by the visit of a Japanese scholar—Professor Tezuka—and it shows the filiation between Heidegger's thought and Japanese toward the affirmation of poetic language, as well as his keen interest in Japanese thought. Heidegger frequently expressed his bewilderment that the Japanese tend to forget the beginnings of their own thinking in their pursuit of the newest and latest trends in European thought.

II

This essay is an exercise in what Giambattista Vico calls *ingenium,* that is, the power of connecting separate and diverse elements in Heidegger and Sinitic thinking. There are formidable, if not insurmountable, difficulties in comparing Heidegger's with Asian thought in a short essay. First, it is obvious that Heidegger himself is a prolific and difficult writer. Second, there is the famous "turn" or "divide" *(Kehre)* between the early and the later Heidegger or, to use William Richardson's expression, "through phenomenology to thought." There is the "left-handed" (that is, "sinister") compliment—certainly, in favor of our present study—that Heidegger's Being is really the Chinese *tao,* for which there is no comparable term in Western thought. Even concerning Heidegger's *Being and Time,* there are two diametrically opposed or conflicting interpretations: some view it as "historicist" because it fails to advance the timeless or eternal truth beyond all ages and cultures, whereas others conclude that it is "ahistoricist" because in it the structures of human reality are meant to be true of all ages and cultures. Both aporetic views are wrong because they misunderstand—each in a diametrically opposing way—Heidegger's conception of historicity *(Geschichtlichkeit):* one ignores it as the redemption of eternity, while the other as the recovery of time. Third, there is a multitude of philosophical thoughts, methods, and approaches in Asia, and several writers have proposed the compatibility of Heidegger's thought with various aspects of Eastern thought. There have been important studies that compare Heidegger with individual Oriental thinkers: the favorite comparison, for good reason, is between Heidegger and Kitarō Nishida. The broadest thematic category of East Asian thought comparable to Heidegger's thought would probably be "Sinism"—the title of the early and pioneering work of Herrlee Creel. "Sinism" was meant to accentuate what is peculiarly or uniquely Chinese in Confucianism, Taoism, and Ch'an or Zen Buddhism, and was formulated to encompass the important aspects of philosophical, religious, and ethical thought of both Japan and Korea as well as the Chinese language or ideography.

From the perspective of Heidegger's early thought, the only legitimate way to comparative philosophy is the identification of the philosophical universe as "pluralistic." Heidegger indirectly intimated this when he expressed bewilderment that the Japanese chased after everything new in European thought. Why such a rush for (Western) truth unless they believe that it is superior to their own? Nishida—the most important twentieth-century Japanese philosopher, who did more than any other thinker to integrate Western and Oriental thought—also believes in cultural pluralism in that the unity of a world culture would be based on the specificity of an individual culture. Parenthetically, it must be pointed out from the very outset that from the standpoint of Heidegger's thought there can be no separation between "truth" and "method," as there is equally no separation between language and thought on the one hand and between language and reality on the other. After all, Heidegger himself advances the notion in *Being and Time* that ontology is possible only as phenomenology. The separation between truth and method has been consummated with the rise of positivism or scientism; while the unitary philosophical claim that the methods of the natural sciences, especially physics, are paradigmatic to all truth-claims has been contested by Hans-Georg Gadamer in *Truth and Method,* which makes an effective argument within the context of Heidegger's philosophical hermeneutics.

Let us transpose the notion of what the one-time student of Heidegger, Hannah Arendt, calls "human plurality" (in her seminal work *The Human Condition*) on to cultural pluralism. According to Arendt, human plurality is the basic condition of both speech and action, and it has the twofold character of equality and distinction. The first refers to the existence of commonality among human beings and human cultures without which we would not be able to understand one another, whether they be "primitive" and "modern" or "Western" and "Eastern." On the other hand, without distinction we would need neither speech nor action to make ourselves understood. This is in essence, I propose, the *principium* of "ontological difference" in Heidegger's thought. The true merit of this philosophical pluralism—the Heideggerian principle of "ontological difference" and the Chinese idea of the complementarity of the two opposites (*yin* and *yang*)—lies in a logic of correlation.[2] Following cues from Hayden White, I have also called this logic of correlation "diatactics." White wishes it to replace—appropriately, I think—the term "dialectics" in order to avoid the ideological overtone of Marx and the transcendental overtone of Hegel's thought: diatactics is neither "paratactical" (conceptually underdetermined) nor "hypotactical" (conceptually overdetermined). As a nonreductive method of correlation, diatactics confirms the complementarity of any two given disparate phenomena. It is also tactile to the extent to which it arouses the intimate sense of touch and accentuates the dialogic, pragmatic side of language-in-use. In this regard, the principle of diatactics, as we will later see, is fundamentally Heideggerian as well when Heidegger defines thinking as a "handicraft." Ultimately, in the logic of correlation—unlike the dialectics of Hegel and Marx—the positive *(yang)* and the negative *(yin)* are not resolved categorically or otherwise in terms of a higher synthesis but preserve the unending flow of their opposition as complementary. In short, the conceptual advantage that diatactics proffers is the following: it rejects the facile monism and dualism as well as the reductionism of all kinds which are likely to fall into the dichotomy of superiority and inferiority in grafting knowledge and action, mind and body, subjectivity and objectivity, language and reality, speech and writing, man and nature, and so on.

III

Questioning, Heidegger declares, is the "piety of thinking" *(Frömmigkeit des Denkens)*. Indeed, questioning has been the quintessence of phenomenology as a philosophical movement. Phenomenology is neither a school, a set of dogmas, a method, nor a technique in the same way that mathematics is a technique for the physical sciences today. The founder of phenomenology, Edmund Husserl—who is also Heidegger's mentor— himself conceives of philosophy as a perpetual beginning, as Socratic ignorance. For the "true thinker," philosophy never ceases to be a riddle and wonder to itself. As a vigilance, philosophy seeks the source of knowledge in the "things themselves." Husserl often used the term "introduction" to characterize a new beginning of phenomenology in his work. Merleau-Ponty was fond of using the term "interrogation" for his philosophical research to insist that the questioner himself is "always already" *(immer schon)*—to use Heidegger's expression—implicated in the question he raises. To paraphrase Merleau-Ponty slightly in order to accent this genealogical spirit in phenomenological thought, the end of phenomenological philosophy is the account of its beginning. In essence, the true phenomenologist is necessarily a perpetual beginner. In this selfsame spirit, Heidegger too defines phenomenology as the possibility of thinking.

The "piety of thinking" is the thematic *abecedarium* of comparing Heidegger with Eastern thought in this essay. As the *principium* of this essay, it heralds the voice of poetic language in the conversation of humankind and ultimately acknowledges the "thinking" poet as the legislator of the world. By delimiting our discussion to the single theme, the "piety of thinking," we do not betray Heidegger's spirit but instead uphold it when he himself affirms that "to think is to confine yourself to a single thought that one day stands still like a star in the world's sky."[3]

In the crisis of man and (his or her) humanity, foremost is the crisis of thinking. We prefer the word "thinking" to "thought" for the simple reason that while the latter is a passive end-product, the former denotes the active process of unending activity: it is indeed "wayward," "on the way." It is, in other words, the *tao*—the unending, often meandering "road." In *What Is Called Thinking?*, Heidegger himself explains the twofold meaning of participles which "participate" or "take part" in two meanings in which the one refers to the other as a pair. In this case, thinking—like "blossoming"—is something thinking and the act of thinking. Be that as it may, what is most needed in our time is a way to think appropriately. There is interest in thinking today as it is engendered by thought-provoking events. Paradoxically, however, Heidegger rightly observes that in our age the most thought-provoking event is that we are still not thinking, a dangerous condition which leads itself readily to the "banality of evil" (to borrow a phrase from Hannah Arendt's controversial reporting of Adolf Eichmann after the model of Heidegger's anonymous "they" *(das Man)*. In such an impoverished state of thinking, we must first clarify the condition of our thinking: this is the primary function of philosophy. The opposite of thinking or "thoughtfulness" is, of course, thoughtlessness. The "banality of evil" refers to the unprecedented phenomenon of evil deeds committed by Eichmann on a gigantic, hideous scale which cannot be traced to any wickedness, pathology, or ideological conviction but to the extraordinary shallowness which is neither monstrous or demonic but rather the "authentic inability to think." What Arendt is interested in pointing out here is not our ability to theorize abstractly or think in abstraction but our ability to make moral judgments based on the *sensus communis* (as in Socratic wisdom, Aristotelian *phronēsis,* or Kantian moral judgment) as the abode of man's humanity. It is thinking as a natural necessity or duty of the "examined" human life which is a faculty of every man who belongs to the species called human. To talk about thinking as the pillar of morality is not to neutralize it but to dig its *archē* itself: thoughtlessness is indeed a moral latitudinarianism. On the other hand, to moralize is to trivialize the essence of human thinking.

According to Heidegger, thinking as autonomous activity is distinguished from both "knowing" (in an epistemological sense) and "acting" (in a pragmatic sense). For it neither produces solely epistemological truths nor is merely instrumental to action whose manifest aim is measured by its pragmatic cash value. Rather, "knowing" and "acting" presuppose "thinking." Thinking as *alētheia* is presupposed in both knowledge and action. As such it is neither scientific, technical, nor utilitarian. In short, genuine thinking is not "calculative." The alternative to calculative thinking *(rechnendes Denken)* is for Heidegger meditative thinking *(besinnliches Denken)*. In the following pages, I will try to show the "meaningful" nexus of thinking as *poiēsis, praxis,* and *technē* in the original Greek sense of the terms.

In Heidegger's ontology, thinking and language are inseparable: language is the house of Being whose guardian man is. We "always already" find ourselves in the midst of language: we are attuned to language as reality rather than as a surrogate of reality. To think of language *is* to think of reality. Let us call man's attunement to language "linguisticality" *(Sprachlichkeit)*—that which makes thinking possible. By linguisticality we denote the following four inseparably related properties: (1) language is intrinsic to human specificity as social; (2) it is inseparable from our conception of reality, that is, it is not a mirror to reflect, copy, or represent it but is reality itself; (3) it is the primary medium of human communication; and (4) it is an embodied phenomenon. In this connection, the most revealing challenge Heidegger poses for comparative philosophy in relation to thinking and language concerns whether Western languages are ineluctably tied to Western metaphysical thinking or instead offer other possibilities of thinking. In Heidegger's thought one would suspect that they are more or less two sides of the same coin.

For Heidegger, our attunement to language and thus to the world is not simply "rationalistic" in the traditional sense of Western metaphysics. Instead, language is an embodied phenomenon, for which reason, as I have already intimated, I use the term "diatactics." In the West, it was Giambattista Vico's linguistic *autopsia* (or anatomy)—in the sense of seeking the evidence of the senses—which discovered language originally as embodied speech *(Sprachleiblichkeit)*. For Vico, words are carried over from human bodies to signify nature, where the "body language" animates inanimate things, and from the properties of human bodies to signify the institutions of the mind, including, of course, what we call the "rhetoric" and "grammar" of language. For Heidegger, too, the hand is more than an organ, altogether it is peculiarly human, that is, the quiddity of being human. In Heidegger's *What Is Called Thinking?* occurs a marvelous passage concerning the many ways of the hand that culminate in thinking as a "handicraft" (handy craft) in the same way that the use of language—both speaking and writing—is the *technē* (art) of the body. It defies paraphrasing and is worth quoting in full:

> We are trying to learn thinking. Perhaps thinking, too, is just something like building a cabinet. At any rate, it is a craft, a "handicraft." "Craft" literally means the strength and skill in our hands. The hand is a peculiar thing. In the common view, the hand is part of our bodily organism. But the hand's essence can never be determined, or explained, by its being an organ which can grasp. Apes, too, have organs that can grasp, but they do not have hands. The hand is infinitely different from all grasping organs—paws, claws, or fangs—different by an abyss of essence. Only a being who can speak, that is, think, can have hands and can be handy in achieving works of handicraft. But the craft of the hand is richer than we commonly imagine. The hand does not only grasp and catch, or push and pull. The hand reaches and extends, receives, and welcomes—and not just things: the hand extends itself, and receives its own welcome in the hands of others. The hand holds. The hand carries. The hand designs and signs, presumably

because man is a sign. Two hands fold into one, a gesture meant to carry man into the great oneness. The hand is all this, and this is the handicraft. Everything is rooted here that is commonly known as handicraft, and commonly we go no further. But the hand's gestures run everywhere through language, in their most perfect purity precisely when man speaks by being silent. And only when man speaks, does he think—not the other way around, as metaphysics still believes. Every motion of the hand in every one of its works carries itself through the element of thinking, every hearing of the hand bears itself in that element. All the work of the hand is rooted in thinking. Therefore, thinking itself is man's simplest, and for that reason hardest, handiwork, if it would be accomplished at its proper time.[4]

In Heidegger, therefore, thinking, speaking, and the hand form a filial unity. He unifies the sayings of Anaxagoras and Democritus which may appear contradictory at first glance: Anaxagoras, who said that man is intelligent because he has a mouth rather than hands, and Democritus, who said that human progress depends on the working of the hand rather than the mind. Heidegger's thought is indeed the diatactics of Anaxagoras and Democritus. As the hand is tactile, so are thinking and speaking. If thought is a handy craft, its opposite, thoughtlessness—which is pervasive and rampant in the modern world, as evidenced in the disembodied (alienated) language and behavior of Eichmann—is an infliction of cutaneous alagia, the condition of feeling no pain in the skin. The "thinking hand" or thinking as a "handy work," of which Heidegger speaks, confers upon us the work of the hand as embodied conduct. As such the hand is not just an "extension" of the body but is the body incorporated. The hand *is* the lived body; it is an organized "corporation." As embodied conduct, the hand is pansensory and synesthetic. It activates the workings of the other senses, for example, hearing, seeing, saying, and singing. Indeed, it embodies the sociability of the senses.

   The import of Heidegger's diatactics of thinking and language—especially speaking—is, I submit, enormous for comparative philosophy. As Heidegger himself is an etymological master, the etymological and paleographical study of Chinese ideography, known as "etymosinology," which began with Ernest Fenellosa and influenced later the poetry of Ezra Pound (for example, in the *Cantos*), should not be left unnoticed. Doubly important, as we will later see in detail, is Fenellosa's view of the Chinese ideogram as an authentic medium of poetry or the poeticized language par excellence. If the notion of "eco/nomy" betokens the genius and gift of Chinese ideograms, Chinese ideography is the exemplar of poetic language. Etymosinology is a dazzling display of the ideogrammic abracadabra by means of which Fenellosa tried to celebrate the meeting of the *yin* of the "markedly feminine" East and the *yang* of the "markedly masculine" West. Although the feminine and masculine allusions may not

be totally appropriate, the correlative logic of the *yin* and the *yang* as one
unity is brought close to Heidegger's "ontological difference."[5]

Chinese ideography—calligraphy in particular—is a kinetic art: it is
the human body in graceful motion. The ideogram as metaphor or
"imagery" of the body is indeed "kinaesthetic," to use Kenneth Burke's
phrase. And the Chinese revere the art of calligraphy as much as painting: calligraphy is the painting of ideograms or—to intimate the spiritual
and personal dimension of artists themselves—"characters."[6] In the genealogy of form, calligraphy is indeed prior to painting. In very significant
measure, Chinese ideography is a choreography of human gestures and,
as a family of signifiers, "a conversation of gestures" which, because of
the presence of meaning, is not the reduction of ideograms to human
physiology. The rhetoric of an ideogram, whether it is "tree," "sun,"
"moon," "stream," "man," "male," "female," "smile," or "cry," lies in its status as a "speaking picture." For instance, the ideographic "gesture" of
human expressivity (for example, "smile" and "cry") is indelibly pan-
tomimic—beckoning for a similar response in return. Picasso's "Swimmer" (1929) and "Acrobat" (1930) are two choreographs of the human
body in fluent and rhythmic motion which are approaching ideography
or calligraphy. They are, in short, balletic and frolicking anthropograms.
Stéphane Mallarmé speaks of the dance as the "visual embodiment of
idea" *(l'incorporation visuelle de l'idée).*[7] In *The Principles of Art,* R. G.
Collingwood observes that every language is a specialized form of bodily
gesture and, as such, that dance is the mother of all languages. In *Not I,*
the Vichian Samuel Beckett "choreographs" the dramaticity of speaking
as the dance of the mouth. With him we can say that in language as gestures the spoken and the written are identical.[8] Since the dance is the
motion of the body in time and space, it may legitimately be claimed as
the "birth-place" of all visual and auditory arts (for example, painting
and music). Moreover, Marshall McLuhan, who had the romantic vision
of writing his antitypographic treatise, *The Gutenberg Galaxy,* in the
ideogrammic medium, thought of the Chinese ideogram as a vortex of
corporate energy—"corporate" in the twofold sense of being bodily and
collective. Several years ago, the Japanese journalist Takao Tokuoka
reported with humor in the editorial column of the *New York Times* the
inventive word *towelket*—a shop sign written in Japanese phonetic characters *(kana)*—which is a combination of the two English words "towel"
and "blanket" (towelket = towel + [blan]ket). What born Joyceans the
Japanese are! Of course, what I have in mind is Joyce's talent or inven-
tiveness for composing chordal vocabularies in *Ulysses* and *Finnegans
Wake.* The Joycean "decomposition" or musicalization of the "abced-
minded" world or the "popeyed world" of the "scribblative" has its structural parallel in Fenellosa's deconstruction or demystification of Chinese

ideograms as simple or complex "corporations." Joyceanism or Joyce's unique stylistic stands out for its tremendous proclivities for making visible words chordal and for thinking in chords after the acoustic model of music, that is, for the production of chordal meanings by obliterating (auditory) content and (visual) form: thornghts (thorn + thoughts), rhythmatick (rhythm + mathematics), paupulation (paucity + population), evoluation (evolution + evaluation), cerebration (cerebrum + celebration), etc. If Fenellosa's etymological and paleographic deconstruction of Chinese ideograms *(kanji)* is correct, the composition of "towelket" is a result of the natural *habitus* of the Japanese mind—in fact, of the Oriental mind that is accustomed to the vorticism of Chinese ideograms. I find the etymolinguistics of Chinese ideography both enlightening and fascinating. Consider the following examples of "hypograms" as the corporate insemination of other ideograms provided by Fenellosa himself: "East" is an entangling of "sun" with "tree" (i.e., the sun entangled in the branches of a tree in the early morning or at sunrise); "old" or "ancient" is a composite of "ten" and "mouth" ("ten" *over* "mouth," presumably referring to what has come down through the mouth for ten generations); and "truth" or "faithfulness" is a composite

Picasso, "Swimmer" (as ideogram). © *S.P.A.D.E.M., Paris/V.A.G.A., New York, 1986.*

of "man" and "word" (man standing *by* his word). Two of my favorite characters are "humanity" and "sage." The former is a composite of "man" and "two" (two men standing together) and the latter is a composite of "ear," "mouth," and "king." As the "king" is the unifier of heaven, man, and earth, the "sage" is the unifier of heaven, man, and earth by speaking and hearing truthfully.

Having shown the correlative logic of thinking and language as embodied phenomena in Heidegger and Chinese ideography, we should go one step further in characterizing language as performance. As the "poetic" is for Heidegger paradigmatic to all thinking, doing, and making, so poeticized or aestheticized language is performance par excellence. This view is of the utmost importance, as we will later show, for accounting for man's moral conduct.

Heidegger regards written language as inferior to or a poor substitute for direct conversation because in writing thinking easily loses its flexibility and it becomes difficult to retain the multidimensionality peculiar to thinking: he is an aural or auditory thinker.[9] Ralph Waldo Emerson, who spoke eloquently of thinking as a "pious reception," also thought that (written) language is fossil poetry.[10] For the same reason, Heidegger rejects the spectatorial view of knowledge embedded in the Cartesian *Cogito*—the logocentric kernel of modern Western philosophy, that is, thinking as disinterested, distanced, and detached.

In his studies of Renaissance art and poetry, Walter Pater views music as the "consummate art," in that all art aspires to attain the condition of music. In *The Birth of Tragedy,* Nietzsche—the last metaphysician of the West, according to Heidegger—echoes and rejoices in the voice of Orpheus, the singer who moves "a world in darkness": "it is only as an *aesthetic phenomenon* that existence and the world are eternally *justified.*" So the Nietzschean aesthetic is epitomized by music: music is for Nietzsche one way to make the aesthetic intelligible and grasp it directly: "Quite generally, only music, placed beside the world, can give us an idea of what is meant by the justification of the world as an aesthetic phenomenon."[11] The prevailing use of auditory metaphors in Heidegger's thought is congruent with his critique of the modern age as the age of "world picture" *(Weltbild),* his general conception of language, thought, and the world in relation to Being: for example, "mood" or "dis/position" and "attunement" *(Bestimmtsein).* There is indeed the semantic kinship or filiation of the German words "to hear" *(hören),* "to hearken" *(horchen),* "to belong" *(gehören),* and "to obey" *(gehorchen).* Moreover, "hearing" and "obeying" have the same etymological root: the Latin *obaudire,* to listen from below, is to obey. In *Being and Time,* Heidegger conceives of mood *(Stimmung)* as a primordial, existential character of man. As a *factum brutum,* mood has an ontological bearing because it is a basic mode of "There-being" *(Dasein)*. As *Befindlichkeit,* it is the basic way of "finding" ourselves in the world. Through it, we attune ourselves to the world: that is to say, we lend a "musical" ear to and obey it at the same time. As disposition, mood is not just the sensitive and emotional side of human consciousness but rather the essential nature *(animus)* of man. "Mood," Heidegger writes, "is never merely a way of being attuned, and letting ourselves be attuned, in this or that way in mood. Mood is precisely the basic way in which we are *outside* ourselves. But that is the way we are essentially and constantly."[12] No wonder, being *outside* ourselves, mood—both sorrowful and joyful alike—is highly contagious in a small circle of spouses and close friends and relatives. In short, mood is the *tonality* of *Dasein* as "Being-in-the-world" *(in-der-Welt-sein).*

The structure of oral poetry is indeed paradigmatic to language as performance. Oral poetry is rhetoric par excellence because rhetoric, as one author defines it succinctly, is "the signifying act that values oral performance."[13] Emerson captures the performative spirit of language when he describes words as actions and conversely actions as a kind of words. In oral poetry, *poiēsis, praxis,* and *technē* are rolled into one. In the genealogy of language (as communication), oral poetry is the "first language," and the oral poet is the "first born." The persona and (oral) poetry of Homer signify the dawn of Western thinking itself. Like Hermes, Orpheus, and even the Muses (the daughters of Mnemosyne or Memory), Homer was a singer or bard. The name of the god Hermes, in whose name hermeneutics celebrates the sacred and magical canon of his spoken words, stems from *herma,* the mute stone monument which also corresponds phonetically to the Latin *sermo* (speech)—as we know, muteness or silence is the "mother tongue." Hermes was the inventor of language and the "magician" of spoken words who was "spellbinding." According to the Homeric "Hymn to Hermes," the Hermetic legend is synonymous with the discovery of the universe (uni-verse) as the sounding orbit. Hermes was a herald *(keryx):* he was a virtuoso of sound-making whose *kerygma* (message) was aired by and encoded in the sound of spoken words. The term "herald" is related to the Latin *carmen* (song) and the Sanskrit *karuh* (to sing) and *karus* (bard), whose sole virtue scales the pitch of the "signifying excellence of voice." As the master of speech, Hermes was the messenger of Zeus; in his capacity as a herald he gave Pandora her voice. No wonder, then, this genuine Olympian was "the friendliest of the gods to men."

The tintinabulation of oral poetry is consonant with the poetic voice of Heidegger, which is resonant with the poet Rilke: *Gesang ist Dasein* where *poiēsis, praxis,* and *technē*—the sung word, the deed, and the art of word-making—come together as unity in the organization of existence or Being.[14] First, oral poetry is oral and auditory (acoustic), that is, in it the mouth and the ear are the main organs of communication. In Homeric oral poetry as shown in the works of Milman Parry, Albert B. Lord, Marshall McLuhan, Eric A. Havelock, Walter J. Ong, and others, speech and music are inseparable simply because it is sung. Second, in oral poetry there is no separation between composition and performance: composition is spontaneous performance. The oral poem—like jazz or any improvised music—is composed not for but in performance. Third, in the Homeric culture the oral *techne* of poetry was the instrument of preserving the dynamic flow of a collective life. *Poiēsis* was *techne*, and *mimēsis* was the poetic technique of communication to preserve the acoustic effects *(pragmata)* of an oral culture. Poetry is an oral performance in the service of the acoustic effects of culture. The dynamic flow of this oral culture was preserved in the cornucopia of poetry, that is, in its repetition, redundancy, and verboseness. The Homeric epic was metaphorically called a "river of song." In essence, oral poetry is speech sung as performative utterances. When a person is making a performative utterance, he is doing something rather than merely saying something that may be true or false, that is, describing or reporting the state of affairs. In language as speech acts, "performance" and "promise" are no longer antithetical lexicons. The spoken word as performative utterance becomes an index of moral value once it is extended to the realm of human conduct: we are, morally or otherwise, what we say (as doing).

The Chinese syntax itself, as etymosinologists have tried to show, is action or performance. The Chinese cardinal moral virtue called "sincerity" is spelled syntactically "word-performed" (for which the Japanese "tragic heroes" from ancient to modern times sacrificed their lives). As it means what we say or perform what we promise in words, it personifies the Chinese conception of the circular unity of knowledge and action in the sense that knowledge is the beginning of action and action the completion of knowledge. There is, of course, a union or family of moral notions connected with sincerity—*jen*, piety, faithfulness, rite, and so on. Faithfulness or fidelity literally means "man-standing-by-his-word," and it refers to the responsibility of the speaker to his word as ethical performance. The Confucian formulation of the "rectification of names" *(cheng ming)*—calling things by their right (rite) names—exemplifies the ethics of language-in-performance. In the *Analects,* Confucius said: "without knowing the (performative) power of words, it is impossible to know man." This affirms the following: the centrality of language to human conduct, the ethics of language embodying the humanity of man, and the spoken word as pre-scriptive. The following passages from the *Analects* express the same idea: (1) when the superior man "is heard to speak, his language is firm and decided"; (2) "the wise err neither in regard to their man nor to their words"; (3) "the virtuous will be sure to speak *correctly,* but those whose speech is good may not always be virtuous"; (4) "the superior man is modest in his speech, but exceeds in his actions"; and (5) friendship with "the glib-tongued" is injurious.

It should not be left unnoticed that in recent years Western grammatologists in literary theory have become fascinated with Chinese ideography because it is perceived mistakenly to have the character of "pure writing" (*écriture*)—the writing that exorcises the phonetic or is devoid of phonetic genealogy. They echo the voice of Oswald Spengler (the author of *The Decline of the West*). Spengler acknowledges writing as an entirely new kind of language that brings about a complete change in the conscious relationships and associations of men and women. The cardinal virtue of writing, as he sees it, is the liberation of human consciousness from the bondage and tyranny of the present embedded in speech. Writing resembles architecture, monument, pyramid, tapestry, cathedral, or the Acropolis where the immortal god of abstraction resides. It is the idea of writing as immortal that Spengler wishes to propagate. Timeless truths are embodied not in speech but only in script. He emphasizes that writing is "the grand symbol of the Far"—the Far East, perhaps—and the will to eternity. In search of the *karma* of the ideogram, the thirteenth-century Chinese scholar Tai T'ung wrote *Six Scripts* after, by his own admission, thirty years of arduous thinking and strenuous work. It is the exegesis of the six different etymological and paleographic roots of Chinese ideography whose tradition has been continued and preserved in the works of Bernard Karlgren. For our analysis here, we ought to mention only the "phonetic" principle or rootage of Chinese writing which traces the "origin" of written figures to spoken sounds. Tai is critical of those etymologists who knew nothing of the principle of phonetic composition. According to him, the written is preceded by the spoken in Chinese: writing makes speech visible. The invisible vapor of speech is distilled, as it were, in visible writing. Chinese ideography is a silent speech as performative. This does not mean, of course, that Chinese writing is reduced to the physiology of phonation. Rather, it only means that Chinese writing is, in important measure, the "abstract" form of the "concrete" speech. It is no accident that the Chinese expressions that denote linguistic activity contain the radical for (spoken) "word." Correlatively, however, without the written, the spoken could not be represented to the eye. The circle of language, whose epicenter is sociality, is made up of the spoken *yin* and the written *yang* as complementary.

IV

What is piety? How can piety be related to thinking in this comparative study? To answer these questions, we must return to the idea that the opposite of "thoughtlessness" is "thoughtfulness." Discussing Eichmann's real thoughtlessness, which led to the "banality of evil," Arendt contends that it was his inability to think from the standpoint of somebody else. That is to say, Eichmann was not thoughtful. He lacked receptive reciprocity for the thought of the other, which is tantamount to the absence of genuine communication. "No communication," Arendt writes, "was possible with him [Eichmann], not because he lied but because he was surrounded by the most reliable of all safeguards against the words and the presence of others, and hence against reality as such."[15]

The definition of piety as receptive reciprocity is like the *yin* principle as contrasted with the *yang* principle of the *I Ching*. In his illuminating discussion of Greek and Roman religion, C. Kerenyi relates the Latin *pietas* to *religio*. In fact, some writers (for example, Cicero) used the former synonymously with the latter. For the "ritually" performed act (rite) belongs to the sphere of *pietas*. By examining the legend of the temple which was built in Rome for the goddess Pietas, Kerenyi observes that

> on the site of this temple, so it was related, a mother had once been imprisoned and had been kept alive by the milk of her own daughter's breast. The story may have been adapted from a Greek original, though this is by no means certain. But it would have been pointless, had it not represented *pietas* in the ideal form in which it appeared to the Romans. The special thing which here stands out is something bodily and spiritual at the same time. *Pietas* here shows itself as a form of absolute reciprocity in nature, a completely closed circle of giving and receiving. In some variants of the story, the mother's place is taken by the father. But the example thus revered is always this same natural circle of reciprocity. While *aidos* presupposes that one can also stand outside it, *pietas* as a matter of course unites those who give nourishment with those who in uninterrupted thankfulness return it, unites the source of life with its creatures from which its sources receive life. The *pii* and *piae* are completely enclosed in this circle.[16]

It is no accident that economists discuss "exchanges" as the reciprocal relations of economic life both primitive and modern, and modern sociologists and anthropologists recognize the "gift" as an anthropological specimen for obligatory reciprocity in human relations. Marcel Mauss's classic study of the "gift" of archaic societies such as Polynesia, Melanesia, and Northwest America is relevant to the understanding of reciprocity in its primordial form. As a form of obligation, the gift is the "necessary form of exchange" and "one of the bases of social life" as carried out by the people on the communal basis in the form of courtesies, entertainment, ritual, dances, feasts, military assistance, marriages, succession to wealth, and so on.

For Heidegger, too, thinking as pious is receptive and reverential. It is a receptive response to the "call" or "voice" of Being: authentic thinking "hears" the voice of Being and "belongs" to it. What must be made absolutely clear from the outset concerning piety as reciprocity is this: like "mood" as the "attunement" or "being attuned" *(Bestimmtsein)*, it is not egocentric (autocentric) but heterocentric (allocentric). For Heidegger as for Kerenyi, piety as absolute reciprocity approximates—as milking nourishes and is being nourished—the "touching" sense of intimacy and thus stands for the incorporation of the spiritual in the corporeal. For, after all, thinking is for Heidegger a "handicraft." There is in Heidegger as in Kerenyi—each in his own different way—a filiality between the "piety of thinking" and "thanking." For Heidegger, the old German word *thanc* is memory, and thinking that recalls is thanking. Moreover, Cicero, who associates *pietas* with *religio,* enshrines the ears, not the eyes, as religious (i.e., the *aures religiosae* of the Attic orators). Although the scriptural words are the best guide for the understanding of God's divine purpose in the universe, St. Augustine, who knew Cicero's writings well and from whom we inherited some of Cicero's lost writings, thought that arts such as music and painting contribute to it. In *De Musica,* however, he contended that music (invisible) is a better guide than painting (visible) for the attainment of man's religious spirituality and the understanding of the divine order. Thus, the former is a higher art than the latter. Piety, associated with "hearing," signifies "nearness," whereas *theōria,* associated with vision, implies distance. It is no accident, therefore, that Heidegger, who regards "speaking" as the primary essence of language and resorts frequently to aural or auditory metaphors, relates reciprocity to the sense of "hearing," "hearkening," "belonging," and "obeying." Hearing is by nature socializing or reciprocating, whereas vision is inherently narcissistic and isolating.[17]

Piety as reciprocity is also genuinely Sinitic—Confucian, Taoist, and Zen. Indeed, it is the thread that weaves all the Sinitic fabric of such important moral notions as humaneness, filial piety, propriety, and rite as "neighboring" concepts. Piety as reciprocity signifies the sacrament of coexistence or, as I call it elsewhere, "social principle."[18] The "social principle" has two distinguishable but inseparable elemental components: (1) homopiety and (2) geopiety. Homopiety refers to the convivial relationships between (wo)man and (wo)man, which may also be called "sociopiety," whereas geopiety is that part of the "social principle" which is concerned with the connatural reciprocity between (wo)man and nature or the earth.[19] Homopiety is dominantly a Confucian principle, whereas geopiety is a Taoist and Zen principle. One may hastily conclude, therefore, that the early "humanistic" Heidegger would be closely Confucian, whereas the later "ontological" Heidegger would be closely Taoist and Zen. Besides the *Tao Te Ching,* to which Chung-yuan Chang has made numerous allusions to Heidegger's "new way of thinking," there are the sayings of Chuang-tzu: man is truly a "cosmion"—"Heaven and earth were born at the same time as I was, and ten thousand things [that is, Nature as material world] are one with me." However, Confucianism does not exclude geopiety, nor do Taoism and Ch'an or Zen Buddhism exclude homopiety. In *Li Chi*, Confucius writes: "To fell a single tree, or kill a single animal, not at the proper season, is contrary to filial piety"—the subject matter which is also taught through the text *Hsia Ching* in the classical education of the Chinese language at early childhood. In this way, the moral objective of filial piety is not confined to the effect of one man's conduct on another but is extended to the effect of man's conduct on other nonhuman beings and things.[20] Conversely, there is no shortage, in Taoism and Ch'an or Zen Buddhism, of allusions to human reciprocity. By the same token, it is wrong to associate the early Heidegger with "homocentricity" or the later Heidegger with the "end" or renunciation of man as such. After all, the "fundamental ontology" of *Being and Time* is the affirmation of man as an earth dweller: *homo* is rooted in *humus*. As Erazim Kohák put it recently, "To recover the moral sense of our humanity, we would need to recover first the moral sense of nature."[21]

Harmony, which is the pitch of musicality and the paradigm certainly of all "performing arts" and perhaps of the aesthetic itself, underscores the piety of thinking and thus the performances of both homopiety and geopiety. It is a "gathering" of many as an ordered whole: it is, musically speaking, a chorus, polyphonic chord, or orchestration of the differentiated many or, as the Chinese would say, "ten thousand things"—including the making of our thoughts. Therefore, reciprocity that generates and sustains harmony requires the simultaneous weaving of both "equality" and "distinction" (difference). For reciprocity without distinction reduces itself to the relationship of indolent anonymity, whereas reciprocity without equality brings about the relationship of rigid hierarchy. To gather our thoughts is to be thoughtful. Gathering denotes "nearness" which approximates auditory rather than visual space.[22] There is an episodic account by J. Glenn Gray of the German word Heidegger uses: *versammeln* which was translated after considerable deliberation and with Heidegger's own approval, as "to gather." It is rooted in the old German *gattern* (to couple, to espouse, or to join in marriage) which in turn was related to the Greek *to agathon* (the good).[23] The Greek *logos* originates from *lego* (to speak) and the root *leg-* is "to gather." *Logos*, like the Hebrew *dabhar*, originally meant "to gather," "to speak," and "to think." The Neapolitan philosopher Vico, who heralded poetry as the "first language" and poetic wisdom as the fountain-head of philosophical thought and to whose rhetorical tradition Heidegger himself belongs, notes the rustic origins of the Latin *lex* as "gathering" or "collecting" and then later "law," the "assemblage" of people, and "reading" (*legere* or "collecting letters").[24]

In Sinism there is a filiality between the aesthetic and the ethical: the beautiful and the good are synonymous. In characterizing Asiatic thought simply as aesthetic in *The Meeting of East and West*, F. S. C. Northrop was not far from describing its essence. Since the seventeenth century many European minds often created the image of the Orient as the aesthetic "paradise on earth." As the aesthetic is the connatural harmony of man and the wilderness of nature (that is, geopiety), so is the good the convivial relationship between (wo)man and (wo)man (that is, homopiety). Harmony is the essence not only of the aesthetic but also of the social, that is to say, it is both geopious and homopious. It cannot be overemphasized that "serenity," "releasement," or "repose" *(Gelassenheit)* is the keyboard on which the idea of harmony—both connaturality and conviviality—are being played out. For it "poeticizes" or "aestheticizes" man and the earth. From *Li Chi*, we also find the ancient Chinese sense of things as an ordered whole in which music plays an integrating role:

> There are heaven above and earth below, and between them are distributed all the (various) beings with their different (natures and qualities):—in accordance with this proceeded the framing of ceremonies. (The influence of) heaven and earth flow forth and never cease; and by their united action (the phenomena of) production and change ensue:—in accordance with this music arose. The process of growth in spring, and of maturing in summer (suggest the idea of) benevolence; those of in-gathering in autumn and of storing in winter, suggest righteousness. Benevolence is akin to music, and righteousness to ceremonies.[25]

Meditative thinking is characterized by serenity—the receptive reverence of things as they are in themselves—while calculative thinking implies dominance, manipulation, and utility. Serenity is nonwilled, nonforced, and nonconcerned activity, that is, an active responsiveness in man to the "natural light" of a thing. It is then "a will-less letting in of everything," the spontaneity that sets a thing free to be nothing but itself. "A higher acting," Heidegger writes, "is concealed in releasement than is found in all the actions within the world and in the machinations of all mankind."[26] Here Heidegger's notion of serenity or releasement parallels the Taoist idea of *wu wei* and the Zen way of thinking and doing—the way of refraining from thinking and doing contrary to the natural and spontaneous way of things. Just as Heidegger's serenity is "a higher acting," so is *wu wei* both nonanthropocentric in man's relationships with nature and nonindividualistic in our multiple relationships with one another (that is, it is both geopious and homopious). It is like the flow of a river that meanders unconcernedly along the contours of the landscape or the splitting of a bamboo with its natural grain rather than against it. The Zen way of perfecting archery, as shown in Eugen Herrigel's classic study, lies in unconcernedness or "purposeless detachment." It is the "artless," effortless, and self-forgetting immersion in the archer in his performance without any ulterior, utilitarian ends in view.

The notion of Nature—*tzu-jan* in Chinese, *ji-nen* in Japanese, and *ja-yun* in Korean—signifies a "serene" or "reverential" composure for the "natural spontaneity" of all things, the "thisness" or "thatness" (or "thusness") of everything living or nonliving. As it is af-filiated with serenity, the poetic discloses or discovers the topology of Being—the topology that tells the "whereabouts" of Being's presence. The poet is destined to discover Being—the ultimacy of thinking—and its true nature which has too long been hidden in the metaphysical closet of Western philosophy. He is the thinker personified who "advocates" the quadrate *(das Geviert)* of sky, earth, gods, and mortals which allows their free interplay. In the *Tao Te Ching,* the same unity is expressed in the circular chain of man that follows the earth; earth that follows heaven; heaven that follows the Tao; and, finally, Tao that follows Nature or the natural order of things *(tzu-jan).*[27] This splendid, simple gathering of the elements in "serenity" is expressed in a haikuesque quality of meaning, style, and subjects in the last lines found in Heidegger's discussion on "The Thinker as Poet":

Forests spread
Brooks plunge
Rocks persist
Mist diffuses

Meadows wait
Springs well
Winds dwell
Blessing muses.[28]

Compare Heidegger's lines with the famous haiku of Bashō, "Furu ikeya/ Kawazu tobikomu/ Mizu no oto," which should be read and heard as "the sound of a frog jumping in the water of the old pond," as a concordant continuum of the natural elements in harmony. So the simplicity and wilderness of *oto* ("sound") is the elemental, all-embracing *principium* of the haiku. The Zen splendor of the simple and wild in Bashō's haiku airs and echoes the sonorous mood that is "being attuned" to the seasonal serenade of Being or Nature. The harmony of the elements is the great topological chain of Being where the reverberation of the water's sound is perceived—better, "conceived"—by the poet in the little creature's consonance with nature or the whole uni-verse as the sounding background of tranquility or beatific repose. The poetic, which is attuned to the topology of Being, is the acme of thinking. It does not surmount the earth in order to exploit and conquer it, but rather it brings man on to, and makes him belong to, the earth: it brings him dwelling on earth. The poetic embodies the quintessence of geopiety.

The aesthetic or poetic may now be contrasted with the technological: it is a stark contrast between *Gelassenheit* and *Gestell* in Heidegger's thought. One is meditative (spontaneous and natural), whereas the other calculative (exploitative and utilitarian). Very few, by now, argue against the conclusion that technology is the consummation of modern civilization, East or West, South or North. It destroys both homopiety and geopiety. Technology is, as it were, the "ontological fix" of modern man everywhere. Thus Heidegger writes:

> What now *is,* is marked by the dominance of the active nature of modern technology. This dominance is already representing itself in all areas of life, by various identifiable traits such as functionalization, systematic improvement, automation, bureaucratization, communications. Just as we call the idea of living things biology, just so the presentation and full articulation of all beings, dominated as they now are everywhere by the nature of the technical, may be called technology. The expression may serve as a term for the metaphysics of the atomic age. Viewed from the present and drawn from our insight into the present, the step back out of metaphysics into the essential nature of metaphysics is the step out of technology and technological description and interpretation of the age, into the *essence* of modern technology which is still to be thought.[29]

Heidegger contends that we have not yet come fully to grips with the nature of modern technocentric or technomorphic culture in which man himself is the "functionary" of technology. To say that the essence of technology is not technological is to deny the idea that technology is merely instrumental. The lethal network of globalized technology or, as Heidegger calls it, "technological frenzy," is a historical nightmare from which we all wish to awaken or a narcolepsy from which we would never awaken. Its unthinkable potential lies in bringing the entire earth into a necropolis. For Heidegger, it is infinitely inadequate to view modern technology merely as *instrumentum* or instrumental facilitation. For it has now acquired the ontological priority over every form of thinking, making, and doing—including scientific activity. The worst consequence of misunderstanding the true nature (essence) of technology merely as instrumental rationality is bound to neutralize it as amoral. Heidegger proposes the idea of "autonomous technology" in place of "instrumental technology" to understand the essence of technology itself. Technology as autonomous is no longer simply a means to human activity. For it is not merely the application of mathematical physical science to *praxis,* but is an autonomous *praxis* itself. The traditional rationale of technology as *instrumentum* that serves the *telos* of man is obsolete and anachronistic.

Means has indeed become end. This, in fact, is the "categorical imperative" of technology as autonomous.

"Representation" is the epistemological keyword, after the Cartesian legacy of the mind's unblinking gaze, in the metaphysics of technology as autonomous. This "representational" metaphysics of technology may be best shown in the television technology that "enframes" modern society. It epitomizes man's "channeled existence" and his visual narcissism in the modern age as the age of "world picture" *(Weltbild)*. Representational metaphysics is a continuation or an extension, therefore, of the Cartesian *Cogito* in which the subjective ("I") and the visual ("eye") viewpoint are brought together in the absolute affirmation and certainty of cognition as "clear and distinct ideas" (i.e., the Cartesian legacy of visual and narcissistic metaphysics).[30] The world viewed as picture in television is an aspect (idea) of *Gestell* ("enframing"). The essence of technology is *Gestell* which, as "to set in place" *(stellen),* is eminently spatial and visual. Television both spotlights and highlights this enframing in our age as the age of world picture. As the essence of all technology as enframing is representing, television too represents as picture or structured image *(Gebild)* the original presence of the world as it is in itself. To be sure, there is the fundamental distinction between "seeing" and "seeing as," that is, seeing a real object and seeing it as a picture, an image, or a mirror. One is fully visual, fully thought, whereas the other only half visual, half thought. We must understand here that to capture the essence of reality by means of representational metaphysics, that is, an anthology of images, is a forever Sisyphean task, for image has only a semblance of knowledge, subtraction of reality, and an appearance of participation.[31]

The advent of technology, as we have stressed, begins to destroy both geopiety and homopiety. For technology "scatters" rather than "gathers" things and our thoughts. The mathematical is basic to the grammar of modern technology as autonomous *praxis*. However, the language of modern mathematics or of the mathematical sciences has little in common with the original expression of the mathematical by Pythagoras or the ancient Pythagoreans—"All is Number" or "Number is all things." With them, it was meant to express the perfect, ontological ordering of invisible (temporal) *harmonia* but not visible (spatial) equations, that is, universal *harmonia* embodied in the mathematical. In the Renaissance, too, the Vitruvian figure inscribed in a square and a circle was a symbol of "sympathy" *(symphonia)* between microcosm and macrocosm, and Leonardo da Vinci obtained a harmonious smile in *La Gioconda* by means of the geometry of a circle. So with Pythagoras the *ratio* or harmonic proportionality of the octave (2:1), of the fourth (4:3), and of the fifth (3:2) was meant to perfect the ordering of the mathematical. The sum of the numbers used in these ratios—1, 2, 3, and 4—is 10, which is for Pythagoras the perfect number. To Pythagoras, this mathematical order came as a revelation of the *harmonia* of the natural (heavenly) and the moral world, each individually and both together. The celestial *harmonia* is the "sound" or "music" of the heavenly bodies. However, we do not hear this harmonious sound of music only because from our birth we hear it constantly. What happens in the modern mathematical sciences with and since Galileo and Descartes, however, is another story. With them the Pythagorean mathematical became converted into a technical method rather than an ontological ordering of the universe. For Husserl, modern mathematics or the mathematization of nature by Galileo into the geometric boxes of triangles, circles, and squares inscribed in the "Book of Nature" is "a garb of ideas" *(Ideenkleid)* in which "true being" (or reality) has been taken for a method. It is the mathematical sublimation of nature which "mirrors" and "represents," that is, falsifies reality, nature, and the world—it falsifies because what is "mirrored" or "represented" is only half true. In modern mathematics and the mathematical sciences, the ontological generality of the mathematical has been replaced by the generality of method: the birth of methodolatry or the mathematical truth sublimated in method. For this reason, it is often said that the invention of method but not the use of mathematics is the hallmark of modern science.

V

In 1969 an important conference on Heidegger and Eastern thought was held at the University of Hawaii to honor Heidegger on the occasion of his eightieth birthday; the invited speakers included the late J. Glenn Gray, Calvin O. Schrag, and J. L. Mehta.[32] Following Heidegger's own hint that a dialogue between him and Eastern thought was inevitable, the conferees expressed a strong sentiment that not only might Heidegger serve to build a bridge between East and West but also his thought might, more importantly, serve as the basis of uniting world philosophies. Today, after seventeen years, a conclusive study on this projected task remains unavailable, and many hard years of work on it are already cut out for students of comparative philosophy and culture. The manifest kinship between Heidegger's thought and Sinism can, of course, be stretched to include not only the philosophical landscape of China as a region but also the other regions of East Asia where Chinese ideography —the indispensable signpost of Chinese influence—has long been accepted as their regular linguistic diet.

Heidegger is truly a philosophical deconstructionist[33]—in exactly the same sense as he himself defines the term—who reenvisions and subverts the long-cherished metaphysical tradition of the West—logocentrism that coincides often with ethnocentrism or Occidentalism of one kind or another (for example, Hegelianism). It is that tradition of inherited thought which is at the brink of unleashing awesome, destructive forces ranging from thermonuclear power to cybernetics—that almighty tradition of calculative power which may summarily be called "politology." An alternative to illusionary and fateful politology is the "piety of thinking" as an *ultima philosophia* which may serve as the yarn to weave the woof of Heidegger's own thought and the warp of Eastern thought—Confucianism, Taoism, Ch'an or Zen Buddhism, and others.[34]

Thought-provoking events should, according to Heidegger, insure the provocation of eventful thought. The eventful decades in which we live would certainly provoke serious thinking. As such, Heidegger's conception of the "piety of thinking" is a seminal thought that teaches us both what and how to think, where truth and method are integrated into one unity. It is the pathway to gather or orchestrate our thoughts—both Eastern and Western. Pious thinking is all poetic thinking that leads both to homopiety and geopiety. This poetic thinking may be against "humanism" or the homocentric view of the world but is never against man as such, that is, for the abolition of man.[35] Following the poet Hölderlin, Heidegger is convinced that what saves grows out of danger, impending danger or what the Chinese call "crisis"—that idea which combines "danger" and "opportunity" or proposes an opportunity in the presence of danger. This saving power does not come about haphazardly or by "makeshift." Rather, it emanates from a radical turn of the mind by "being attuned" reverentially to Being or what the Orient calls Nature. This saving power is predicated upon the ready acknowledgment and pious reception of the poet as the supreme and consummate legislator of the world. By speaking the voice of poetry in the conversation of humankind, the thinker as artist is able to subvert the monopoly of established reality by virtue of the reversibility of Heidegger's thought and the thought of the East or Orient which, as Heidegger calls it, is the "land of dawn." *Mutantis mutandis*, "belonging" (as reciprocity)—two in one and one in two—is also "be-longing."

Notes

I wish to dedicate this essay to James J. Heller, who, as the academic dean at Moravian College, has given me his support and encouragement for my work in every way he could for about twenty-five years.

An earlier version of this essay appeared as "The Piety of Thinking: Heidegger's Pathway to Comparative Philosophy," in *The Phenomenology of Man and of the Human Condition*, Part II (Analecta Hussertiana, vol. 21), ed. Anna-Teresa Tymieniecka (Dordrecht: D. Reidel, 1986), pp. 337–368.

1. In a recent collection of essays that explore the status of phenomenology in Japan, it is claimed that in Japan phenomenology became "a field of scholarship [the Japanese] could explore, evaluate and appropriate in their own terms: ultimately, as it seems, it became a genuine mode of Japanese philosophizing. The result is a *Japanese* phenomenology, that is to say: a reflection which is unmistakenly heir to Husserl, but reflects as much the Japanese intellectual legacy and the philosophical quest of contemporary Japan, from the Meiji era to World War II and the present" (Yoshihiro Nitta and Hirotaka Tatematsu (eds.), *Japanese Phenomenology,* Analecta Husserliana, vol. 8 [Dordrecht: Reidel, 1979], p. x). It should be noted that a new East-West dialogue in the movement of phenomenology might very well have begun in earnest with the recent publication of *Phenomenology of Life in a Dialogue between Chinese and Occidental Philosophy,* Analecta Husserliana, vol. 17 (Dordrecht: Reidel, 1984).

2. The twentieth-century Chinese philosopher Tung-sun Chang propounds the logic of correlation as uniquely Chinese. See "A Chinese Philosopher's Theory of Knowledge," in *Our Language and Our World,* ed. S. I. Hayakawa (New York: Harper, 1959), pp. 299–324. In *The Theoretical Foundations of Chinese Medicine* (Cambridge: MIT Press, 1974), Manfred Porkert elaborates on the Chinese systems of "kinaesthetic" correlation or correspondence.

3. Martin Heidegger, *Poetry, Language, Thought,* trans. Albert Hofstadter (New York: Harper and Row, 1971), p. 4.

4. Martin Heidegger, *What Is Called Thinking?,* trans. Fred D. Wieck and J. Glenn Gray (New York: Harper and Row, 1968), pp. 16–17.

5. See my "Misreading the Ideogram: From Fenellosa to Derrida and McLuhan," *Paideuma* 13 (Fall 1984): 211–227. Cf. Zhang Longzi, "The *Tao* and the *Logos*: Notes on Derrida's Critique of Logocentrism," *Critical Inquiry* 11 (March 1985): 385–398. For a comparative analysis of Heidegger's thought and the Chinese language, see Johannes Lohmann, "M. Heidegger's 'Ontological Difference' and Language," in *On Heidegger and Language,* trans. and ed. Joseph J. Kockelmans (Evanston: Northwestern University Press, 1972), pp. 303–363. Lohmann writes: "A dominating trait manifests itself here in the relationship between Chinese thought and Indo-European, or Greek and Western, thought, a trait which is manifested equally in the relationship between Chinese and European cultures. As Humboldt has pointed out for languages, this trait is unique in the relationships of languages and of cultures to one another; it can be briefly characterized as a total difference within the context of an equally total comparability. One can observe this trait in various aspects of a culture—from such formalities as the mourning color (white or black) or the place of honor (left or right) to the overall *habitus* of philosophical thought and of the conception of life and world view. There is obviously not only a question of 'two extreme realizations of the possibilities of man's language which are related to one another in polar opposition,' but a question of two realizations of human possibilities, each of which in its own way is perfect. From this the incomparable, paradigmatic value which the Chinese language as well as the Chinese culture and its history have for us becomes evident" (pp. 337–338). For the most comprehensive study of Oriental thought in this connection, see Hajime Nakamura, *Ways of Thinking of Eastern Peoples,* ed. Philip P. Wiener (Honolulu: East-West Center Press, 1964).

6. For an excellent discussion of the kinesthetic relationships of calligraphy to painting, sculpture, and architecture, see Chiang Yee, *Chinese Calligraphy,* 3rd rev. and enl. ed. (Cambridge: Harvard University Press, 1973). A unique, interesting side of Chinese ideography *(kanji)* is the invention of a kind of Rorschach

test based on *tsukuriji* ("made-up words") to test the attitudes of the Japanese youth. See George Fields, *From Bonsai to Levi's* (New York: Macmillan, 1982), pp. 102–105.

7. In *Puzzles and Epiphanies* (New York: Chilmark Press, 1962), Frank Kermode writes that ". . . [the American dancer Loïe] Fuller is a kind of Ideogram: "*l'incorporation visuelle de l'idée,* a spectacle defying all definition, radiant, homogeneous" (p. 25). For an elegant justification of dancing as the consummate art, see Havelock Ellis, *The Dance of Life* (Boston: Houghton Mifflin, 1923), pp. 36–67.

8. Somewhere in the genealogy of language we must insert the "savage" body itself as "a cuneiform tablet," inscription, and/or graphics. See Alphonso Lingis, *Excesses: Eros and Culture* (Albany: State University of New York Press, 1983), pp. 24–25. For a sociology of the body in relation to contemporary culture, see John O'Neill, *Five Bodies* (Ithaca: Cornell University Press, 1982).

9. In this Heideggerian tradition, Albert Hofstadter writes that "the statement, as a form of oral language, articulates in sound. Not only does it articulate being, both objective and subjective in their unity, but it makes it audible. *Written language is a score for oral performance,* except in extreme cases of artificial symbolic language-construction. Human being becomes audible in the articulate form of the declarative sentence. The serial ordering of different phonemes, making use of their sound qualities, rhythms, and other characteristics, constitutes an utterance which is heard as the uttering of the self-world, subject-object complex just described, and which therefore is the means by which that complex is itself heard as just that complex. . . . In the end, every feature of language, from vocabulary, case, tense, and mood to synonymy-antonymy, logic, rhyme, rhythm, and rhetorical order, is intelligible as a functioning constituent of a medium that articulates human existence. Language is the act by which man brings himself out as man" (*Truth and Art* [New York: Columbia University Press, 1965], pp. 82–83; my italics).

10. The following passage from "The Poet" is one of the most eloquent passages in the entire corpus of Emerson's writings: "The poets made all the words, and therefore, language is the archives of history, and, if we must say it, a sort of tomb of the muses. For, though the origin of most of our words is forgotten, each word was at first a stroke of genius, and obtained currency, because for the moment it symbolized the world to the first speaker and to the hearer. The etymologist finds the deadest word to have been once a brilliant picture. *Language is fossil poetry.* As the limestone of the continent consists of infinite masses of the shells of animalcules, so language is made up of images, or tropes, which now, in their secondary use, have long ceased to remind us of their poetic origin. But the poet names the thing because he sees it, or comes one step nearer to it than any other" (*Essays: Second Series* [New York: Lovell, Coryell, n. d.], p. 21; my italics).

11. Friedrich Nietzsche, *The Birth of Tragedy,* trans. Walter Kaufmann (New York: Random House, 1967), pp. 52, 141.

12. Martin Heidegger, *Nietzsche,* vol. 1, *The Will to Power as Art,* trans. David Farrell Krell (New York: Harper and Row, 1979), p. 99. The acoustic side of Zen or Zen's "record of things heard" is brought forth by David Applebaum in "On Turning a Zen Ear," *Philosophy East and West* 33 (April 1983): 115–122.

13. Geoffrey H. Hartman, *Saving the Text* (Baltimore: Johns Hopkins University Press, 1981), p. 120.

14. See my "Martin Heidegger and the Homecoming of Oral Poetry," *Philosophy Today* 26 (1982): 148–170.

15. Hannah Arendt, *Eichmann in Jerusalem: A Report on the Banality of Evil,* rev. ed. (New York: Penguin Books, 1977), p. 49.

16. C. Kerenyi, *The Religion of the Greeks and Romans,* trans. Christopher Holme (New York: Dutton, 1962), p. 119. Cf. the following stanzas of "pious" John Donne's "Valediction: Forbidding Mourning" (which is quoted from Hartman, *Saving the Text,* p. 153):

> If they be two, they are two so
>   As stiffe twin compasses are two,
> Thy soule the fixt foot, makes no show
>   To move, but doth, if th'other doe.
>
> And though it in the center sit,
>   Yet when the other far doth rome,
> It leanes, and hearkens after it,
>   And growes erect, as that comes home.
>
> Such wilt thou be to mee, who must
>   Like th'other foot, obliquely runne;
> Thy firmnes makes my circle just,
>   And makes me end, where I begunne.

For my treatment of reciprocity or sociality as the absolute ground of Sinism in general and Confucianism in particular, see "*Jen:* An Existential and Phenomenological Problem of Intersubjectivity," *Philosophy East and West* 16 (July–October 1966): 169–188 and "Confucianism and Existentialism: Intersubjectivity as the Way of Man," *Philosophy and Phenomenological Research* 30 (1969): 186–202.

17. We have already noted etymological and semantic filiation of the German words *hören* ("to hear"), *horchen* ("to hearken"), *gehören* ("to belong"), and *gehorchen* ("to obey") in addition to the Latin *abaudire* that has the double meaning of hearing and obeying. Hans-Georg Gadamer points further to the familial intimacy of these auditory words when he notes: "It is the Greek word *oikeion,* i.e., that which pertains to the household, to the *oikos.* It is an ordinary expression for relatives and house friends, i.e., for all who belong to the household. Oikos, household, thus has the broad sense of an economic unit such as the Greek household characteristically was. But oikeion is just as much an expression for that place where one feels at home, where one belongs and where everything is familiar. We too have usages similar to the usage of the Greek oikeion which display this double aspect in the conceptual field of household. In German, *hoi oikeioi* is rendered as *die Angehörigen,* and in abstraction from this normal usage we have come to speak of *das Angehörige,* meaning everything which pertains to the household and not only those people who belong to it" (*Dialogue and Dialectic,* trans. P. Christopher Smith [New Haven: Yale University Press, 1980], p. 18). For a discussion of ecology based on the auditory model of sound as performance, see my "The Orphic Voice and Ecology," *Environmental Ethics* 3 (1981): 329–340.

18. See Hwa Yol Jung and Petee Jung, "Toward a New Humanism: The Politics of Civility in a 'No-Growth' Society," *Man and World* 9 (1976): 283–306.

19. The themes of homopiety and geopiety are inspired by the Heideggerian historical semantist Leo Spitzer in his *Classical and Christian Ideas of World Harmony: Prolegomena to an Interpretation of the Word* "Stimmung," ed. Anna Granville Hatcher (Baltimore: Johns Hopkins University Press, 1963). I am greatly indebted to the geographer Yi-Fu Tuan for my understanding of geopiety, which is distinctly Heideggerian. From reading his works, I learned that geogra-

phy is not confined to the reading of maps but is a philosophical and humanistic discipline. Among his writings, see especially "Geopiety: A Theme in Man's Attachment to Nature and to Place," in *Geographies of the Mind: Essays in Historical Geosophy in Honor of John Kirtland Wright,* ed. David Lowenthal and Martyn J. Bowden (New York: Oxford University Press, 1976), pp. 11–39. For expositions on geopiety in Heidegger's thought, see J. Glenn Gray, "Heidegger's Course: From Human Existence to Nature," *Journal of Philosophy* 54 (1957): 197–207; Vincent Vycinas, *Earth and Gods* (The Hague: Martinus Nijhoff, 1961); and Michael E. Zimmerman, "Toward a Heideggerean *Ethos* for Radical Environmentalism," *Environmental Ethics* 5 (1983): 99–131.

20. In the *Western Inscription,* the eleventh-century Chinese neo-Confucianist Chang Tsai writes: "Heaven is my father and Earth is my mother, and even such a small creature as I find[s] an intimate place in their midst. Therefore that which fills the universe I regard as my body and that which directs the universe I consider as my nature. All people are my brothers and sisters, and all things are my companions" (Wing-tsit Chan, *A Source Book in Chinese Philosophy* [Princeton: Princeton University Press, 1963], p. 497). With this passage, Chang Tsai opens up a philosophical gateway to treat the Confucian concept of *jen* as the all-encompassing *élan vital* of social principle.

21. *The Embers and the Stars* (Chicago: University of Chicago Press, 1984), p. 13.

22. Color and sound are two radically different ways of organizing the human sensorium and the world. There is a qualitative difference in human experience between the visual and the acoustic. As music is the organized movement of sound, the spatiality of sound is most fully actualized in the tones of music. Color does not separate itself from the object, whereas sound separates itself from its source (e.g., voice or the sound of a musical instrument). In other words, color is a dependent attribute of an object, whereas sound is not. While the color we see is the property of a thing itself and we confront color in space, the tone we hear is not the property of anything and we encounter it out of or from space. Color is locatable and localizable in one single position with the object, whereas sound, once separated from its source, has no definite topological property or determination although its source is locatable. Sound travels in no one direction, it travels in all directions. Musical tones have no locatable places: they are neither "here" nor "there" but everywhere (i.e., placeless or ubiquitous). In *Poetic Thinking: An Approach to Heidegger* (Chicago: University of Chicago Press, 1981), David Halliburton writes that "In the performance of a symphony, . . . responsibility may be seen in the interconnecting indebtedness of each constituent: the musicians, as users of equipment (instruments, chairs, music stands, and the like), together with their skills; the artisans responsible for the preparation of the equipment; the members of the audience, together with their capacity to hear and to sustain attention; the score, a being with a thingly character that allies it with equipment even as it carries an already constituted inclination (the totality of the composer's notations); the composer, as one who brings forth within the same order as the artisan; that artisan who is the printer of the score; the manner (in the sense of melody, timbre, tone) of the score as performed; the space of time in which that manner emerges through the concerned composure of performance; the space of time of the tradition without which the music could not move into its own articulation—without which, as the temporal structure that preserves the reciprocal responsibility of all the constituents, it would not be music; and finally, the space of time which is the world play's manner of moving, through all that is thus indebted to its own disclosure" (p. 217).

23. J. Glenn Gray, "Heidegger in Remembering and Remembering Heidegger," *Man and World* 10 (1977): 62–63.

24. See my "Vico's Rhetoric: A Note on Verene's *Vico's Science of Imagination*," *Philosophy and Rhetoric* 15 (1982): 187–202.

25. *Li Chi: Book of Rites,* 2 vols., trans. James Legge (New Hyde Park: University Books, 1967), 2:102–103. Speaking of the locus of the personal as moral performance embodied in the Confucian thought of rite, Herbert Fingarette writes: "We would do well to take music, of which Confucius was a devotee, as our model here. We distinguish sensitive and intelligent musical performances from dull and unperceptive ones; and we detect in the performance confidence and integrity, or perhaps hesitation, conflict, 'faking,' 'sentimentalizing.' We detect all this *in* the performance: we do not have to look into the psyche or personality of the performer. It is all 'there,' public. Although it is there *in* the performance, it is apparent to us when we consider the performance not as 'the Beethoven Opus 3' (that is, from the composer perspective), nor as a 'public concert' (the *li* perspective), nor as a 'post-Mozartian opus' (the style perspective), but primarily as this particular person's performance (the personal perspective)" (*Confucius—The Secular as Sacred* [New York: Harper and Row, 1972], p. 53).

26. Heidegger, *Poetry, Language, Thought,* p. 61.

27. David Farrell Krell sketches *das Geviert* as envisioned by Heidegger in the following pictogram in which the crossing of Being is not a crossing *out (Durchstreichung)* but a crossing *through (Durchkreuzen):*

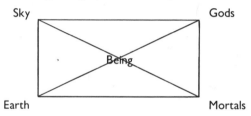

See "Analysis," in Martin Heidegger, *Nietzsche,* vol. 4, *Nihilism,* trans. Frank A. Capuzzi (New York: Harper and Row, 1982), p. 289. For a fine discussion of Taoism in this connection, see Kuang-ming Wu, *Chuang Tzu: World Philosopher at Play* (New York: Crossroad, 1982).

28. Heidegger, *Poetry, Language, Thought,* p. 14.

29. Martin Heidegger, *Identity and Difference,* trans. Joan Stambaugh (New York: Harper and Row, 1969), pp. 51–52.

30. For a scathing critique of Cartesianism, see Richard Rorty, *Philosophy and the Mirror of Nature* (Princeton: Princeton University Press, 1979). In *The World Viewed,* rev. ed. (Cambridge: Harvard University Press, 1979), Stanley Cavell uses the term "automatism." The significance of automatism for our discussion here is twofold. First, as mechnical reproduction or representation, photography, for example, is of reality but not reality itself, photographic automatism removes the human agent from the task of reproduction or representation. Second, photography is not hand-made but mechanically reproduced—and what is mechanically reproduced is an absence of the human hand in forming its objects. To put it in the Heideggerian terminology, in photography thinking is no longer a "handicraft."

31. See Susan Sontag, *On Photography* (New York: Dell, 1977).

32. See *Philosophy East and West* 20 (July 1970).

33. Cf. Robert Magliola, *Derrida on the Mend* (West Lafayette: Purdue University Press, 1984), which is an interesting three-way speculation on Heidegger, Derrida, and Eastern thought.

34. In the *Politicus,* Plato, interestingly, likens the practical art of statesmanship (political *praxis*) to the art *(technē)* of weaving—the wholesome *handicraft* which I consider to be the opposite of politology.

35. In *Zen and Western Thought,* ed. William R. LaFleur (Honolulu: University of Hawaii Press, 1985), Masao Abe argues that "Dōgen grounds his existence on the radically dehomocentric, cosmological dimension whereas Heidegger is not altogether freed from homocentrism, though he emphasizes transcending towards the world" (p. 65). Heidegger's later philosophical orientation would, however, make superfluous Abe's contention concerning Heidegger as contrasted with the Zen master Dōgen.

David Michael Levin

Mudra as Thinking: Developing Our Wisdom-of-Being in Gesture and Movement

Introduction

According to the Tibetan tradition of Buddhism, *mudra* is a form of embodiment manifesting the dynamics of enlightenment. According to Heidegger, authentic thinking is an individual human existence in which our potential-for-being is actualized. I therefore see a way to bridge the chasm which separates Tibetan Buddhism, as a spiritual life identified with its origin in the East, from the thinking of Martin Heidegger, a philosopher whose interpretation of the spiritual life identifies him with the tradition rooted in the West. Building this bridge, however, is not so easy, since Heidegger leaves the *embodiment* of thinking largely unthought, while the Buddhist teachings appear to present the wisdom of *mudra* as an antidote for too much thinking. So I need to interpret Heidegger in a way that brings out the embodiment implicit in his thinking, and I need to emphasize that Heidegger breaks away from his tradition by interpreting what he calls "thinking" as a recollection of Being, and not as the abstract cognitive activity of a pure ego-logical subject. By the same token, however, it will also be necessary for me to interpret the teachings of *mudra* in a way that seems to have been alien to them. I will attempt to clarify my sense that these teachings *demonstrate* enlightenment by embodying it in exemplary forms, idealized corporeal schematizations. It is, I believe, the distinctive function of the various *mudras* to help the practitioner get access to a wisdom carried by the body which is, when we translate it back into the language used by Heidegger, a powerful recollection of Being. The bridge I shall be attempting to build, therefore, is one which could perhaps enrich both traditions, giving to each a new self-understanding by way of the other.

Mudra, a Sanskrit word born in the spiritual culture of India, eventually emerged within the profoundly hermeneutical tradition of Tibetan Buddhism, where it was translated by the words *phyag-rgya*. According to kLong-chen rab-'byams-pa, one of Tibet's most eminent scholars and teachers (A.D. 1308–1364), *phyag* basically means "to hold to," in the sense of a commitment that binds one to going beyond Samsara, or a commitment to grasp and adhere to the significance of Buddhahood, while *rgya* means "to seal" Samsara with the vow to achieve enlightenment.[1] At another level of understanding, however, *phyag* may be taken to mean "a pristine, primordial awareness of the intrinsic openness of Being" *(phyag ni stong pa'i ye-shes te)*, while *rgya* may be taken to mean our "liberation from the fact of Samsara" *(rgya ni 'khor-ba'i chos las grol)*. And since, for the Tibetans, the human being always participates in three fields, levels, or dimensions of Being, namely, incarnation, speech, and mind, *mudra* is understood as taking place in three distinct but interdependent fields, levels, or dimensions of Being: corporeal *mudra (lus-kyi phyag-rgya)*, speech *mudra (ngag-gi phyag-rgya)*, and Dharma *mudra (chos-kyi phyag-rgya)*, which is *mudra* participating with full awareness, or full presence, in the dimensionality of Being as a whole.

In terms of our self-development as human beings, participation in this third dimension, this most open, most primordial field of Being, is of the utmost importance. The teachings of *mudra* facilitate our entrance into this field by activating an ontological understanding that is already present in our corporeal nature. The importance of *mudra* for our access to this bodily wisdom lies in the fact that we are situated in a field that breaks down our ego-structured encapsulations and opens us up to the being of other sentient natures. Thus, *mudra* contributes to our self-development by anchoring our life in the compassion of a transpersonal field.

As a matter for discourse, the essential nature of *mudra* is much too vast for our comprehension. In this essay, we will focus on *mudra* in relation to our incarnation: the body of motility; the body, that is, of gesture and movement. Even so, we cannot hope to encompass its nature, its significance. What I propose for our consideration, therefore, is my conviction that, on the one hand, what Heidegger brings to light through the concept of *das Gebärde des Denkens* ("the bearing of thought") can be fruitfully specified and opened up when it is understood in correlation with the concept of *mudra,* and that, on the other hand, Heidegger's illuminations of gesture and movements can serve us well as the ground of a bridge to span the distance which continues to separate our Western conception of motility from the conception which holds sway in the life-world of Tibetan Buddhism. This essay is accordingly aimed at a simultaneous clarification of Heidegger and Tibetan Buddhism. Beyond that, however, it aspires to disclose the potential for spiritual self-development which it is within our capacity to enjoy, by grace of that wonderful and most precious gift, the gift of a human embodiment. Binding ourselves to this goal, we shall attempt to formulate the "potential-for-being" that is always already implicit, inwrought, in our gestures and movements, and we shall see how the teachings of *mudra* enable us to *actualize* this wisdom, this potential.

Part One: Thinking with Our Hands

According to our tradition of metaphysics, the human body is not capable of thinking. Thinking takes place only in the "mind." And this "mind" is contingently located in the region of the head—which, for that reason, is often not counted as part of the human "body." Furthermore, our tradition is very deeply committed to this dualism of "mind" and "body," because it is tightly bound to the Judaeo-Christian ideal of asceticism and its path of renunciation. When we read Descartes, for example, it becomes quite evident that the epistemological and ontological dualism of "body" and "mind" is, in the final analysis, a reflective manifestation of the dualism in our *religious* experience of good and evil: we have tended to see a radical split in our moral nature, a split which reverberates as a painful split in every dimension of our being. The body is evil; it is a source of sin, moral weakness and limitation, cognitive error, perceptual illusion. When separated from the body, the "mind" is essentially unpolluted and free of evil. Nothing so noble, so "lofty" as thought could ever take place in the "lower" body. Unfortunately, however, this understanding only perpetuates the moral and spiritual affliction. (Nietzsche, I believe, was the first Western philosopher to recognize this problem.)

If we want ever to break out of the suffering reflected by this tradition, we must first of all acknowledge that we can think (for example) with—or in—our hands. Until we acknowledge this, it will not be possible for us to retrieve for the future the primordial and inherently liberating experience of the presencing of Being. At the present time, our technological sensibility tends to conceal this primordial presencing of Being, immeasurably deep in its "meaning," behind modes of presencing which are derivative, and not as rich or deep, but which correspond to the instrumental technology of the Western Will to Power. We fall into a pathological fixation on the two modes of presencing, being-ready-at-hand *(Zuhandensein)* and being-extant *(Vorhandensein),* that reflect the historical unfolding of our samsaric affliction, our inveterate tendency to pattern all experiences of Being in terms of our attraction, our aversion, and our indifference in relation to the beings we encounter. What differentiates Heidegger's sense of "thinking" from the more familiar sense still dominant in our tradition, however, is precisely the fact that "thinking" in his sense—most certainly *not* an activity of the Cartesian *res cogitans*—allows us, for the first time, to understand a nondualistic and embodied experience of thinking against the background of Western philosophical discourse.

Merleau-Ponty observes that skillful typing is a "knowledge in the hands, which is forthcoming only when bodily effort is made, and [which] cannot be formulated in detachment from that effort."[2] Our unwillingness to acknowledge this wonderful intelligence inwrought in the hands themselves makes us profoundly indifferent, not only to the "ontological difference" between beings and Being-as-such, but also, in consequence, to the ontological potential-for-being of which we are capable by virtue of the gift of our hands. Etymology tells us that "to gesture" means "to bear," "to bring forth," "to give birth," and "to make appear." The gesturing of our hands is a *technē,* a skill, an articulatory capacity. But what do our gestures bring forth? To what do they give birth? What kinds of beings do they make appear in the world of their restless activity? Our hands are a most precious gift. We need to reciprocate this gift by giving them, in return, the gift of our thought.

In *What Is Called Thinking?,* Heidegger undertakes a sustained meditation on the hands and their craft.

> "Craft" literally means the strength and skill in our hands. The hand is a peculiar thing. In the common view, the hand is [merely] part of our bodily organism. But the hand's *essence* can never be determined, or explained, by its being [just] an organ which can grasp. . . . The hand is infinitely different from all grasping organs—paws, claws, or fangs—different by an abyss of essence. Only a being who can speak, that is, *think,* can have hands and can be handy in achieving works of handicraft.
>
> But the craft of the hand is richer than we commonly imagine. The hand does not only grasp and catch, or push and pull. The hand reaches and extends, receives its own welcome in the hands of others. The hand holds. The hand carries. The hand designs. . . . Two hands fold into one, a gesture meant to carry man into the great oneness. The hand is all this, and this is the true handicraft.[3]

And Heidegger then points out the *need* for giving the maintenance of thought to our hands:

> Every motion of the hand in every one of its works carries itself through the element of thinking; every bearing of the hand bears itself in that element. All the work of the hand is rooted in thinking.[4]

Now if we hear this last sentence in the old *metaphysical* way, we will miss Heidegger's point. He is not saying that the hand is rooted in the thinking *(cogitationes)* of the mind (the *ego cogitans*). Rather, he is asserting that the ontical *comportment* of the hand is to be rooted in *its* ontological thoughtfulness. In other words, there is a thinking of Being which is rooted in the work of the hands: in the very bearing of our hands, we can give thought to the presencing of Being.

It is crucial to understand, here, that we are not at all denying the "ontological difference" between beings and Being-as-such (the Being of beings) when we affirm the idea that the hands can give thought to Being-as-such *without* abandoning their *ontical* involvement with various manipulable beings. In other words, it would be a misunderstanding of the ontological difference, or of the difference between the ontic and the ontological, to believe that our hands cannot maintain their ontological awareness, their relationship with Being, while being, and as their way of being, ontically concerned with particular beings. The ontological is not in opposition to the ontic; rather, it safeguards the *openness* of the ontic: it is the dimension into which, and as which, the ontic opens; or, in still other words, it is the open dimension of Being as a whole which *comes to a focus* in the ontic. Pre-ontologically, that is, without explicit, reflective awareness and understanding, we are, through our hands, *always and already in a relationship* with the Being of beings. So the deepening ontological understanding for which this relationship calls can take place nowhere else than in the *ontic* field of our activity, whenever we lend our hands to an opening up of the ontic field.

There is a *tactful* way of handling things, a way of manipulating, which is mindful of their dimensionality, and which maintains them *in the dimensions of their Being,* that is, in the tangibly open dimension of the ontological difference. The hands give to Being our gift of thought *whenever* they handle things with a skill that *cares for* the richness, the inexhaustible depth, of their being. Thus, Heidegger wants to call our attention to the traditional craftsmen—the cabinetmaker, for example, who "makes himself answer and respond above all to the different kinds of wood and to the shapes slumbering within the wood."[5] With such skillful gestures of thought, patient, gentle, responsive, and caring, the craftsman is not just relating to a "thing"; he is also in touch with the very *being* of that thing. Through his ontical way of being—with the wood, the thing he is making—he is receptive to, and therefore participates in, its whole depth of ontological meaningfulness, its whole field of Being.

In maintaining beings in their ownmost dimensionality of Being, we are accordingly involved, at the same time, in the maintenance of Being itself—although, to be sure, there are *also* ways for the hands to give themselves more "directly" and "fully" to this maintenance. Here, what I have in mind are, for example, sacred theatre, religious rituals, and prayer.

Now according to Heidegger, beings in our everyday world are primarily present for us in two modalities: in terms of their being present-at-hand *(Vorhandensein)* and in terms of their being ready-to-hand *(Zuhandensein)*. The latter mode of being is the way things are when they are present to us as "handy," as "useful" and "readily available," within the contexts of our projects; and it therefore characterizes that dimension of our world which is pervasively determined by technological relationships and their contexts of instrumental operations. Foremost among these contextual project-relationships are, as the word Heidegger uses itself suggests, the instrumental operations and activities initiated by our hands—by our hands, that is, and the tools which extend the mastery of their operations. The *former* mode of being is what (how) a thing appears to be, or appears *as* being, in regard to "its own" inherent possibilities of being, and therefore in regard to its being independent of human being, and not reducible to, nor completely determined by, the instrumental and cognitive projects that constitute the human "world."

What still remains in question, however, is whether or not (despite this distinction between two modes of being) the very terms of this distinction, or perhaps the way the distinction is drawn, could be said to give evidence, symptomatic evidence, of a pervasively technological, pervasively manipulative and control-oriented com-prehension of the Being of beings—a grasping of the gift and the givenness of Being which is, in fact, quite distinctive of the deep affliction destroying our modern historical epoch.

Since I believe that there are many kinds of meaningful and appropriate responses to our crisis, I do not wish to be misunderstood as an advocate of psychologism; but I do certainly want to suggest that a "psychological focus" on our experience of holding, handling, grasping, and touching could be extremely helpful in releasing us from the tenacious grip of our technological world-view. If our experience of beings, and of the Being of all beings, is indeed powerfully determined by our technological world-epoch, and if this technological world-epoch can be traced back to a life-world shaped by the activity of our hands, then it would seem reasonable to suppose that, should we find within ourselves the capacity to cultivate an awareness which modifies our way of relating to things we touch and handle, we could indeed begin, albeit with small and insignificant gestures, to break out of the reductive nihilism of our present historical epoch, and begin, in truth, to hold open for human existence a new historical possibility. This new historical possibility is to be found, I submit, right in our hands.

In the modern technological epoch, the way of being-present which Heidegger calls *Vorhandensein* (being present-at-hand, being sheerly extant) is *reduced* to a constant and totally comprehensible, totally controllable *standing presence,* a constant and permanent presence, while the way of being present (the way of presencing) which Heidegger characterizes as *Zuhandensein* (being-ready-at-hand) is reduced to a being which is constantly and immediately ready-to-hand, always right at hand and ready for immediate use at any time. Underlying this historical transformation through technology, however, is the historically situated, historically changing character of the human *will,* which is embodied, in the first instance, in hands that reach out after an all-encompassing "embrace" of domination, and are moved by the intense desire, the intense, but false "need," to grasp and control and permanently secure. If another way of being-present with things, and with Being itself, is ever to be granted us, however, then it seems clear that we must renounce the willful approach: we must not attempt to grasp and seize; rather, we must be prepared, first, to *let go*—and to remain, as it were, utterly empty-handed. (I mean "empty-handed," here, in a sense which does not preclude our actually holding or keeping something in our hands. I mean to characterize an attitude.) For, the overcoming of nihilism, and the coming-to-pass of a new way-of-being in the world of technology, would seem to require (although this could never be sufficient) hands which *willingly embody* wonder and awe and reverence, and which know how to question and hold themselves open in "the piety of thinking." That would be the primordial experience of presence (the presence of Being as such), out of which, alone, a radically different technological relationship to the presencing of beings might eventually come within reach and fill our hands with its gifts.

Since the child's first concepts *(Begriffe)* are schemata of comprehension formed in the process of grasping *(greifen)* and manipulation, it is only to be expected that our experience of tangible beings, and of Being itself, will tend to be determined in ways that correspond to the initial character of the inquiring, learning gesture. The circumstances of early life, and the gestures they elicit—gestures made in anxiety, gestures of violent emotion, seizing or rejecting—set the predominant character of the original concept. If we are concerned about pathologies in the character of comprehension, we should look to afflictions in the character of our prehensions. If we are distressed by the nihilism which increasingly threatens us in this epoch of advanced technology, we would do well to attend to the ways we "use" our hands, and the ways we experience their "activity." For, if the "origin" of technology is in our hands, then the key to the overcoming of technological nihilism—a radically new historical initiative—may also be found in our hands. The question is: Can we retrieve a new concept of technology from the ontological awareness-of-Being still implicit in the grasp of our hands?

It is with these considerations in mind, I believe, that Heidegger takes up the question of "proper use." His analysis of use brings out the essential nature of our hands and helps us to define the gestures of which we, as thinking mortals, are most worthy.

> 'Using' does not mean utilizing, using up, exploiting. When we handle a thing, for example, our hand must fit itself to the thing. Use implies fitting response. Proper use does not debase what is being used—on the contrary, use is determined and defined by leaving the used thing in its essential nature. But leaving it that way does not mean carelessness, much less neglect. On the contrary; only proper use brings the thing to its essential nature and keeps it there . . . safe in its essence.[6]

According to Heidegger, then, we are appropriately caring when we relate "to the thing in hand according to its nature, thus letting that nature become manifest by the handling."[7] The grasp of technology cannot reach into the essential nature of things, for its operations reify: they are tactless transgressions. The tender touch, which *feels* what it touches with a reverence that is also active "aesthetic" appreciation, gets in touch with a thing's essential nature more deeply and closely than the hand which willfully grasps and clings, moved by desire (by the poisons of attraction and aversion), or than the hand which is indifferent to the beauty of the thing in the disclosure of its truth, its ontological difference. As the mode of our original understanding (our pre-comprehension of things in a mood of openness), feeling is our most tactful way into the opening depth of things. Touching with respect, handling with tact, we have things whole and intact. And we let them yield their more intangible nature, their deeper and otherwise inaccessible nature.

What *is* our capacity to be touched, and moved, by that which we are given for our touching? What is the character of our touch? By what are we touched, by what moved? Touching presupposes our capacity to be touched, and this implicit reciprocity calls into question our inveterate tendency to polarize the tactile field into a subject and its object. At a deeper, more primordial level, this polarization does not appear; ontologically, the touching and the touched take part in a dynamic of reciprocity, mere "inflections" in a field of energy. Are we capable of touching things, capable of handling and manipulating things, with the sensibility of *Gelassenheit*? The "properly human" gesture, in touch with the "value" of Being, will skillfully practice a movement of neutrality and nonattachment. Touching a deep, and deeply hidden truth, the thoughtful maker of cabinets touches the wood he is using with fingers sensitive to the precise needs of the wood. He takes pride in his tools, and handles them with care. In his movements we observe poise and grace; and in his gentle touching and holding, we may sense a visible tact. Every gesture elicits the concealed, and is, in this sense, hermeneutical.

For Heidegger, our gestures bespeak capacities.[8] These capacities are in turn deeply motivated by their inborn skillfulness *(Geschicklichkeit):* the gift *(Geschenk)* we are given at birth. At birth, we are given a gift of nature and sent *(geschickt)* on our way. Whatsoever we do with that gift, how we experience the potential inherent in our skillfulness, decides our story *(Geschichte),* our individual fate, our mortal destiny *(Geschicklichkeit, Schicksal).* Some of us will, in the course of time, realize the gift in this skill; some will not. But in any case, it is appropriate *(schicklich)* that we realize the true measure of our articulatory capacities, in that we have appropriately experienced our indebtedness and belongingness *(Zugehörigkeit),* appropriated our capacity to develop, and responded in the most appropriate way to the original, unchosen appropriation of our articulatory being (our mortal *legein).* Since the skill we develop *is* a gift, and in truth a "dispensation" of Being, the most appropriate way of realizing it will be through a responsiveness that deeply and fully *inhabits* our gestural being and transforms every act of articulation into a fulfilling gesture of rejoicing and thanksgiving.

Part Two: Lending a Hand to Being

In "The Turning" *(Die Kehre),* Heidegger observes that "thinking is genuine activity, genuine taking a hand, if to take a hand means to lend a hand to . . . the coming to presence of Being."[9] This observation focuses the "Question of Being" (the *Seinsfrage)* on the gesturing of our hands. Of what are we capable? What do we bring forth with our hands? And how? And why? To what do we offer our hands? The "Question of Being" calls our gesturing, our motility in general, into question. The Question questions our motivation; it touches us in our innermost being and moves us; it moves us to recollect the true dimensionality, the very essence, of our gestural being. The Question motivates a *shift* in our focus, our awareness. It formulates the "ontological difference" as a difference between our gesturing in the forgetfulness of our ontical everydayness and an ontologically deepened gesturing which is mindful of the tangible givenness of Being. It formulates a task which challenges us to take the measure of our gesturing by situating our motility within the immeasurable dimensionality of the tactile field of Being as a whole. Our gestural capacities bear within their motility an ingrained "destiny": a potential we are called upon to make our own. And we appropriately own up to "destiny" as we begin to realize the extent of our commitment to the maintenance of Being.

We can lend a hand to Being in many ways. We can lend it, in fact, every time we give a hand to other mortals; and we can lend it every time the hand we give to the various things we touch and handle is a gesture of care, a gesture of thoughtful maintenance in touch with the field of their being. The thoughtful maintenance of beings, moving out of respect for their ownmost, and even their most intangible ways of being, never fails to lend a hand to the coming-to-presence of Being.

In his *Existential Foundations of Medicine and Psychology,* Medard Boss points out that "to exist *as Da-sein* means to sustain and maintain the clearness of a world-spanning realm of perception, to hold open this realm into which whatever can be may shine forth and be perceived in its meaning and its place."[10] As Boss experiences it, "the human being exists *as* a spanning, hearing, and holding-open of a realm of perception that is responsive to the presence of whatever phenomena reveal themselves in it."[11] The Question of Being is a question of truth which holds us open, *as* beings who gesture, to the tangible openness, the span, of Being: the sensible dimensionality of the ontological difference. (*Alētheia* is Heidegger's word for this hermeneutical experience of opening, and of the openness itself.) It focuses us on our capacity to gesture, to articulate through gesture, in a way that holds beings and keeps beings within the openness of this dimensionality. It focuses us directly on the tactful character of our capacity to touch and hold and manipulate the various beings of our world in a way that maintains their rich contact, and ours, with the primordial clearing of space that lets them, and us, first meet in presence.

There is, for our purposes, an especially important passage, in *The Existential Foundations of Medicine and Psychology,* where Boss begins to articulate the transition, the shift, from the merely ontic to the deeper, more ontological dimensionality of the thoughtful gesture. It is worth paying attention to the succession of steps, or moves, by means of which he shifts from an ontical experience with which we are all very familiar to the threshold of a deeper, more ontological experience: an experience with which we may not be so familiar, but which we will surely undergo as we begin to give thought to our gesture. Here (with my indications of the steps in brackets) is what he writes:

> When I direct someone toward a windowsill with a gesture of my right hand, my bodily existence as a human being does not end [1] *at the tip of my index finger.* While perceiving the windowsill . . . [2] *I extend myself bodily far beyond this fingertip to that windowsill.* In fact, bodily [3] *I reach out even further than this to touch all the phenomena of my world,* present or merely visualized re-presented ones. . . .[12]

Just how far, emotionally, can we reach? What is the reach and range of our compassion? Are we completely open, or even open as much as we feel we could be, to extending ourselves, reaching out to others, reaching out to help those beings who need our help? By what are we touched? When, and by what, are we visibly moved? Are we moved, are we *visibly* moved, by the power of compassion? Or are we moved, mostly, by avarice and self-interest? What is the *character* of our touch? Is it tender and gentle? Is it graced by consideration? Is it a caring caress? How (that is, with what quality of feeling) do we reach out and grasp, touch, hold, handle, manipulate, and maintain? Do we cling tenaciously to what we love? Is our hold in any way destructive? Can we really *feel* what we are touching? Could we deepen, or expand, that feeling? How do we give a hand? When, how, and to whom do we *offer* a helping hand? And when another human being gives *us* a hand, or offers to do so, how do we greet and receive it? Do we go about with two tightly clenched fists, or are the hands relaxed and open? These are thought-provoking questions: questions which may bring into focus for us the tact and contact of our being; questions which may move us to give more thought to how we, in the time of our dwelling, touch upon the lives of others. And not only that. These are questions which help us to get in touch with a "guardian awareness" (etymologically, a *Wahr-nehmung,* an understanding already protecting and preserving our ontological attunement) always implicit in all our gestures; and they help us to *situate* our gestural experience in *a more open dimension,* so that our gestures are made visible, and can be felt, in the appropriateness of their belonging to the maintenance of Being.

Traditional Western metaphysics would assert that our motility and gesturing *(legein)* depend upon, and are in need of, a "rational" grounding *(logos).* But the concept of this "rational" grounding is the historical product of a reflection depriving itself of feeling and sensibility, a reflection that, in reaching the historical stage of formal metaphysics, has virtually lost all touch with the bodily felt truth of its original and elemental field of Being. The "pathology" characteristic of its traditional ontology requires a new concept of ground and grounding, a concept brought forth in our gestures and movements themselves, and as an experience of our deepening contact with the more elemental grounding of the sensible field of motility.

As we are understanding it here, Heidegger's Question of Being functions "methodologically" to *challenge* our gestures and movement, to *draw them out* into the openness of the dimensionality we call "Being." This is certainly very different from the traditional understanding of the ontological task proposed by the Western metaphysician. I would like to suggest that Heidegger diverges from the Western tradition on two points. (1) The Question of Being does not call for, nor does it need, an absolutely Cartesian foundation. What makes the question itself and our response to it genuinely "ontological" is to be found, rather, in its way of continually drawing us out, as beings who gesture, into a deeper, more meaningful dimensionality of embodied experience. (2) Instead of calling for a methodological *epochē,* a reflective turning-away-from, holding-back, and disengaging (as in Descartes and Husserl), Heidegger's Question of Being functions to direct our attention, our available awareness, into the very heart of our experience of motility. The Question of Being questions our experience of motility; it invites us to go into that experience, into its bodily feeling; and it asks us to move and gesture with an awareness that is attentive to the openness and depth of the field in which our comportment takes place. Thus, as we get more deeply and fully in touch with the "felt sense" of our basic motility, we begin to get a "feel" for the layout *(legein)* of opportunities by grace of which we could deepen our capacity to maintain the presencing *(alētheia)* of Being in the very field of our comportment.

I submit that this very different method of reflection, which works, not by endistancing, but by *permeating* the body of our gesturing and moving with a more thoughtful awareness, is a genuine *anamnēsis,* a "recollection of Being," in the sense that (1) it is concerned with our returning to, and retrieving, that which, from the very first, we have always and already been *given* to understanding (that is, a pre-conceptual, pre-ontological understanding of our mortal being in its relation to Being as a whole), and (2) it is concerned with our capacity to recollect the presencing of Being. But Heideggers's "recollection" takes the form of a reading of the history of metaphysics as a history of Being. Thus, his notion of "recollection" remains for the most part disembodied—and to that extent, it unfortunately perpetuates the very metaphysics it sets out to deconstruct. By contrast, the "recollection" I am effecting here—inspired, I must admit, by my initiation into Tibetan Buddhist practice—attempts to locate this recollection as a process taking place, first of all, in the experiential body. We are bodying forth a relationship with Being long before there is any philosophical consciousness.

Part Three: The Genesis and Unfolding of Human Motility

Our motility takes place in a field. Our being, as beings gifted with the capacity we call "motility," is dependent upon this field. Our being is organized by, and grounded in, the topology of this field. The field of our motility is the layout of a field of Being: it is how Being manifests, how Being presences, in relation to our motility. Consequently, in the light of the Question of Being, even our motility is at stake. The Question becomes a question for our being as beings for whom there is *(es gibt)* this capacity we call "motility." Specifically, then: Of what are we capable? This question focuses attention on our capacity to *develop* the character of our primordial relationship to the topology of Being-as-a-whole *by virtue of* our motility. What is at stake? Our groundedness, our rootedness, our balance and steadiness of gait, our bearing and carriage,

our path, and the goals on this path: every aspect of our motility in relation to Being-as-such.

In its disclosure of the primordial *logos,* our ontological interpretation
accordingly calls our attention to an inveterate human tendency to lose
touch and forget, err and stray, stumble and fall. Can we regain lost
ground? Can we get our foothold? Can we recover our balance? Can we
find our way? Can we get to know our own pace? The retrieval of the
body's ontological awareness (that is, a recollection of our pre-ontological attunement-to-Being), is a disclosure of the primordial "claim"
("call") of Being, recalling us to ourselves. We are thus responding to the
Question of Being by formulating the task of fundamental ontology as an
articulation of our most fundamental Topology. And we are thinking this
Question in terms of a process of embodiment whose experience of
motility has been called into question and intensely motivated to move
towards a more thoughtful life of "authenticity."

Since the being of motility is, in its deepest truth, a sensuous-emo-
tional field of motivating energies, a field of tensions whose intertwining
is a tendency to constitute bodily centers of ego-logical (subjectively- and
objectively-polarized) comportment, the possibility of authentic existence refers us to the question of "Care": the being of motility must be
understood as the fulfillment of "solicitude," the openness in our way of
being-with-others. For the intertwining is *already* a primordial form of
"solicitude," and the encompassing field therefore becomes a compass of
compassion. As regards human motility, we must conclude that the "calling" which most deeply touches our nature, and moves us in its service, is
to be *felt* as *a strongly grounded motivation* to act in the world, visibly
moved by a deeply rooted compassion for the sufferings and needs of all
other sentient beings. *Compassion is: moving and being-moved for the
sake of others.* Compassion is a calling which lays claim to our motility
from the very beginning.

The authentic human being, whose ontologically experienced motility
we have been schematizing, understandingly appropriates the topological configuration of corporeal capacities as a local disclosedness, a local
field of highly motivated energy, "originating in" and "emerging from" a
still more primordial clearing of Being. According to this interpretation,
our motility claims our attention at this level as the "animation" or "acti-
vation" of an elemental *flesh* inseparable from its situational field and
functioning as an immediately meaningful disclosure, both in and of
Being. This open field, this expansive space of disclosure, is a dimension
of motility whose primordial topological presence is a truth concealed
not only by our "normal" everyday mode of motility, a motility characteristic of everyone and anyone, but concealed also by its projection in
the present-at-hand ontology of our tradition of theoretical reflection.

From "the very beginning" (that is, always and already), the field of motility is an *elemental syntax* of motivations, an array or layout of possible routings, orchestrating and choreographing our bodily postures, gestures, attitudes, and comportments. Our ontological interpretation calls attention to, articulates, and thereby opens up, the basic overall layout of the motility-field for human existence; it is a reflective disclosing of its depth and dimensionality, its most fundamental openness-to-Being. Our interpretation is an attempt at clarifying the way that this layout, as a place *(topos)* for the primordial "working" of the *logos,* orchestrates and lays claim to our motility as the field of its most deeply meaningful existential possibilities and opportunities.

The human being "begins" life endowed with a body genetically pre-coded, genetically pre-programmed, for movement. This infantile body of movement is, however, an *ancient* body, a body which, from the very beginning, belongs as much to the culture of our ancestors as it does to nature. The earliest stages of development constitute a phase in our human life during which the motility is *without* an ego-logical subject or agent; that is to say that the infant's motility-body and the enabling field of clearing are still relatively undifferentiated. Since the motility-body has not yet been personally "owned," it belongs primordially to Being-as-a-whole, which presences "for" it in the worldly form of a reliable ground and a field of clearing. The infant's body, and *a fortiori* the "sublimated" body of the child which *we* still carry around with us in the course of our normal adulthood, belong to, and are charged by their primordial attunement to, the worldhood of the motility-field as a whole. By grace of this topological belonging and attunement, that body of motility exists in the world with a *pre-ontological understanding* of Being.

The child's body of motility becomes, of course, progressively more socialized, more "humanized." The child's body is shaped, according to the image of its culture, into the well-tempered body of everyone-and-anyone: the primordial orchestrations of motility opened up for him pre-ontologically gradually fall into line, constituting a life-world already regulated by social conventions, cultural styles, ethnic identifications, role-introjections, and especially significant associations. The original routings are routinized; a free motility finds itself sedimented into habitualities; the archetypes, functioning primordially as corporeal schemata, are increasingly fixed into typical patterns of movement, habitual styles of gesturing and posturing, a familiar signature. The motility characteristic of *das Man,* of *Jedermann,* manifests our "inveterate tendency" to become absorbed in an unnecessarily narrow, needlessly restricted world-field of purposive, and mostly self-centered action. There is no (felt) sense of the larger field, the open horizon, the background, and the ground underlying; no sense of a more pervasive and more universal field-continuum as the more original source of motility, and as having already laid out for us a certain elemental configuration, a certain life-world, of *possible* movements, *possible* courses and routings. There is no understanding of our deeper inherence, our intertwining, in the topology of Being.

But we are not necessarily "stuck" in this restricted field, not necessarily immobilized by the boundaries which are imposed on us by virtue of our initiation into a social world and our education into the ways and traditions of our culture. There can be no doubt that each generation of mortals has needed, and continues to feel a need for, this corporate initiation and education. The motility characteristic of everyone-and-anyone is a *necessary* acquisition for our natural, normal, and spiritually most fulfilling development. But there is *no need* for us to restrict ourselves, in our egological adulthood, to such standard and typical forms of motility. Heidegger's recollection of Being as our primordial topology calls into question the adult ego's standard of normality and the ontology which reflects it. We will only understand this question, though, if we let ourselves be moved by its truth. We must go *into* our experience of movement, finding in its depth the hidden topology of our primordial, elemental, pre-ontological openness-to-Being. The calling we will encounter is a bodily felt sense of the true nature of our motility as a dynamic mode of being-in-the-world; it calls us into the region of existential struggle and decision: that standpoint, namely, from which we begin to understand that neither the worldly, practical egological motility of everyone-and-anyone, nor the present-to-hand ontology to which it gives rise, can constitute the *ultimate* source of meaningfulness.

But how do we shift, how move, from the everyday motility characteristic of everyone-and-anyone (in our technological epoch) into the more authentic motility of the outstanding individual, the one who lives and dwells in the dimension of ontological openness, the dimension where the body of motility is intensely energized and renewed, deeply moved by its relationship to the openness of the primordial topology? It is not enough to speak of a "radical refelection"; nor does it suffice to speak of a gesture of ontological-existential "recollection" *(anamnēsis)*. What we need to think about, rather, is a dynamically reflective process which gets us more deeply and fully *in touch* with our implicit com-pre-hension of motility, our *bodily felt sense* of its nature, as a way-of-being-in-the-world: we must reclaim our bodily felt sense of motility in its pre-ontologically attuned openness-to-Being.

The narrowing, restraining, and self-limiting experience of motility that is characteristic of the ego-logical adult in our modern technological world has indeed a genesis—and a cultural history—that we can clearly trace, not only recollecting its primordial, and more open, pre-ontological orchestration, but disclosively reading and articulating, from our present standpoint, our felt sense of its inherent possiblities for a development and unfolding *beyond* the unsatisfactory motility of everyone-and-anyone. Since symbolism is appropriate in the story of our genealogy, our onto-genesis, I would like to suggest that the body of motility is rather like a primordial text very much in *need* of existential, ontological, and hermeneutical interpretation. Since the topology of Being is a *logos* which, in laying down the vectors of the motility-field, *pre-inscribes* this layout into the elemental flesh of our being, the topology is a *topography.* The *logos* is a writing, a *grammar* of motility, a topology pre-inscribed like an esoteric text upon the primordial flesh; and it gathers this flesh into the shape of a motility-body at the center of a spatial field. The body of motility is like a *palimpsest* of endlessly interpretable fields of sense: a multi-layered text of mortal experience woven from the intertwining codes of Being.

Our collaborative reading of this hidden, or anyway obscure, text returns us to the ancient symbols of the "collective unconscious," an excluded archetypal understanding of the body's inherence in the original ecstasy of Being. This deeply fundamental awareness, resident in our embodiment, is open to the presencing of Being in its more primordial, and therefore concealed, determination of our motility-field; open, that is, to the round-dance of elemental energy, bringing forth a space, a field, and a ground for our motility.

In closing this abbreviated interpretation, based on Heidegger, of the being of the body of motility, I would like to cite a Tibetan (Buddhist) rDzogs-chen text from the eighteenth century. The text, written by 'Jigs-med gling-pa, is called, in its English translation by Dr. Herbert V. Guenther, "The Tantra of the Reality of Transcendent Awareness [symbolically referred to as] Kun-tu bzang-po, the Quintessence of Fulfillment and Completion."[13] It offers a very deep interpretation of Being as it is registered in our experience of motility, our experience as beings who are capable of moving and being moved.

In the first chapter, "Explaining the Ground and the Gates to Samsara and Nirvana," we are told about the Being of the "ground," the ground of our being, and the paths of suffering and liberation which articulate our passage in relatedness-to-Being. This discussion is basic for our understanding of motility and its potential-for-development, since all motility takes place in an open space or clearing, and on a supportive ground. How this ground is experienced and understood, not only theoretically, but in our motility itself, makes all the difference for our ontological fulfillment as beings-who-move. In this hermeneutical text, the "ground" is disclosed in its primordial truth, that is, as an *Es gibt* for our motility, described in a hermeneutic language which contests the distinction between psychology and cosmology; it is called "a pervasive medium in which the intentionality of a mind does not yet operate." This is a phenomenological description of the primordial being of the ground, or the field, as it is lived pre-ontologically. Out of its dynamic, however, a certain configuration of "motility *(rlung)*, present in the analytic and synthetic functions of a mind and activated by the traces of positive and negative actions and of the emotively toned patterns of attraction, antipathy, and indifference, . . . begins to stir." Out of the dance, the primordial ecstasy of energy, there takes place in open space a settling of the ground and a clearing of the field. Emerging from within this field, centers of ego-logical energy arise, tending to solidify into habitual patterns of attractions, antipathy, and indifference that determine the character and directionality of our postures, movements, and gestures.

According to that text:

> In this way the activity of the six senses awakening to their objects marks the emergence of the subjective mind operating in the subject-object dichotomy *(yid)*. In favoring the emotively toned and constituted aspect of mind, . . . which is the egocentricness of conscious life, it occasions the five basic emotively toned action- and reaction-patterns, the twenty subsidiary ones, the fifty mental events, and the eighty-four thousand interpretations and judgments, so that everything without exception is set for the origination of Samsara [that is, the world of human existence as a realm of suffering, misery, and all forms of destructiveness].

Here we are reading an interpretation of the body of motility as the body of a living being, a being whose flesh is deeply inscribed by its experiencings of pain and suffering and sorrow. We are reading an existential-ontological interpretation of the motility-life of everyone-and-anyone, the normal adult who is living in the everyday world at an ego-logical stage (level, stratum) of development. This interpretation hermeneutically traces the genesis of the human way of being as a psycho-physical process of ancient provenance, emerging from an elemental field of motility and developing or unfolding itself into the spatiality of an ego-logical structure, an ego-logical configuration of disclosive spatiality already implicit as an "inveterate tendency" within the primordial layout *(logos)* of the field-as-a-whole. The Tibetan text is thus a "recollection" of the history of Being as an errant, wayward, and fallen modality of human motility. As Guenther remarks, "The underlying assumption is the psychologically verifiable fact that man is capable of ascending to the highest levels of spiritual awareness and also of falling into the deepest abyss of misery and suffering." It is an interpretation which *situates* the human motility-body, *as* a psycho-physical process of existential-ontological development, within a cosmological dimension of Being. (Experientially speaking, we must ask, for example: what happens to our motility, and to our understanding of its (felt) sense, when our individually and culturally characteristic gestures, gestures typical of everyone-and-anyone, and the gestures which correspond to our technological epoch, are explicitly *situated* in a transpersonal, and indeed cosmological field of meaningfulness? Do we feel a shift, a new reach? Is there a sudden shift in the intensity-level, the experienced energy, of our motility?)

The text also articulates the *truth* of this process in terms of a motility so *related* to its field-of-Being-as-a-whole that it finds itself in the *fulfillment* of its various capacities. Thus we read:

> Although the transcending awareness which knows reality as it is in reality, is, in view of its continuity, not a different substance from the pervasive medium of the all-ground, it is said to be a change in its modality. It is like awakening from deep sleep. But although here the senses wake up to their objects, they are not affected by the appearance of these objects. . . .

And the motility-body which *incarnates* this transcending awareness is accordingly said to be, at the level of its greatest spiritual self-fulfillment and self-realization, "a free unimpeded movement." "Samsara," says Guenther, "is basically a descriptive term for the observable fact that man, in ignorance of his real being, is driven by his actions and emotions, while Nirvana refers to the experienceable passage beyond suffering." The chapter concludes with the observation that

> inasmuch as this capacity cannot be thwarted by reification into external objects and by avidity and listlessness, everything is set for the origination of Nirvana [that is, the world of human existence as a realm of well-being, a realm in which human motility understands itself as, and is, a clearing for the truth of Being in the depth of its beauty and goodness].

The second chapter, "explaining the Split into Samsara and Nirvana," emphasizes that we need very much to "know what the ground is," since its presencing "comprises both a path of freedom and one of errancy."

As Guenther points out, "there is a danger . . . we may center all our attention on the developmental phase [of ego-logical adulthood] and lose sight of the 'all-ground,' or even identify the 'all-ground' with the ground underlying one particular direction of the development." As such, of course, the field of motility is not "sullied by karmic actions and emotively toned action- and reaction-patterns." Whence, and why, do such patterns of errancy arise, constituting the world of Samsara, the world we know most familiarly, the everyday world of everyone-and-anyone? The third chapter answers as follows:

> When the noetic capacity by its inherent dynamic has stirred from the all-ground and is about to meet its object, the all-ground cognitiveness *(kun-*

gzhi'i rnam-par shes-pa) has risen; it is as if the (indeterminate) psychological make-up (or the pervasive medium which makes a "mind," in the strict
sense of the word, possible) has been roused from its deep sleep. The concrete objects of the five senses are not yet really present; but a very subtle
cognitive capacity which tends to grasp its objects *has* risen and makes itself
ready in every respect to receive the impressions of the objects of the discursive mind, like a mirror. This receptivity is confronted with [a field of]
objects [organized] by the five senses operating according to their structure
(rtsa) and their specific motor activity *(rlung)*. . . . Then, through emo-
tionality and mentation it arranges the action- and reaction-patterns of
attraction, antipathy, and indifference, and so sets up the cause-and-effect
[world] of Samsara in a total manner. . . .

By contrast, a motility that is *thoughtfully in touch* with its encompassing and underlying field, a motility, therefore, which is *free* of emotively
toned dualities, enjoys a life-world whose "ground" is a great initial gift,
"the path a great self-authentication, and the goal a great self-freedom."
According to the text, "Nirvana" may be said to "begin" when our motility is *deeply in touch* with the five senses and their respective fields and
zones (vision, hearing, tactility, taste, and smell); for, at the level of syn-
aesthesia, the stratum of "intertwining," there arises the potential for a
"great transcending awareness," and our motility-body is *moved* by a
vision which the author of this text, inspired by Kun-tu-bzang-po,
describes—for our benefit—in a chapter entitled "The Path of the Magnificent Appearance of the Ground." His description, at once phenomenological and symbolic (hermeneutical), reaches us in these terms:

> Out of its realm the radiant light of the magnificent appearance of the
> ground, representing a pattern of communication in the highest perfection,
> comes as a self-arising appearance where the light shed by the lamp of self-
> arisen analytical awareness marks the beginning, that of the lamp of distant
> vision marks the gates through which the ground appears, that of the lamp
> of pure value reveals the beauty of the ground that has appeared, and that of
> the lamp of glittering colors illumines the distinct features of the ground that
> has appeared.

When our motility, which rests in a field represented by the concept of
"an ultimate continuity," is (1) thoroughly integrated with the four lamps
of vision (that is, when our motility is in touch with, and arises from, the
stratum of a synaesthetic and synergic intertwining), then (2) "the felt
knowledge of reality becomes more and more intense, (3) cognition
attains its fullest measure, and (4) reality reigns alone." The existential
"goal," which is "self-freedom," is then "perfectly present in the light of
the path," a path which it would be appropriate to call a path of "self-
authentication."

According to the Tibetan tradition, the path of such an existence lays claim to a motility whose essence is to be found in its "communicative-ness." And the *heart* of this "communicativeness" is a motility-body moved by, and in the service of, the greatest and most far-reaching compassion. Since the communicativeness of this compassion originates in the intertwinings and synergies of the field-continuum, the realizing or actualizing of the body's capacity to be *moved* by compassion is a process determined by the depth of our rootedness in this transpersonal field-continuum, as well as by the depth of the contact into which our motility has entered.

Summarizing the significance of the text as a teaching of unsurpassable wisdom, Guenther writes that

> two basic paths are open. Man may give himself over to the world and its ultimately futile aims, or he may see the fleeting character of the world and give himself over to his [ownmost] existential possibilities in the face of transcendence. In this connection, the tradition that derives from Vimalamitra expressly speaks of a path upward to, and being, a path of freedom, and a path going downward and getting lost in a maze of bewilderment, in the flickering appearances distorted by subjective aims and biases. It here so happens that man strays away from "existence" *(sku)* into mere "organismic being" *(lus).* . . .

When, however, we are resolved to appropriate our human way of being in relation to Being-as-a-whole, then (as Guenther puts it) "there reigns the freedom of the spirit moving in a realm of values which alone can give [fulfilling] meaning to human life." I propose to take these words as an existential-ontological interpretation of that motility-body whose distinctive potential-for-being we have always and already experienced, experienced even here and even now, experienced, therefore, even in our most errant and most ungraceful moments.

Part Four: Mudra

"It is one's own spiritual nature in enlightenment that responds to the 'external' world, comes into contact with objects, raises the eyebrows, winks the eyelids, and moves the hand and legs." D. T. Suzuki, *Essays in Zen Buddhism*[14]

"In holding fast, or grasping, the whole universe vanishes. In letting go, or releasing, the individual world appears, in which everyone asserts his true existence." Katsuki Sekida, *Two Zen Classics: Mumonkan and Hekiganroku*[15]

"I exercise occult and subtle power,/ carrying water, shouldering firewood." Zen Master Koji[16]

"Isan kicked over the pitcher. So wonderful is his Zen that every movement of his foot and hand is shining with the truth." Shibayama Zenkei, *Zen Comments on the Mumonkan*[17]

Heidegger struggled to break free of the metaphysical tradition which nurtured him. Steadfast in his thinking, he did partially succeed. More than this cannot, of course, be expected of him. So we may be thankful that he articulated, against the background of Western philosophy, at least the possibility of a new "thinking": a thinking of Being which would take place *in the practical world of human existence*. But, when we ask his texts for some guidance in understanding the process of *embodying* this thinking, we find that he has virtually nothing to say. In this respect, Heidegger was indeed still caught up in the theoretical metaphysics of Western culture, which has consistently, from the time of its very beginning, denied the role of the body in the process of spiritual self-development.

In the Western world, wherever the Judaeo-Christian spirit has prevailed, we will find an intense hatred, an intense fear, of the human body. Only among the "savages" and "primitives"—in brief, wherever this ascetic spirit has not succeeded in destroying the indigenous cultures— can we still find teachings of great power concerning the "incarnation" of spiritual wisdom. At the present time, however, the most powerful, most deeply articulate teachings, teachings constitutive of a genuine tradition of embodiment, can only be found, I believe, in the Tantric Buddhism of Tibet.

In a lovely book called *Gesture of Balance,* Tarthang Tulku, a teacher and scholar in the Tibetan rNyingma lineage, carefully demonstrates for us that "we have the opportunity to recreate our bodies through positive energy."[18] His words are not abstract theoretical propositions in a metaphysical system, but actual transmissions of an ancient wisdom. He speaks from out of an old tradition of spiritual teachings—a tradition, in fact, of embodiment, which *schematizes* practical wisdom as the embodiment of the tradition. The Tibetans understand that a spiritual tradition needs to be kept alive through its ongoing renewal. They also understand that a spiritual tradition needs to be embodied, otherwise it fails to enter, and transmute, the patterns of daily life. They understand, therefore, that this tradition of teachings must be a tradition of embodiment (that is, a tradition that teaches its embodiment), and that it is the embodiment of this tradition that keeps it really alive.

Buddhism has survived precisely because its practitioners appreciated the human body as primary bearer (or "signifier") of hermeneutical process. In the West, the human body has been systematically degraded to the status of a physical object. This is not at all surprising, considering the domination, in the West, of what Merleau-Ponty calls "objective thinking." But in the countries where Buddhism has flourished—in Tibet, for instance—the human body is considered to be an extremely precious gift: an "auspicious occasion" for the achievement of enlightenment.

Mudra is a multi-dimensional phenomenon.[19] Thus, when we speak of *mudra,* we must specify the sense we have in mind. For example, we may note that *mudra* is an elegant and lucid manifestation of enlightenment, the very embodiment of enlightenment as an existential experience, and a paradigmatic experience of enlightenment as embodiment. Ontologically speaking, *mudra* is a cosmological pattern of Being itself, manifesting through the motility of human beings, rather like the *legein* of the *logos* for Heraclitus. But, from another point of view, namely the development of the human potential-for-being, *mudra* refers to *spiritual practices* in which the practitioner develops a deeper understanding of the teachings by receiving their transmission in ritualized and symbolic disciplines for the body, in liturgically or pedagogically prescribed gestures, postures, and attitudes. In the remaining pages of this essay, I should like to concentrate on this particular aspect of *mudra.*

First of all, since *mudra* as a practice requires us to imitate and repeat ancient gestures of deep spiritual significance, it teaches us in the most direct and incontrovertible way, in terms of our lived experience, that the human body is not, first and foremost, a material object, a physical substratum devoid of intrinsic significance. Practicing *mudra,* one can actually *feel* the significance: it is tangibly *present* in the body, inhabiting the gesture, coursing through the frame from our toes to our head, and forming powerful concentrations of energy in the major regions of the body. As we meditatively practice prescribed *mudras,* we may gradually discover ontological dimensions of our being and realize, in the medium of our motility, our participation in and openness to the transpersonal field-continuum, a manifestation of Being as a whole. As we learn through *mudra* of our inherence in this field-continuum, we enter into the cosmic flow and dance of energies and we are opened to a dimension of Being in which the old Western metaphysical dualisms of subject and object, subject and world, body and environment, myself and others, as well as the boundaries and shapes of Euclidean-Newtonian space that define the local ego's human body, finally begin to dissolve.[20] Since the openness of this dimension is transpersonal, our access to this relatedness facilitates the emergence of a motility responsive to the needs of compassion. In developing our bodily felt sense of *Mitsein* (our being-with-others), *mudra* cultivates our rudimentary gestures of compassion.

Our word *religion* stems from a Latin root which refers us to the vow, the commitment, the binding contract: a decisive moment, that is, in the choice of a spiritual path. The practice of *mudra* bears a similar significance. The *mudra* is not only, however, the taking and binding of a *vow;* it is also the binding of the *body,* the mimetic shaping and conforming of the body itself to the schematized, ideal body that represents the living patterns of enlightenment. Thus, we may say that *mudra* is the instancing living of those teachings, and the very presence of a full-bodied truth or wisdom. The repeated practice of these corporeal schemata thus constitutes the attempt to realize the intrinsic capacity for enlightenment which is always already given to us, implicitly inwrought into the gift of our human embodiment.

The ritual practice of *mudra* makes use, in effect, of corporeal schematizations—ideal schemata, or symbolic images, of a more enlightened human embodiment. These schemata prescribe meditative postures and gestures, and the imitative repetition of these patterns helps us to focus on our bodily felt experience in a way that puts us in touch with the intrinsic potential that calls for development. The process of "focusing" puts us in touch with the "felt sense" of the gesture, so that we allow the gesture's depth of sensitivity, its innate resources of awareness, to develop. In this way, we cultivate a skill whose potential of energy is, as we discover, *always already with us*.

Our everyday gestures originate in, and never entirely lose contact with, a refreshing, open reserve of nondual energy, a primordial gestation of holistic, bodily felt experience. This motivating energy, an energy by grace of which our motility is made possible, is anonymous and prepersonal. Since the ego is not only a psychic structure, but also an inveterate tendency, or pattern, of embodiment, the meditative practice of *mudra* makes accessible to us the gift of resources in motility which can facilitate the transformation of egological gestures, postures, and behaviors. Anonymous primordial energy becomes selfless worldly action; prepersonal incarnations of Being become gestures of compassion extended beyond the limits that have determined our merely personal concerns. In practicing *mudra*, we cut right through the ego's three kinds of poisonous gesture—gestures in the grip of desire, hatred, and confusion—and contact the powerful, but undeveloped nondual energies of Being. By working directly with these energies, we allow them to change our way of being-in-the-world. Thus, ego-forming gestures haunted by an *anonymity* which belongs to a more infantile stage of life can actually become practiced gestures of *selflessness*: open and spontaneous gestures that are no longer bound by the unwholesome patterns of ego. Likewise, the young child's charmingly open and natural manner of gesturing, whose *pre-personal* character continues, irrepressibly, to animate and inflect even the most standardized, thoughtless, and habitual gestures of our adulthood, may undergo a fulfilling metamorphosis, once the energies of that gesture are not inhibited, but openly felt. Through the practice of *mudra*, our gestures may become not only much more personal (that is, existentially authentic, directly grounded in our own heartful experience), but also much *more* than personal, being perpetually enriched and strengthened by a religious tradition which values the "transcendent" or "transpersonal" gestures of openness that stretch to reach *beyond* the merely personal realm of karmic action, and even beyond the time-and-space of "ordinary reality." And as for the qualitative, *pre-conceptual* bearing of our gestures, it too may be touched and changed, so that our gestures are charged with a meaningfulness which feels very much richer, and much more skillfully creative, than what our conceptual vocabulary is accustomed to grasp and re-present.

When we have fully developed the reserve of inborn skills latent in the human gesture, everything we touch and handle, and even just point to, at once becomes tangible in a *mandala* of the most profound meaningfulness, which brings out, from that depth, whatever beauty and value the thing may have to offer. With every gesture, we weave around the beings we encounter, and are ourselves woven into, a wondrous *mandala* of Being. With every gesture, the Being of beings is invited to presence, like a vast assembly of deities, surrounding and embracing the being which our gesture has singled out for special celebration and thanksgiving.

Above all, however, the practice of *mudra* seals our desire to develop the intrinsic compassion of our gestures, so that, through the continuum of communicativeness and responsiveness, all beings, and even the Being of beings itself, can touch and move us. Helping us to enter into the *continuum* of the field of motility, *mudra* teaches us that there could be no gesture which does not recognize a primordial kinship already entrusted with binding value. Even at a distance, we can be touched by compassion. Even at a distance, we can touch others with our compassion. Even at a distance, all beings are bound together, sealed by *mudra* into the weaving of Being. *Mudra* reminds us of our original communion with *all* beings, both sentient and nonsentient. It reminds us that we, as mortals, have an elemental affinity with *all* beings in Nature. *Mudra* reminds us that our gestures are not ours alone, but belong to a transpersonal "thought" which is unfathomably "older" than we ourselves. After great exertion in practice, though, it may come to pass that the experienced "source" of our gestures will withdraw from the ego-body into the primordial mystery of Being as such, and the practitioner's gestures will no longer be "his" or "hers," but will belong, rather, to the primordial Buddha, the Buddha Samantabhadra; and, from out of this field, they will begin to enact the archetypal wisdom, the elegance and grace, the healing patterns, of a cosmological dance of energy.

Notes

1. See Herbert V. Guenther, *Buddhist Philosophy in Theory and Practice* (Boulder, Colorado: Shambhala, 1976), p. 194. Also see Guenther's *Tibetan Buddhism in Western Perspective* (Berkeley: Dharma Publishing, 1977).

2. Maurice Merleau-Ponty, *Phenomenology of Perception,* trans. Colin Smith (London: Routledge & Kegan Paul, 1962), p. 144.

3. Martin Heidegger, *What Is Called Thinking?,* trans. Fred Wieck and Glenn Gray (New York: Harper and Row, 1968), p.16.

4. *Ibid.*

5. *Ibid.,* p. 14.

6. *Ibid.,* p. 187.

7. *Ibid.,* p. 195.

8. See Heidegger, *Early Greek Thinking,* trans. David Farrell Krell and Frank Capuzzi (New York: Harper and Row, 1975), p. 68ff.

9. Heidegger, "The Turning," in *The Question Concerning Technology and Other Essays,* trans. William Lovitt (New York: Harper and Row, 1977), p. 40.

10. Medard Boss, *Existential Foundations of Medicine and Psychology,* trans. Stephen Conway and Anne Cleaves (New York: Jason Aronson, 1979), p. 131.

11. *Ibid.,* p. 142.

12. *Ibid.,* p. 102.

13. Guenther, "Indian Buddhist Thought in Tibetan Perspective," in *Tibetan Buddhism in Western Perspective,* pp. 115–138.

14. D. T. Suzuki, *Essays in Zen Buddhism,* First Series (New York: Grove Press, 1961), p. 234.

15. Katsuki Sekida, *Two Zen Classics: Mumonkan and Hekiganroku* (New York: John Weatherhill, 1977), p. 329.

16. *Ibid.,* p. 263.

17. Shibayama Zenkei, *Zen Comments on the Mumonkan* (New York: New American Library, 1974), p. 291.

18. See Tarthang Tulku, *Gesture of Balance* (Berkeley: Dharma Publishing, 1977), p. 65.

19. See Guenther, *The Tantric View of Life* (Boulder: Shambhala, 1976) and *Buddhist Philosophy in Theory and Practice,* p. 193.

20. See the various *mudra* practices in Tarthang Tulku, *Time, Space, and Knowledge* (Berkeley: Dharma Publishing, 1978).

Contributors

Paul Shih-yi Hsiao studied Chinese philology, philosophy, and psychology at Peking University before receiving his Ph.D. in philosophy from the University of Milan. In 1941 he published an Italian translation of the *Tao Te Ching* by Lao-tzu. During the fifties and sixties he taught Chinese language and philosophy in Freiburg and published a number of articles on these topics in German periodicals. He was Professor of Philosophy at Fu-Jen University in Taipei, Taiwan, from 1974 until his death in 1986.

Hwa Yol Jung is Professor of Political Science at Moravian College in Pennsylvania. He specializes in political philosophy and has a strong interest in the European Continental tradition of phenomenology, existential philosophy, and hermeneutics. He has published extensively in these areas as well as in the philosophy of the social sciences, philosophy of technology, environmental ethics, and literary criticism. He has just completed *The Diatactics of Language: Prolegomena to Political Philosophy* and *Rethinking Political Theory*.

Tetsuaki Kotoh received his degrees in philosophy from Kyoto University, having focused mainly on the thinking of Heidegger and on subsequent developments in hermeneutic philosophy. He is currently an assistant professor in the Division of Comparative Culture Studies at Hiroshima University. He has published several articles in Japanese philosophical journals on the topic of language, especially in its relation to the phenomenon of silence.

David Michael Levin is Professor of Philosophy at Northwestern University. He is the author of a book on Edmund Husserl and numerous articles in phenomenological psychology, hermeneutical phenomenology, and aesthetics. His most recent work, focused on the body of felt experience, draws most of all on the work of Heidegger, Merleau-Ponty, Freud, and Jung. He has recently published two books: *The Body's Recollection of Being* and *Pathologies of the Modern Self.*

J. L. Mehta received his Ph.D. from Banaras Hindu University in Varanasi, India. He studied as a Humboldt Foundation Fellow with several prominent Heidegger experts at the universities of Cologne and Freiburg, and was for many years a visiting professor at the Center for the Study of World Religions at Harvard. He is the author of one of the definitive books on Heidegger's thought, *Martin Heidegger: The Way and the Vision,* and has recently published a collection of essays under the title *India and the West.*

Kōhei Mizoguchi received his degrees in philosophy from Kyoto University, the last being a doctorate for a thesis on "Heidegger and the Problem of Time." He has taught philosophy at a number of universities in the Kansai area of Japan, and since 1983 has been Associate Professor of Ethics at Osaka University. He has published a number of articles on the philosophies of Heidegger and Gadamer and on other topics in contemporary hermeneutics and ontology.

Keiji Nishitani graduated from Kyoto University and was subsequently appointed assistant professor there. In 1943 he was given the Chair of Philosophy at Kyoto University, a position which he held for over twenty years, and is now Professor Emeritus of Philosophy and Religion at Otani Buddhist University in Kyoto. He is the author of numerous books on Eastern and Western philosophy, the most important of which has appeared in English translation: *Religion and Nothingness.*

Graham Parkes studied philosophy and psychology at Oxford and the University of California at Berkeley, and is now Associate Professor of Philosophy at the University of Hawaii at Manoa. He has published articles on Nietzsche and Heidegger (mostly from a comparative point of view), and on topics in the philosophy of literature and the visual arts. He is currently working on a book-length manuscript which articulates Nietzsche's psychology, borrowing in part from the frameworks of the psychologies of Plato, Freud, and Jung.

Otto Pöggeler studied philosophy at the Universities of Bonn and Heidelberg. He is the author of several major books on Heidegger (*Der Denkweg Martin Heideggers* [1963], *Philosophie und Politik bei Heidegger* [1972], and *Heidegger und die hermeneutische Philosophie* [1983]), Hegel (*Hegels Idee einer Phänomenologie des Geistes* [1973], *Études*

Hegeliennes [1985]), and on the philosophy of art and poetry. Since 1968 he has been Professor of Philosophy at the Ruhr University in Bochum, and is also director of the Hegel Archives there.

Joan Stambaugh received degrees in philosophy from Vassar College, Columbia University, and the University of Freiburg. She is currently Professor of Philosophy at Hunter College in the City University of New York. She is the author of two books on Nietzsche: *Untersuchungen zum Problem der Zeit bei Nietzsche* and *Nietzsche's Thought of Eternal Return,* and has published numerous articles, mostly on topics in German philosophy. She is the translator of a number of Heidegger's works, and recently completed a new translation of *Sein und Zeit.*

Akihiro Takeichi received his degrees in philosophy from Kyoto University and has been Professor of Philosophy there since 1976. He has published several articles in Japanese and German journals on topics in phenomenology, hermeneutics, and other aspects of modern Western philosophy. He is co-editor of the *New Iwanami Seminars* in philosophy, a sixteen-volume anthology of studies in contemporary Japanese philosophy.

Yasuo Yuasa studied philosophy, economics, and literature at Tokyo University, and is currently Professor of Ethics at Tsukuba University, near Tokyo. He has published numerous books on topics such as contemporary Japanese philosophy and existentialism, the psychology of C. G. Jung, the philosophy of Watsuji, and Japanese religious consciousness, both ancient and modern. His current research focuses on the mind-body relationship from the perspectives of oriental medicine and meditation practice.

Author-Title Index

Subject Index